Northwestern University
STUDIES IN *Phenomenology & Existential Philosophy*

Phenomenology in Psychology and Psychiatry

Herbert Spiegelberg

Phenomenology in Psychology and Psychiatry

A Historical Introduction

Northwestern University Press
Evanston 1972

Library of Congress Catalog Card Number: 74–154833
ISBN 0–8101–0624–8
Printed in the United States of America
Second Paperback Printing, 1986

Herbert Spiegelberg is professor of philosophy emeritus
at Washington University, St. Louis.

To Eldora Haskell Spiegelberg—
psychologist in action, healing peacemaker,
philo-phenomenologist—
sine qua non

Contents

Preface

> To write a history is always a questionable affair. For even with the most honest intent one is in danger of being dishonest. In fact, whoever undertakes such an account states in advance that he will highlight some things and put others into the shade.
>
> J. W. Goethe, Introduction to the *Theory of Colors*

SOME TEN YEARS AGO, when I had to call a halt to my snowballing enterprise of preparing a historical introduction to the Phenomenological Movement, I made a point of acknowledging one of its gravest defects: its failure to include an account of the impact of phenomenology on areas other than philosophy. Short of such an account, a movement with the aspirations and ramifications of phenomenology cannot be fully appraised. Yet, to provide a meaningful survey of all the fields which phenomenology has affected would at this stage require more than one person's time—and background knowledge. Fortunately, this wider task is not yet very urgent. However, I realized at the outset that there is one area where the incompleteness of my attempt is especially serious: that of psychology and its adjacent disciplines, psychopathology and psychiatry. Hence I added to the preface to my earlier book: "At the moment all I can do is to openly admit this shortcoming and to express the hope that someone, if not I myself, will be able to fill the gap." Thus far, to my knowledge, no one has picked up this challenge. Nor had I any right to hope that anyone would do so, especially in accord with my specifications. True, there have been the two books by Ulrich Sonnemann and Anna-Teresa Tymieniecka, which have entered the field independently, as well as shorter chapters in more comprehensive works and separate articles. But the scope and quality of these first treatments could not fill the need as I saw it.[1] Thus,

1. Ulrich Sonnemann's *Existence and Therapy: An Introduction to Phenomenological Psychology and Existential Analysis* (New York: Grune & Stratton, 1954), p. xi, tries to lead from a sketch of Husserl's phenom-

it became increasingly clear to me that I would have to accept my own challenge. This realization helped me in overcoming my initial reluctance to take on another large historical assignment whose scope could not be clearly foreseen.

At first, I had hopes that part of this task had been taken care of by the historians of psychology and psychiatry. But most of their accounts let me down completely. For example, Gardner Murphy's *Historical Introduction to Modern Psychology* (1929) does not even mention phenomenology. Neither does G. S. Brett's three-volume *History of Psychology* (1953). J. C. Flugel's *A Hundred Years of Psychology* (1964) mentions "Husserl's phenomenology" only once as historical background for Gestalt psychology; W. B. Pillsbury's *The History of Psychology* (1929) speaks only of the influence of Brentano's psychology on "Hus-

---

enology, through a brief outline of Heidegger's "existentialism," to Binswanger's conception of therapy. While this plan makes sense and the author is on the whole better informed than most of his rivals, its execution leaves much to be desired by way of presentation and expression. Also, the author himself disclaims "a detailed historical analysis of the movement" as "too indirect an introduction to it" (p. x). Anna-Teresa Tymieniecka's *Phenomenology and Science in Contemporary Thought* (New York: Noonday Press, 1962), Vol. XXII, embraces an even larger assignment by selecting basic ideas of Husserl, Jaspers, and Heidegger and trying to show their applications in all the sciences. Psychology and psychiatry figure especially in the Husserl and Heidegger sections (but not in the one on Jaspers), with short samples. Again, the purpose of this smaller book is not historical (p. xvii), and unfortunately much of the incidental historical information and many references are misleading, if not erroneous.

Pertinent chapters in larger books, such as Henry F. Ellenberger's "Clinical Introduction to Psychiatric Phenomenology and Existential Analysis," in *Existence,* ed. Rollo May, Ernest Angel, Henri F. Ellenberger (New York: Basic Books, 1958), pp. 92–126, give cross-sections through the field, yet with little philosophical foundation and no historical claims. The Appendix to the second edition of Kurt F. Reinhardt's *The Existentialist Revolt* (New York: Ungar, 1960), pp. 244–67, in addition to paraphrasing May's texts, adds something about Christian depth psychologists.

Very helpful are several articles in magazines, among which I would like to single out two by Adrian Van Kaam: "The Third Force in European Psychology—Its Expression in a Theory of Psychotherapy," Psychosynthesis Research Foundation (Greenville, Del., 1960), and, more detailed, "The Impact of Existential Phenomenology on the Psychological Literature of Western Europe," *Review of Existential Psychology and Psychiatry,* I (1961), 63–92. Stephan Strasser has followed up his earlier judicious survey of "Phenomenological Trends in European Psychology," *Philosophy and Phenomenological Research,* XVII (1957), 18–34, with a paper on "Phenomenologies and Psychologies," *Review of Existential Psychology and Psychiatry,* V (1965), 80–105, in which he distinguishes four stages of phenomenology without tracing in detail how they are reflected in psychology.

serl's school of philosophy." Gregory Zilboorg's *A History of Medical Psychology* (1941) has nothing to offer on phenomenological psychiatry.

The latest work in the field that has come to my attention, the *History of Psychology: An Overview*, by Henryk Misiak and Virginia Stout Sexton (New York: Grune & Stratton, 1966), contains two long chapters on "Phenomenological Psychology" (27 pages) and "Existentialism and Psychology" (28 pages). While at an earlier point this helpful collection of, and first orientation about, much of the material might easily have released me from my struggles, closer inspection showed that more was to be done by way of firsthand research than this textbook presentation with its necessary, and some unnecessary, limitations. Also, the attempt to divide phenomenology and existentialism appears here to be unworkable and is often misleading. Besides, in accordance with their plan, the authors omit psychopathology and psychiatry.

Fortunately, Edwin G. Boring's misnamed classic, *A History of Experimental Psychology*,[2] presents the history of modern psychology practically in terms of a contest between "phenomenology," which he considers a characteristic of German science, and objective and behavioristic psychology. This interpretation makes it clear, however, that he understands phenomenology much more broadly than anyone else, since he includes even physiologists such as Johannes Müller and Ernst Heinrich Weber among the phenomenologists. Actually, he defines it simply as "the description of immediate experience, with as little scientific bias as possible" (p. 18) and consequently includes Franz Brentano and Carl Stumpf without qualification among the phenomenologists. However, the Phenomenological Movement in the sense of the present book does not figure in the Table of Contents; it receives its main treatment in the middle of the chapter on Gestalt theory as one of its "antecedents." Husserl is mentioned only in the section on Carl Stumpf (pp. 367 f.). Thus, while Boring's conscientious and almost always reliable account provides excellent background for the story which I have to present, it leaves at least three major needs unfulfilled:

1. It deliberately avoids discussing the philosophical background and the philosophical sources of developments in psychology.

2. Within the period covered, it treats phenomenological

2. 2d ed. (New York: Appleton-Century-Crofts, 1929).

psychology only within Gestalt psychology: in fact it overestimates the ties between the two.

3. It ends with the early Husserl and omits the whole story of phenomenological psychiatry.

Hence most of my job remained to be done or redone by going back to the original sources. It was, of course, clear to me from the very start that the demands of such an interdisciplinary project would be formidable and that I was not sufficiently at home in psychology and psychiatry to undertake it. To do more than a dilettante job I needed preparation, help—and time. Specifically, I needed access to the sources and particularly to the living sources of the story, a good many of whom, fortunately, were still alive. The chance for the collection of such material came to me on the occasion of a Fulbright Lectureship at the University of Munich in 1961–62, which allowed me to visit some of the key witnesses to the original introduction of phenomenology into psychiatry; to these I am deeply indebted. Thus, by the time I returned to the States I had assembled most of the materials for an enriched story. However, I had also come to realize the vast scope of my new assignment, although by now I no longer felt free to withdraw from it. The new data which had fallen into my hands, and the vistas and insights which they allowed, demanded recording and communicating. Also, the help that I had accepted from my informants constituted a trust which I had to justify.

To discharge this trust, however, seemed impossible after my return to my former teaching position at Lawrence College. My transfer to Washington University gave me at least much better library facilities. But it was not until I had received a grant from the National Institute of Mental Health, giving me a year of half-time and two semesters of full-time leave, that I could begin the actual writing of the story. Without such a boost it might well have remained unwritten.

Under these circumstances it may not be irrelevant to mention something about the genesis of the original manuscript—for it grew in a somewhat unusual form. It seemed wise to begin with the limited studies of individual phenomenological psychopathologists in Part II as the best way to immerse myself in the most challenging materials, using them as test cases for determining the most appropriate approach and for developing sensible hypotheses. The first studies covered such key figures as Jaspers and Binswanger but later, where the tracing of phenomenological influences seemed particularly instructive, even younger men were added. In presenting these "clinical" cases, I could make use of the pattern which I had developed in my earlier book: I had always started by trying to determine the place of the thinker I was examining in the context of the Phenomenological Movement; then I discussed his basic concern and his conception of phenomenology; finally, I added examples of its applications to concrete subjects. However, in the present book I have not attempted a concluding appraisal of my subjects, especially not of their scientific contributions. Instead, I have tried to present a sober estimate of the role of phenomenological philosophy in their enterprises. My main job has been to understand, to aid in understanding, and wherever possible to awaken understanding.

Next, I turned to the more comprehensive tasks of Part I, where I wanted to provide an over-all perspective of the phenomenological contribution to general psychology and psychiatry as well as to their more specialized fields. Here my first hope was that it would be possible to run over the traditional branches of research and to plot for each one of them what phenomenology has added to its stock. But this did not work out as I had hoped. For it turned out that much more solid information about the main contributors and contributing groups was required before their findings could be tabulated and evaluated. Hence I decided to arrange the materials mostly around the individuals and schools. I also felt that, especially for readers without particular interest in or access to my earlier book, I should begin with a survey of what the major phenomenological philosophers themselves had undertaken in psychology. This introductory section is followed by the main burden of Part I: an account of what the psychologists and psychiatrists have done with phenomenology, arranged according to major areas but stressing primarily the interpretation and use of phenomenology by each investigator or group of investigators.

Only after carrying out these specific studies did I feel in a position to try a more comprehensive interpretation of my findings and to write a systematic introduction. I did not wish to enter a territory so new to me with any preconceived patterns or even hypotheses. I wanted these to crystallize in interaction with the materials. I began with nothing but questions. Having secured at least some of the answers, I gathered the necessary confidence for formulating some defensible interpretations. They are expressed in the following introduction. Only now that I had an explicit focus and some degree of unity did I begin to revise and rewrite the bulk of the book.

If I have been reasonably successful in my approach, I would hope that my efforts can serve as a model for similar enterprises and that further studies will show how phenomenology has affected fields other than philosophy and psychology—from mathematics to the study of religion. And let me dispel any doubt about the fact that I shall not compete with them. After some fifteen years of engaging in metaphenomenology, historical and methodological, I would like to leave this line to others better qualified in the specialized fields. My own commitments for the future call for doing phenomenology directly once more.

In closing, let me repeat what I said, with only partial success, in the preface to my earlier book: This book is not an attempt to write a history, let alone a definitive history. I am too much of a historical skeptic to believe that this can ever be done, especially in dealing with the history of the immediate past. But this conviction does not absolve us from an effort to achieve a perspective which can keep the avenues to history open rather than block them. I want to offer an introduction, in fact a phenomenological one in the sense that it should convey history as given to us only through appearances, which are more or less adequate. I consider the supreme historical virtue to be self-critical humility. There is no such thing as the proverbial History (with a capital *H*) which will some day tell us how it all really happened and whose achievement or fault it was. Hence we had better drop all pretense of a finality based merely on the fact that we no longer have to fear the protests of those forever silenced by the grave.

In this respect an attempt to write the history of the living past is much fairer—though riskier. But it also involves the problem of how far the historian is under an obligation to spare the feelings of those still alive, particularly if he has been entrusted with confidential information. There have been occasions when such questions of historical ethics have bothered me. I may have toned down some formulations out of consideration for living witnesses. But I feel at least reasonably sure that I have never suppressed evidence that I considered essential. Nevertheless, I foresee that some day, and not only because of new evidence, some of my evaluations could and should be modified. My hope is that at least my evidence will not have become irrelevant.

It remains for me to give public recognition of the debts

which I have incurred in undertaking a task which I could never have tackled without considerable help and encouragement.

As I have already mentioned, the most concrete support I received was that of the National Institute of Mental Health, which by three grants (MH 7788) to Washington University made it possible for me to have a year's leave from my teaching. But I also owe a debt to the Fulbright Commission, since it was during my year in Germany in 1961–62 that I collected the major new material for this story.

Next I should mention the personal support I enjoyed, especially from the major victims of the second part of the story, who also acted as informants. One of the nicest rewards of this project was their personal acquaintance and confidence.

Direct help in putting together the final text was given by my colleagues Saul Rosenzweig of the Department of Psychology of Washington University and George Psathas of the Department of Sociology, now at Boston University. I am indebted to them for their critical reading of Part I and for detailed constructive suggestions.

Mrs. Janice Feldstein, far beyond the call of a copyeditor's regular duties, helped to give final shape to the manuscript, especially through her labors on the Bibliography. Philip and Jane Bossert of Washington University helped me efficiently with the proofreading.

In conclusion, the preface of this book calls for a public accounting of its dedication. Eldora Haskell Spiegelberg, a school psychologist, with a primary allegiance to Rogerian psychotherapy, has been more than the usual marital victim of her husband's literary follies. She has kept me in touch with psychology in action. To supply a sympathetic non-phenomenologist like her with a clear, informative book was a special challenge to me. She has been my constant consultant on pertinent subjects and stylistic matters. And in the end she was my first critical sounding board for the completed text. If the result should prove helpful to others, they too owe a substantial debt to one whose major commitments are in the field of action for peace and freedom.

Introduction

> The fact that a basic philosophical attitude is inevitable for a science does not imply the necessity of bogging down in philosophy.
>
> Karl Jaspers, *Allgemeine Psychopathologie*

[1] Limiting the Task: On Phenomenology and Existentialism

One major threat for the present enterprise is that it has no natural boundaries. Hence, the first need is for me to stake out my claim. But I also want to supply some of the rationale for putting down the stakes where I do. My primary purpose in writing this book was to provide students of contemporary psychology and psychiatry with a shortened and reliable approach to the philosophical sources for the main phenomenological currents in their fields. The area here presented is of course merely a section of a wider territory which includes the entire range of phenomenological philosophy. It would be a senseless duplication if I should try to repeat here information which I presented in my earlier book.[1]

Thus, while I shall try not to shower the patient reader with cross references, he should realize that a complete understanding of the context will depend on consulting the fuller account of my earlier introduction to philosophical phenomenology. As a preliminary substitute he can also make use of my article on Phenomenology, which first appeared in the 1966 edition of the *Encyclopaedia Britannica.*

However, even in this book I owe the reader the kind of working understanding of what phenomenology is all about that my previous studies have tried to facilitate. Perhaps some briefing is also necessary about the relations between phenomenology and

1. *The Phenomenological Movement: A Historical Introduction,* 2d ed. (The Hague: Nijhoff, 1965).

existentialism which, especially in the Anglo-American world, have become inextricably connected, if not merged. I want to do my best to keep them at least distinguishable, if only in order to limit my job as far as can be justified. For a first orientation about the main names and events in chronological order, the reader might be helped by the diagram on pages xxx–xxxi.

Phenomenology grew out of a more general attempt to develop a widened conception of experience than a sensation-bound positivism allowed for. Its motto "To the things" involved a turning away from concepts and theories toward the directly presented in its subjective fullness. Franz Brentano, its major forerunner, had formulated the idea of a descriptive psychology or psychognostics. Husserl, after first reasserting the right of mathematics and logic against a merely inductive psychology, had developed the conception of a new fundamental science which was to support other studies based on an intuiting investigation of the structures of pure consciousness, made accessible by a special suspension of belief in the reality of our natural and scientific world, the so-called phenomenological reduction, in which the constitution of the phenomena according to intending acts and intended contents was studied in detail ("transcendental phenomenology"). The older Phenomenological Movement represented by Alexander Pfänder and Max Scheler had laid special stress on the exploration of essential structures and essential connections in and between the phenomena. Heidegger, in his quest for the meaning of Being, had tried to enlist an enlarged hermeneutic phenomenology for the task of uncovering the meanings of human existence as a first step toward his goal.

At this stage phenomenology began to merge with the philosophy of existence, whose roots go back to Kierkegaard and beyond, and which had found in Karl Jaspers a philosophical supporter who, however, opposed phenomenology in philosophy because of its scientific pretensions. The primary concern of this philosophy was substantive, not methodological. However, in France these two interests merged in Gabriel Marcel and especially in Sartre, whose synthesis of the two resulted in the adoption of the term "existentialism." Phenomenological existentialism as the phenomena-based philosophy of human existence has found its most persuasive expression in the work of Merleau-Ponty.

A study of these developments does not yield a unified conception of phenomenology. At first sight it may give the impression of a dispersal into a variety of phenomenologies without a common denominator. Despite these appearances I have tried to single out essential features of phenomenology on a graduated scale. Descriptive phenomenology is an attempt to intuit, analyze, and describe the data of direct experience in a fresh and systematic manner, guided especially by the patterns of intentionality. Essential or eidetic phenomenology explores the essential structures on the basis of imaginative variation of the data. The phenomenology of appearances pays special attention to the different perspectives and modes in which the phenomena are given. Constitutional phenomenology investigates the way in which the phenomena establish themselves in our consciousness. And hermeneutic phenomenology tries to interpret the meaning of the phenomena, especially that of human *Dasein*.

The close link-up, if not identification, of phenomenology with existentialism in psychology and psychiatry since the forties may also make it desirable to explain briefly how I am going to use the more fashionable term "existentialism" in relation to "phenomenology." Existentialism, the offspring of existential thinking that began long before the phenomenological movement, can be defined primarily and best by its central theme, "existence," a term used by Kierkegaard in a new sense, more limited than it had been before, colloquially and philosophically, for the way in which a single individual experiences his being in the world. This orientation toward a neglected and poignant phenomenon does not commit existentialism to any peculiar approach. Kierkegaard was certainly not "scientific," especially not in Hegel's sense of "science," and Jaspers rejected all kinds of objectification, including that ascribed to Husserlian phenomenology. Thus the new phenomenological existentialism differs from the original one by maintaining that existence *can* be approached phenomenologically and studied as one phenomenon among others in its essential structures. That in this process the phenomenological method underwent further development in the direction of a "hermeneutic" rather than descriptive direction makes for some methodological differences as well.

Existentialist phenomenology or, because of the primary emphasis on the subject matter better called "phenomenological existentialism," should not be identified with phenomenological psychology as such. There was and still is a phenomenological psychology that is not existential, inasmuch as the "psychic" does not coincide with the existential. Prime examples of non-

Chronological Survey of the Major Trends in Phenomenological Philosophy †

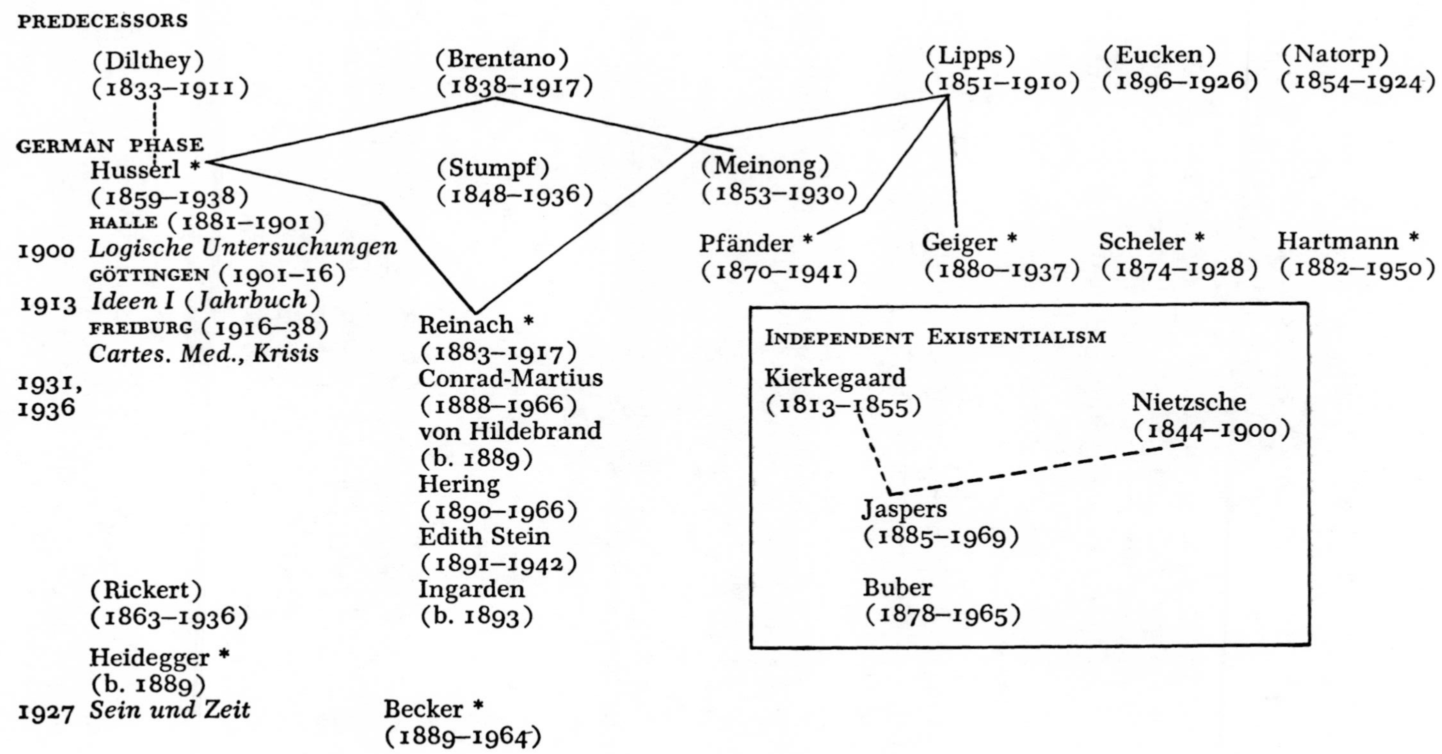

FRENCH PHASE

Marcel
(b. 1889)
1927 *Journal métaphysique*
Sartre
(b. 1905)
1943 *L'Etre et le néant*
Merleau-Ponty
(1908–1961)
1945 *Phénoménologie de la perception*
Ricoeur
(b. 1913)
1950 *Philosophie de la volonté*
Dufrenne
(b. 1910)
1953 *Phénoménologie de l'experience esthétique*

OTHER MAJOR REPRESENTATIVES SINCE WORLD WAR II

GERMANY	FRANCE-BELGIUM	ITALY	USA
Fink (b. 1905)	Berger (1896–1960)	Paci (b. 1911)	Cairns (b. 1901)
Gadamer (b. 1900)	de Waelhens (b. 1911)		Gurwitsch (b. 1901)
Kuhn (b. 1899)	Van Breda (b. 1911)		Schutz (1899–1959)
Landgrebe (b. 1902)			Tillich (1886–1965)
Löwith (b. 1897)			Wild (b. 1902)
Reiner (b. 1896)			

† Asterisks indicate the editors of Husserl's phenomenological yearbook, *Jahrbuch für Philosophie und phänomenologische Forschung* (1913–30). Unbroken lines indicate student-teacher relationships; broken lines mean influences, parentheses indicate predecessors.

existential phenomena can be found in the phenomenology of such perceptual fields as touch or smell, even though these are not free of existential significance.

This book, like its predecessor, is meant to be primarily an aid. The reader is merely invited, but not expected, to study it from cover to cover. Obviously, I hope that I have been able to present a coherent story with a pervasive theme. But I do not share the self-defeating arrogance of so many writers who tell their potential readers that they are under obligation to read every single word of the text before they have the right to judge it. Every reader should feel free to take as much of it as he can absorb at any given time. My hope is that I can provide enough vistas as he moves along to lure him further, into even more forbidding territory.

In trying to adjust the reader's expectations to what I have to offer I shall first discuss the nouns in my title. By "phenomenology" I shall understand what I called previously "phenomenology in the broad sense," i.e., the approach advocated by the original group of Husserl's early collaborators and their successors, who interpreted the motto of "going to the things" as a faithful description of what was intuitively given, including not only particular phenomena but also their essential structures. This broad sense is to be distinguished from the *strict* sense in which the ways in which these phenomena appear are studied, as well as from the *strictest* sense implied by the introduction of Husserl's phenomenological reduction—i.e., the operation of "bracketing" or suspending the belief in the reality of the immediately given, an operation leading to "transcendental phenomenology." On the other hand, phenomenology is not to be taken in that *widest* sense of the term which would include everyone who, regardless of his relation to the movement, has adopted either consciously or unconsciously one or the other of the techniques mentioned above. More specifically, my plan is to show the role of the movement initiated by Edmund Husserl around 1910 in the intellectual context of the time. In addition to Husserl himself this movement includes his original collaborators, Alexander Pfänder, Adolf Reinach, Moritz Geiger, and Max Scheler, as well as their successors, Martin Heidegger and the French phenomenologists. But I shall omit figures such as Alexius Meinong and his Graz school, influential though they were along channels very similar and often parallel to those of full-fledged phenomenology in the broad sense here defined, though this will not exclude occasional side glances whenever they prove illuminating.

To widen the frame even further and to include, for instance, such predecessors and even such inspirers of the Phenomenological Movement as William James not only would make this project unmanageable but would also blur the edges of my attempt to show as clearly as possible how a definite philosophical movement can affect an area of studies such as psychology. However, going to the other extreme of narrowing down the scope of phenomenology to Husserl's strictest sense would have reduced the yield to a trickle, considering Husserl's growing purist tendency to disown his earlier, and even his later, followers inside and outside the "walls." It would also cut out some of the most creative interpretations—and misinterpretations of his work. Nevertheless, although phenomenology will be interpreted in the broad sense given here, special attention will also be given to the stricter senses.

I see little need for stating my interpretation of the term "psychology" as used in the title. While I am fully aware of the unresolved, if not insoluble, problems attaching to any philosophic formulation of the nature of psychology, I merely want it to be understood that I intend to sample the field of empirical studies which nowadays goes by that name. I shall leave it undecided whether or not they can all be adequately defined in terms of organismic behavior, a definition which would immediately raise the question of the meanings of "organismic" and of "behavior," if not of "behaviorism," whose possible phenomenological reinterpretation is one of the most significant items of current methodological debate.

There is more reason for explaining how, for purposes of this book, I define the term "psychiatry." First of all, although it was necessary to keep the title simple, it should be understood that I mean to include psychopathology (or abnormal psychology, as the odd American label has it), the theoretical study of abnormal psychic phenomena. I do not want to minimize the distinction between psychopathology and psychiatry, which is much more pronounced in the European tradition. Yet, the connection between the two is an intimate one. Even Husserl's distinctions between logic as a practical and as a theoretical science in the first volume of his *Logical Investigations* have made it plain that practical logic as a technology depends on theoretical logic. In this light I should perhaps point out that, though using the more current term "psychiatry," I want to stress the psychopathological foundations rather than the therapeutic implications of this study, and certainly not the "practice" of psychotherapy.

What is even more important, however, is to bring out that in the perspective of phenomenology the whole distinction between psychology and "psychopathology" appears in a new light. This is actually the best reason for combining in this book the two fields, each of which may seem vast enough to call for more than one researcher's efforts. Even before phenomenology entered the scene, the division of normal and abnormal psychology into two academic "faculties," sometimes not even located on the same campus, was a source of discomfort and doubt. This is not the place to discuss the reasons why the division between the studies of the normal and the abnormal were made so much wider in the psychic than in the somatic field. It did not take phenomenology to break down these barriers. Freud's psychoanalysis probably deserves the major credit. On the whole, the initiative seems to have come largely from the medical side. But phenomenology, in its impartial interest for all phenomena, normal as well as abnormal, and in its presuppositionless readiness to question such dichotomies as the one between the normal and the abnormal, may well have accelerated this trend, which has not only reduced the disjunction to the polarity of a spectrum but has helped to bring out the common roots of both. The phenomenological psychopathologists especially have invaded the field of phenomenological psychology to such an extent that they no longer seem to recognize the whole distinction. Most of them clearly have felt that they had to build their own psychology. If this is not fully true of Jaspers, it certainly applies to Binswanger and most of his followers.

I am anxious to point this out because I want to forestall a misunderstanding of the reasons for the division of this book into two parts. At first sight it might look as if Part I deals only with psychologists and Part II only with selected psychopathologists and psychiatrists. However, a closer look at the content of Part II should reveal that, especially toward the end, several clinical psychologists join the psychiatrists. While it is true that the outstanding figures in Part II were originally psychopathologists with a medical background, the aim in Part II, as its title suggests, is to study in depth the key figures who introduced phenomenology into both psychology and psychiatry. The fact that the psychiatrists call for intensive studies more than the psychologists is hardly accidental. For, especially in the clinical field, they were in need of new foundations which only a new psychology, beginning with psychoanalysis and followed by phenomenology, could supply. Under these circumstances I certainly do not want to uphold a segregation of psychology and psychiatry which was fading even before phenomenology entered the field and which is even more evanescent in its new light.

Next, I should explain the relation between phenomenology and psychology-psychiatry which is implied by the seemingly innocuous preposition "in." The main implication is that phenomenological philosophy has not only influenced psychology and psychiatry from the outside but has invaded them and is now firmly ensconced inside them. I would like to track down such infiltrations as concretely as possible. This can be done at times by textual documentation, at least in the case of quotation-minded scientists. However, quotations are no reliable measure of dependence and may have been stuck in for all sorts of reasons, relevant and irrelevant. Besides, there are scholars, philosophers as well as scientists, who neglect and even despise such trimmings of "learnedness." In a sense this could even be good phenomenology, which goes to the things and not, or at least not primarily, to the literary sources. Also, in a case such as phenomenology, after the first period of infiltration an influence becomes so pervasive that it forms part and parcel of the atmosphere, though unfortunately it also very often becomes diluted and distorted. The real measure of phenomenological "presence" is its active role in ongoing research. Thus we shall have to watch not only for loans (or plagiarism) but for the reproductive use of phenomenological inspirations in the form of additions to and corrections of the phenomenological imports. In short, my plan is to examine how far phenomenological philosophy has been a live force within psychology and psychiatry, rather than an intruder from the outside.

One more feature of my title deserves underlining; in this case it is a negative one: the absence of any definite or indefinite article. I am not speaking about *the* Phenomenological Movement or *the* psychology of the twentieth century. This ambiguity is more than a stylistic matter. For I do not want to promise that the present account will be exhaustive, either with respect to the entire invading phenomenological movement or with regard to the invaded psychology and psychiatry. This would have been impossible, certainly for me personally, given my limitations in background, time, and inclination. But I even doubt that it would have been desirable. What I believe is needed more than a complete Baedeker is a study in depth of some of the leading motifs and trends. Filling the gaps and following up minor developments will then be relatively easy and more meaningful. But a luxuriant field like ours had better not be cluttered by too many varieties and subdivisions which may even interfere with growth. Enough if I can give more intensive accounts of some of the more developed structures and leave this study open-ended. Surely I want to give more than arbitrarily selected and scattered samples. But their representativeness must not block the way to curiosity about lesser known men and studies. To the best of my knowledge I shall always try to indicate where we might expect to find them. My goal throughout has been to shorten the approach to the growing edge of research—and ultimately to the phenomena themselves.

As an example of what may well be considered a serious gap in my panorama of phenomenology in psychology and psychiatry, I would like to bring up the case of Helmuth Plessner (b. 1892). While his central concern is philosophical anthropology, enough of this ill-defined territory includes segments from phenomenological psychology and psychopathology—and does so particularly in the case of Plessner—to call for more than this passing mention. But in admitting this seeming omission, I would like to plead several mitigating circumstances:

1. Plessner's main base is in philosophy, not in psychology or any of the sciences; as such he would have qualified better for my earlier work, or at most for the first chapter of this book, which reviews the contributions of the philosophers to the area of the present volume.

2. Although Plessner was a student of Husserl's in Göttingen in 1914 and was associated with Scheler in Cologne, he has made it clear that he considers not only Husserl's phenomenology but the entire idea of phenomenology as a philosophy to be gravely misconceived. At most he grants phenomenological description an important role at the start of anthropological philosophy, but even then it has to be supplemented by hermeneutic interpretation in the style of Dilthey.

3. Among the many provocative ideas in Plessner's writings, which especially abound in his book on the strata of organic life and man (*Die Stufen des Organischen und der Mensch* [1928]) and in his study on laughing and weeping (*Lachen und Weinen* [1941]),[2] several, such as his thesis about the positionality of organic life (as being centered and set off from its surrounding)

2. English translation, *Laughing and Crying: A Study of the Limits of Human Behavior,* trans. James Spencer Churchill and Marjorie Grene (Evanston, Ill.: Northwestern University Press, 1970).

and the eccentricity of man (as knowing also his own knowing about this positionality), merit the attention of phenomenologists. But it is far from clear how far these findings are supposed to be based on phenomenological observation and description. Especially in the remarkable studies of laughing and weeping as limits of human behavior, one may miss the concrete description of what is actually going on in subjective experience, while being told about the occasions and the significance of these forms of behavior.

For thorough discussion of the role of phenomenology in Plessner's anthropology, I would like to refer to a study by Felix Hammer which was apparently approved by Plessner himself.[3]

[2] Toward a Phenomenology of Influence: Its Nature and Its Varieties

My immediate purpose, then, is to give a picture of how philosophical phenomenology has "infiltrated" psychology and psychiatry, in an attempt to determine how much it has been able to fill a genuine need. Such infiltration goes by the name of "influence." However, I confess to a considerable dissatisfaction with this oversimplifying term, a dissatisfaction which extends to all sorts of historical and human situations and studies, and which is ultimately a phenomenological concern. For what exactly goes on in the relationship between what influences and what is influenced? How is this influence experienced, especially on the side of its recipient? Thus far I have not been able to obtain much light from methodological discussions about the nature and the variety of the relationships involved.[4] In the present case it is particularly important to get a clearer idea of the variety of possible and actual relations. This is one reason why I want to insert here some more general reflections about the spectrum of these relationships.

I would like to begin with an observation which may seem to be almost etymological. The English word "influence," as well as its equivalent in other languages, is clearly a metaphor. Un-

3. *Die exzentrische Position des Menschen* (Bonn: Bouvier & Co., 1967), esp. pp. 42–53, 141–53.

4. For a general awareness of "influence" focusing on the problem of acceptance, see D. Shakov and D. Rapaport, *The Influence of Freud on American Psychology* (New York: International Publishers, 1964), pp. 7 ff.

derlying it is the picture of a flux or flow of something from above into something below. Now it seems to me that one important implication of this metaphor is that it points to the fact that nothing can flow into something unless there is a receptacle ready for it—a river bed into which the flood can descend—if it is not to result in a diffuse inundation of the countryside. There can be no influx without a waiting bed or, to change the metaphor, no growth without a soil prepared for the seed. There is in this sense no such thing as a one-way influence. It depends on the more or less active collaboration of the recipient. Jaspers could not have been influenced by Kierkegaard without "discovering" him; and he could not have discovered him without having looked for an awakener like Kierkegaard.

However, within this general frame there are all sorts of possible variations. This is clearly not the place to study them exhaustively. Such a study would also have to determine the relation of influence to causation in general and, more pertinently, to human motivation in particular. But even without discussing and clarifying these much wider issues, I think it makes sense to distinguish more concretely the main types of influence which the present study will have to consider and keep apart. They can be arranged according to different dimensions: I shall begin with some relatively superficial ones.

A. *Non-Personal and Interpersonal Influence*

All "influences" in intellectual history are of course personal to the extent that at least the recipient of the influence must be a person. But the source of the influence may be impersonal: it can be an idea or a book. Normally, the testimony of the recipient of the influence who admits his "debt" is prima-facie evidence of such influence. It is true that he may be mistaken in his judgment and even may give credit for such irrelevant reasons as scholarly display or ingratiation. Hence mere footnote quotations should never be considered sufficient proof of influence. As a matter of fact, in some cases recipients of influences have changed their estimates of such influences in retrospect, sometimes minimizing them (e.g., Jaspers' estimate of Husserl's influence on himself), sometimes magnifying them (e.g., David Katz's estimate of a corresponding influence from Husserl).

The matter is more complex in the case of interpersonal influences, when one person consciously attempts to influence another person, as in the cases of persuasion, suggestion, and some kinds of preaching and teaching. Here we also have to know, secondly, about the intent of the influencer, who may actually exert an influence without realizing it or against his will, and, thirdly, about the actual correspondence or non-correspondence between intent and result. Husserl had very little influence in the latter sense. But his impact in directions he hardly foresaw and never intended was all the greater. Heidegger influenced Protestant theology without meaning to do so. But he did try to change the interpretation of literary texts (as in the case of Hölderlin), though with but limited success. It is the more general, non-personal influence from ideas and persons which will chiefly matter in our enterprise.

B. *Direct and Indirect Influence*

Not all influence is transmitted directly from person to person or even from idea to person. For example, Socrates' tremendous influence on posterity was indirect. Sometimes it even becomes impossible to determine the source of such indirect influences at all with sufficient certainty. Nevertheless they exist. A good deal of the influence of phenomenology was certainly indirect, especially after it had begun to permeate the *Zeitgeist*. Such influences may pass through channels not expressly acknowledged or any longer known. Thinkers may on principle or by neglect fail to credit their predecessors or contemporaries, or ideas may be picked up from the general atmosphere. What happens in such cases is what is known in physics as osmosis, the seeping through the "permeable membranes" of our minds.

C. *Degrees of Influence*

The degrees of influence which have particular bearing on the study of the influences of phenomenology can be arranged in a descending scale, from total influence via partial influences to the absence of all influence.

1. Total Influence. By total influence I understand a situation in which the recipient gives in completely or where he is "swept off his feet," as it were. He takes over an idea from the source of influence not only by entertaining it but by accepting it and making it his own, perhaps even to the extent of propagating it himself. A clear case is that of a "loan" freely acknowledged and incorporated into the recipient's way of thinking. Of course such influences are apt to become distorted, not only because

the contexts will be different but also because of misunderstandings and misapplications. Nevertheless, in the recipient's mind this may appear as a mere syphoning operation in which he infuses himself with what flows from the source into his own receptacle.

2. Partial Influences. By partial influences I understand those which fail to be completely transmitted into the recipient, although they have a substantial and even decisive impact on him; they make at least "a dent." However, the incompleteness of the partial influences is by no means all there is to them, since there are positive and creative aspects as well. In this respect I shall distinguish the following types of partial influence, which depend largely upon the phase of development at which they take effect:

(a) Stimulation. In this case the influence sets off or releases a movement in the recipient which may soon become very different from the stimulus and owe to it not much more than its start. The way in which the scholastic concept, or rather the term, "intention" released all kinds of exploration and new discoveries in Husserl may be a case in point. Such stimulation can even be negative in the sense that it arouses opposition, which leads to dialectical antithesis and countermovements that reverse the trend of the stimulus. In man, the contrary animal par excellence, stimulation may well act as one of the most powerful forces, both for progress and retrogression.

(b) Reinforcement. A particularly important case is that of an influence which meets a parallel development that is already underway and then modifies its direction by adding its new momentum. It may also act as a catalyst, perhaps at the very start, without entering permanently into the mainstream of the development. We shall see how phenomenological philosophy has often acted as a reinforcer and even as a stopgap in a number of groping psychological trends.

There is also the case of mutual reinforcement, where the impact of the influence has a recoil effect on its source. Such interaction may lead to cumulative reinforcement when the exchange between two congenial movements encourages them mutually. Such a relationship may even amount to something comparable to "resonance" in physics and chemistry, where vibrations at the same frequency in two bodies lead to reinforced vibrations in both.

(c) Corroboration. It may be that the parallel or convergence of two developments is discovered only in retrospect. In that case there is of course no longer any influence on the actual course of events. But once the parallel is discovered, it can still serve as a confirmation in the literal sense of fortifying independent developments by stabilization. More important, such parallels can serve as historical control experiments that will provide relevant, if not conclusive, evidence of the legitimacy of both courses. This is what seems to me to have taken place in what I would call the grassroots development of phenomenological psychology in America. Its adoption of the word phenomenology occurred in almost complete ignorance of the original philosophical phenomenology. Of course, after discovery there is room for fruitful development and interaction.

[3] The Thesis

Keeping these types of "influence" apart seems to me of major importance for a full and sober appraisal of the role of any idea, person, or movement in history—and especially so in the case of a movement as fluid and undogmatic as phenomenology. For its influence cannot and should not be measured by the number of definite loans and quotations. Perhaps its main value consists in the "partial influences," the stimulation and reinforcement it has provided for independent developments. For phenomenology bids us to go not to the literary and personal sources, which are still indirect, but "to the things," to the phenomena, as the direct sources of all phenomenological insight. To have provided such inspiration may well have been the most important role of phenomenology in its relation to recent psychology and psychiatry. In fact, in this century phenomenology has influenced psychology and psychiatry more than any other movement in philosophy; it is rivaled only by the contribution of Ernst Cassirer, who himself had considerable connections with phenomenology. However, it is not the purpose of this book to make competitive claims for phenomenology. To establish these would presuppose a full-scale investigation of the influences exerted by other movements, such as positivism, naturalism, pragmatism, and Neo-Kantianism. My only concern is to present concrete evidence of specific contributions of phenomenology to developments in psychology and psychiatry, leaving it to the future to make comparative evaluations. What seems to me much more important at this stage is to show that philosophy, of any brand, still and again has significance for science, and for psychology and psychiatry in particular. In this sense, phenomenology is to serve only as an example.

More specifically, what I propose to show is this: Phenomenology as a philosophy has made a significant difference in the fields of psychology and psychiatry. By replacing the restrictive methodologies of a narrow positivism and naturalism, it has made room for new phenomena and new interpretations. It has broken the strait jacket of behaviorism without denying its relative value. It has also contributed to the overcoming of atomistic associationism. Concretely, it has helped in reforming the psychology of perception, of the emotions, and of the will and has added to such specialized enterprises as the study of the self and social psychology. In psychiatry it has made room for a much wider and deeper understanding of pathological phenomena and has helped to open the way for new therapies.

The main burden of this book will be to show concretely how much of this has been accomplished and in what ways.

[4] The Approach

The demonstration of these influences could be attempted by several routes. One method would be to go over the map of psychology and psychiatry and show what phenomenology has contributed in each area. Desirable though this would be for anyone interested in assessing the change that phenomenology has brought about in the total picture, I am afraid it would not be feasible—certainly not for me. For it would require a conspectus of the entire field with its major and some minor divisions before plotting the addition of phenomenology to each one of them.

Another approach might be to explore the major channels of influence either from the start or from the end. In the former case the major figures in phenomenological philosophy would have to serve as fountainheads, and their influences upon each one of the psychologists and psychiatrists in question would have to be enumerated. This might be the most impressive way of building up a credit sheet for each philosopher, and it is a method I considered very seriously. My chief reason for deciding against it was that I doubt its usefulness for those who want to understand what is going on in psychology and psychiatry today. Also, it presupposes more knowledge about the final stage, the effects, than I think I could and should expect. I must even admit that I myself had to learn a lot about these effects before I felt in a position to trace their ancestry.

This was one of the reasons why I decided to approach the story from the end, beginning with an examination of major figures in psychology and psychiatry, and going back from there to their sources in phenomenological philosophy. Even so, in the present frame, I intend no monographs on these figures. All that seems possible is to focus on the phenomenological ingredients in their work as seen against the background of the general pattern of their thinking and research. This means, of course, that the influence of each philosopher is scattered over the whole book. Whoever is primarily interested in this side of the story and particularly in what either Husserl or Scheler or Heidegger has added to the developments in these fields will therefore have to make frequent use of the indexes. Chapter 1, which deals with the psychological work of these philosophers themselves should also provide aids.

Otherwise, I hope the layout of the book as indicated in the Table of Contents will speak for itself. Let me repeat: the two major sections are not meant to coincide with the crumbling divisions between psychology and psychiatry. Thus the real division is that between the area studies which deal mostly with the psychologists, and the studies in depth which for the most part are devoted to the psychiatrists. Clearly, this is no hard and fast division, and it is certainly not a neat one. If this book laid any claim to comprehensiveness, this arrangement would certainly be a serious defect. But the very fact that the second part stresses studies of individual figures should make it clear that no such purpose was in my mind, and as I entered the jungle I realized how futile it would be to consider it. My attempt at an introduction is, as in my earlier book, merely an attempt to cut clearings. Much cleaning up and even more pioneer work remains to be done. It would be even phenomenologically misleading to present a neatly laid out map of a cultivated plain. A birds-eye view like mine must not conceal how confused and tangled the views are from below.

On the whole, this is not a story for purists. Certainly most of it would be rejected by Edmund Husserl, the founder of pure phenomenology, who came more and more to see the whole Phenomenological Movement as a corruption of his increasingly radical project of a rigorous science founded on transcendental phenomenology. There is, however, ample reason to see this "corruption" in a much wider perspective without diluting the purity of Husserl's intention to the vanishing point of mere lip service and window dressing. Seen in the context of the intellectual development of the Western world, phenomenology in the new Husserlian sense is really only a branch of a much wider stream, a wave superimposed on a much longer ground swell. By this ground swell I mean the countermovement to the wave of abstractive science initiated by Galileo with his suppression of the mathematically unmanageable world of the qualitative and the "subjective." The first highlight in the larger countermovement, which wanted to "save the phenomena" (in a sense different from Plato's) and recover the full breadth and depth of qualitative experience, was Goethe's theory of color, a theory opposed to Newton's. As a first attempt in that direction, it was even more effective than the Romantics' anti-scientific revolt against all science.[5] Hegel's "phenomenology" as an attempt to recover the concrete universal and the "colorful bark" of history belongs in this trend. Ewald Hering in his theory of the light sense, in opposition to Helmholtz' physicalistic approach, stressed the need for phenomenological description, prior to explanation, without using the name phenomenology. Even positivism, if not controlled by the "nothing-butters," had its phenomenological aspects, and even Ernst Mach and Ludwig Boltzmann employed the term "phenomenology," a fact not unknown to Husserl. Seen in this light Husserl's phenomenology, in adopting the pre-existing term and utilizing the attempts of his immediate predecessors Franz Brentano and Carl Stumpf, merely superimposed his new phenomenology on the wider and less pronounced movement. Husserl, too, attempted to reconcile the recovery of the full range of the phenomena with the rationality of a rigorous science.

It is true that Husserl's phenomenology differed from these pre-phenomenologies in its radicalism and its "purism." But if there is anything to this "purity," it should be able to purify its impure anticipations and imperfect rivals, thus providing the best possible preparation for the development of a more consistent phenomenology. One of the functions of the present enterprise could and should be to show how much the infusion of some of the elements of such a philosophical phenomenology

5. See A. N. Whitehead, *Science and the Modern World* (New York: Macmillan, 1925), chap. V ("The Romantic Reaction").

has already accomplished in molding psychology and psychiatry. There is no reason to think that this process has reached the end, particularly since new ingredients can be helpful in solving some of the old and new "crises" in empirical science.

Perhaps there is an even stronger case for a more liberal attitude toward unorthodox phenomenology: If it is true that phenomenology goes first and last "to the things," then it is to be expected that more than once it can and will arise spontaneously "from the grassroots." In this case, it would be anything but surprising if phenomenology should appear independently and repeatedly in different places and times. After all, Husserl's own phenomenology claimed to be one "from below." [6]

This observation does not mean that phenomenology should carefully insulate itself from the tradition, including its own tradition, in favor of exclusive communion with "the things." While it is good to have separate strands of phenomenology attack the phenomena independently, if only as controls, it stands to reason that ultimately even phenomenology will thrive best as a cooperative enterprise, and that exchange and mutual check on one's findings will help even one's own seeing. It is in this sense that the role of philosophical phenomenology for "grassroots phenomenology" in psychology and psychiatry seems to me worth exploring and recording for its own sake as well as for the sake of those who have a stake in doing phenomenology.

6. Spiegelberg, *Phenomenological Movement*, p. 111 n.

PART I

Contributions of Phenomenology to Psychology and Psychiatry: General Orientation

1 / Phenomenological Psychology in Phenomenological Philosophy

[1] Introductory Remarks

The chief purpose of the present chapter is to serve as a reminder. Most of the material brought together here in abridged form is contained in the pertinent chapters of my earlier book, where it can be found best by consulting the Index of Subjects under "psychology, phenomenological." However, there the main point was to show the connection between the general philosophical foundations of the phenomenologists under discussion and their concrete psychological studies. Thus the total contribution of phenomenology to psychology remained scattered. The function of the present recapitulation is to draw together the main results as a background for the new materials in the following chapters. No additional reading is necessary for those who are merely looking for a first orientation. Although my emphasis here is different, I shall follow the selection and sequence of the major figures in my earlier account.

The significant question to be answered in this chapter is whether and how far the philosophical ideas of our phenomenologists have affected their psychological research. In trying to answer it one has to bear in mind that in the academic setting of European universities philosophy and psychology were usually so closely connected that psychology was not more than a branch of philosophy. Wilhelm Wundt and Oswald Külpe, for example, combined both fields in one person and made distinctive contributions even in extra-psychological philosophy. Thus their interest in psychology was not a mere personal intrusion of the philosopher into a psychology department. To separate the strands of philosophy and psychology in the work of individual phenomenologists is far from simple. I shall begin with the major predecessors of phenomenology.

[2] Franz Brentano (1838–1917)

The role of psychology in Brentano's reformed philosophy was central: to provide the scientific foundation for all the branches of his new philosophy, including ethics. But not all of Brentano's psychology, written "from an empirical standpoint," can be claimed for phenomenology, quite apart from the fact that the term is almost completely absent from his vocabulary. Only his "descriptive psychology" (or "psychognosis"), as distinguished from "genetic psychology," which was to deal with causal explanations, would qualify. However, Brentano himself never progressed beyond the range of descriptive psychology. This psychology mostly explored general structures as revealed not to ordinary experience but to a kind of idealizing abstraction (*ideale Anschauung*) that clearly went beyond the experience of customary empiricism. This was indeed incipient phenomenology.

A full account of Brentano's phenomenology would therefore have to include most of the content of Volume I, and what in the second edition became Volume II, of his *Psychologie*,[1] omitting only his opening reflections about psychology in general and adding some of the posthumous materials edited by Oskar Kraus. But such a restatement would serve little purpose in the present context.

Instead, I shall merely mention some of the most original features of this descriptive psychology:

(1) *a new phenomenon*, "intentionality," or better, *reference to an object*, the most important distinguishing characteristic of psychic phenomena in contrast to physical phenomena. References differ in quality in such acts as perceiving, imagining, judging, willing, etc.

(2) *a new act*, inner perception as the simultaneous awareness of our own acts, an act that is "self-evident" and even infallible as far as it goes.

(3) *a new order of the phenomena*, the classification into three basic groups of psychic phenomena—representations

1. *Psychologie vom empirischen Standpunkt*, 3 vols. (Leipzig: Meiner, 1924–28).

(*Vorstellungen*), judgments, and feelings of "love" and "hatred." The latter two groups, in contrast to the first one, are distinguished by their polarization into positive and negative opposites.

Clearly, these features are only examples and are merely identified rather than described and evaluated. But they have been particularly influential both inside and outside Brentano's school.

Brentano's influence can be seen in the work of Carl Stumpf, as well as in the writings of Alexius Meinong's Graz school. Although the achievements of Brentano's psychology, such as intentionality, were not referred to explicitly, descriptive discoveries like Ehrenfels' *Gestaltqualitäten* were fitting developments of the Brentano approach to the psychic phenomena.

What does Brentano's psychology owe to his philosophy? Underlying his interest in psychology was his concern for a new philosophy built on scientific grounds. His expectation was that psychology would supply these grounds. Seeing that the existing associationist psychology was unable to fill this need, he attempted a new psychology that started out from a description of the data unfettered by positivistic blinkers. Obviously, this did not mean any loans from philosophy, but rather the opposite: Philosophy was now based on psychology. But the new psychology was phenomenology in the making. Phenomenological psychology received from Brentano the decisive impulse for its emphasis on description rather than explanation. Not all of his first results may have been discriminating enough. But some were left as cornerstones for full-fledged phenomenology.

[3] Carl Stumpf (1848–1936)

Stumpf is known chiefly for his pioneering contributions to the "psychology of sound." But in later reviewing his own work, it was precisely this "psychology," labeled so with reluctance, that he listed as *Phänomenologie*. In annexing it to phenomenology one has to bear in mind that Stumpf in his philosophy of science assigned to phenomenology a new sense, not taken up by others: that of exploring the contents of our experience as distinguished from the "functions" or acts in which they were experienced, which he called "psychology" in the narrower sense. This phenomenology was one of several "presciences" (*Vorwissenschaften*) preceding both philosophy and science.

However, the restricted meaning of Stumpf's term did not imply that his own research fell outside the range of phenomenology in the broad sense as used in this book.

There is only one circumstance which may make one pause: Stumpf's phenomenology is to a large extent experimental. And those who think of phenomenology as an a priori science hostile to experience may think that a fortiori it is also anti-experimental. It is therefore important to pay attention to the nature and purpose of Stumpf's experiments. Their primary purpose was not the statistical establishment of correlations between physical stimuli and psychological responses, but the discriminating and controlled exploration of the subjective phenomena, such as overtones, fusions, etc., in a way which makes their reproduction and checking possible even on an intersubjective basis. The means for such a systematic exploration was the experimental variation of the stimuli. In this manner Stumpf, in the two volumes of his classical but incomplete *Tonpsychologie,* managed to establish a number of basic facts about sound and its dimensions, their unity and their differences, about fusion and consonance, and also about the spatial character of sounds. Besides, he explored the properties of other sense phenomena and established such "attributes" as intensity as common to both auditory and visual sensations.

Another example of Stumpf's phenomenological studies concerned space perception. His "nativist" theory of the idea of space involved the rejection of the "empiricist" thesis, according to which the spatial organization of our sense world was learned gradually. The implied recognition of spatial perception as primary and underived was of course in line with a phenomenological approach and opposed to an associationist analysis. But it did not imply that the idea of space was innate or even an a priori form in Kant's sense.

These concrete examples may give the impression of a piecemeal approach. And it is true that Stumpf never produced a comprehensive work on psychology or philosophy. His main strength was concrete research. But that he did not lack philosophical penetration and perspective was shown in his Berlin Academy treatises. Psychology and phenomenology had definite and specific places in his system of the sciences. Although it would be hard to find any more specific influence of Stumpf's philosophy on psychology, his very conception of phenomenology was a result of his over-all view of the structure of reality and of human knowledge.

Stumpf's contribution to phenomenological psychology was important. It not only consisted in his additions to the descriptive knowledge of the phenomena of sound, but it included his utilization of experimental techniques for refining phenomenological observations and making them more intersubjective. Even more important was the fact that under Stumpf's aegis phenomenology became for the first time an established part of psychology. I submit that Stumpf's plea for phenomenology in Berlin had a lot to do with its subsequent adoption by the gestaltists and their American followers. It is also significant that, notwithstanding serious and increasing disagreements between Stumpf and Husserl and his associates, Stumpf always stood up for the phenomenology of Husserl's *Logische Untersuchungen.* This meant that not only Brentano's but Husserl's phenomenology had privileged access to subsequent psychology.

[4] Edmund Husserl (1859–1938)

Obviously, an appraisal of Husserl's role in the relation between phenomenology and psychology is of central importance. But it is also far from easy. Too often Husserl's historical struggle against psychologism has been considered proof of his hostility to all psychology. The first volume of his *Logische Untersuchungen* (1900) supplied the major support for this belief, and certain passages in his manifesto on "Philosophie als strenge Wissenschaft" (1911) attacking naturalistic philosophy seemed to confirm it. His relations to the leading psychologists of his time were bad or non-existent, as shown for instance by his intervention at the 1914 Göttingen Congress for experimental psychology. Although admittedly he failed to keep up with the literature and simultaneous developments, this did not prevent the psychologists from paying increasing attention to his work.

This paradox is reflected in Husserl's ambivalent attitude toward psychology. To understand it one has to sketch its development. It began with the "psychological analyses" of his habilitation thesis on the concept of number (1887). During this first period of an attempt to find foundations for the philosophy of arithmetic in the psychology of his master Franz Brentano, Husserl clearly thought of himself as a descriptive psychologist. The subsequent emancipation of his "pure logic" from psychology and the battle against psychologism showed him at the farthest remove from actual psychology. But the search for a foundation for this new logic in a non-psychological phenomenology led him back to the abandoned site. Yet not until the twenties did this interest in psychology again become thematic to the extent of special psychological studies. Two lecture courses on phenomenological psychology were given by Husserl in 1925 and 1928. His article "Phenomenology," prepared for the *Encyclopaedia Britannica,* with a first section on "Pure Psychology," was followed by the Amsterdam lectures on "Phenomenological Psychology" given in 1928.[2] Finally, the last part of *Die Krisis der europäischen Wissenschaften und die transzendentale Phänomenologie* (III), and especially its incomplete Part B, deals with psychology as one of the "ways" to the new philosophy. In fact, even in this last phase there seems to have been a development. In the Freiburg lectures Husserl was aiming at giving a solid foundation for all psychology through a pure psychology on philosophical grounds. In the Amsterdam lectures he used this phenomenological psychology (based on a "psychological reduction" to the purely psychic phenomena) as a stepping stone toward transcendental phenomenology (based on a more radical reduction than the "psychological" one needed for the purification of the psychic phenomena alone). At the last stage of the *Krisis* phenomenological psychology was claimed to coincide with transcendental phenomenology itself, which seemed destined to absorb it; in other words, here was only a difference in degree, not in kind, between pure psychology and phenomenology as a philosophy. Thus Husserl seemed to have come full circle. While initially philosophy had been converted into psychology, now psychology was on the point of becoming transcendental phenomenology.

The ambivalence in Husserl's relation to psychology can perhaps best be understood in the light of the basic role of consciousness in his philosophy. As he saw it, consciousness was on the one hand a basic fact of pure psychology. Treated as a mere fact of such a psychology, it could become a threat for phenomenology, which could not accept any facts without questioning their epistemic credentials. For such a "transcendental" phenomenology even pure psychology could involve (transcendental) psychologism. On the other hand, phenomenology offered a chance for a fundamental examination of psychological consciousness, thus making a special contribution to psychology.

2. *Husserliana IX*, 237–349.

But psychology could also provide a particularly good stepping stone to phenomenology, showing its need and sharing with it at least the same phenomenon, though seen in different ways.

The Husserl Archives in Louvain contain the copy of a five-page typewritten letter by Husserl dated June 28, 1927, addressed to Karl Bühler in reply to Bühler's gift of his *Die Krise der Psychologie*. This letter is remarkable for several reasons.

1. Husserl states at once that he has read Bühler's book with the greatest interest, a fact which is borne out by the unusual number of marginalia in the copy now at the Archives. This fact even suggests that this was one of the books which started Husserl's thought about the "crisis" of the European sciences.

2. At the same time Husserl acknowledged that his studies had made it impossible for him to follow the psychological literature, thus confirming an impression based on the absence of any references to psychologists after Brentano and Stumpf in his writings.[3]

3. Most of the letter develops the claim that pure phenomenology, while primarily aiming at a transcendental philosophy, can at the same time be used as an a priori foundation for empirical psychology, something which psychologists have overlooked thus far.

4. Husserl recommends to the psychologists the return to the concrete, live experience (*konkrete lebendige Erfahrung*) of the world of life as the meaning of a priori and transcendental phenomenology.

5. The letter reveals Husserl's disappointment about the fact that even such psychologists as Bühler, who had made use of his *Logische Untersuchungen*, had failed to take account of the possible contributions of the work he had done since the *Ideen*. We shall have occasion to see later whether Bühler, who had actually tried to call on Husserl shortly before this letter, merited this complaint.

However, in the present context, the last phase in Husserl's

3. This must not make one overlook the fact that Husserl was aware of some of the uses made of his work by psychologists, e.g., by the Würzburg school, and that he even envisaged the uses of their methods by phenomenology. Witness the following passage from *Ideen* III (*Phaenomenologica* V, 32) written before 1912:

> As an academic teacher I have for a good many years discussed the possibility of artificial measures for the providing of exemplary intuitings (*Anschauungen*) and have taken the very first studies of the Würzburg school about the experimental psychology of thinking as an occasion for discussing the methodological experiment in exactly the same sense in which I am doing it here (my translation).

relations to psychology, also characterized by his rejection of gestaltism as another form of naturalistic psychology, seems to be of minor significance for psychologists, especially in view of its incompleteness. Here I would like to concentrate on two phases in Husserl's relations to psychology: the actual contributions of his earlier work and the potential contribution of his most explicit and extensive piece of psychology, the Freiburg lectures on phenomenological psychology.

Husserl's first contributions to phenomenological psychology were not always announced under this name. They began with his early efforts, still belonging to his Brentano period, to find psychological foundations for a philosophy of arithmetic. Descriptions of the acts of collective unification, of counting, of elementary and higher arithmetic operations, were distinguished and discussed, if not fully described. The explicitly phenomenological accounts began with the second volume of the *Logische Untersuchungen.* Acts of signifying (bestowing meaning and supplying intuitive content) and various kinds of abstraction (isolating and generalizing) were distinguished and exemplified. In particular, the whole phenomenon of intentionality was now unfolded in its essential structure and in its variations. In so doing Husserl soon stepped beyond the range of merely logical acts, especially when he explored sensuous and non-sensuous ("categorial") intuiting (*Anschauung*), thus passing completely beyond Brentano's pioneer distinctions. Then Husserl extended the scope of his phenomenological psychology even further. His lectures on the inner consciousness of time, published in 1928 and now augmented by the texts published in *Husserliana* X, reveal a new picture of memory, distinguishing acts of retention and recall, protention and expectation. In his *Ideen* phenomenological psychology was enriched by the study of perception and various dimensions of belief ("doxic" modifications). Axiological and practical acts were considered, though it is true that in his publications Husserl never explored the non-theoretical phenomena, beyond blocking out the field for their study. Increasing emphasis was placed on the ego in its various roles and acts, which had been omitted from the phenomenological sections of the second, phenomenological volume of the *Logische Untersuchungen,* but was eventually considered under the odd label "egology." In the later studies one almost always finds stimulating beginnings, though it must be admitted that the concrete descriptions became rarer and sketchier. The remarkably full accounts of pre-predicative and predicative experience in *Erfah-*

rung und Urteil (1939), edited by Ludwig Landgrebe, belong to much earlier periods.

The lectures on "Phenomenological Psychology" (in *Husserliana* IX), as well as the full text of the *Britannica* article, so badly telescoped (from 7,000 German to 4,000 English words) in the translation for the 1929 *Britannica*, and the text of the two completed thirds of the Amsterdam lectures, did not become accessible until their posthumous publication in 1962 and thus have had little chance to exert any actual influence. But their content justifies a preview, until a translation becomes available. For here is the most sustained development of Husserl's idea of a phenomenological psychology.[4] The importance of these lectures, though unpublished at the time, can perhaps better be understood in the light of a passage from a letter written to Husserl by Martin Heidegger on October 22, 1927, relating to the latter's attempts to help Husserl with the preparation of his article for the *Britannica*.[5] In this letter Heidegger touched on the lack of a psychology in Husserl's sense in the science of his day. Indeed, Husserl's claim that a psychology free of all references to physical ingredients was the ambition of the psychology of the time may strike one as a strange illusion about the actual state of contemporary psychology. This text then provides at least the badly needed illustration of what was in Husserl's mind when he talked about such a pure psychology. Even so it is important to point out at the very start that the lectures contain no *system* of phenomenological psychology. Much more than his *Ideen zu einer reinen Phänomenologie*, this work would deserve the title "Guiding Ideas Toward . . ."

What Husserl had in mind, according to the Introduction, was an a priori psychology of our inner experience designed to describe its essential structures, analogous to, but still quite different from, pure geometry with its limited system of axioms (*Husserliana* IX, 50). Such a psychology was to provide the basis for empirical psychology. The actual content of the lec-

4. For the relation of the conception of Husserl's phenomenological psychology to his general phenomenology and to empirical psychology, see H. Spiegelberg, *The Phenomenological Movement: A Historical Introduction*, 2d ed. (The Hague: Martinus Nijhoff, 1965), pp. 149–52. For a fuller account and discussion, see Aron Gurwitsch, "Edmund Husserl's Conception of Phenomenological Psychology," *Review of Metaphysics*, XIX (1966), 689–727.

5. *Husserliana* IX, 601: "You remarked repeatedly during the past days: Actually [*eigentlich*] there is not yet any pure psychology." Heidegger then referred to three unspecified folders among Husserl's own writings whose publication could fill the gap.

tures consists of forty-five systematic sections, of which the first twenty deal with general methodological questions of phenomenology. Only the remaining twenty-five take up psychological topics specifically, and these without any claim to comprehensiveness. However, they include some very suggestive ideas concerning the strata of the psychic life (*Stufenaufbau des Seelischen*), as based upon the passive impersonal life on which the ego-centered personal life is founded; here Husserl also pays brief attention to the psychic permeation (*Beseelung*) of the living body (*Leib*) (§21). Perception, one of Husserl's major themes, figures next with some significant developments of his earlier accounts. Then come the modifications of perception in recollection, phantasy, and expectation. The ego enters as the subjective pole of all psychic experience. But there was apparently no time left for discussion of the affective and practical life. The final retrospect makes it clear that what the lectures had offered was at best a sketch, a series of reflections about what phenomenological psychology might do and would have to do on a systematic scale.

In Husserl's case it may appear almost superfluous to raise the question of how far this phenomenological psychology was the fruit of philosophy and particularly of pure phenomenology. While Husserl's phenomenology was deliberately developed "from below," it is clear that the basic patterns of interpretation came "from above." This can be seen particularly in the lectures on phenomenological psychology. This approach is manifested in the discussion not only of the methods employed, i.e., the eidetic and especially the transcendental one, but of the pattern of intentionality, which was basic for all of Husserl's descriptive undertakings. True, Husserl would never have tried to impose these patterns upon the phenomena as they presented themselves. But these patterns certainly served as guidelines for the structural investigation.

What, if any, were Husserl's concrete contributions to phenomenological psychology? One must be on guard against overestimating them. For not only did Husserl fail to give a complete outline of his phenomenological psychology, but one finds surprisingly few concrete traces of his specific psychological insights in the subsequent literature. This may be partly due to the fact that such analyses were concerned too directly with the more technical parts of his work. It may also have something to do with the fact that Husserl himself, at least in his publications, largely ignored the work of psychologists, including William James, for whom he had such high regard, and the phenomenological psychologists. Thus it was not Husserl, the phenomenological *psychologist*, who proved to be the major contributor to the development of psychology. It was the *philosopher* Husserl whose general conception of phenomenology as the science of intentional consciousness, to be described in its essential structures, provided the major impulse for the future.

[5] Alexander Pfänder (1870–1941)

Except for his *Logic*, originally a side-line in his work, Pfänder is known thus far chiefly for his work in phenomenological psychology. In fact, among the members of the early phenomenological group he was the only one who published book-length studies in this field. But although most of his work in psychology was either explicitly or implicitly phenomenological, this does not mean that he developed a true system of phenomenological psychology.

Actually, Pfänder's first major book, the introduction to psychology as a whole (*Einführung in die Psychologie*) preceded the beginning of the Phenomenological Movement and his contact with Husserl. But it followed Pfänder's own *Phenomenology of Willing* of 1900, which appeared the year before Husserl's studies in "phenomenology and theory of knowledge" (*Logische Untersuchungen*, Vol. II). However, it must be realized that Pfänder's early phenomenology was to all intents and purposes identical with Brentano's descriptive psychology and with the analytic psychology of his own teacher Theodor Lipps. Thus it did not yet stress the need and the uses of Husserl's essential intuitings (*Wesensschau*). Even his later descriptive studies were not geared to Husserl's terminology. What they did offer was a vast enrichment in range and depth of the descriptions of psychological phenomena, combined with a penetrating grasp of their essential structures, relations, and varieties. But for Pfänder more perceptive description was only another step on the road to interpretive understanding. Thus his last and most ambitious work, on "Man's Psyche" (*Die Seele des Menschen*), meant an extension of phenomenological description in an attempt to understand the descriptively enriched picture dynamically. Here Pfänder explored the why as well as the how, yet always painstakingly showing the intuitive bases for his interpretations.

However, in the present context it might be more helpful to point out some of the more exemplary and effective pieces of Pfänder's descriptive phenomenology. In selecting these I would like to stress Pfänder's primary interest in the practical life of the psyche, an interest which differs significantly from Husserl's in its theoretical functions. The following points deserve special notice:

(1) the distinction between willing and the more general phenomenon of striving, a distinction which makes the taking of a position (*Stellungnahme*) the central characteristic of willing;

(2) the contrasting of motivation with causation and similar phenomena, which shows that motives in the strict sense become motives only because the ego espouses them as supports for its decisions;

(3) the study of the directional sentiments (*Gesinnungen*) such as love and benevolence, which describes them as acts flowing toward their objects with a characteristic emotional temperature, confirming or denying their right to be, and which also explores such general dimensions of psychic acts as degrees of genuineness, artificiality, definitiveness, etc.;

(4) the distinction of such qualities as texture, size, flow, and tonus in the structure of human personalities (characterology), descriptions in which Pfänder often uses daring metaphors;

(5) a widening in the conception of perception, which was given a key position in Pfänder's philosophy as the ultimate foundation of all claims to knowledge, including perception not only of theoretical objects but also of values and ideal requirements, and distinguishing between probing and scanning perception, the latter clearly having little if any epistemological weight.

How far can phenomenological philosophy claim credit for these psychological contributions? There is certainly little explicit trace of Husserl's phenomenological philosophy in Pfänder's psychological writings. And Pfänder's own version of phenomenology was still very much in the making when he published his most influential papers in phenomenological psychology. Nevertheless, certain underlying philosophical conceptions permeate Pfänder's psychology implicitly. However, they form not dogmatic presuppositions but merely anticipations to be tested in actual research. A particularly good instance is his distinction between fundamental and empirical essences, fundamental essences being what a certain being is "basically" or "at bottom," or in its fully developed form or "idea." In our empirical lives these essences are developed either not at all or only very imperfectly. But it is part of our full knowledge of such entities as living beings that they contain such undeveloped essences. For Pfänder, this is a conception that only phenomenology can underpin.

Some of Pfänder's phenomenological psychology made considerable impression on Ludwig Binswanger and José Ortega y Gasset. His descriptions of genuine and spurious phenomena prepared the way for the later doctrines of authenticity (*Eigentlichkeit*) and inauthenticity. Lately, Paul Ricoeur's interest and tribute suggest that Pfänder's day may still arrive even elsewhere.[6]

[6] Moritz Geiger (1880–1937)

Like Pfänder, Moritz Geiger, his junior by ten years, came from the school of Theodor Lipps; but he had also studied in Leipzig under Wundt and in Göttingen under Husserl. He had even visited in the United States, before finding an outlet there during his last four years. Ranging much more widely than Pfänder, though without Pfänder's systematic scope, he had a strong stake in phenomenological psychology. His most brilliant contribution to it was a study on the phenomenology of esthetic enjoyment, one of the best examples of the psychology of aesthetics, a field in which Geiger was the first to take a phenomenological interest. He made some valuable distinctions in exploring the metaphor of "depth," which led him into existential psychology. He also did discriminating work in the field of empathy, particularly the empathy of moods. He was also the first to raise the problem of the unconscious on phenomenological grounds, though not yet in connection with psychoanalysis.

Phenomenological philosophy entered into these psychological studies only indirectly, but in his methodological discussions

6. See especially Ricoeur's plea for Pfänder as a guide for the linguistic analysis of the language of willing in his still unpublished Munich paper of 1971 on "Phénoménologie du vouloir et approche par le langage ordinaire."

Geiger made it plain that to him empirical and experimental research made sense only on the basis of preliminary phenomenological distinctions. This position implied the espousal of a broader empiricism, not restricted to sense data, and the rejection of the reductionism of positivistic "nothing-butters" and nominalists who denied general essences. While this was common ground for the early phenomenological movement, Geiger's concrete research included some particularly effective applications. Limited though they were, they must not be lost.

[7] Max Scheler (1874–1928)

Compared with the contributions of other phenomenological philosophers to the spread of phenomenology into psychology and psychiatry, Scheler's were the most immediate and most pervasive, though he never wrote or even planned on a systematic phenomenological psychology. Whatever he ejected along his meteoric path was incidental to his major concern of developing a philosophical anthropology along personalistic lines. It is significant that his first two phenomenological contributions to psychology, the ones on self-deceptions (*Über Selbsttäuschungen*) and on *ressentiment*, appeared in a new journal for "patho-psychology" (*Zeitschrift für Pathopsychologie*, I [1911] and II [1912]), and established a first connection between the new movement and psychiatry. Scheler's classic book of 1913 on the phenomenology of sympathy contained the first phenomenological discussions of Freudian psychoanalysis, negative but not unsympathetic.[7] But his major constructive contributions to both fields are scattered over his major works and do not lend themselves to a systematic summary in such a narrow frame as the present one. All I can do here is to single out some of his more influential descriptions, more or less in the sequence of their publications.

Scheler's first and foremost interest in phenomenological explorations was in the emotional area. This field was of particular significance to him in view of its central role in man's relations to the world of values. A more discriminating phenomenology of

7. *Zur Phänomenologie und Theorie der Sympathiege Fühle und von Liebe und Hass* (Halle: Niemeyer, 1913; 2d ed., Bonn: Friedrich Cohen, 1923). English translation by Peter Heath, *The Nature of Sympathy* (Hamden, Conn.: Archon Books, 1954). For Scheler's interest in Freud, see also Lou Andreas-Salomé, *In der Schule bei Freud* (Zurich: Niehans, 1958), pp. 197–203.

our emotional life promised to Scheler not only a phenomenological harvest for its own sake but the means for freeing the emotions from the traditional charge of total and hopeless subjectivity. What Scheler hoped to show was that even the emotions contained essential structures connecting them meaningfully with one another and with values as their intentional referents, and that hence they obeyed a priori laws of meaning (*Sinngesetze*). In order to show this, Scheler had first to demonstrate the inadequacy of an ethics based upon mere sympathy, a phenomenological study which revealed not only the variety of the phenomena involved, but also the secondary nature of sympathy. In this respect sympathy differed basically from love as an act in which Scheler saw an essential and primary orientation toward value. In his central work on ethics, he offered an even more elaborate positive phenomenology of the emotions, distinguishing especially between non-intentional and "intentional," i.e., object-directed, feelings (*Wertfühlen*), which opened up the possibility of genuine value cognition. In addition, Scheler explored different strata of these feelings—the merely sensuous, the vital, the purely mental (*seelisch*), and the spiritual (*geistige*) emotions—all with different relations to values.

But while Scheler's most solid work centered in the phenomenology of the emotions, his interests gradually spread over all of psychology. Most important to him was his theory of act and person, the person being actually a unity of acts, and as such not objectifiable. Thus its phenomenological description posed special problems.

Another instance of Scheler's phenomenological pioneering was in the philosophy of religion. Here phenomenological psychology was charged particularly with the exploration of the religious acts, among which Scheler mentioned—though he did not explore in detail—entreaty, thanksgiving, reverence, etc.

Finally, there is the area of perception, in which Scheler became involved particularly in connection with his attempt to make a phenomenological case for realism against Husserl's growing idealism. Here Scheler paid particular attention to the experience of resistance, as manifested in our perception of reality. It must also not go unmentioned that Scheler made an impressive case for the possibility of the direct perception of other selves contrary to any theories basing our knowledge on inference or on empathy.

Similar phenomenological studies can be found in a vast number of scattered places, some in separate essays. Those on *ressentiment* and on suffering may serve as examples. In the field of psychopathology an essay on *Rentenhysterie* (pension neurosis) is indicative of the range of his marginal psychological and psychopathological interests.

Scheler's phenomenological psychology was clearly guided by certain philosophical prejudgments—at times perhaps misguided ones. But these prejudgments also helped him in finding new phenomena of which he gave pioneering accounts. Thus, without the conception of intentionality he would hardly have been able to develop his new theory of emotions. His theory of the emotional a priori opened up the whole question of structural relationships among our psychic phenomena and their referents. This was certainly phenomenological psychology with a philosophical foundation.

Scheler was the great stimulator of phenomenological psychology, though he was not always its most convincing spokesman. His name occurs more frequently in the psychological and psychopathological literature than that of any of the early phenomenologists, Husserl included. This may also be due to the fact that he paid much more explicit attention to the work of the empirical psychologists than other phenomenologists did. To give only a few examples: The philosophical anthropology of Paul-Ludwig Landsberg, Helmuth Plessner, and Wilhelm Hengstenberg would not have been possible without Scheler. In psychopathology Kurt Schneider, H. C. Rümke, Paul Schilder, and V. E. von Gebsattel were at least temporarily under the spell of Scheler's ideas. This is also the case with such biologists turned psychologists and philosophers as Viktor von Weizsäcker and F. J. J. Buytendijk.

[8] Martin Heidegger (b. 1889)

Heidegger's influence on psychology and psychiatry differs vastly from Scheler's. There was nothing deliberate about it. Actually, Heidegger's Ph.D. thesis was an attack on psychologism. In the beginning of *Sein und Zeit* (§ 10), he set apart his existential analytics from psychology as well as from anthropology and biology, charging psychology, along with the other disciplines, with the neglect of its ontological foundations. For Heidegger, psychology, in particular, fails to explore the mode of being basic for psychological phenomena. This mode of being is and remains Heidegger's absorbing interest. The fact that lately he has taken some responsive and even spontaneous interest in the work of such existential psychiatrists as Medard Boss and Viktor Frankl hardly indicates any psychological, let alone psychiatric, ambitions.

Thus Heidegger's impact on psychology and psychiatry is really an unplanned side effect, based in part on a misunderstanding of his central objective. His role here is fundamentally similar to the one he played in the genesis of French existentialism, which adopted him as one of its founders largely because of a misinterpretation of *Sein und Zeit*. It is true that Heidegger's failure to top the analytics of human existence with an ontology of Being left the existential sections of the book as the only "functioning" part of his project. Under these circumstances, it is not surprising that in the hands of his first interpreters the study of existence soon developed into existentialism. Likewise, it is no wonder that psychology and anthropology as well as the other human sciences made use of what seemed exciting and fruitful enough for their own interests without waiting for the missing culmination of *Being and Time*, which would have brought the ontological coping stone, the sense of Being itself. No matter how unintentional this new use was in Heidegger's own perspective, the effect cannot be denied, even though Heidegger may have disclaimed it, especially in the case of Ludwig Binswanger's *Daseinsanalyse*.

That Heidegger's phenomenological ontology contains ingredients which are immediately relevant to phenomenological psychology is obvious from the titles of some of the sections of *Sein und Zeit* which refer to fear (*Furcht*), anxiety (*Angst*), and care (*Sorge*). But what kind of phenomenology is invoked? Here it must be realized that Heidegger's version differs from Husserl's in several regards, as he himself has recently stated explicitly.[8] While he too thinks of phenomenology as a direct approach "to the things," he has repudiated Husserl's version of it as a "distinctive philosophical position," i.e., transcendental idealism. Even in *Sein und Zeit* he by-passed descriptive phenomenology in favor of what he now called "hermeneutic phenomenology," a phenomenology whose major function was the interpretation or unveiling of the meaning, often a hidden meaning, of the "phenomenological," as distinguished from the "vulgar," phenomena. Hence Heidegger's contribution to phe-

8. Prefatory letter to William J. Richardson, *Heidegger: Through Phenomenology to Thought* (The Hague: Nijhoff, 1963), p. xv. See also *Zur Sache des Denkens* (Tübingen: Niemeyer, 1969), pp. 69 ff.

nomenological psychology was clearly not straight description but an interpretation comparable to the kind of hermeneutics sought by Wilhelm Dilthey, to whom Heidegger often paid guarded tribute.

The most conspicuous cases of Heidegger's interpretations of psychological phenomena in the usual sense occurred in the context of his characterization of *Dasein* as being-in-the-world, in the preparatory section I of *Sein und Zeit.* Analyses of situations (*Befindlichkeiten*), especially in the form of moods (*Stimmungen*), were introduced as the most revealing clues to the modes of being (*Seinsweisen*) of *Dasein.* In this context Heidegger also explored fear (*Furcht*). He paid special attention to the ways in which everyday *Dasein* can "fall away" (*Verfallen*), discussing curiosity (*Neugier*), for instance, as indicative of man's flight from his being. He then analyzed anxiety (*Angst*), which he distinguished from fear by the absence of a definite object and interpreted as giving access to the fundamental character of *Dasein,* concern (*Sorge*). Anxiety (*Angst*) was interpreted even more fully in *What is Metaphysics?* as a pulling away from nothingness. In considering these often puzzling, if not startling, interpretations one must bear in mind that Heidegger was not after a description of the ordinary phenomenon in its entirety but tried to determine its "meaning," and more specifically the way in which, in its very structure, it is related to Being. Such a limited and slanted analysis may catch a significant part of the total phenomenon, but it must not be mistaken for an all-embracing one.

In section II of *Sein und Zeit,* the "Fundamental Analysis," further psychological themes enter, but they are mostly related to such ethical topics as conscience and its call. In later works such subjects became rarer. His new interpretations of "thinking" (in the sense of meditation or *Andacht*) or of calmness (*Gelassenheit*) still have a certain affinity with psychological topics. But Heidegger would be the last to claim these treatments as psychological, which does not rule out the possibility that others may do so. What must always be realized is that Heidegger is interested in such phenomena only to the extent that they reveal Being, represent a "clearing" (*Lichtung*) within Being, as Heidegger now often characterizes human "ek-sistence," i.e., as "standing out" into Being.

In view of these relatively brief and almost incidental discussions, Heidegger's impact on the psychologists and especially the psychiatrists is truly amazing. The explanation lies deeper than these isolated analyses of familiar psychological topics can reveal. What has to be remembered is that Heidegger's analyses of the modes of being of man (*existentiale Analyse*) cannot be carried out in isolation from the analysis of man's entire existence (*existentielle Analyse*). Hence Heidegger's ontological insights are inextricably connected with ontic insights about man, including his psychological structure. It takes only a switch in interest and emphasis to make these aspects explicit.

It is from the highly original themes of this wider ontic analysis that the real inspirations of Heidegger's phenomenology for psychology and psychiatry originated. By introducing such themes as Being, *Dasein*, world, time, and death, Heidegger placed man and his psyche before a vast cosmic background that psychology had never before considered in this manner. What now emerged was that a real understanding of man, normal or abnormal, was possible only by seeing him in relation to this most comprehensive setting. How does man relate himself to Being? What is his world and his place in it? How does he experience time? Heidegger's phenomenological hermeneutics provides the horizon against which man's psyche stands out in depth. In its light, man is a being who is ultimately defined by his relation not only to other beings but to Being itself and its fundamental characteristics. It is thus Heidegger's new ontology which has ultimately revolutionized psychology and psychiatry.

[9] Nicolai Hartmann (1882–1950)

It is by no means clear that Nicolai Hartmann should be included among the philosophers of the Phenomenological Movement. But his relations with it were so close and so historically important that he must not go unmentioned, and even the psychological implications of his thought have to be considered. However, in spite of his encyclopedic interests, which resulted in a new type of system, Hartmann took comparatively little direct interest in psychology. There were incidental discussions of psychological questions in his largely phenomenological ethics, such as his accounts of value consciousness and its varieties, and even in his critical ontology, where he introduced a group of "emotional-transcendent acts" capable of giving us access to transcendent reality.[9] But they did not add up to a phe-

9. *Zur Grundlegung der Ontologie* (Berlin: de Gruyter, 1935), pp. 177 ff.

nomenological psychology and do not seem to have had much influence on non-philosophical psychologists.

There was, however, one more general doctrine in Hartmann's ontology which did have such an effect. For his ontology asserted a pervasive "law" according to which reality has a stratified structure. Its higher strata are supported by lower strata, which form their necessary condition; yet the higher strata remain autonomous in their novelty with regard to the lower ones.[10] Hartmann even asserted that this fundamental "law of categories" was confirmed by the "phenomena," apparently in the sense of his own phenomenology (IV, 14–17). Now Hartmann himself applied this law merely to the relation between the psychic (*seelisch*) phenomena and the spiritual (*geistig*) phenomena which rested upon them. But he did not claim that the psyche itself has within it a hierarchic structure, a principle that came to be defended in the strata theories of Erich Rothacker and Philipp Lersch. Lersch in particular, gave special credit for this conception to Nicolai Hartmann.

[10] Gabriel Marcel (b. 1889)

Psychological interest is more pronounced among the French phenomenologists than among most of the German ones. This may be explained in part by the new emphasis on human existence, which now has become for the French the focus of phenomenological attention. Even the interest in Scheler, the first phenomenologist to make a real impression in France, had its center in his psychological and anthropological writings.

Among the French philosophers Marcel was the first to do original phenomenology. However, his ultimate concern was clearly not psychology but "metaphysics," and more specifically the "ontological mystery" of Being and man's participation in it. Among the forms of this participation are such existential acts as commitment, hope, and faith. The primary focus for this "mystery," our own body, is experienced in different ways. Such "situations" give rise to Marcel's diary-style reflections, which often throw new and striking light on psychological phenomena. However, even his essay-length elaborations of these entries are

10. *Das Problem des geistigen Seins* (Berlin: de Gruyter, 1933), pp. 15 ff.

not, and are not meant to be, exhaustive phenomenological analyses but mostly existential appeals. Yet the stimulating effect of these samples of firsthand phenomenology must not be underestimated.

Marcel's incipient phenomenological psychology is guided by his ulterior philosophical objectives and his underlying "metaphysical" conceptions of existence and being. What he contributed to existential psychology was the pioneering interest in phenomena not yet seen in this light and now shining with a new radiance.

[11] JEAN-PAUL SARTRE (B. 1905)

SARTRE'S STAKE in phenomenological psychology is particularly high. Academically, it even precedes his work in general philosophy, at least as far as the record of his book-length publications is concerned, which begins with his two books on the imagination and the one on the emotions. However, even in the selection of these topics one may discover indications of his underlying philosophical concerns, chiefly about freedom, which he found especially evident in the phenomena of the imagination and most severely threatened by the passions.

Phenomenology, which Sartre studied in Berlin by reading Husserl, Scheler, and Heidegger, along with Jaspers and the psychoanalysts, gave him the tools for exploring these phenomena much more confidently than his prior academic training had allowed, and for separating what is phenomenologically certain from what is merely empirically probable. His most explicit reflections on the relations between psychology, phenomenology, and phenomenological psychology occur in the Introduction to his *Sketch of a Theory of the Emotions,* where, after trying to show the inadequacies of a merely empirical psychology in accounting for human existence, he introduced phenomenology in both the Husserlian and Heideggerian style as the basis for a phenomenological psychology capable of assigning meaning to the facts in the context of human existence. The brief treatise itself is meant as a mere sample of such a phenomenological theory and not even as an exhaustive one. A more highly developed piece was Sartre's second book about the imagination, the first one having been merely critical and programmatic. The later book actually includes both phenomenological and empirical psychology. The first of its four parts, giving the phenomenological description of what is certain, chiefly studies the "intentional" structure of the imagination.

Sartre's interest in phenomenological psychology has not ended with his first psychological monographs. Occasions for psychological digressions occur in his more philosophical writings as well as in his literary work. To enumerate them here would be both unnecessary and futile. A few examples should suffice.

In *Being and Nothingness,* the descriptions of bad faith are of particular interest, a phenomenon which in Sartre's existential psychoanalysis was to take the place of the Freudian unconscious and the mechanisms of repression. Existential psychoanalysis, as the attempt to "decipher" man's actions and especially his neurotic behavior by going back to his fundamental choices, became the most original and most ambitious part of Sartre's phenomenological psychology. However, admittedly the development of this new psychoanalysis can in no way approach the work of Freud, though Sartre has given a good many illustrations of his psychoanalytic method in his literary case studies on *Genet, Flaubert,* and *Baudelaire,* and in his *Portrait of an Anti-Semite.* His studies of the gaze (*regard*) in the context of his social phenomenology are also characteristic of his originality—and of his limitations. So are his studies of the body-consciousness and of such social attitudes as love, indifference, and masochism as ways of coping with the conflicting freedom of other people. But while there is a comparatively detailed, though slanted, treatment of the inauthentic modes of behavior, there is only the barest hint as to the possibility of authentic alternatives, let alone phenomenological descriptions of them.

A characteristic example of Sartre's penetrating slant is his account of "nausea." Its chief description occurs in the diary-novel of the same title, which actually was Sartre's first major literary success. Compared with it, the treatment of this experience in *Being and Nothingness* is pale and peripheral. If one contrasts Sartre's analysis of nausea with the remarkable but neglected study of *Der Ekel* by Aurel Kolnai in the tenth volume of Husserl's yearbook, presumably unknown to Sartre, two things stand out: (1) What Sartre deals with is a very special type of nausea, i.e., a reaction to Being as such, in this sense an ontological nausea. Even when he relates it to specific materials such as the viscous (in his "psychoanalysis of matter"), he clearly is not interested in exploring the phenomenon of nausea for its own sake. (2) There is no detailed analysis and description of the structure of the phenomenon. His primary concern is nausea as a response to Being as such in its contingency and its overpowering proliferation. Thus, increasingly Sartre's phenomenological psychology served the purposes of his wider ontology and existential anthropology, which of late are trying to come to terms with Marxism. Its merit lies chiefly in its fresh attack on relatively unexplored phenomena which happen to fit into Sartre's preconceived ontological scheme.

Sartre's phenomenological psychology owed its primary inspiration to Husserl's pure phenomenology. But this does not mean that Sartre remained permanently dependent on it. He is much too original in his application as well as in his theorizing to subscribe to any orthodoxy. His most important contribution is the impulse he has given to the cause of an indigenous phenomenological psychology in the French world. His idea of an existential psychoanalysis, never meant as a therapeutic enterprise, may not have attracted much following. But indirectly it has reinforced other currents both in France and elsewhere, if only in their protests against it.

[12] Maurice Merleau-Ponty (1908–1961)

The French phenomenologist with the greatest stake and record in psychology was clearly Maurice Merleau-Ponty. This is evident not only from his major works up to about 1945, but also from the fact that his first appointment at the Sorbonne was in psychology and specifically in child psychology.[11]

However, the nature of Merleau-Ponty's contributions differs considerably from Sartre's. They do not consist in the identification of overlooked or neglected phenomena, in whose exposure Sartre excels. Instead, Merleau-Ponty seems to stay with such familiar phenomena as perception or sensation. What is new is his phenomenological reinterpretation of these phenomena.

In this sense his first major contribution was the phenome-

11. From the Sorbonne period stem his lectures on "The Child's Relations with Others," published in *Les Cours de Sorbonne* and translated by William Cobb for the volume edited by James M. Edie, *The Primacy of Perception* (Evanston, Ill.: Northwestern University Press, 1964). Lately, the student notes of five more such courses, approved by the lecturer, have been published in the *Bulletin de psychologie*, XVIII (1964), 109–336, along with fuller versions of the other two courses.

nological reclamation of the concept of behavior from its impoverishment at the hands of a narrow behaviorism. For to Merleau-Ponty, behavior emerged as a *Gestalt* or form which embraces both the external and the internal phenomena, consciousness and movement, in inextricable interfusion. Both were aspects of one and the same phenomenon.

Merleau-Ponty's largest work, *The Phenomenology of Perception,* was also his most ambitious undertaking. It was, however, less a work in phenomenological psychology than in philosophy, for which perception was to serve as the ground level. The "return to the phenomena," which was Merleau-Ponty's way out of the impasse of the usual psychology of perception and sensation, led him first to a consideration of the phenomenal field, in which the body and the world as perceived were the most important topics to be explored and described. Perception was studied primarily as the way in which we are related to the world. It was finally interpreted as an existential act by which we commit ourselves to a certain interpretation of the "sense" of experience as it presents itself to us.

There are of course any number of incidental phenomenological observations in Merleau-Ponty's other writings. But it would be hard to isolate them from their contexts. Merleau-Ponty clearly did not wish to add to a phenomenological "picture book," as Husserl had called this kind of piecemeal phenomenology. His most remarkable contribution lay in the new existential interpretation of the phenomena as he conceived of them.

One significant difference between Merleau-Ponty and Sartre can be seen in their respective attitudes toward psychoanalysis and Freud. While Sartre found in psychoanalysis a challenge which phenomenology and existential philosophy had to take seriously, he himself rejected Freud's theory as mechanistic and speculative rather than phenomenological. All he could accept was the psychoanalysis of one of Freud's renegades, Wilhelm Stekel. Merleau-Ponty's attitude toward Freud was much more sympathetic. As he expressed it, particularly in his preface to the book by A. Hesnard, the senior Freudian psychoanalyst and president of the French Society for Psychoanalysis,[12] he believed in a convergence between phenomenology and psychoanalysis, once they are properly understood in depth, but not in their merger.

The role of phenomenological philosophy in Merleau-Ponty's

12. *L'Oeuvre de Freud et son importance pour le monde moderne* (Paris: Payot, 1960), Preface, pp. 5–10.

psychology is pervasive without being obtrusive. Thus his conviction that there is sense, though limited sense, throughout the experienced world pervades his study of sensation and perception. His first concern is the "return to the phenomena" plain and simple. This does not prevent him from searching for their sources in the workings of "functioning intentionality" (*fungierende Intentionalität*) in the manner of the later Husserl.

Compared with Sartre's psychological studies, those of Merleau-Ponty have permeated the work of non-philosopher psychologists much more widely. But there are no direct pupils and no "school."

[13] Paul Ricoeur (b. 1913)

Ricoeur's still incomplete magnum opus, his *Philosophie de la volonté*, has as its basis a phenomenology of the will. This is especially true of the first volume, a descriptive study of the voluntary and the involuntary factors of practical conduct in their reciprocal relationship.[13] It actually represents a revival of descriptive phenomenology, which in the case of the will has been built in part on Pfänder's work, which Ricoeur knows and appreciates. But he also expands it considerably, since his study of the will is part of a much vaster project with ultimate implications for metaphysics and the philosophy of religion. Furthermore, Ricoeur is not satisfied with descriptive phenomenology but appeals to such new branches as hermeneutics for exploring aspects of the phenomena not accessible to direct description. The possibility and need of thus expanding phenomenology has led Ricoeur to a searching examination of the hermeneutic method as used in psychoanalysis in the light of phenomenology. In so doing he insists that Freud's psychoanalysis be taken seriously and not diluted, as has been done by many Neo-Freudians.

Ricoeur's book-length essay on Freud[14] is primarily an attempt at a philosophic interpretation of the Freudian enterprise. But ultimately it also aims at clarifying the idea of hermeneutics in connection with Ricoeur's own philosophy. Phenomenology

13. Translated by Erazim V. Kohák under the title *Freedom and Nature: The Voluntary and Involuntary* (Evanston, Ill.: Northwestern University Press, 1966).

14. *De l'interpretation: Essai sur Freud* (Paris: Editions du Seuil, 1965).

figures as one of several methods of justifying Freud's valiant enterprise epistemologically. And, after examining comparable attempts to fit it into scientific methodology, Ricoeur concludes that no other philosophy has come so close to making room for the Freudian conception of the unconscious as the phenomenology of Husserl and his followers, such as Merleau-Ponty and de Waelhens. But Ricoeur does not minimize the fact that ultimately Freud's purpose and method differ considerably from Husserl's. Hence, while in a sense phenomenology prepares the ground for psychoanalysis, it cannot support it. For such a support it has to go elsewhere, for instance to Hegel's phenomenology.

Aside from the area of the will, Ricoeur has also paid phenomenological attention to "sentiment," respect, and sympathy. But such psychological studies are usually undertaken in the interest of wider objectives in the philosophy of man and, ultimately, in the philosophy of religion.

Ricoeur's ultimate objective is transphenomenological. But his way of studying the phenomena is based on a solid knowledge and use of classic phenomenology, especially its Husserlian version, in which Ricoeur is thoroughly at home. However, Marcel's philosophy has perhaps even greater appeal to him as far as its final goals are concerned. What Ricoeur has contributed to psychology thus far has not yet been of large influence beyond philosophical circles. But there is evidence of his appeal to some psychiatrists (such has Henri Ey and von Baeyer) of the Heidelberg school.

[14] An Appraisal

It is obvious that thus far there has been little cooperation among the philosophical phenomenologists who have taken an interest in psychology and psychiatry. Consequently, their psychological work as a whole gives the impression of a piecemeal approach. At best the results can be brought together from scattered sources and places. There has been little attempt at any such thing as a comprehensive system of "phenomenological psychology." Nor does the recent use of the title for collections of essays by Aron Gurwitsch and Erwin Straus imply such claims.

However, it would be possible to arrange the independent findings of the philosophical phenomenologists in a pattern that would be helpful in determining whether or not there were any unifying threads in their work. The following list contains the scaffold for such a survey. Topics are listed in approximate historical order, followed by the names of those philosophers who have done the most work in the particular area.[15]

Perception and Sensation: Husserl, Wilhelm Schapp, Pfänder, Scheler, Merleau-Ponty
Imagination: Fritz Kaufmann, Eugen Fink, Sartre
Feelings: Pfänder, Geiger, Scheler, Heidegger, Ricoeur
Willing: Pfänder, Hans Reiner, Ricoeur
Self: Husserl, Pfänder, Traugott Konstantin Oesterreich
Personality (Character): Pfänder
Body-Consciousness: Husserl, Pfänder, Scheler, Marcel, Sartre, Merleau-Ponty
Social Psychology: Adolf Reinach, Scheler
Abnormal Psychology: Scheler
Psychology of Value: Scheler, Dietrich von Hildebrand, Pfänder, Hartmann
Psychology of Art: Geiger, Roman Ingarden, Mikel Dufrenne
Psychology of Religion: Scheler, Kurt Stavenhagen

But such a compilation, while practically useful, would fail to establish any claim for the unity of phenomenological psychology. For the fact is that the findings of the men listed here have been based on individual investigations, with no attempt at correlation and indeed little, if any, cross-checking. Not all of these philosophers were really at home in the fields to which they applied phenomenological methods. In some cases their only advantage over the specialists was their philosophical background. Nevertheless, I maintain that what they have seen and described is not without psychological merit and should find its place in a real system of phenomenological psychology. As we have seen, their findings lack the comprehensiveness and depth that comes from concentration on the subject and the lively exchange that is the great virtue of empirical and experimental research. There is no reason why this could not yet be achieved by phenomenology; but the fact remains that up to now it has not been done.

This indicates the need to listen to those specialized psychologists who have tried to apply some of the phenomenological

15. First names are given for phenomenologists not discussed in this chapter. In most cases, further information can be found in *The Phenomenological Movement*.

techniques to their own discipline. There is after all no good reason for thinking that only trained philosophers can practice phenomenology; there is no such thing as a phenomenological license. The next chapter, therefore, will explore the achievements of the phenomenological method in the hands of psychologists who have tried to utilize it consciously in their own field.

2 / Phenomenological Philosophy in Some Major Schools of Psychology

[1] Introductory Observations

In the preceding chapter the protagonists were philosophers with a more or less pronounced interest in psychology, but usually not with a firm foothold in the experimental field. It is therefore not surprising that their attempts to put phenomenology to psychological use have not made much of an impression on the professional psychologists. All the more important is it to determine what phenomenology has been able to contribute when handled by the psychologists themselves, and how it has fared in the process.

In trying to tell this story, I shall again not aim at an encyclopedic survey. Instead, I shall concentrate on the major schools that have been demonstrably influenced by philosophical phenomenology. But in view of the fact that these schools themselves were never rigorously set off from each other, there is no reason to omit some adjacent outsiders.

Even so, the scope of my assignment remains formidable, especially for someone who is not a psychologist in his own right. Fortunately, as far as the nineteenth-century background and most of the biographical and bibliographical material is concerned, I can simply refer to Edwin G. Boring's history, to which I am so heavily indebted.[1] My objective, as defined in the Introduction, is anyway a much more limited one: namely, to determine how far these schools were influenced by phenomenological philosophy, and particularly by Husserl's ideas.

1. *A History of Experimental Psychology,* 2d ed. (New York: Appleton-Century-Crofts, 1929). See above p. xxi.

The picture as presented by Boring depicts psychology as emancipating itself during the nineteenth century from the leading strings, if not from the stranglehold, of philosophy. There is enough truth to this view to make it antecedently plausible. But that does not make it ultimately correct. It can even be shown that the real reasons for this emancipation were philosophical in nature. For a start independent of philosophy was called for, not by the factual failure of a non-empirical approach but by philosophy's essential inability to provide an account and an understanding of the actual phenomena. These reasons persisted even in the new positivistic phase.

But now something new happened. New philosophical stimuli appeared at the periphery of psychology, and soon new philosophical infiltrations began. To write the full history of these infiltrations, which would have to include positivism, pragmatism, and logical atomism as well as phenomenology and existentialism, would obviously be a major undertaking. In this respect my attempt to show the contributions of phenomenology will be merely an illustration of the continued, though changed, significance of philosophy for psychology. I have no intention of giving a systematic justification for these one-sided and sometimes two-sided influences. Only by way of a hypothesis, to be tested through this book, would I suggest that even today's scientific psychology needs a philosophy of psychology for clarification of its fundamental concepts and assumptions in relation to those of other sciences and to science as such. However, psychology may also draw on philosophy for the kind of guiding ideas or "frames" which are basic in the life of the "scientific imagination." I submit that precisely in the case of phenomenological philosophy the main significance of philosophy is that of providing such new "frames." These "frames" are based on the full exploration and utilization of direct experience, which opens up new avenues for empirical research and permits its more meaningful interpretation.

[2] The Initial Situation

A. *Husserl's Psychological Contemporaries*

I SHALL BEGIN by discussing briefly the early relations of the new philosophical phenomenology to the surrounding psychologies. The early years of Husserl's phenomenology in Göttingen were certainly not marked by cordial and fruitful relations with the leading psychological schools. Carl Stumpf in Berlin, his senior friend and supporter from their common years at the University of Halle, maintained a friendly, though clearly diminishing interest in Husserl's new work. Presumably he also drew the attention of his psychological students to Husserl's *Logische Untersuchungen*. More important, he probably was responsible for the momentous interest of his colleague Wilhelm Dilthey in Husserl. For Dilthey entertained high hopes that Husserl's phenomenology could aid him in his attempt to develop a new psychology for the *Geisteswissenschaften*, until Husserl's attack on historicism alienated him for good. Relations with the heads of the other major schools ranged from indifferent to bad. Husserl's campaign against psychologism had spoiled the climate. And Husserl himself did not improve matters when he met psychologists in person, as he did at the one professional meeting which we know he attended, the Congress of Experimental Psychology in Göttingen in 1914, where he insisted that "pure phenomenology is neither descriptive psychology nor does it contain anything from any other psychology." [2]

Wilhelm Wundt (1832–1920), the leader in the experimental psychology of this period, was Husserl's chief antagonist among the psychologists. This is not particularly surprising in view of the fact that Husserl had attacked him in the first volume of his *Logische Untersuchungen* (§ 23), as one of the protagonists of *Psychologismus*, to which Wundt had retaliated by branding Husserl's phenomenology as *Scholastik*.[3]

Along with Wilhelm Wundt, Theodor Lipps (1851–1914) was the main German target of Husserl's assault on psychologism. But Lipps, quite apart from the interest of his students, felt increasingly that his own analytic and descriptive psychology had much in common with Husserl's phenomenology and admitted that his own psychological interpretation of logic had been at least misleading. Nevertheless, Lipps's psychology was at best a parallel to Husserl's phenomenology, leading to some peripheral stimulation, in Husserl's case, to the extent that he took up Lipps's key concept of empathy, modifying it, however, considerably. On the whole, the interaction did not lead beyond a sense of partial mutual corroboration of one another's findings.

2. *Bericht über den VI. Kongress für experimentelle Psychologie in Göttingen vom 15–18 April, 1914* (Leipzig, 1914), p. 144.

3. "Psychologismus und Logizismus," *Kleine Schriften* (Leipzig: Kroner, 1910–21), I (1910), 613.

Oswald Külpe (1862–1915) trained originally in Wundt's laboratory, but developing his own independent experimental school at Würzburg, which in opposition to the Leipzig school tackled also problems of thinking and willing, showed no immediate interest in Husserl's phenomenology of thinking. There is no definite proof—though there is at least circumstantial evidence—that only Külpe's students August Messer and Karl Bühler introduced Husserl's ideas to Külpe. But even then Külpe stressed particularly the differences, objecting, for instance, to Husserl's attempt to interpret imageless thought as a special type of non-sensuous intuiting (*Anschauung*).[4] Eventually Külpe also distinguished his own descriptive phenomenology as a science of reality (*Realwissenschaft*) from Husserl's science of essences.[5] Besides, in his philosophical work Külpe, the "critical realist," while paying tribute to the importance of phenomenology, always expressed reservations based on its methodological imperfections and its inadequate treatment of reality.[6]

In Husserl's Göttingen Georg Elias Müller (1850–1935) was at the head of perhaps the second best experimental laboratory in Germany. He had widened the field of his research beyond that of Wundt's psychophysics, particularly in his research on memory. But he was also the least philosophical, if not the most anti-philosophical, of the German psychologists of the time. All the evidence available indicates that the relations between him and Husserl, who was a faculty member with only relatively precarious status (since he held a personal chair created for him by Friedrich Althoff, the Prussian Minister of Education, against the will of his colleagues), were far from cordial. There is even an oral tradition, which I learned through a letter from Dr. Rosa Katz, wife of David Katz, that Müller used to refer to Husserl's philosophizing as verbal hairsplitting (*Wortklauberei*). Müller's monumental three-volume work on memory—published toward the end of Husserl's Göttingen period—which at times comes very close to some of Husserl's themes, never mentions his name, although the second volume contains at least one section (§68) on "phenomenological givenness."[7]

4. *Die Realisierung* (Leipzig: Hirzel, 1912), I, 129. See also Husserl's protest against Külpe's misunderstanding in *Ideen* I (1913), § 3 n.

5. *Vorlesung über Psychologie* (Leipzig: Hirzel, 1920), p. 21.

6. *Die Philosophie der Gegenwart in Deutschland,* 7th ed. (Leipzig: Teubner, 1920), pp. 130 ff.

7. *Zur Analyse der Gedächtnistätigkeit und des Vorstellungverlaufs,* Part II, in *Zeitschrift für Psychologie und Physiologie der Sinnesorgane,* Ergänzungsband, IX (1917), 252–59.

This may also be the best place to mention relationships between philosophical phenomenology and two great psychologists of Husserl's generation—E. B. Titchener and William Stern—relationships which should be interpreted not as instances of full-fledged influence but as cases of at least one-sided awareness and partial convergence. But before examining them I would like to mention a rather surprising, but telling testimony about Husserl, which occurs in the autobiography of C. E. Spearman (1863–1945), the British-American pioneer of statistical intelligence research, in his account of his visit to Göttingen in 1906. After giving his impressions of G. E. Müller's teaching, Spearman adds the following paragraph about Husserl:

> At the same university, that of Göttingen, I had the further advantage of attending the lectures of Husserl, in his way, as great a man as Müller. But their ways lay worlds apart. In fact, the sole thing that seemed common to the two was the inability of each to appreciate the other! To Müller, Husserl's fine analyses seemed to be a revival of the Middle Ages (as, indeed, they largely were, but not necessarily to their disadvantage). To Husserl, Müller's attempt to cope with psychological problems by means of experiments was like trying to unravel lace with a pitchfork. And yet Husserl's own procedure—as he described it to me himself—only differed from that of the best experimentalists dealing with similar problems in that he had nobody but himself as experimental subject.[8]

I shall consider first the case of Edward Bradford Titchener (1867–1927), the British psychologist who worked at Cornell. According to Boring, Titchener actually represented the German psychological tradition in America, particularly that of Külpe. Titchener's relation to phenomenology apparently had two aspects, perhaps even two phases. The first and the only documented one was expressed in the context of his criticism of act psychology, beginning with that of Brentano, which he rejected as being incompatible with his own anti-philosophical stand, based largely on the positivism of Mach and Avenarius. Titchener examined not only Stumpf's and Lipps's version of act psychology, but also that of Husserl. In fact, according to Boring, he stated that he had spent one day less than a year in understanding Husserl, that he now understood him, and that "there is nothing in him." [9] The fruit of this study can be found

8. *History of Psychology in Autobiography*, ed. Carl Murchison, 3 vols. (New York: Russell & Russell, 1930), I, 305.

9. *History of Experimental Psychology*, p. 420.

in five pages in his posthumous *Systematic Psychology,* which contain many footnote references to "Philosophie als strenge Wissenschaft," the *Logische Untersuchungen,* and the *Ideen.* These pages, which had been first published in an article in 1922, do not quite bear out such a completely negative verdict, although they present Husserl's phenomenology as purely philosophical and indifferent to descriptive psychology.[10]

However, this rejection of Husserl's philosophical phenomenology along with all other act psychologies does not mean that Titchener had rejected all forms of phenomenology. For, again according to Boring, during his last decade, while rejecting the "phenomenology of Würzburg," he

> was greatly impressed by the "newest" psychology in Germany, the work on perception of the Gestalt school and the new method of experimental phenomenology; now, however, he was ready to have his students try—phenomenologizing. He always distinguished between the constrained and rigorous report of introspection and the free reports of phénomenology, but it is plain that he put considerable faith in the new method. Since he never published on this subject, and the papers that have come from his laboratory with his sanction are very specialized, it is useless to try to guess whither Titchener was tending.[11]

One might well have expected to learn more about it in the unwritten fourth chapter on Method of the *Systematic Psychology.* Boring's hints suggest that this may have amounted to a seconding for the unfolding phenomenology of the gestaltists. At least one such example of Titchenerian phenomenology can be found in a study from the Cornell laboratory under the title of "The Phenomenological Description of Musical Intervals" by E. M. Edmonds and M. E. Smith.[12] The kind of description it illustrates is anything but naïve; for it appeals specifically to a "phenomenological attitude" (p. 290), not easy to achieve, and opposed to the "analytic attitude." As the chief model for this "phenomenological description," the authors refer to C. C. Pratt's first study on "Some Qualities of Bitonal Complexes,"[13] which also talks of "phenomenological description" but mentions only Carl Stumpf's *Tonpsychologie* as background.

There is also reason for discussing the relation between the

10. *Systematic Psychology* (London: Macmillan, 1929), pp. 213 ff.; *American Journal of Psychology,* XXXIII (1922), 54 ff.
11. *History of Experimental Psychology,* p. 416.
12. *American Journal of Psychology,* XXXIV (1923), 287–91.
13. *American Journal of Psychology,* XXXII (1921), 490–518.

Phenomenological Movement and the psychology of one of its major representatives in the Germany of this time, William Stern (1871–1938), who, however, was also the creator of the philosophy of personalism. His influence on Gordon Allport's psychology of personality opened up further new channels for phenomenology.

At first sight the attempt to link up Stern with phenomenology may seem farfetched. There was certainly little, if any, personal contact between Stern and Husserl or the other phenomenologists. Phenomenology is mentioned only rarely in his major psychological writings, though always sympathetically.[14] However, while Stern's systematic account lists descriptive psychology as the first task of psychology, it distinguishes the "phenomenal description" of Husserl, Scheler, Heidegger, and apparently Pfänder, from general description by its concern with the essential (p. 16; Eng. trans., pp. 10 ff.) and also credits Husserl's phenomenology with having inspired the Würzburg school in its psychology of thinking (p. 368; Eng. trans., pp. 271 ff.). There is even more explicit evidence of Stern's near-identification with the phenomenological approach in the form of a retrospective characterization of his first psychological studies, notably in his autobiography of 1926. Thus, in mentioning his descriptive work on the apperception of change and the specious present (*Präsenzzeit*) and his unpublished habilitation thesis, he remarked:

> Today I regret that the rather voluminous manuscripts never reached publication; for to my knowledge they represent one of the earliest attempts of what is called today "Phenomenological Description," and might have expected, regardless of their imperfection, a certain attention in the phenomenological work of the next period.[15]

Actually Stern may never have known that these two studies played a considerable role in Husserl's early phenomenological studies on time, in which Stern's work and especially his conception of *Präsenzzeit* is quoted and discussed, to be sure not as the final word but clearly as the most significant contribution to the subject since Brentano and Meinong.[16]

14. *Allgemeine Psychologie auf personalistischer Grundlage* (The Hague: Nijhoff, 1935). English translation, *General Psychology from the Personalistic Viewpoint* (New York: Macmillan, 1938).

15. *Die Philosophie der Gegenwart in Selbstdarstellungen*, ed. R. Schmidt (Leipzig: Meiner, 1927), VI, 129–84. Translated in Murchison, *History of Psychology in Autobiography*, I, 335–88.

16. "Phänomenologie des inneren Zeitbewusstseins," *Husserliana* X, pp. 20, 21, 59, 196, 213, 220, 232, 405 ff.

While such convergences and even influences indicate a definite affinity, the real proof of historically important relationship appeared only at a later period, when Stern's personalism, in spite of its independent roots, offered a development reinforcing phenomenology and reinforced by it.

B. *The "Second Generation"*

Considering this lack of resonance to Husserl's work among the heads of the psychological schools who were his contemporaries, Husserl's impact on the second generation was all the more remarkable. One might attribute it to the typical revolt of a new generation which looks for outside inspiration and support for its dissents from the masters. But there may be even more positive reasons for the change of outlook. All German experimental psychologies were, after all, still psychologies of consciousness and hence in this widest sense phenomenologies. Where could their supporters find a philosophical backing for this approach more outspoken than in Husserl's phenomenology?

To be sure, there was very little immediate infiltration at the Wundtian citadel in Leipzig. His successor Wilhelm Wirth, originally a student of Lipps, while a friend of Pfänder's, expressed continued opposition to Husserl. It was only in the new Leipzig school of Felix Krüger, with his psychology of wholeness (*Ganzheitspsychologie*), that things changed considerably.

The impact of Husserl's phenomenology was much more immediate among the students of Theodor Lipps. Here the revolt against the master's psychologism had prepared the ground for the discovery of Husserl. Among the "deserters," Pfänder and Geiger, joined later by Scheler in 1907, were particularly interested in psychology. But they were also philosophers to such an extent that I discussed their contribution in the preceding chapter and in my earlier book.

Much more interesting, therefore, are the schools intermediate between those of Wundt and Lipps, in which the influence of phenomenology is less sweeping but more related to concrete and original research.

I shall omit here such independent circles as the Graz school of Alexius Meinong, whose students Stefan Witasek, Vittorio Benussi, and, perhaps most influential, Christian von Ehrenfels, often followed a course parallel to Husserl's, but deliberately independent. The similarity is explained by Meinong's slightly earlier secession from Brentano and the emphasis on mutual independence that resulted from Meinong's unfortunate priority feud with Husserl over Meinong's theory of objects, after which each avoided references to the other.[17] This did not prevent a mutual awareness, even after the dropping of all literary credit relations. It may also deserve mention that a late Meinong student, Fritz Heider, since his coming to the States, has developed a pronounced interest in phenomenology.[18]

This leaves as the most important case material for the present chapter the Würzburg school of Oswald Külpe, the Göttingen school of Georg Elias Müller, and the Gestalt school of Frankfurt and Berlin, which had no single head. I shall begin with the Göttingen school, in spite of the fact that chronologically the Würzburg school was the first one to show Husserl's influence in its publications. The influence of Husserl was of course much more direct in Göttingen. Also, the phenomenological inspiration led here to much more original work and proved to be of more lasting effect, especially in the case of the work of David Katz. The reason for putting Gestalt psychology last is almost obvious: it comes later in time, and its connections with phenomenology were much more tenuous, especially in the beginning.

One general observation might be worth making here, since it affects the entire history of phenomenology after Hitler. One could call it the melting-pot effect of exile on the emigrated psychologies. In the new setting, differences between such schools as Gestalt psychology and phenomenology, for example, have become less important, and their common elements, in fact their complementary nature, have become clear. Thus we shall see the gestaltists referring to phenomenology as their basic method, and phenomenologists such as Aron Gurwitsch adopting gestaltist principles in their theory of perception. The former aloofness and even rivalry have given way to an attitude of sympathetic mutual support. This clearly involves the danger of syncretism, as the lumping together under such labels as "the Third Force" would

17. H. Spiegelberg, *The Phenomenological Movement*, 2 vols. (The Hague: Nijhoff, 1965), I, 98 ff. Since I wrote the earlier book, Roderick M. Chisholm has shown me the microfilm of an extensive Meinong typescript of 1917 containing a detailed critical discussion of Husserl's *Ideen*.

18. *The Psychology of Interpersonal Relations* (New York: Wiley, 1958); *On Perception and Event Structure and the Psychological Environment* (New York: International Universities Press, 1959), esp. pp. 85 ff. Also, see below, pp. 81–82.

indicate. There is a difference between spontaneous convergence and the compression of an incongruous mixture by outside conditions.

[3] Phenomenology among the Göttingen Psychologists

To recapture today the intellectual atmosphere of the Göttingen psychology during the period of Husserl's unfolding phenomenology is no longer possible. What is clear is that, rejected by most of his colleagues, Husserl nevertheless exerted an increasing attraction on the new generation of students, especially the circle which around 1910 became organized in the Göttingen Philosophische Gesellschaft. But it must be realized that this group was by no means "orthodox." Specifically, they did not follow Husserl in the direction of his emerging transcendental phenomenology, with its emphasis on the "reduction" and its incipient idealism. To this group Husserl was primarily the liberator from traditional theories, who invited them to go "to the things" directly and to describe them as they saw them. It must also be realized that at that time the only book of Husserl's available to them in print was his *Logische Untersuchungen*.

This group, inspired but not directed by Husserl, was not confined to philosophers. It included mathematicians, historians, theologians, and particularly psychologists. Actually, psychology, not being segregated academically as an independent department from philosophy, was its closest faculty neighbor. Thus Husserl's students could not fail to be exposed to the psychology of Georg Elias Müller. And at least to some extent, Müller's students had to take account of what went on in Husserl's classes. Some of Husserl's students also took part as subjects in the experimental work of the Göttingen laboratory, and names such as Heinrich Hofmann, Jean Hering, and Alexandre Koyré figure in their protocols. It is therefore not surprising that some of Husserl's ideas began to influence Müller's students and assistants. Since at that time Müller's laboratory was one of the best training grounds for experimental psychologists, they were of course of particular importance as possible carriers of the new phenomenological psychology. Probably the most important ones to pick up some of the new ideas were, in chronological order, Erich Jaensch, David Katz, and Edgar Rubin.

This influence is not always easy to trace. Contrary to what we shall observe in the case of the Würzburg school, very little of it went through literary channels. For the Göttingen psychologists had the live Husserl and his live followers as sources of their information and inspiration. David Katz in particular attended Husserl's lectures and seminars, but clearly the others too did so to some degree. According to Jean Hering, however, they took no special part in the activities of the Philosophische Gesellschaft. Although it is no longer possible to determine, it is not very likely that the Göttingen psychologists had much personal contact with Husserl; one might suspect that the tension between Husserl and Müller had something to do with this situation. It is all the more remarkable that Husserl's influence did not stop short of the psychological laboratory. Clearly, to the young Göttingen psychologists Husserl was mostly the stimulator, example, and to some extent the catalyst, not the source for their phenomenological ventures.

A. *Erich Jaensch (1883–1940)*

The first definite trace of Husserl's influence can be found in the early Göttingen writings of Erich Jaensch, whose later fame was based on his studies of eidetic imagery and the eidetic type of personality. However, there is no evidence of a connection between this discovery and Jaensch's early phenomenological interests, unless one sees an affinity between the phenomenological interest in intuiting (*Anschauung*) and the kind of pictorial imagery characteristic of the eidetic personality.

But there is concrete proof for Jaensch's early attachment to Husserl, confirmed also by personal information from Husserl's daughter Elly (Mrs. Jakob Rosenberg), in the form of ten letters that Jaensch wrote to Husserl between 1906 and 1922 that are now in the Husserl Archives in Louvain. They establish the fact that Jaensch not only attended some of Husserl's lectures but had enrolled in his seminar in the winter semester of 1905/6, one of the decisive years in the development of Husserl's phenomenology. While Jaensch, in sending Husserl his doctoral dissertation of 1909 on visual perception, did not make any phenomenological claims for his experimental work, he did announce such plans with regard to his second forthcoming book on the perception of space, stating that he had become convinced of the general importance of phenomenology for psychology. "Most of the errors in this discipline, thus far studied primarily by physiologists, can be explained by the fact that purely phenomenological description of what is given immediately in appearance has never been carried out with sufficient care . . ." (letter to Husserl of December 31, 1909).

The book itself, Jaensch's thesis for habilitation as a lecturer in Strassburg, clearly showed traces of Husserlian inspiration.[19] A final footnote (pp. 486 f.) questioned the result of the entire experimental study with the remark that "attempts to interpret such phenomena could be successfully made only if they were preceded by a detailed *phenomenology* of the elementary functions under investigation," a demand that was even doubly valid for a study of the "more complex ones." In this connection Jaensch referred those who declare such knowledge impossible to the first volume of Husserl's *Logische Untersuchungen*. Even more significant is the fact that Jaensch himself not only spoke of a phenomenology of depth impression as a prerequisite for its explanation but presented what he himself called a "phenomenology of empty space" (Chapter VI). On December 29, 1917, Jaensch announced to Husserl studies in which he would show "the alpha and omega of all psychology, the intentional acts in their whole range from the wrongly labeled physiology of the senses up to religious philosophy." But these studies do not seem to have materialized. For in a last letter of January 1, 1922, Jaensch merely acknowledged the stimulation and guidance he had received from Moritz Geiger by his manner of relating psychology and phenomenology.

However, there is no sign of phenomenological influence in Jaensch's later work, and particularly not in the weird and perhaps pathological aberrations of his last theory of personality types into the kind of racism which was to victimize his erstwhile fellow students, Katz and Rubin.

B. *David Katz* (1889–1953)

Katz was the Göttingen psychologist with whom Husserl's influence went deepest and remained most lasting. He was also the most original in developing it further. This very originality makes it relatively difficult to determine the exact extent and nature of Husserl's role in his work.

19. "Über die Wahrnehmung des Raumes," *Zeitschrift für Psychologie*, Supplement, VI (1911).

Katz's References to Husserl's Phenomenology

An attempt to evaluate Katz's debt to Husserl has to begin with Katz's own testimony, which does not seem to have been sufficiently heeded. Since it also underwent some changes, as Katz looked back to his Göttingen beginnings, the main evidence may be worth recording.

There was surprisingly little mention of Husserl in the first edition of Katz's classic book on color. His only reference to Husserl here appeared in a short paragraph in the second section of the text, in which he made a new distinction among the modes of appearance (*Erscheinungsweisen*) of the colors: [20]

> I think that to a certain degree I have been influenced by the lectures and seminars [*Übungen*] of Professor Husserl in stressing the phenomenological analysis of the color phenomena more strongly than has been customary thus far. That this analysis means nothing completely new to the psychology of color is attested by the often quoted discussions of Hering. This influence is to be understood more in the sense of (the adoption of) the general phenomenological attitude and less of concretely developed analyses; for color analyses of the type carried out here have not been presented by Professor Husserl in his lectures and seminars.[21]

This seemingly grudging admission of Husserl's role not only disappeared from the second edition of 1930 but was replaced by the following two sentences in the first paragraph of the Preface:

> [My] method is that of the unprejudiced description of the phenomena, for which the designation "phenomenological method" has become current. My introduction to Husserl's phenomenology took place in lectures which I as a young student attended with the founder of modern phenomenological philosophy, to whom I would like to express the cordial thanks I owe him.[22]

In his later publications, Katz became even more outspoken in his adherence to the phenomenological method. Thus his book

20. "Die Erscheinungsweisen der Farben und ihre Beeinflussung durch die individuelle Erfahrung," *Zeitschrift für Psychologie: Ergänzungsband,* VII (1911), 30.

21. Some indications of Husserl's interest in the phenomenology of color appearances can be found, however, in *Ideen* (1913), § 41 (*Husserliana* III, 93).

22. P. x. Unfortunately, these sentences have been omitted from the abridged translation by Robert B. MacLeod and G. W. Fox, *The World of Colour* (London: Kegan Paul, Trench, Trubner, 1935), pp. 11–28.

on *Gestaltpsychologie* [23] contains a special chapter on "The Phenomenological Method," in which he goes so far as to say that "comprehension of contemporary psychology necessitates an understanding of the phenomenological method" (p. 24; Eng. trans., p. 18), and adds that "the critique which Gestalt psychology directs against the older psychology, and its own positive contributions as well, stand or fall on the merits of the phenomenological method." To be sure, Ewald Hering is mentioned as its first practitioner. "A philosopher, Husserl (1901–1902), made a systematic use of it and expanded its application,"—the date being a clear reference to the Husserl of the *Logische Untersuchungen* rather than to the pure phenomenologist of his later writings.

But the most impressive tribute that Katz paid to Husserl occurs in his autobiography:

> To me phenomenology, as advocated at that time [i.e., during Katz's student days] by Edmund Husserl, seems to be the most important connection between philosophy and psychology. None of my academic teachers, with the exception of G. E. Müller, has more deeply influenced my procedure and my attitude in psychological matters than Husserl by his phenomenological method.[24]

In this context Katz also mentioned his friendly relations with Max Scheler, "another philosopher who showed a sympathetic attitude toward psychology" and who at that time belonged to the Göttingen circle. He added that "both Husserl and Scheler took an ardent interest in analyses of the kind I have published in my two books on color and touch sensation." Unfortunately, it is no longer possible to establish whether this meant that they actually subscribed to Katz's findings.

One may wonder whether for Katz Husserl's role did not grow in retrospect, unless one thinks he toned down his initial tribute in order not to offend Müller, his principal teacher in the field of psychology. Apparently, the realization of Husserl's significance for psychology grew on Katz in the manner of a delayed response. In the end he left no doubt about the fact that he considered not only phenomenology but Husserl's part in its development to be decisive for modern psychology and particularly for his own research. For with all his admiration for the experimental training

23. *Gestaltpsychologie* (Basel: Schwabe, 1944; 2d ed., 1948). English translation by Robert Tyson, *Gestalt Psychology* (New York: Ronald Press, 1950).

24. *History of Psychology in Autobiography,* ed. Edwin G. Boring et al. (New York: Russell & Russell, 1952), IV, 194.

which he had received in Müller's laboratory, Katz, like Jaensch, felt that this psychology "needed psychologizing, paradoxical as it may seem." Müller's treatment of perception was purely in terms of psychophysics "almost exclusively from a physiological standpoint . . . supplemented by speculative ideas. . . . Psychological questions were touched upon only slightly. . . . This lack of psychology in the treatment of a field so rich in fascinating phenomena, and, moreover, the lack of psychological data in the literature dealing with the field, troubled me very much and was one of the reasons why I started the research on color" (p. 189). The phenomenological method proved to be Katz's principal answer to this deficiency. And Husserl was its main practitioner within reach.

However, before accepting Katz's self-interpretation and his tribute to phenomenology, one has to consider his conception of phenomenology and its actual role in his research.

Katz's Conception of Phenomenology

Apparently Katz believed that his conception of phenomenology was identical with Husserl's. But the fact that he referred to Ewald Hering, the physiologist (who himself never used this term and of whom Husserl took little notice [e.g., *Husserliana* IX, §4, p. 302]), is indicative of his peculiar perspective.

The first explicit formulation of the Husserlian method can be found in the preface of the second edition of the color book, where Katz speaks of "the unprejudiced description of the phenomena." There is no reference to Husserl's own specifications, not even to those in the *Logische Untersuchungen*, let alone in *Ideen*. In 1937, in his studies in comparative psychology,[25] Katz introduced the phenomenological method into animal psychology as "the method giving the greatest possible freedom," its aim being to describe the psychologically meaningful behavior of animals just as it finds it (p. 46). "This approach we will call the 'phenomenological method.' " This sounds like a personal redefinition of the term. And it is true that Katz here includes not only "looking at animals without preconceived ideas" but "feeling oneself into the animals' situation under the most natural conditions possible." As examples of this method Katz mentioned Köhler (observations on chimpanzees) and Kurt von Frisch (study of

25. *Mensch und Tier* (Zurich: Gonzett and Huber, 1948), chap. III. English translation by Hannah Steinberg and Arthur Summerfield, *Animals and Men* (New York: Longmans, Green, 1937).

the language of the bees), who themselves did not invoke phenomenology, at least not in this context. But even for this widened use, Katz claimed that the unbiased description of the phenomena was fundamental.

Compared with this first explicit discussion of phenomenology, the special chapter on the phenomenological method that appeared in Katz's book on *Gestalt Psychology* sounded more restrained and conservative. Here the phenomenological method was characterized as the simple undistorted description of the phenomena as they appeared (p. 24; Eng. trans., p. 22). They "were allowed to speak for themselves, as it were" (p. 24; Eng. trans., p. 18). The need of this method was illustrated by the "stimulus error," which confuses the knowledge of physical causes with the sensations they elicit.

None of these characterizations introduced the full-fledged phenomenological method of Husserl and other phenomenological philosophers. However, in his autobiography Katz moved at least one step further when, in his account of Husserlian phenomenology, he mentioned "relations of insight (*Wesenseinsichten*)" not only as included in phenomenology but as relevant to the psychologist, e.g., in the "geometrical arrangement of colors, which cannot be based on mere factual experience or statistics." [26] But there is no mention of such features of Husserl's pure or transcendental phenomenology as the phenomenological reduction.

The fact that Katz's accounts of the phenomenological method do not include all the features which other phenomenologists, and particularly Husserl, specify is no proof that he avoids them in actual practice. The way to decide whether or not he does is to watch his phenomenology in action.

Katz's Practice of Phenomenology

Katz's major and most original contributions to phenomenological psychology are his two books on color and touch. In order to determine the kind of phenomenology they embody, one might begin with a consideration of the titles and tables of contents and then turn to a consideration of some aspects of the actual texts.

A comparative look at the 1911 and 1930 editions of the color book, which are quite different, will prove instructive. To begin with, the titles differ. The first title read somewhat cum-

26. *History of Psychology in Autobiography*, ed. Boring, IV, 195.

bersomely: *Die Erscheinungsweisen der Farben und ihre Beeinflussung durch die individuelle Erfahrung* (*The Modes of Appearances of the Colors and Their Modification by Individual Experience*). The second title was simply *Der Aufbau der Farbwelt* (*The Structure of the World of Color*), a title which paralleled that of Katz's second book on *Der Aufbau der Tastwelt* (*The Structure of the World of Touch*) of 1925. One might wonder about the meaning of this change in title. Katz himself, in the preface to the second edition, spoke only about the omission of the second part of the first title (*Their Modification by Individual Experience*), which he now considered misleading, since the result of his study had shown the relative unimportance of individual factors. This might also suggest that only general, if not essential, features determine the structure of the phenomena of color. But Katz did not explain why he replaced "the modes of appearance" by "structure" and "the colors" by "the world of color." Without putting too much emphasis on these substitutions, one can use them as clues for pointing out some characteristic aspects in Katz's developing phenomenology.

Katz's use of the term *Erscheinungsweise* (mode of appearance), which continued, if not in the title, at least in the text of the second edition, may remind one at first of Husserl's precedent and of his synonym for it, *Gegebenheitsweise* (mode of givenness), which puts Katz even closer to Husserl's conception of the intentional structure of experience, according to which each thing appears in different perspectival modes. However, one must realize that this was not Katz's primary concern. For him the prime example of different modes of appearance of color were the two phenomena of film color (*Flächenfarbe*) and surface color (*Oberflächenfarbe*). These are simply different types of color in different settings, not different modes of appearance of one and the same color. They have a common substratum (*Materie*). But in their respective contexts they change their identity. In this light it might be more appropriate to call them different manifestations or "incarnations" of the same color. Hence Katz's change of title to *The World of Color* by no means implies that he was abandoning Husserl's conception of phenomenology as an exploration of the modes of appearance.

What was more significant was the introduction of the term "world" into the titles of both the books on color and touch. The preface to the book on touch spoke specifically about the fascination of the "almost inexhaustible richness of the touchable world" and about the surprisingly vast realm of distinctive touch configurations, which in certain regards exceeds even those of color as revealed in the earlier book. Thus the term "world" functions chiefly as a means for emphasizing the abundance of phenomena in the sensuous field, an abundance which prephenomenological psychology had largely overlooked.

Finally, the introduction of the word "*Aufbau*" (structure), omitted from the translation of the title, which is likewise not explained by Katz himself, may be interpreted as an expression of his interest in the relations among the elements of the world of color, rather than in a complete account of all the contents of the world of color after the manner of Goethe's theory of colors (*Farbenlehre*).

Even more important, of course, are the actual contents of the book. A first look at the Table of Contents of the first edition of the color book would not make one suspect that this was the most sustained study in phenomenological psychology thus far. But even this text hardly mentioned the word "phenomenology." Only after the paragraph of acknowledgments in §2 (where Husserl is mentioned) did Katz speak of his own "presuppositionless phenomenological analyses of color phenomena" as new, with only some of Ewald Hering's studies as precedents (p. 30). In retrospect one almost has the impression that Katz did not want to advertise his phenomenology before having shown its fruits. By contrast the second edition not only displayed the term "phenomenology" in the title of the very first section (*Phänomenologie der Beleuchtung und das leeren Raumes*) but began the new Preface with an explicit espousal of the phenomenological method, which was credited with the success of his first edition. Especially in subsection §7, phenomenology was invoked for showing the difference between luminosity (*leuchten*) and illumination (*Beleuchtung*) as different phenomena.

The earlier book on the world of touch was not yet as explicit in parading the term "phenomenology" in its titles. But it did talk much more prominently about the *phenomena* of touch (*Tastphänomene*) as equivalent expressions for *Erscheinungsweisen* (ways of appearance); the term *Farbphänomene* (phenomena of color) is less prominent in the first edition of the color book.

However, the decisive test for Katz's phenomenology is its place in the actual texts. It would make little sense to give a detailed analysis of the books without at the same time reporting their content. Any condensation here would do them an injustice. Phenomenologically, the beginning sections are always the most revealing, since in the later ones Katz became understandably more interested in the exploration of the causal dependencies of the phenomena upon extra-phenomenal factors.

The first part of the book on color introduced an entirely new differentiation of the phenomena, beginning with the distinction between film colors (*Flächenfarben*), with no definite location in three-dimensional space, and surface colors (*Oberflächenfarben*), characterized by their role as surfaces of spatial objects. These two types were followed by colors spread through definite areas in space. Transparent colors, reflecting colors, luster, luminousness, and glow were introduced as distinct phenomena. By the use of a special method of "reduction" (looking at them through a perforated screen)—clearly not Husserl's phenomenological reduction—they could be transformed, Katz felt, into film colors. But this was no good reason for giving film colors priority qua phenomena.

All this is quite original and has proved to be a permanent contribution to the phenomenology of color. Katz made no attempt to relate these new distinctions to Husserl's work, nor was there any definite reason for doing so. But there is some reason for pointing out a parallel between Katz's and Husserl's conceptions that suggests a certain stimulation, especially in the case of Katz's distinction between film colors and surface colors. Here I am thinking of Husserl's interpretation of perception in terms of "intentionality," according to which it consists in the intending viewing of "sense data" (*hyle*) as properties of "intentional" objects. Thus, in his *Ideen* (§41), Husserl discussed the way in which color appears in continuous perspective shadings (*Farbenabschattungen*). These are "animated" (*beseelt*) by interpretations (*Auffassungen*) which perform an objectifying function, resulting in what we call the appearing of the original color. Obviously, Husserl's terminology did not refer to any such thing as surface colors explicitly. But I submit that the whole picture of the relation between the film color and the surface color is related to Husserl's distinction between color and its perspective shadings (*Abschattung*). Katz's film colors are "reduced" surface colors, which are normally seen as surface colors, just as perspective shadings are usually interpreted as properties of objects. Granted that Katz never referred to "intentionality" as a basic structure of all sense perception, it was nevertheless implicit in his distinction between the two types of color.

In several ways, and not only phenomenologically, Katz's second major work on the world of touch was even more remarkable than the one on color and would certainly deserve a selective translation. While on the whole Katz followed the procedure of his earlier book and organized it in a parallel manner, his findings have additional interest. For instance, they result in a reappraisal of the data of touch as supposedly a "lower sense." Katz's phenomenology reveals not only the amazing variety of touch data but also the fact that they are anything but a disjointed jumble. Both by content and by order they form a "world" in Katz's sense. Hence he objected to the assignment of touch to such "lower senses" as taste and smell. In fact Katz pleaded for the primacy of touch over sight and hearing as far as cognitive value was concerned; for touch is more indispensable, if not as variegated, as they are. However, Katz did not deny that the world of touch is inferior to the world of color as far as "polyphony" is concerned; it is "monotonous" in its basic material (*Urmaterie*), which consists of pressure data. Variety is present only in the modes of appearance (*Erscheinungsweisen*) in which this monotonous material is organized. In this respect the world of touch is fully the equal of the world of color.

A survey of the "phenomena of touch" in the second chapter reveals, for instance, the same difference of film phenomena and surface phenomena which occurs in the world of color. Some of the touch phenomena have spatial depth (such as air). Some touch *qualia* are transparent in the sense that we can touch through them. Thus we can touch through a glove, but we can also touch through whole layers of tissue, as in medical percussion. Subsequently, modes of the surface *qualia* such as hardness and smoothness are considered, differences in touch of natural and artificial materials taken up, continuity and discontinuity of the touch field examined, and the specific differences of figure and ground in touch configurations pointed out. The memory touch datum, analogous to the memory color, of an object receives attention. Another chapter explores movement as a formative factor in the appearance of touch phenomena. This suggests a trend in the direction of Husserl's constitutive or genetic phenomenology.

The longest section of the book reports experiments and measures in detail the functions of the sense of touch. But in addition to establishing quantitative relations, it adds considerable qualitative detail and brings out the relation of touch data to those of other senses, such as the sensations of temperature. A last section incorporates the results of Katz's studies of the sense of vibration, which he placed between touch and hearing as a separate new sense. This sense can even account for the enjoyment of music by the deaf, which Katz and Révész had studied intensively.

It should be pointed out that the parallel between color and touch phenomena, which Katz utilized a great deal for comparative purposes, by no means led him to assimilate the two. Among the differences which emerged are the greater "objectivity" of the color phenomena, in which the seeing subject is not consciously involved, compared with the touch phenomena, which are essentially "bi-polar," since here both the touching subject and the object touched have a prominent place in each actual experience. Obviously, the mere mention of such items can do little more than suggest the richness of the phenomenological content of this book. I would like to hope that these samples can attract some readers to a closer study of the original.

The Role of Philosophical Phenomenology for Katz

On the basis of these samples, what, beyond Katz's own testimony, can be said about the significance of phenomenological philosophy for his psychology?

That there has been an influence, in fact almost a delayed-reaction influence, seems undeniable. But how essential was it? Certainly its traces are not conspicuous, especially not in the (abridged) translation of the color book, or even as they emerge from an examination of the concrete studies contained in other publications. Did Katz deceive himself about the importance of Husserl's and Scheler's role for his phenomenology? There is obviously no way of telling whether and in what direction Katz's phenomenology would have developed, had he not been exposed to Husserl and to the atmosphere of his circle. Katz's primary inspiration for his study of the color phenomena and his interest in their better description clearly came from Ewald Hering, although he seems to have felt a lack of differentiation in Hering's survey of the color phenomena. It is this intensification of Hering's "phenomenology" that may need explanation.

Of course in the case of as original and open-minded an observer as Katz, his insights need not be explained by outside influences. A cautious interpretation of what happened would be the following: Katz, like so many of the new psychologists engaged in enriching the psychological field after a period of positivistic impoverishment, was in need of a new methodology as a justification of his practice. This is what phenomenology could supply better than other philosophies. Phenomenology also encouraged the turn toward the concrete, inasmuch as even philosophical phenomenologists had become involved in descriptions of phenomena on their own, unconcerned about possible trespassing. In addition, the live exchange, especially with such men as Scheler, seems to have had an invigorating effect on Katz's own research. There is a possibility that some of the specific ideas in Husserl's phenomenology, such as his intentional theory of perception, had a remote effect on Katz's differentiation between film and surface qualities. At best, however, this influence was corroborating rather than initiating. Katz's phenomenological psychology was indeed indebted to the general conception of Husserl's phenomenology—and not only in his own late perspective. It acted upon him as a support and, in this sense at least, as an accelerator and probably as a general stimulant by way of osmosis from Husserl's seminar to Müller's laboratory.

In claiming Katz for phenomenology to this extent, one must of course not overlook his many wider interests and commitments in psychology. Thus he sided more and more with Gestalt psychology, though not without reservations, while stressing its phenomenological foundations, claiming that his own phenomenology had provided evidence against atomism and for "wholeness" as an essential character of the psychological phenomena. He was also influenced by William Stern and Ernst Cassirer. But such open-mindedness did not conflict with what Katz himself clearly considered his primary methodological commitments to a phenomenology and "phenomenological elucidation [*Klärung*]" as the foundation for all other psychological research, and as "the greatest of all psychological virtues." [27]

C. *Edgar Rubin (1886–1951)*

The Danish author of the book on visually perceived figures, *Visuell wahrgenommene Figuren*,[28] with its celebrated distinction between figure and ground and their reversible nature, may at first sight seem unrelated to phenomenology. Never does Edgar Rubin mention phenomenology explicitly in this book, and the name of Husserl occurs only once (p. 201), and, as a matter of fact, in a skeptical vein, though with a definite quotation from

27. *Gestaltpsychologie*, p. 83; Eng. trans., pp. 84.

28. (Copenhagen: Glydendalske Bokhandel, 1915). A German translation was published by Glydendalske in 1921. Subsequent page numbers refer to the German edition.

his *Logische Untersuchungen.* However, in his memorial article Rubin's friend Katz stated that, in addition to G. E. Müller's "decisive influence on Rubin's thinking," he, "like other experimental psychologists, was deeply impressed by the phenomenological viewpoint, which at that time had pervaded the scientific atmosphere of Göttingen as a consequence of the spell cast by the ideas of Husserl. This outlook became apparent in his chief work." [29]

Looking at Rubin's work in this light, one can also point out that he characterized his visually perceived figures as *erlebt,* i.e., as pieces of lived experience.[30] He also told us not to ascribe to these phenomena properties which we may know as belonging to the "objective" world (p. xi), i.e., presumably those which we know from physical science. In this connection it may also be significant that Rubin made the perception of figure not a matter of attention, a factor stressed chiefly by G. E. Müller, but of *Erlebnis.*

Rubin's best-known contribution to psychology is the detailed study of the phenomena of figure and ground and their psychological conditions. Actually it has been Gestalt psychology rather than phenomenology which has made the greatest use of his discoveries. However, Rubin's book is not restricted to these phenomena. The whole second section, with its observations on the plane figure, the contour and the stroke, is worthy of attention, especially his demonstration of the phenomenon of the contour as a line without breadth and color at the transition between two differently colored plane figures, which we may "follow" (*verfolgen*). Here even the "pure ego" is invoked as the being which moves along the contour, and its description shows clearly the Göttingen style of phenomenologizing (p. 153).

Rubin was certainly not a mere follower of Husserl's phenomenology. But quite apart from Katz's testimony, Rubin's actual research makes it plain that he had absorbed the spirit of the new approach, both creatively and critically.

D. *Géza Révész (1878–1955)*

The range of this remarkably versatile and enterprising Hungarian was certainly much wider than phenomenology. But during his Göttingen period his interest in phenomenology was

29. "Edgar Rubin," *Psychological Review,* LVIII (1951), 87.
30. *Visuell wahrgenommene Figuren,* p. ix.

sufficient to make him call one of his first publications "Phenomenology of the Series of Sensations."[31] He is also known to have attended Husserl's lectures. Yet his final adherence to phenomenology was by no means unqualified. Thus, in his most ambitious work, his two volumes on the forms of the world of touch[32] (whose title is reminiscent of the earlier work of his friend David Katz), his explicit discussion of the phenomenological approach is highly critical. True, he does not minimize its importance:

> In the recent history of psychology I know of hardly a methodological thought which could rival in importance and results the phenomenological approach. . . . The significant progress which we have achieved by this insight has amply justified the path taken by Brentano, then by Hering, Husserl, Külpe, and Lipps (I, 75).

But he warned strongly against its subjectivity, especially in the hands of untrained and "autocratic" phenomenologists, "who reject the variations of the experiment" (I, 71); in this context he referred to Wilhelm Schapp, whom Katz regarded highly, and Herbert Leyendecker, both students of Husserl, as "warning examples." Nevertheless, Révész's magnum opus contains several sections in which phenomenology is invoked, for instance in the study of acoustic space and in the discussion of the heterogeneity of optic and haptic impressions, where he pays special tribute to Katz's work (I, 65).

Thus phenomenology had an important part in launching Révész in his psychological work, but his allegiance to phenomenology was not comparable to that of Katz.

E. *Wilhelm Schapp (1884–1969)*

A full understanding of the relationship between the phenomenological psychologists of Göttingen and the Husserl circle involves close examination of the work of two of Husserl's students who acted as go-betweens—Wilhelm Schapp and Heinrich Hofmann—whose dissertations dealt with largely psychological phenomena. Of the two, only Hofmann was a close friend of Katz's. But, as Hofmann pointed out, when he and Katz discov-

31. "Phänomenologie der Empfindungsreihen" (Budapest: Atheneum, 1907). See also Bibliography on Révész in *Acta psychologica*, XII (1956), 208–15.

32. *Die Formenwelt des Tastsinnes*, 2 vols. (The Hague: Nijhoff, 1937).

ered that they were working on the same topic, they decided to avoid it in their conversation. Hofmann, however, was one of Katz's principal experimental subjects. Schapp, philosophically the more creative of the two, especially in his later production, was apparently not equally close to the work of the Göttingen laboratory. Nevertheless, in the second edition of his book on color Katz mentioned Schapp's dissertation on the phenomenology of perception as a definite contribution to the discussion of the cognitive value of the color phenomena. Some of Schapp's observations on touch also figure in Katz's second book.

Schapp's dissertation [33] had considerable influence even outside Göttingen as one of the most original and fruitful demonstrations of concrete phenomenology. Yet, while Schapp gave Husserl the major credit for his findings, he referred to him only very rarely in the text, and his style of thinking and writing was certainly very different from Husserl's. His discipleship consisted mostly in "going to the things" by himself and reporting his findings as vividly as possible, mostly in the first person singular. As he put it: "I only hope that I did not write down anything which I did not see myself." Consequently, the dissertation includes hardly any references to the professional literature, although it does not exclude the mention of the great philosophers from Plato to Hegel.

Schapp's unusually rich and lively study of some 160 pages dealt chiefly with the ways in which the world of things of our everyday experience is given in perception. A first section studied the means by which the world is presented—primarily through color, sound, and touch—and their relations. In the end Schapp explored the question of what it is that is so presented, i.e., space and the spatial world of things. What Schapp was anxious to show was not only that these senses deliver to us directly their specific qualities—color, sound, and pressure—but that through them we see, and do not merely infer, such qualities as hardness, elasticity, fluidity, etc. The second section explored in detail how and under what conditions one such quality, namely color, reveals to us the world of things and analyzed the role of illumination, luster, and distinctness in this process. Although all this was much in line with Katz's slightly later book, Schapp's investigations lack Katz's experimental support. In its place, he added important epistemological considerations.

33. *Beiträge zur Phänomenologie der Wahrnehmung* (Göttingen: Kaestner, 1910; 2d ed., Erlangen: Palm & Enke, 1925).

F. *Heinrich Hofmann (b. 1883)*

Hofmann's investigation of the concept of sensation [34] was much more closely related to both Husserl's and Müller's work than Schapp's. While claiming independence from Husserl's approach, Hofmann recognized that his lectures of 1904 and 1907 had presented similar studies about the constitution of the spatial thing from the perceptual modes of givenness, something which he called analysis of strata (*Schichtenanalyse*) (p. 100). There would be little point in an abstract of Hofmann's investigations, important though they became because of their influence on Ortega y Gasset. But it should be mentioned that Hofmann rejected the traditional concept of sensation as untenable. What he finally put into its place were the perspective aspects through which the seen object appears, a conception for which he gave explicit credit to Husserl. Katz's studies on colors were also often mentioned approvingly.

G. *In Retrospect*

To attempt further reconstruction of Göttingen psychology under Husserl's immediate shadow would be rather difficult and hardly advisable in the present framework. All that the preceding samples were meant to convey was that psychology in Göttingen had considerable ties with philosophical phenomenology and particularly with Husserl's early version of it. Most of Husserl's influence seems to have occurred without his taking a hand in it. The plain fact was that several groping young psychologists turned to Husserl, rather than that he annexed them. One might think of plotting their closeness to Husserl by drawing concentric circles around him. Hofmann and Schapp would then form the innermost ring, Katz would be the first ring among the experimental psychologists, with Révész being on the outermost shell followed by zones of indifference and hostility.

Looking back over the evidence which I have tried to present in this section, I believe that the following estimate would best describe the situation of phenomenological psychology in Husserl's Göttingen: Experimental psychology developed a decided trend toward a more descriptive approach. This influence was not a matter of deliberate infusion. Nor was it a matter of direct loans or takeovers. What philosophical phenomenology did for psy-

34. "Untersuchungen über den Empfindungsbegriff," *Archiv für die gesamte Psychologie*, XXVI (1913), 1–136.

chology during this period was chiefly to act as a catalyst, reinforcing and corroborating a more open and direct approach to the psychological phenomena.

[4] Phenomenology in the Würzburg School

As far as literary traces were concerned, the echo of Husserl's work among the psychologists in Würzburg preceded that in Göttingen. But literary quotations are hardly a reliable index of influence, and even less of the importance of such influence. Thus Husserl's role in the thinking of the Würzburg group could best be introduced as the first instance of his action at a distance. For there is no evidence of his ever having visited with the Würzburg group, nor any trace of significant correspondence with any of its members at the time. Nevertheless, there are signs of mutual awareness and of some interaction, which makes this relationship, hardly studied thus far, worth exploring. The fact that Husserl himself, purist that he was, does not seem to have been very appreciative of the echo to his work in Würzburg, though he was aware of it (see p. 9), does not impair its historical importance.

As is well known, the main objective of the Würzburg school was to explore by experiment the "higher psychological functions," such as thinking and willing, in open disregard of Wundt's veto. These experiments chiefly made use of the critical introspection of trained observers. What they yielded was the unexpected fact that thinking and likewise willing did not consist exclusively or primarily of sensuous images. Both the method and the findings themselves ran counter to the prevailing principles of scientific psychology. In both respects phenomenology seemed to offer aid and comfort.

The most original work of the Würzburg school was carried out by Oswald Külpe's assistants and students, though it was clearly supervised by Külpe, who often served as a subject. When in 1901 A. Mayer and I. Orth published their study of association, in which the subjects were to describe their thinking, Husserl's *Logische Untersuchungen* was not yet generally known. This is also true in the case of the even more important studies by Karl Marbe, which for the first time demonstrated that introspection contained judgments of comparative weights in which no sensations or images were present and introduced the concept of the imageless *Bewusstseinslage* as a new phenomenon in consciousness. Henry J. Watt, the British member of the new team, launched, in addition to a more painstaking method, the task (*Aufgabe*) resulting in an attitude (*Einstellung*) as the decisive factor in imageless or image-poor thinking. But even in 1905, Husserl's views on non-sensuous or "categorial" intuition were apparently not yet on the map in Würzburg. At least Watt never seems to have mentioned Husserl by name.[35] Nor did Husserl's name occur in the first book by Narziss Ach (1905) on the act of will (*Über die Willenstätigkeit und das Denken*) (see below, p. 63).

A. *August Messer (1867–1937)*

The first of the group to refer to Husserl by name seems to have been August Messer. His experimental investigations of thinking (1906) credited Husserl in at least three places with the clarification of such concepts as distinctness, fullness, vividness, sensation, and meaning in general.[36] There is probably no longer any chance of finding out how Messer, trained in Giessen, where he had started teaching before coming to Würzburg in 1904–5 to do experimental work under Külpe, had discovered Husserl. The proximity of Marburg, where Natorp had begun to spread Husserl's fame, is hardly an adequate explanation. But there is also the strong possibility that Karl Bühler told Messer about Husserl when he came to Würzburg from Berlin, prior to becoming a *Privatdozent* and Külpe's assistant in 1906.

More significant than these first incidental references is the impact Husserl made on Messer's important book on sensation and thinking of 1908. Its introduction contains a special paragraph with the following sentences:

> One additional work, not primarily psychological, that can bring much clarification in these matters is to be mentioned here: Hus-

35. It is puzzling that Husserl referred to Watt in the *Ideen* (*Husserliana* III, 185) as implicitly attacking him in the criticisms of Theodor Lipps that were contained in Watt's report about recent work on the psychology of memory and association in the *Archiv für die gesamte Psychologie* of 1907 (Vol. IX). "Although my name is not mentioned, I think I may consider his criticism to be directed also against me . . ." This footnote is also indicative of how much closer, at this time, Husserl felt to Lipps than he had when he attacked Lipps as a chief exponent of psychologism.

36. "Experimentelle psychologische Untersuchungen über das Denken," *Archiv für die gesamte Psychologie,* VIII (1906), 1–224, especially the footnotes on pp. 85, 112, 149. Boring's formulation understates Husserl's influence on Messer by mentioning one single reference (*History of Experimental Psychology,* p. 408).

> serl's *Logische Untersuchungen.* It includes much that is of great significance for a psychology of thinking, and besides it draws with great precision the distinction, often so difficult to make, between the psychological and the logical approach to thinking.[37]

Actually the whole structure of the book is based on Husserl's ideas about intention and the intentional act. Thus intentionality, in the sense of a meaning reference, is traced first in perception and subsequently in thinking, abstraction, and judgment. Also, Husserl's doctrine of non-sensuous intuiting (*unsinnliche Anschauung*) plays an important part in the sections on the interpretation of thinking. The book ends with a ringing repudiation of all psychologism. Thus Husserl, as Messer himself had put it in his autobiography,[38] had supplied him with the philosophical tool for overcoming the sensationalism of the associationists, while his own experimental work had given him empirical confirmation.

However, Messer's seemingly total adoption of Husserl's position in the *Logische Untersuchungen* did not mean that he followed him on his way toward the pure phenomenology of the *Ideen.* Thus, when Husserl published his manifesto on "Philosophy as a Rigorous Science," in 1911, Messer responded in an essay on "Husserl's Phenomenology in Its Relation to Psychology,"[39] in which he took exception to Husserl's seeming repudiation of all experimental psychology (not quite fairly, since Husserl had made an exception at least for Carl Stumpf). Clearly, Messer felt that the experimental work of the Würzburg school deserved a better mark and was compatible with Husserl's program.[40] Otherwise, the article is still a strong plea for Husserl's phenomenology as pure psychology and as philosophy.[41] This did not imply that Messer saw in phenomenology the last word in philosophy rather than the penultimate one. Thus, in

37. *Empfindung und Denken* (Leipzig: Quelle & Meyer, 1908), p. 7.

38. Schmidt, *Die Philosophie der Gegenwart in Selbstdarstellungen,* Vol. III (1924), pp. 147–78, esp. p. 157.

39. "Husserl's Phänomenologie in ihren Verhältnis zur Psychologie," *Archiv für die gesamte Psychologie,* XXII (1911), 117–29.

40. In this spirit Messer also paid tribute to the psychological work done in Göttingen by Katz and Schapp, giving special credit to Katz's experimental procedures. "Die experimentelle Psychologie im Jahre 1911," *Jahrbücher für Philosophie,* I (1913), 269.

41. This did not appease Husserl. Thus in the *Ideen* (§ 79, last note) he complained that Messer had completely misunderstood and misrepresented him, chiefly because Messer had failed to recognize the peculiar nature of phenomenology as a doctrine of essences (*Wesenslehre*).

his survey of contemporary philosophy,[42] Messer took up Husserl's phenomenology just ahead of the saving word of the "critical realism" of Külpe. He remained skeptical of Husserl's essential intuition (*Wesensschau*) and obviously did not go in for his final transcendental idealism .

For Messer, then, the phenomenology of Husserl's *Logische Untersuchungen* provided the liberation from the narrow prison of sensationalism in general. It also gave him the means for a structural description of the most important higher function in psychology, thinking. This meant more than reinforcement and corroboration. Phenomenology supplied an active ingredient in Messer's interpretation of his own findings.

B. *Karl Bühler (1879–1963)*

The fact that Bühler's first reference to Husserl's work followed Messer's by one year [43] hardly proves Messer's priority in discovering him. In any case, Bühler's first reference to Husserl amounted to considerably more than a footnote. For he took a whole paragraph close to the beginning of his article (pp. 298–99) to commend the fruitfulness of Husserl's approach compared with the approaches of his predecessors and returned to him several times in the course of the article. He also acknowledged specifically the adoption (*Annahme*) of viewpoints (*Gesichtspunkte*) and ideas from the *Logische Untersuchungen* (p. 300).

The actual circumstances of Bühler's relations to Husserl and his work can probably no longer be established. The fact that Bühler came to Würzburg via Berlin makes it not unlikely that he had learned about Husserl from Carl Stumpf, with whom, according to Albert Wellek, Bühler had worked in Berlin. This also makes it likely that he was the one to spread Husserl's fame in Würzburg, as Boring, who also thought that it was through Bühler that Külpe learned about Husserl, suggested. As to personal contacts between Bühler and Husserl, Charlotte Bühler, to whom I am indebted for this information, states that he was "definitely in personal touch with Husserl." But since she got to know her husband only considerably after the Würzburg

42. *Die Hauptrichtungen der Philosophie der Gegenwart* (Munich: Reinhardt, 1916).

43. "Tatsachen und Probleme zu einer Psychologie der Denkvorgänge," *Archiv für die gesamte Psychologie*, IX (1907) 297–365, and XII (1908), 1–23.

years, she is not sure whether Bühler went to see Husserl or whether they saw each other on some later occasion. Anyhow, these personal contacts were hardly of much consequence. As to correspondence, only the typed copy of a letter written by Husserl to Bühler on June 28, 1927, has survived, which mentions Bühler's unsuccessful attempt to pay Husserl a visit in Freiburg, inviting him to repeat it. Nevertheless, with the possible exception of Messer, Bühler seems to have been the most direct link between Würzburg and Göttingen.

However, the important thing is the role of Husserl's ideas in the context of Bühler's psychology. Any attempt to determine it has to take account of the fact that Bühler's interests ranged far beyond the original interests of the Würzburg school, e.g., into the areas of Gestalt phenomena, developmental psychology, and the theory of language. A full account of the role of phenomenology for Bühler would have to study all these aspects of his work as well.

In the present context, Bühler's interest in the psychology of thinking as explored at Würzburg is most relevant. Here Bühler credited Husserl with a kind of "transcendental method," according to which we could derive from our knowledge of the ideal logical norms something about the processes in our thinking which correspond to them. But while Bühler commended this method, in which he saw a break with the Kantian approach and which he considered "extraordinarily fruitful," he himself wanted to establish this correspondence by a direct experimental method of exploration (*Ausfragemethode*). Having established that his subjects in their attempts to understand some fairly difficult quotations had no imagery but only "thoughts" (*Gedanken*), Bühler tried to analyze the positive characteristics of these thoughts. Here, after distinguishing between consciousness of rules, relations, and "intentions," he drew on Husserl's *Logical Investigations* in analyzing their structure, which thus supplied him with both a philosophical background for his study and with the means to interpret his results.

After Bühler had left Würzburg and the Würzburg school had become a matter of history, he published a book on color as part of a larger but uncompleted work on the nature of perception.[44] It dealt with the same kind of phenomena as Katz's first book, of which the title immediately reminds us. In fact, Katz, along with Hering and Helmholtz, provided the point of depar-

44. *Die Erscheinungsweisen der Farben* in *Handbuch der Psychologie*, Vol. I (Jena: Fischer, 1922).

ture for this new study. Repeatedly, Bühler referred to his own new studies as phenomenological. But there is only one explicit reference to Husserl and no specific attempt to make use of any of his insights. The descriptive work is matched by experimental research.

Still later Bühler turned to the theory of language. Here again he started out from a discussion of Husserl's semantic studies in the *Logical Investigations*.[45] Besides, throughout the book, Husserl's views are among those most frequently and most appreciatively considered. Bühler even took sympathetic account of the further development of Husserl's views on language in his *Formal and Transcendental Logic* (1929) and his *Cartesian Meditations* (1931). This did not prevent him from contradicting "the revered author" (p. 10) and from developing a new theory which added to the two functions of language that Husserl's scheme had distinguished, i.e., expression and presentation, a third function, i.e., appeal.[46]

What then is the place of phenomenology in Bühler's psychology? In 1927, Bühler published a programmatic book on *The Crisis in Psychology*, a subject much debated at the time in Germany. He even sent a copy to Husserl, which elicited Husserl's intense interest and the letter mentioned above. For Bühler, this crisis consisted of the contest between the three rival psychologies of conscious experience (*Erlebnispsychologie*), behaviorism, and psychology as *Geisteswissenschaft*. Actually, Bühler saw in this crisis merely a sign of growth and a transition to a new synthesis which would integrate these three aspects of psychological reality. Phenomenology as such did not figure by name in this new synthesis. But Bühler mentioned specifically his adherence to Husserl's "semasiology" in pointing out the significance of the concept of meaning for his new synthesis. One might therefore assume that phenomenology remained a basic part of the new psychology, as such included in the aspect of conscious experience, though it was hardly the only part of this

45. *Sprachtheorie* (Jena: Fischer, 1934; 2d ed., 1965).

46. There is additional evidence for Bühler's continued interest in Husserl's phenomenology during the thirties. Thus, in his preface to the second edition of the *Sprachtheorie*, the editor, Friedrich Kainz, mentions the fact that, while Bühler himself did not want to identify too closely with Husserl's phenomenology, his Vienna Institute undertook "detailed Husserl studies" (p. xi). To these Bühler himself seemed to be referring in the text of the book, where he mentioned an able critical study of the progress of Husserl's phenomenology in linguistic theory by one of his own students, which was to be published in the near future (pp. xxx, 232).

aspect. There is no reason to believe that in Bühler's last phase, particularly during his period in the United States, when he returned to Gestalt problems on a broader scale, he modified this appraisal significantly.

C. *Narziss Ach (1871–1946)*

Messer and Bühler were not the only members of the Würzburg school aware of Husserl's early phenomenology. It figured also in the studies of Narziss Ach and Otto Selz, though in the latter case it played only a minor role.

Narziss Ach studied chiefly the act of will by means of the new experimental methods. Although in his first book on the act of will and thinking[47] he used the term "phenomenological" only in passing as an equivalent of "phenomenal" (e.g., pp. 106, 199, 215), in his second book[48] he spoke much more prominently about his "phenomenological" results, always trying to describe the phenomenological aspect of the act of will and in so doing making use of Husserl's terminology (e.g., "*Moment*") with special reference to the *Logische Untersuchungen*. But such loans hardly indicate a very substantial debt.

D. *Otto Selz (1881–1944)*

Apparently this debt was even weaker in the case of Otto Selz, who wrote the most substantial work on the psychology of thinking to come out of the Würzburg school.[49] True, even here Husserl was quoted repeatedly as a support. But his relative role was much smaller than it had been for Selz's predecessors.

E. *Albert Michotte (1881–1965)*

This would seem to be the proper place for introducing the work of the first phenomenological psychologist outside the German area, the Belgian Albert Michotte. For while his work outgrew the world of the Würzburg school and he established his own school at Louvain, it was, as he put it in his autobiography,

47. *Über die Willenstätigkeit und das Denken* (Göttingen: Vandenhoeck & Ruprecht, 1905).

48. *Über der Willensakt und das Temperament* (Leipzig: Quelle & Meyer, 1910).

49. *Die Gesetze des geordneten Denkverlaufs,* Vol. I (Stuttgart: Spemann, 1913); Vol. II (Bonn: Cohen, 1922).

in Würzburg that "I discovered the works of Brentano, Mach, Meinong, Husserl, Stumpf, von Ehrenfels, and others." [50] The mediator was Külpe, who had met Michotte (as he had Messer) at the Congress for Experimental Psychology in Giessen in 1904, and had attracted him to Würzburg after three years in Leipzig. By the time of Michotte's residence in Würzburg (1907–8), Messer and Bühler had already published their papers, but Bühler was still there as a *Privatdozent.*

However, this does not mean that Michotte became immediately involved in phenomenology as a tributary to the work of the Würzburg school, let alone that he was attracted by Husserl's philosophy. Michotte was and remained primarily an experimental psychologist and one of the most original at that. He was, however, an experimentalist with a difference, who put his experience to new uses, including uses relevant to philosophy. But, as to phenomenological philosophy, Michotte kept at a respectful distance. This became particularly clear to me when in 1953 I had the privilege of being shown some of the perceptual experiments in his laboratory, which was then under the same roof with the Institut supérieur de philosophie in Louvain, where the Husserl Archives were housed beginning in 1939. At that time he expressed great puzzlement about the possible relation between his own phenomenological psychology and the phenomenology studied in the Archives above him. In fact, to my knowledge his publications never referred to Husserl, though they often mentioned the gestaltists and Katz and Rubin.

Michotte made no claim to having solved philosophical problems by his experimental demonstrations. All he wanted to show was the indisputable evidence of the phenomena without claiming that they reflect ultimate reality. In this he was perhaps more phenomenological than he himself realized. As to his peculiar interpretation of phenomenology, he seemed to think that only the work that he did after 1939 (the very year of the arrival of the Husserl papers in Louvain) was phenomenology.[51]

> The year 1939 was a turning point in my career and marks the beginning of a period during which I attacked, still using the experimental method, certain fundamental problems of phenomenology, the problems of causality, of permanence, and of apparent reality in our experience (p. 227).

50. *History of Psychology in Autobiography,* ed. Boring, IV (1952), 227 ff.

51. *Ibid.,* pp. 213–36, esp. pp. 215, 227, 235.

But he added that this work of phenomenology was "the result of a whole life of research and meditation" (p. 235).

What was this phenomenology in Michotte's sense? To my knowledge he never defined it in print. But it is fairly obvious that it implied for him the thorough exploration, if possible by experimental techniques, of the phenomena in all their concreteness experienced by his subjects. This interpretation, of course, was hardly different from the phenomenology of such members of the experimental school as Carl Stumpf. But Michotte also explicitly disclaimed all epistemological ambitions, particularly in the preface to the second edition of his book on the perception of causality.[52] Thus, in the case of perception he was concerned only with the *impression* of causality rather than with its veridical *cognition*. This did not imply that he considered his phenomenological findings irrelevant to the epistemological question. In fact, Michotte made it quite clear that without his interest in the philosophical issues, and without the challenges of David Hume's denial of a perception of causality and Maine de Biran's affirmation, he would never have undertaken his research. The role of the experiment in Michotte's work was simply that of showing concretely how unfounded Hume's assertions were, since they could not be based on anything but superficial observations or crude experiences which lacked all precision and especially the working precautions indispensable in psychological research (p. 252; Eng. trans., pp. 255–56). He did so by specifying the precise conditions under which such impressions as those of causality, materiality, or permanence do or do not arise. After Michotte's demonstrations there could no longer be any reasonable doubt that we do have definite and describable immediate impressions of causal influence, no matter what their ultimate validity may be, particularly in the eyes of a critical realist in the Külpe or Neo-Scholastic tradition like Michotte.

Michotte's manner of introducing the causal impressions may at first throw doubts on the relevance of these impressions in establishing real causation. For he merely used such artificial visual patterns as dots and lines without any causal connection between them. He quoted one of his philosopher colleagues with approval: "In effect you start from an illusion in order to prove

52. *La Perception de la causalité* (Louvain: Nauwelaerts, 1954), p. v. The English translation by T. R. and Elaine Miles, *Perception of Causality* (London: Methuen, 1963), contains an important new chapter by the author in the appendices.

the reality of the causal impression and to demonstrate its objectivity" (p. 226; Eng. trans., p. 228). But he conceded that the objectivity thus proved was no more than phenomenal intersubjectivity. In any case this phenomenon now became so tangible as to undercut all nominalistic skepticism. For Michotte not only showed causal impressions but also distinguished several distinct types elicited by different arrangements of his stimuli. Specifically, he demonstrated in detail such causal impressions as (1) launching (*lancement*)—a definite *Gestalt* connected with the perception of two movements where the two moving objects part company—and (2) entrainment (*entraînement*)—where both objects move on together in unison. These have many subdivisions (release, expulsion, self-movement, etc.). What is common to them is the phenomenon of spread (*ampliation*) of movement from an agent to a patient. This spread includes the impression of productiveness, overlooked especially by Hume's naïve idea of causation (pp. 218 ff.; Eng. trans., pp. 221 ff.). Thus perception can give us immediately the impression of a "generation," not merely of a dependence, as in the case of the release effect. However, Michotte did not think that "qualitative causality" (one quality causing another) allows for comparable perception. All we can see here without movement is a succession of qualities.

Michotte's other "phenomenological" experiments contributed relevant data for the solution of three philosophical problems:

(1) animal movement, as manifested by specifiable characteristics which can also be produced artificially, leading to phenomenal impressions of purposiveness ("intentionality") or teleology;

(2) phenomenal permanence in changing impressions;

(3) apparent reality.

What Michotte claimed as his chief result was that sensory experience is infinitely richer than one could have supposed. Clearly, Michotte has broken new ground and not only has shown new phenomena but, by experimental techniques, has made them intersubjectively accessible. Both the enrichment of the world of phenomena and their experimental analysis represent major achievements for the development of phenomenology, even beyond the experimental range. Their philosophical utilization leads beyond Michotte's laboratory.

In the meantime, phenomenology in the more philosophical sense can claim to have contributed at least to the climate in which Michotte's research was started by the Würzburg school. Obviously, even before 1939, most of his work on the phenomena of the will was in the broadest sense phenomenological.[53] What he did after 1939 differed from what he had done before chiefly in his choice of problems in the perceptual range. The fact that Michotte called this work "phenomenological" has to be understood in the context of his distinction between phenomenology and epistemology: he wanted to avoid all premature epistemological claims. This remarkable modesty made the significance of his findings all the greater.

[5] Phenomenology in Gestalt Psychology

> It was not only the stimulating newness of our enterprise which inspired us. There was also a great wave of relief—as though we were escaping from a prison. The prison was psychology as taught in the universities when we were still students.[54]

The above sentences from Köhler's Presidential Address before the American Psychological Association in 1959 sound strikingly like early enthusiastic pronouncements of Max Scheler, otherwise no friend and no kinsman of Köhler, on the new Phenomenological Movement as a liberation from the imprisonment of modern man.[55] That both Gestalt psychology and phenomenology have a similar concern in liberating modern man for a fresh approach to reality is clear enough. But this similarity can be overrated. Especially in the American perspective, there is an understandable tendency to overestimate the historical closeness of the two, a misinterpretation expressed for instance in the way in which Boring introduced phenomenology in his chapter on Gestalt psychology as merely a precursor of the latter. Not only did Gestalt psychology have other and closer ancestors, but phenomenology had several non-gestaltist

53. Thus the study by Michotte and Prüm on "Le Choix volontaire" (*Archives de psychologie*, X [1911], 113–320) often uses the term "phenomenological" as a synonym of "descriptive" and an antonym of "explicative" and even contains a special section called "La phénoménologie de l'acte de volonté" (pp. 310 ff.).

54. Wolfgang Köhler, "Gestalt Psychology Today," in *Documents of Gestalt Psychology*, ed. Mary Henle (Berkeley, Calif.: University of California Press, 1961), p. 4.

55. *Vom Umsturz der Werte* (1915), in *Gesammelte Werke*, Vol. III (Bern: Francke, 1954), p. 339; see also *The Phenomenological Movement*, p. 240.

descendants, beginning with the Göttingen group (which Boring does mention among the "antecedents") and some members of the Würzburg school.

To begin with, any influence of phenomenology on Gestalt psychology would have been one of action at a distance. The gestaltist triumvirate, Max Wertheimer, Kurt Koffka, and Wolfgang Köhler, apparently met Husserl and other leading phenomenologists only late and casually. The centers of phenomenology in Göttingen, Freiburg, and Munich differed from those of the gestaltists in Frankfurt and Berlin, and there was little overlapping at the periphery. Only after the center of gravity of Gestalt psychology had moved to the United States, with Koffka in Northhampton (Smith College), Wertheimer in New York (New School of Social Research), and Köhler near Philadelphia (Swarthmore College), did a more direct exchange with the emigrated younger phenomenologists become possible and to a limited extent actual.

What must also be considered is that none of the three founders of Gestalt psychology had a primary interest in philosophy. Presumably this interest developed only as they became fully aware of the implications of their findings. Especially when they had to confront the challenge of behaviorism did they feel a need for philosophical foundations for their position. This happened primarily in the United States. At this stage phenomenology seemed to offer some of the needed methodological buttressing.

Of course Gestalt psychology as a new configuration in the field of psychology could not help being aware of the field from which it had emerged. Even before it crystallized in 1911, when Wertheimer published his studies about the seeing of movement, and achieved consciousness of its identity around 1920, when Koffka made first contributions to the psychology of Gestalt, the gestaltists were connected with the predecessors and the first psychological offshoots of phenomenology. Wertheimer had started his studies in Prague and had been in touch with Ewald Hering, the independent phenomenologist of sight, and with Christian von Ehrenfels, the discoverer of the *Gestaltqualitäten*, who reflected Brentano's approach as developed by Meinong. From 1901 to 1903 he was in Berlin, where Stumpf was formulating his own phenomenology. He took his Ph.D. in Würzburg under Külpe, to be sure too early for the Husserl infiltration that began with Messer and Bühler. Koffka began his studies in Berlin under Carl Stumpf [56] and, after his habilitation in Giessen, must have imbibed some of the Würzburg spirit through Messer, as his dedication to Külpe "in Erinnerung an Würzburg 1909" makes quite plain. Köhler entered the world of wider phenomenology in Berlin, where he took his Ph.D. under Stumpf.

However, one must also realize that by 1911 Husserl's phenomenology had become part of the general atmosphere, and that it no longer makes sense and is no longer necessary to trace specific influences as in the case of the Würzburg school of the preceding decade. By now the general ideas of Husserl's *Logische Untersuchungen* were common ground. However, with the *Ideen* of 1913 phenomenology had also taken a turn toward a new transcendentalism. And this is one more reason why the gestaltists were no longer very eager to identify with it, sight unseen.[57]

Some details of the gradual reception of phenomenology by the gestaltists are so instructive that they merit more individualized tracing.

A. *Max Wertheimer (1880–1943)*

It was generally acknowledged, particularly by his generous collaborators, that Wertheimer, their senior, was the seminal mind of the group. But he was also the one who published the least. No unified book of his came out during his lifetime, and his trail-blazing papers cannot give an adequate idea of his inspiriting influence. This is one of the reasons why one must not expect to find in his publications explicit references to his relations with philosophical phenomenology or any evidence of the influences that he experienced from it. Wertheimer was not given to lavish quoting. In a sense he was too phenomenological to start from the literature rather than from the original phenomena. The only place where Husserl's phenomenology is mentioned explicitly is in his posthumous book on *Productive Thinking* of 1935, in which phenomenology is characterized as "stressing the essentials in 'phenomenological reduction.'" But it is mentioned only as the first of several schools which brought about "new conceptions, new directions in the theory of think-

56. "He gave the first impulse to my scientific thinking," *Zur Analyse der Vorstellungen und ihrer Gesetze* (Leipzig: Quelle & Meyer, 1912), p. vi.

57. For further material on the gestaltists, see the article, "Gestalt Theory," by Solomon Asch, in *International Encyclopedia of the Social Sciences* (1968), VI, 158–175, esp. 170 ff.

ing," and this fact alone does not make clear what Wertheimer's attitude toward phenomenology was. However, circumstantial evidence makes me believe that Wertheimer, especially in his American period, was highly sympathetic to the general purposes of phenomenological philosophizing. In fact, in his conversations with Dorion Cairns, he seemed to have shown considerable interest in some of the more esoteric problems of Husserl's transcendental phenomenology (Cairns's letter to Husserl of January 17, 1934).

In order to determine how far Wertheimer's approach was genuinely phenomenological, one has to take a look at his actual procedure, beginning with his break-through study on the seeing of movement in 1912. It starts with the bold assertion:

> One sees a movement; it is not the case that the object moved, is now in a place other than where it was before, and hence that one knows that it has moved . . . but one saw the movement. What is psychologically given here? [58]

Wertheimer considers this "clear and distinctly given phenomenon a psychological enigma" (p. 6). But what has to be asked is: "What is psychically given when movement is seen. . . . What constitutes these impressions?" For Wertheimer the primary task is to describe and explore the given under experimentally clearly defined conditions. The result is that, given a certain speed in the successive occurrence of *a* and *b*, an additional phenomenon of movement is unmistakably seen, a phenomenon for which he now coined the term "Phi-phenomenon" (presumably after the Greek word *phora*). Later he distinguished between principal phenomena (*Hauptphänomene*) and intermediate phenomena (*Zwischenphänomene*).

There is certainly no justification for identifying the gestaltist concept of the phenomenon with that of phenomenology, though it clearly differs from that of positivism. What makes it nevertheless congenial is the readiness of a gestaltist like Wertheimer to acknowledge a phenomenon even when it has no recognized place in the reductionist world of the sensationalist empiricists. The gestaltist phenomenon is at least the legitimate cousin of that of the phenomenologists.

Wertheimer's phenomenological approach also manifested itself very clearly in his attempt to show the difference between

58. "Experimentelle Studien über das Sehen von Bewegung," *Zeitschrift für Psychologie*, LXI (1912), 162. Also in *Drei Abhandlungen zur Gestaltheorie* (Erlangen: Weltkreis, 1925), p. 2.

mere "and-connections" (*Undverbindungen*) and genuine Gestalts. He introduced the difference at the very start of his second study on the doctrine of Gestalt, which began with the account of a typical perceptual situation: "I am standing at the window and seeing a house, trees, sky. And now, for theoretical reasons I could try to count off and say: 'There are . . . 327 brightnesses' "—a counting which we obviously do not perform, since we see complete configurations, not elements.[59]

But this readiness to accept and describe irreducible phenomena is not the only feature common to both Gestalt theory and phenomenology. As early as in his study on the seeing of movement, Wertheimer had spoken about the "*a priori* proposition that movement is inconceivable without an object or a seen thing that moves." Here is the equivalent of the essential laws of phenomenology.

It is impossible to say how far Wertheimer was consciously aware of such parallels when he developed his ideas. But it can hardly be doubted that, as far as he was aware of them, they had a corroborating effect on his thinking.

B. *Kurt Koffka (1885–1941)*

Koffka was the member of the original team of gestaltists most interested in establishing contacts with the philosophical camp. He also seems to have gone farthest in identifying the method of Gestalt psychology with that of phenomenology. This happened especially in his most systematic work, the *Principles of Gestalt Psychology*, published first in English in 1935, where he devoted to "the phenomenological method" a special subsection of his second chapter, in which he had developed his conception of the environmental field as the matrix for all psychological explanations.[60] By-passing all other accounts, he called phenomenology simply "as naïve and full a description of direct experience as possible." But he also made a special point of distinguishing it from introspection, by which he understood an "analysis of direct experience into sensations or attributes or some other systematic but not experiential ultimates"; this interpretation of introspection can also be found with Köhler.

Koffka did not mention philosophical phenomenologists in this context. He only referred to Husserl as the sworn enemy of

59. *Psychologische Forschung*, IV (1923), 301 f.
60. *The Principles of Gestalt Psychology* (New York: Harcourt, Brace, 1935), p. 73.

all *Psychologismus* (p. 570), a psychologism of which he thought Gestalt psychology was innocent in its effort to establish an intelligible connection between the realms of logical relations and the psychological facts which are organized in accord with these relations. Husserl's phenomenology as it developed after the Prolegomena of the *Logische Untersuchungen* is not even mentioned. It is therefore fairly clear that Koffka's conception of phenomenology was still very much in line with that of Carl Stumpf, his first teacher in Berlin. But this does not mean that Koffka was simply a disciple of Stumpf, as he himself was anxious to make clear.

In order to understand Koffka's relation to phenomenology, one had best start from what is certainly his major work, the *Principles of Gestalt Psychology.* In this case the title "Principles" meant more than just a collection of fundamental assumptions. It was also indicative of Koffka's philosophic intent. This intent, as becomes increasingly clear, was an attack on "positivism" or "empiricism" in its denial of meaningful relations among the data of human life. Integration was Koffka's goal. Phenomenology was to be a major weapon in this battle for the recognition of meaningful connections, however limited.

In this light even a quick look at Koffka's intellectual development proves illuminating. From Stumpf's Berlin laboratory Koffka had moved to Külpe's Würzburg school. While contributing to its experimental work he nevertheless stated in retrospect that the work of the Würzburg school was unsuccessful, since it resulted only in introducing such *x*'s as the *determinierende Tendenzen.* It was not until 1911 when, together with Köhler, he joined Wertheimer (who had also passed through Würzburg) in Frankfurt, that he got sight of the new principle of *Gestalt,* which represented a positive phenomenon capable of supplying the missing link not only for the understanding of the higher processes but for finding meaning even in perception.

However, in Koffka's case one can find a definite interest in Husserl as early as the Würzburg period, e.g., in his first book, an "experimental investigation" concerning the analysis of representations and their laws,[61] a work dedicated to Külpe and still consciously in the Würzburg tradition. In the last section about our understanding of words, Koffka inserted a special section on Husserl (*Kurzer Hinweis*, pp. 380–81) in which, on the basis of a careful study of passages from the *Logische Unter-*

61. *Zur Analyse der Vorstellungen und ihrer Gesetze* (Leipzig: Quelle & Meyer, 1912),

suchungen, he pointed out differences rather than similarities, with the final conclusion that his own analyses were concerned with factual experiences, while Husserl was chiefly interested in the "objective" and in experiences as such, i.e., in the study of essences (*Wesensforschung*).

In 1913 Koffka, now at Giessen, began his "contributions to a psychology of Gestalt and the experiences of movement,"[62] with the program "on the one hand to describe the phenomena as accurately as possible, on the other to find law-like dependencies between them and the objective processes (experiences and stimuli)." But he added at once: "We renounce any kind of postulated consciousness and unnoticed sensations, or activities and consider ourselves methodically entitled to this" (p. 353). This pronouncement signaled the abandonment of the principle of constancy.

Koffka was the first and boldest gestaltist in formulating the implications of the new approach in printed form. His contribution to the composite handbook of philosophy by Max Dessoir[63] was a 100-page presentation of the "new psychology" as contrasted with the old, i.e., associationism. Here he attacked the latter's dogmas, especially the dualism of stimuli and phenomena based on the assumption of a constant correlation between the two (*Konstanzannahme*) and the assumption of unnoticed phenomenal correlates to the stimuli. He introduced the new answer under the title of "Phänomenologie" (the only time he used it in German), and its prime function was to show the experienced difference between "and-relations" (*Undverbindungen*) and *Gestalten*. This phenomenology was to describe carefully the nexus among the phenomena observed, regardless of the relations among the stimuli. Gestalt psychology in this sense undertook the investigation of the *Gestalt* in itself, looking for its "laws," e.g., the law of good *Gestalt,* a configuration that is clearly related to the essential laws of phenomenology, opposed to the merely contingent connections among the chaotic and-relations.

Around the same time, in his first article written in English, Koffka spelled out even more explicitly the position that the phenomenal aspect is independent of the physical one.[64]

62. *Zeitschrift für Psychologie,* LXVII (1913), 353–58.

63. "Psychologie," in *Die Philosophie in ihren Einzelgebieten,* ed. Max Dessoir (Berlin: A. G. Ullstein, 1925), pp. 497–608.

64. "Introspection and the Method of Psychology," *British Journal of Psychology,* XXV (1924), 149–61.

Introducing it as a third way between introspection and behaviorism, he proposed the "study of the organism in its own surroundings, including consciousness, which we may refer to as the phenomenal world. . . . We cannot assume a point-to-point correspondence between the objective and the phenomenal world" (p. 155).

However, Koffka's major presentation of his new conception materialized only after his move to America. Thus his *Principles of Gestalt Psychology* remained the most important statement of his systematic position. It also attempted to relate it to the predominant trend of American behaviorism and to incorporate the best of it into Gestalt psychology. The key concept in this gestaltist interpretation of behaviorism was that of the behavioral environment, which Koffka contrasted with what he called the geographical environment. His work may well be one of the most significant attempts to rethink and deepen the concept of behavior, which had become externalized in orthodox behaviorism. Psychological behavior, as Koffka, following William McDougall, saw it, is molar, as opposed to molecular, behavior. And such behavior is primarily behavior in relation to an environment. But this environment is no longer the geographical one as described in the objective categories of measuring science, but the behavioral one which must be described in terms of the experiencing individual. In this sense the behavioral environment coincides with the phenomenological environment.

There were other places where Koffka made clear the priority of the phenomenal data over the physical ones and introduced new phenomena beyond the pervading one of *Gestalt*. Particularly significant was his introduction (in Chapter VIII, in which he discussed action) of the ego as the central figure, the "hero of the play." To Koffka the ego appeared as an indispensable part of the behavioral field. Many of Koffka's characterizations of the ego were new and important, such as the emphasis on its complexity, its subsystems, and its variability. However, though there is no indication of any direct connection with Husserl's rehabilitation of the ego, the parallel between the two is all the more striking.

But it is important to realize that neither Koffka nor the other Gestalt psychologists were satisfied with mere description. Psychology was to go beyond the descriptively given to functional concepts (*Funktionsbegriffe*). The fact that the new phenomena could be approached only via description did not justify their reduction to purely phenomenological data but left the task of determining their relation with the transphenomenal physical world unfinished. It was at this point that Gestalt psychology became aware of the fact that there is no strict one-to-one correlation between phenomenon and stimulus. The breakdown of the "constancy principle" in the face of the kind of behavior in man and animals which was involved in the response to relative, rather than to absolute, stimuli made it plain that the phenomena were much more independent of the stimuli than had been admitted thus far. Gestalt psychology was too phenomenological to escape into postulating unnoticed sensations and other inferred illusions, as Stumpf had suggested. Only one hypothesis seemed legitimate: that of Köhler's physical *Gestalts* as *correlates* to their psychic counterparts. This was a hypothesis which required merely that the phenomena be taken first at their face value and described much more conscientiously than before. Abandoning the constancy principle meant also, as Gurwitsch has spelled out most clearly, acknowledging the priority and primacy of phenomenology.

Koffka was the gestaltist who made the fewest qualifications in subscribing to the phenomenological method. But this did not mean that he attached himself to Husserl or any other member of the philosophical movement, although judging from some of his references he seems to have been in touch with less orthodox members such as Geiger and Scheler. His connections were even closer with David Katz and Edgar Rubin.

It would hardly be safe to assert that the phenomenological method, however liberally interpreted, was instrumental in directing Koffka's concrete research. But as he came to reflect on his method it certainly corroborated his methodology, especially in his battle with introspectionism and behaviorism.

C. *Wolfgang Köhler (1887–1967)*

Köhler, the youngest member of the original triumvirate, was also the one who went furthest in giving open support to phenomenological philosophy, if only by joining the editorial board of *Philosophy and Phenomenological Research* after 1941. However, he was much slower than Koffka in expressing this support publicly. He had of course no reason to refer to phenomenology in his classic research on *The Mentality of Apes* (1917). In the book on physical *Gestalts*,[65] with its interest in the physical

65. *Die physichen Gestalten in Ruhe und im stationären Zustand* (Braunschweig: Vieweg, 1920).

equivalents of psychic *Gestalts,* the term "phenomenology" was mentioned merely to characterize Wertheimer's point of departure (pp. 177, 185, 187), and Husserl's work figured only in a footnote (p. 58) as not pertinent to Köhler's problem. Even in the *Gestalt Psychology* of 1929, with all its critical discussion of behaviorism and defense of direct experience, Köhler never appealed to phenomenology as such.

All the more striking was Köhler's adoption of phenomenology as well as its name in his William James lectures of 1934–35, published in 1938 soon after his permanent settlement in the United States.[66] Here phenomenology was invoked as the foundation for a study not only of values but of all psychological facts. However, while Köhler discussed Husserl as the main representative of phenomenology, not mentioning any others, he accepted Husserlian phenomenology only with considerable reservations. He subscribed to its motto "to the things," as opposed to the "naturalistic" and empiricist neglect of what is directly given prior to any explanatory hypotheses. In his brief sketch of this phenomenology he mentioned with obvious approval Husserl's plea for insights into essential relationships other than mere contingent factual ones. But then he drew the line. He did not believe in a strict separation between the world of essences and the world of facts, thus rejecting Husserl's "eidetic reduction." He even suspected him of completely discarding the world of facts on the basis of his "phenomenological reduction." By contrast, his own phenomenology was openly concerned with facts. Essences as such were never mentioned.[67]

However, the delay in Köhler's discussion of phenomenology did not mean that he was not aware of it and, what is more important, that he did not practice it. In many ways Gestalt psychology was merely another one of the revolts against the narrowness of positivist psychology. It implied a new open approach to the phenomena and, in particular, the repudiation of atomic elements in favor of the total *Gestalts* as given in direct experience.[68]

Perhaps the most momentous step in Köhler's rapprochement

66. *The Place of Value in a World of Facts* (New York: Liveright, 1938).

67. See also my review of the book in *Philosophy and Phenomenological Research,* I (1941), 377–86.

68. See also Köhler's Princeton lectures on *The Tasks of Gestalt Psychology* (Princeton, N.J.: Princeton University Press, 1969), esp. chap. 1.

to phenomenology was his rejection of unnoticed sensations, a rejection which actually involved a departure from his teacher Stumpf.[69] Stumpf had defended their existence as required by the logic of the elemental sensations. How could *a* be unequal to *c* if *a* was really equal to *b* and *b* equal to *c*? To Stumpf this proved the existence of unnoticed inequalities behind the supposed equalities. Köhler rejected this reasoning. Could not the relation between *a* and *c* show an entirely new *Gestalt* of inequality without any new physical stimulus? He claimed that the introduction of hypothetical sensations merely for the purpose of defending the constancy hypothesis led to a falsification of the data. Blaming illusions or errors of judgment prevented "a resolute exploration of the primary causes of the illusions." Such an exploration would indeed lead to a "phenomenological description and theoretical treatment of the visual field, which runs contrary to the fundamental assumption of the psychology under investigation" (p. 70).

However, it must be realized that Köhler's ultimate interest was never phenomenological. His first major work, *Die physischen Gestalten* (1920), showed that from the very start his real concern was to anchor the *Gestalt* phenomena in transphenomenal nature, i.e., in the physical *Gestalts* which the latest physics of field forces had made accessible. Nevertheless, even this book mentioned phenomenology, apparently in Stumpf's sense, as an indispensable foundation of this enterprise (p. 189).

The book on *Gestalt Psychology* (1929) was not only the first attempt to present a systematic introduction to the new approach, but it was also addressed to American readers at a time when phenomenology was still practically unknown to them—a fact that may be a partial explanation for the absence of the term from this trail-blazing work. Köhler's book confronted not only the old Continental enemy of associationism but the new American challenge of behaviorism. In so doing, Köhler tried to show that the gestaltist approach differed fundamentally from the objectionable introspection with which phenomenology is so often confused. But this did not mean the absence of the phenomenology. For the key term of his new "liberal" approach was "direct experience," which, with its "subjective" and "objective" features, was defended as the indispensable starting point.

69. "Über unbemerkte Empfindungen und Urteilstäuschungen," *Zeitschrift für Psychologie*, LXVI (1913), 51–80.

This direct experience as described by Köhler was clearly the experience of what was immediately given in the world of our daily living.

This is not the place to show in detail the fruits of Köhler's phenomenological approach. Suffice it to mention the fact that it enabled him to make a case for values as constitutive parts of direct experience. These values were given in the form of the perception of objective requiredness as distinguished from subjective interests, a perception that had also been advocated by Max Wertheimer. Besides, Köhler pleaded the case for the direct givenness of such phenomena as force. On this phenomenological foundation he believed that, by means of scientific inference, he could go beyond mere phenomenology in an attempt to defend his theory of isomorphism, according to which phenomena such as value have their objective correlates in the objective equivalents to phenomenal *Gestalts* in fields of forces, a correlation which anchored the subjective phenomena in a "world of facts." Thus eventually phenomenology proved to be for Köhler the foundation for an ambitious philosophy of value rooted in a philosophy of nature.

Philosophical phenomenology had clearly no immediate influence on the origins of Köhler's psychology and on his eventual philosophy. In the beginning he simply thought through the implications of Wertheimer's and his own factual discoveries in perceptual and animal psychology, which led him to an increasing awareness of the "autonomy" of the phenomena. Apparently, it was only when he had to defend his emerging systematic position that, short of a methodological philosophy, he found in the general principles of phenomenology his most valuable backing. One might say that, in the case of Köhler, philosophical phenomenology had largely the role of a foundation added at a later stage in order to underpin a structure which proved to be increasingly in need of such buttressing. But when Köhler came out openly for phenomenology he did so with an outspokenness which could hardly have been outdone. As he put it: "Phenomenology is the field in which all concepts find their final justification." [70]

D. *Aron Gurwitsch (b. 1901)*

Thus Gestalt psychology only gradually approached and adopted phenomenology as its philosophical ally. Among those

70. *Place of Value in a World of Facts*, p. 102.

who played an important part in this rapprochement were Aron Gurwitsch and Karl Duncker.

In 1928, Gurwitsch, originally a mathematician and then a philosopher, published his Göttingen dissertation in the gestaltist journal *Psychologische Forschung.*[71] In general it was based on Husserl's *Ideen,* but it also made a determined effort to show the relationships between phenomenology and certain motifs in the thought of such gestaltists as Wertheimer, Koffka, and Köhler. Gurwitsch's most important point was that the abandonment of the constancy principle by the gestaltists had led them to a position very close to that of Husserl, since it implied the need to study the phenomena by themselves without primary regard for their objective stimuli. In his later work Gurwitsch also tried to show how gestalt psychology can contribute to the phenomenology of perception and particularly to an understanding of the constitution of the perceived phenomena.[72]

E. *Karl Duncker (1903–1940)*

Duncker's field was primarily psychology, but he had a much stronger background in both mathematics and phenomenology than most other gestaltists. His studies of the phenomena of "induced movement," productive thinking, and motivation showed an unusually wide and thorough acquaintance with the phenomenological literature, even beyond Husserl. He also prepared explicitly phenomenological treatments of such topics as the "phenomenology of pleasure" and the phenomenology of the consciousness of objects. In his studies of problem solving he showed concretely how the solutions are based on the directly experienced and describable reorganization of problematic material into new insightful patterns.

Duncker's premature death cut off what might well have developed into the most fruitful synthesis of Gestalt psychology and phenomenology.

71. "Phänomenologie der Thematik und des reinen Ich: Studien Über Beziehungen von Gestalt theorie und Phänomenologie," *Psychologische Forschung,* XII (1929), 1–102. English translation by Frederick Kersten, "Phenomenology of Thematics and of the Pure Ego: Studies of the Relation between Gestalt Theory and Phenomenology," *Studies in Phenomenology and Psychology* (Evanston, Ill.: Northwestern University Press, 1966), pp. 175–286.

72. "The Phenomenology of Perception: Perceptual Implications," in *An Invitation to Phenomenology,* ed. J. M. Edie (Chicago: Quadrangle, 1965), pp. 17–30.

F. *Kurt Lewin* (1890–1947)

The "supporting" role of phenomenology was not restricted to the inner circle of the Gestalt psychologists. While a complete survey is again out of the question, at least two of the more independent members of the wider circle deserve to be singled out, partly because of their independent and persisting importance in the States—Kurt Lewin and Fritz Heider.

Like Köhler, Kurt Lewin began as a student of Carl Stumpf, acknowledging his lasting debt in his obituary for Stumpf.[73] So he was clearly exposed early to the pre-Husserlian type of phenomenology. It is in this light that one has to read one of his earliest studies, which he himself called a chapter from the "phenomenology of the landscape," entitled "*Kriegslandschaft.*" The main point of this extremely rich descriptive study was to show how the landscape of war (actually that of the stationary warfare of World War I) is limited and polarized with a front and a rear, as compared with the unlimited and unpolarized landscape of peace.[74]

Lewin's other German writings also showed a certain amount of interest in phenomenology. Thus his important studies on action and affective psychology [75] included a section on phenomenological conceptualization (*Begriffsbildung*) as contrasted to a conditional-genetic one, but only in order to warn against overemphasis on phenomenological questions. Another study on experiment and law in psychology [76] pointed out a "certain similarity" between laws for types and the "essence" in the sense of phenomenological logic, and even referred to phenomenological *epochē* (p. 381), mentioning in passing Husserl's *Ideen* (p. 391).

Under these circumstances, the near total absence of any reference to phenomenology in Lewin's later, especially his American, production, is puzzling. One may suspect that he now saw in phenomenology merely a Husserlian enterprise with which he did not want to be identified. Besides, his commitment to a Galilean, as opposed to an Aristotelian, approach may

73. *Psychological Review,* IV (1937), 189–194.
74. *Zeitschrift für angewandte Psychologie,* XII (1917), 440–47.
75. *Psychologische Forschung,* VII (1925), 307, 309.
76. "Gesetz und Experiment in der Psychologie," *Symposium,* V (1925), 373–421.

have turned him away from a philosophy which was opposed to Galileo's mathematical abstractionism.

But there are also more positive reasons for Lewin's moving beyond mere phenomenology. For his primary interest was clearly in a psychology of action, of will and needs, which finally resulted in a study of the dynamics of human personality. Phenomenology, as he understood its descriptive aims, was not in a position to help him with these tasks.

This is not the place to pursue the development of Lewin's psychology of the will into a dynamic theory of the individual personality and finally into group dynamics with its ambitious social goals. However, there is reason to mention the fact that in many ways his field theory led him closer to Husserl's late phenomenology of the life-world than he himself may have had a chance to realize. For when Lewin placed practical behavior in the context of a topological field, he saw that this field was not the physical field of science but the life-space of the experiencing organism. In fact, occasionally Lewin characterized this field as "phenomenal." But he himself avoided any renewed entanglement with "phenomenology." Yet there is much in his development of the structure of the "topological field," with its regions, accesses, and barriers, and with the self in relation to this field, which would lend itself to phenomenological interpretation and assimilation. But the mere historian has no right to indulge in such posthumous "annexations."

G. *Fritz Heider (b. 1896)*

Fritz Heider too is one of the European psychologists who after coming to America became increasingly involved in Gestalt psychology and thus to some extent also in phenomenology. Actually, Heider had started out from the Graz school of Meinong and his followers, and his doctoral thesis on "Thing and Medium" still largely reflects this spirit. He never was close to the centers of phenomenology nor, for that matter, of Gestalt psychology. His Continental academic career led him via the Hamburg of William Stern and Ernst Cassirer, who by then of course also reflected the new phenomenological climate.

Heider's primary concern is perception in all its aspects. Phenomenology as such would hardly have interested him except insofar as it could throw light on perceptual phenomena. Thus he calls special attention to phenomenological features not only in Kurt Lewin's work but also in the "phenomenological descriptions of the psychological environment in the work of Marcel Proust." [77]

But where phenomenology becomes most prominent in Heider's own work is in *The Psychology of Interpersonal Relations,* for which he had laid some foundations in an essay on "Social Perception and Phenomenal Causality," [78] Heider not only refers often and approvingly to works of Scheler and even Sartre and Merleau-Ponty (though Husserl's name does not seem to occur) but is also aware of Schutz's social phenomenology and draws attention to Duncker's phenomenological studies of perception. He characterizes his own objective as "to describe the phenomena faithfully and allow them to guide the choice of problems and procedures." [79] Thus he begins with the study of the common-sense psychology of interpersonal relations as the indispensable start "regardless of whether its assumptions and principles prove valid under scientific scrutiny" (p. 5), and bases it on a study of the "subjective environment of life space." Phenomenal description is everywhere the starting point, though not the terminus, of investigation. It presents one facet, but it cannot reveal the genetic sources of interpersonal behavior (p. 298). What is needed first is "pre-theory," i.e., unformulated and intuitive thinking about behavior (p. 195). Heider's objective becomes particularly clear when, in discussing Gilbert Ryle's approach via ordinary language, he states that the analysis of words and meanings can be only a means, and that the end must be "to make explicit the system of concepts that underlies interpersonal behavior."

It is not hard to see that what is at stake here is a fundamental phenomenology of the social life-world on a purely descriptive scale. The concreteness and cautiousness of these investigations show all the earmarks of a firsthand but nontechnical phenomenology.

H. *Martin Scheerer (1900–1961)*

Another student of William Stern's, Martin Scheerer, a colleague of Fritz Heider's at Hamburg and again later at the University of Kansas, and a close collaborator with Kurt Goldstein in America, also deserves a place in this survey. His phenome-

77. Heider, *On Perception,* pp. 85 ff.
78. *Psychological Review,* LI (1948), 358–74.
79. *On Perception,* p. ix.

nological interests appear first in his large German book on Gestalt theory,[80] in which Scheerer begins the first methodological part by tracing the *Gestalt* in the phenomenal range. In addition to other occasional references to phenomenology, an appendix on the subjectivating method, which is to Scheerer an integral part of Gestalt theory, shows particular familiarity with the phenomenological literature.

A later source of Scheerer's interest in phenomenology is his work on "social cognition." This becomes particularly clear from his article in Lindzey's *Handbook of Social Psychology*.[81]

[6] Phenomenology in Continental Psychology since World War II

At this point I shall abandon all pretense of a historical orientation. Instead, I want to give something like a frog's-eye perspective of the present scene in Continental psychology as it appears to me from a distance on the basis of samplings of the literature and brief visits. All I intend is to give enough impressions of the contemporary scene in European psychology so as neither to raise expectations for the future nor to dash them unduly. My aim is to aid the reader in his own discriminations and observations.

In speaking about Continental psychology I shall not attempt a census country by country. I simply have no means except second- and third-hand information to scan the literature for such countries as Italy or Poland, in spite of the fact that in view of their lively philosophical climate, they are more than likely to show interesting developments in phenomenological psychology as well. Thus my samples are taken from the traditional areas, where I have better access. The discussion will focus on the German scene, with some extensions into Switzerland and the Netherlands.

A. *Phenomenology in German Psychology*

To obtain a fair picture of the state of phenomenology in today's German psychology would be a forbidding task. In a sense, phenomenology seems to be everywhere and nowhere,

80. *Die Lehre von der Gestalt: Ihre Methode und ihr psychologischer Gegenstand* (Berlin: de Gruyter, 1931).

81. See "Cognitive Theory," in *Handbook of Social Psychology*, ed. G. Lindzey and E. Aronson (Reading, Mass.: Addison-Wesley, 1959), pp. 91–142, esp. pp. 122 ff.

permeating practically all textbooks, monographs, and papers, which are more or less studded with references to specific philosophical sources of such infiltrations. The latest monument of German encyclopedism, a handbook of psychology, is a good indication of this trend. Planned to comprise twelve volumes, but already proliferating into additional half-volumes of more than a thousand pages, it shows no unifying conception other than the inclusion of the top psychologists, some of them from abroad.[82] The word *Phänomenologie* is ubiquitous. But none of the sections that have appeared thus far are labeled specifically as "phenomenological." It is also revealing that the editor of the first volume, *Allgemeine Psychologie*, Wolfgang Metzger, deplores in the preface the absence of a "systematic phenomenology of the acts of perceiving" in contrast to the abundance of studies of what is perceived (p. vii). Nor are there many independent works which explicitly claim to be examples of phenomenology. A brief look at some of the representative works by leading German psychologists may be a good test of this impression.

Thus Metzger's own gestaltist *Psychologie* of 1940, in its third edition (1957), now openly dedicated to the founders of Gestalt psychology, does not refer in its layout to phenomenology, but presupposes it as its basic postulate for that part of psychology which deals with the immediately given. Here Goethe is invoked as the model phenomenologist on the same level with the phenomenologists among academic philosophers.

A more explicit plea for phenomenology can be found at the end of Albert Wellek's ten essays on *Ganzheitspsycholgie und Strukturtheorie*,[83] in the form of a lecture on "Consciousness and the Phenomenological Method in Psychology" which he had presented first before the 14th International Congress for Psychology in Montreal in 1954.[84] Here, without rejecting such other methods as operationalism, Wellek defended phenomenology as an essential ingredient of all psychology, including depth psychology and characterology. But again, except for an essay on the phenomenology of the joke,[85] there is no general section on phenomenology to support his defense.

82. *Handbuch der Psychologie*, 12 vols. (Göttingen: Verlag für Psychologie, 1960——).

83. *Ganzheitspsychologie und Strukturtheorie* (Bern: Francke, 1955).

84. See also *Perspectives in Personality Theory*, ed. H. V. Bracken et al. (New York: Basic Books, 1955), pp. 278–99.

85. "Zur Theorie und Phänomenologie des Witzes" (1949), in *Ganzheitspsychologie*, pp. 151–80.

Philipp Lersch in his influential text on the structure of personality [86] lists phenomenology as the second of the three tasks of general psychology between "systematics and classification" and "etiology." Phenomenology is identified with descriptive psychology in Husserl's "original" sense. But only in a few places are descriptions of personality structures characterized as "phenomenology."

Another characteristic instance is that of Hans Thomae in his book on human decision.[87] While this book is meant to be a comprehensive psychological study, based on a systematic collection of empirical case material about difficult decisions, the second and third of its five chapters go specifically by the titles "General Phenomenology of Decision" and "Phenomenology of the Types of Decision." After the first chapter had surveyed the surrounding territory (*Umfeld*) for preliminary sampling, the chapter on general phenomenology investigates the characteristic initial situation, the attempts of reorientation, and the termination of indecision. The discussion of differential phenomenology brings out essential differences in the types of decision according to ways of decision and specific social situations. It is only on this basis that Thomae approaches the question of the conditions for decision and of their final meaning for life and personality, which he no longer considers phenomenological questions.

Worth mentioning in this context is a series of phenomenological-psychological studies edited by C. F. Graumann and J. Linschoten.[88] Published subsequent to a German translation from the French of Aron Gurwitsch's book on *The Field of Consciousness*, however, the first original piece of phenomenology included in these studies was a work by Graumann himself. It was followed by Linschoten's exegetic study of William James's phenomenological psychology,[89] and by a German translation of Merleau-Ponty's *Phenomenology of Perception.*

Graumann's book on the foundations for a phenomenology and psychology of perspectivity [90] is an instructive example for

86. *Der Aufbau der Person,* 7th ed. (Munich: Barth, 1956).

87. *Der Mensch in der Entscheidung* (Munich: Barth, 1960).

88. *Phänomenologisch-psychologische Forschungen* (Berlin: de Gruyter, 1960).

89. *Auf dem Wege zu einer phänomenologischen Psychologie: Die Psychologie vom William James* (Berlin: de Gruyter, 1961). English translation by Amedeo Giorgi, *On the Way Toward a Phenomenological Psychology* (Pittsburgh, Pa.: Duquesne University Press, 1968).

90. *Grundlagen einer Phänomenologie und Psychologie der Perspektivität* (Berlin: de Gruyter, 1960).

the present interaction between pure phenomenology and empirical psychology. After a brief introduction, the first part presents a phenomenology of perspectivity, based on a study of perspective as a subjective form of presentation in drawing, followed by a survey of the role of the concept of perspective in philosophy, beginning with Leibniz, in which the essential structure of perspectivity is determined as a totality of references within a horizon (*horizontale Verweisungsganzheit*). This formulation is meant to indicate that perspectives refer beyond themselves to the complex whole of an object which comprises them, an object which in turn lies within a horizon surrounding the spectator, which cannot be exhausted. The ensuing part on the foundations of a psychology of perspectivity deals with the range (*Geltungsbereich*) and with motivational-features of perspectivity. Under the first heading special attention is given to the modes in which we become aware of the givenness of perspectives characterized by their intuitiveness and non-intuitiveness. Then motivational research tries to trace some of the conditions for the constitution of these perspectives; here Graumann utilizes a good deal of the so-called *Aktualgenese* of the Leipzig school of Fritz Sander, which investigates the way in which Gestalt phenomena establish themselves in our perception. All through his study Graumann refers to the phenomenological literature and particularly to Husserl's work, including the second volume of his *Ideen.* He also quotes frequently from the American literature on perception, especially James Gibson and Floyd H. Allport, both in close touch with, or sympathetic to, the gestaltist-phenomenological approach.

There would be no chance for and little point in an attempt to collect and sample more of the recent German studies in phenomenological psychology. Merely as a promising example, I would like to single out one that has impressed me as a conscious effort to explore a phenomenon in the spirit of Husserl as interpreted by J. Linschoten in *Phänomenologisch psychologische Forschungen* (p. 23): Gerhard Kölbel, *Über die Einsamkeit: Vom Ursprung, Gestaltwandel und Sinn des Einsamkeitserlebens* (Munich: Reinhardt, 1960).

B. *Phenomenology in Swiss Psychology*

Among the Swiss psychological philosophers interested in phenomenology, the following must not go unmentioned: Hans Kunz and Wilhelm Keller. On the surface both emphasize primarily the anthropological concern for a fuller understanding of man. But in their approach to this goal, they adopt more or less explicitly phenomenological procedures and refer constantly to such phenomenological precedents as Scheler, Heidegger, and Pfänder.

In his two-volume work on the anthropological meaning of the imagination [91] Kunz characterizes his own approach as phenomenological analysis, descriptive of the essential characteristics, a goal which, to be sure, can never be completely reached. But he repudiates phenomenology in the sense of a particular school. Nevertheless, his actual returns are not only impressive but show the stimulating influence of the "school." Kunz is also remarkable for his sober sense of the limitations of the phenomenological approach.[92]

Wilhelm Keller approached the anthropological problem on an even wider scale but in a less differentiated manner.[93] He sees his "critico-anthropological" approach (*Sehweise*) as a "phenomenologically determined" synthesis between phenomenology and depth psychology (*Das Selbstwertstreben*, p. 28).

C. *Phenomenology in Dutch Psychology*

Until recently phenomenological psychology has been especially flourishing in the Netherlands. Here the fountainhead and central figure has been and still is F. J. J. Buytendijk, to whom I have devoted a fuller study in Part II. Those interested in the kind of colorful vignettes that are characteristic of Dutch phenomenology may, if they are sufficiently at home in Dutch, obtain a good idea of its output by looking into a volume of contributions to phenomenological psychology published in 1956.[94] Those restricted to English, French, and German can receive a similar picture from two volumes which include non-Dutch contributors.[95] The papers on the handshake and keeping to one's bed (*garder le lit*) by J. H. Van den Berg, on the hotel room,

91. *Die anthropologische Bedeutung der Phantasie* (Basel: Verlag für Recht und Gesellschaft, 1946).

92. *Über den Sinn und die Grenzen des psychologischen Erkennens* (Stuttgart: Klett, 1957).

93. *Vom Wesen des Menschen* (Basel: Verlag für Recht und Gesellschaft, 1943); *Psychologie und Philosophie des Menschen* (Munich: Reinhardt, 1954); *Das Selbstwertstreben* (Munich: Reinhardt, 1963).

94. *Persoon en Wereld*, ed. J. H. Van den Berg and J. Linschoten (Utrecht: Bijleveld, 1956).

95. *Situation: Beiträge zur Phenomenologischer Psychologie und Psychopathologie*, ed. J. H. Van den Berg, F. J. J. Buytendijk, M. Y. Langeveld, and J. Linschoten (Utrecht: Het Spectrum, 1954).

on the psychology of driving by D. J. Van Lennep, and on aspects of sexual incarnation and "The Road and the Endless Distance" by J. Linschoten can supply a vivid taste of the originality of this school. So does Linschoten's more sustained study on the phenomenology of falling asleep.[96]

Another important figure in Dutch phenomenological psychology is Stephan Strasser, a native Austrian who came to the University of Nijmegen via Louvain. I referred to his more philosophical work in my book on *The Phenomenological Movement.* Of particular relevance to phenomenological psychology is his book on affectivity,[97] though it transcends it by its "metaphysical philosophy."

D. *A Note on Phenomenology in British Psychology*

The omission of countries outside the European Continent in this survey of mid-century psychology may create the impression of its non-existence. That this would be mistaken will become sufficiently clear from Chapter V on the American scene. But this still leaves a conspicuous gap with regard to the British situation, which the section on phenomenology in British psychopathology will not close.

Now it seems to be true that, apart from isolated articles in journals, there is nothing like a flourishing phenomenological trend in British psychology. But there is something going on among British philosophers which comes close to a phenomenological psychology and goes by the name of philosophical psychology. The leading exponent, if not the initiator, of this trend is Gilbert Ryle, with his pioneer work on *The Concept of Mind.*[98] Ryle had started out in the twenties as an eager student of German phenomenological philosophy but had later turned against it stridently in the forties.[99]

What Ryle does in his book is ostensibly merely an analysis of the concepts embodied in our ordinary talk about psychological phenomena. But actually such a study requires so much consideration of the phenomena as referents of these concepts that Ryle himself has sometimes spoken of his work as "my phenomenology of mind." Under these circumstances it is not without significance that recently *Mind,* under his editorship,

96. "Über das Einschlafen," *Psychologische Beiträge,* II (1955) 70–97, 266–98.

97. *Das Gemüt* (Utrecht: Het Spectrum, 1956).

98. (London: Hutchinson, 1949).

99. See *The Phenomenological Movement,* p. 623.

published an article on "Phenomenological Psychology," which among other things pointed out that Ryle's conceptual analysis is no different from Husserl's phenomenology properly demystified.[100]

But all this does not add up to more than a new interest within British philosophy, not unrelated to phenomenology in the language of psychology. Thus far it has not resulted in a substantive psychology or had a demonstrable effect on British empirical psychology.

E. *Some Conclusions: Interim Balance*

At closing time for this chapter, the situation for phenomenological psychology is anything but reassuring. In the wider context of contemporary movements and schools, phenomenology remains a minor trend, even after the decline of strict behaviorism. In the narrower context of the new "humanistic" psychologies, it plays not much more than the role of an auxiliary, more invoked than practiced. Even in several areas where phenomenological psychology previously had shown a remarkable vitality and productivity, such as in the Netherlands and Switzerland, there seems to be something like a recession, to say the least. But this may not be altogether a bad thing for the very development of phenomenological psychology, lest it become an undisciplined fad. It needs to be challenged, even by a critical opposition. Once some of the more recent trends toward statistical research have run their course, the need for phenomenological understanding may become all the more urgent, both for the examination of the basic concepts used in such research and for the evaluation of its results.

In the meantime, signs of a continuing and renewed interest in phenomenology are not wanting. A new *International Journal of Phenomenological Psychology*, with German, American, and Belgian editors,[101] and recent introductory psychology texts claiming phenomenological foundations are straws in the wind.[102] But such prolegomena are no substitute for new substantial contributions.

100. D. C. S. Osterhuizen, "Phenomenological Psychology," *Mind*, LXXIX (1968), 487–501.

101. *International Journal of Phenomenology and Psychology*, ed. C. F. Graumann (Heidelberg), A. Giorgi (Duquesne University), and G. Thinès (Belgium) (Berlin: Springer).

102. See, for example, A. Giorgi, *Psychology as a Human Science: A Phenomenologically Based Approach* (New York: Harper & Row, 1970).

3 / Phenomenology in Psychopathology and Psychiatry

THIS CHAPTER should be prefaced by a reminder of a statement I made in the Introduction (p. xxxiv): in the case of phenomenology the whole distinction between psychology and psychiatry loses its previous meaning, even though it has not yet completely disappeared. Thus the separate treatment of the abnormal phenomena no longer makes sense except on historical, practical, and pedagogical grounds. Whether eventually it will disappear completely is something which need not be decided at this point. The important thing to realize is that the distribution of the materials in this book will be based largely on academic tradition.[1]

One additional warning had better be given immediately: This chapter will omit the two protagonists of the play, Karl Jaspers and Ludwig Binswanger. They will be studied separately in Part II. In this part they will figure only in their role as landmarks along the road of the historical development. I realize that this decision is debatable. But I hope it will be justified eventually by greater clarity in the total picture and by the chance to do

1. A more unified treatment of phenomenological psychiatry seems to be promised by the title of a book by the French psychiatrist-philosopher Georges Lantéri-Laura, *La Psychiatrie phénoménologique* (Paris: PUF, 1963). However, thus far it merely offers introductory studies of the phenomenologies of Hegel, Husserl, Heidegger, Sartre, the gestaltists, and Merleau-Ponty, with reflections on the significance of their views for psychiatry. The fulfillment of the promise expressed in the title can be expected only from the second study promised in the preface. But in view of the author's frustration at the findings of his search for a unified phenomenology, which yield only a vague "phenomenological attitude," one wonders whether one still has a right to expect a concrete demonstration of the fruitfulness of this attitude.

fuller justice to the unity of the work and achievement of Jaspers and Binswanger.

[1] Psychopathology before Jaspers[2]

In order to understand the origin and role of phenomenology in psychopathology and psychiatry, one has to consider the development of the concept of mental disease. It has been anything but easy for mankind to extend the concept of sickness from the anatomical and physiological field to the kind of behavior where "endogenous" abnormalities appear without any traceable somatic concomitants. Even today we witness such healthy shocks to "*The Myth of Mental Illness*" as those given by Thomas Szasz.[3] It is therefore not surprising that mental diseases were at first interpreted as cases of demoniacal possession. When such pre-scientific conceptions were finally abandoned, the real problem was how to fit these recalcitrant phenomena into the available patterns of understanding. Omitting here all intermediate and more or less speculative interpretations, one can well understand that the most successful one, i.e., scientific materialism, as expressed, for instance, in cell pathology, seemed the most promising hypothesis for the explanation of mental abnormalities. This approach culminated in the bold thesis that "mental diseases are brain diseases" advanced by Wilhelm Griesinger (who, however, should be cleared of the charge of a crude materialism, since his own system was anything but completely somatic).

The real crisis developed when it was realized that Griesinger's program had no chance of early fulfillment, and that it would not do to merely wait for the progress of brain pathology in order to pin down the anatomical and physiological changes that went along with mental abnormalities. At this point it became clear that the immediate need of scientific investigation was the proper distinction and classification of the phenomena.

2. For a fuller discussion of the pre-history of phenomenology in psychiatry, see Kurt Schneider's helpful article on "Die phänomenologische Richtung in der Psychiatrie," *Philosophischer Anzeiger*, IV (1926), 382–404. For a very informative report with a critical slant about developments since about 1900 by a less involved participant observer, see Arthur Kronfeld, "Über neuere pathopsychisch-phänomenologische Arbeiten," *Zentralblatt für die gesamte Neurologie und Psychiatrie*, XXVIII, (1922), 441–59.

3. (New York: Harper & Row, 1961).

The first one to undertake this job in a systematic and critical way was Emil Kräpelin (1865–1927). The basis for his classification could only be descriptive in the widest sense of the term, since causal explanation had to be postponed. Kräpelin's primary consideration was prognosis. Even psychiatric therapy had to wait. In utilizing his vast collection of case material, he focused on larger patterns of disturbed behavior. This procedure has actually been called phenomenological. But while Kräpelin, student of Wilhelm Wundt that he was, did not exclude patients' reports about their subjective symptoms, his prime interest was in objective features of the various syndromes. As Jaspers saw it:

> Kräpelin's fundamental perspective [*Grundgesinnung*] remained somatic, which he, like the majority of the physicians considered the only medical one, an approach which took not only precedence, but was absolute. The psychological discussions of his textbook, in part excellent, were successful against his own intentions, as it were: he considered them temporary stopgaps until experiment, microscope, and test-tubes had made everything objectively explorable.[4]

But Jaspers was not the first to feel this defect and the need to overcome it. Actually in 1900 and 1901, the years when Husserl's *Logische Untersuchungen* appeared, W. Weygandt, in warning against the overestimation of the study of the central nervous system, had stressed the priority of inner experience over material factors. And in 1903 Robert Gaupp had called for a determined turn toward the study of inner experience as indispensable for psychiatry, if it wanted to make real progress.

But the first organized attempt to reform psychopathology along lines of descriptive psychology came from a group around the Munich psychiatrist Wilhelm Specht. This group started a new journal, the *Zeitschrift für Pathopsychologie* (a term coined in 1912), which included among its coeditors Henri Bergson, Hugo Münsterberg (definitely not a phenomenologist), and Oswald Külpe. Max Scheler contributed to the first volume. Karl Jaspers was represented only in the second. Specht and Münsterberg distinguished between pathopsychology and psychopathology by stipulating that pathopsychology was primarily psychology, not pathology; "pathological" was to be merely the method here to be applied to psychology. But the psychology thus developed was to serve the psychiatrist too. Its foundation was to

4. *Allgemeine Psychopathologie*, 4th ed. (Heidelberg: Springer, 1946), p. 711.

be the careful description and analysis of the pathological phenomena.

Specht's programmatic article mentioned the term "phenomenology" only in passing. He referred to Husserl's programmatic article on "Philosophy as a Rigorous Science" at the very start, denying that the new psychology was scientifically unsound. Actually, two years before the publication of Husserl's *Ideen*, he was acquainted with Husserl's distinction between the natural and the phenomenological attitude and agreed that a phenomenology of the psychic phenomena ought to precede experimental psychology. That Specht had considerable sympathy for phenomenology as a philosophy can be gathered also from his continuing connections with Pfänder and Scheler.

Even more direct evidence for the infiltration of philosophical phenomenology into pathopsychology was Specht's tripartite article in Volume 2 (1914) on the phenomenology and morphology of pathological perceptual illusions.[5] It began with a "Phenomenological Part," creditable in its own right by its cautious thoroughness and concreteness. Scheler's work proved to be one of his major supports. Husserl (*Logische Untersuchungen*), Brentano, Adolf Reinach, and especially Wilhelm Schapp also figured. Thus, contrary to Specht's original program, it was actually phenomenology, not pathology, which was to throw new light on psychology. In fact, the main burden of Specht's programmatic article on "The Value of the Pathological Method in Psychology and the Necessity of Basic Psychiatry of Pathopsychology" was an attempt to show the inadequacy of a brain-centered psychopathology, with its epiphenomenalistic attitude toward the psychic, compared with a primarily psychological approach to the mental diseases. He also suggested that only such an approach could provide psychiatry with its proper foundation. Phrases such as the "loving penetration into the patient" and the "exploration of his life history" indicated the bases for the insight needed by the therapist and to be conveyed to the patient. He mentioned psychoanalysis as the only other not brain-centered approach, but the arbitrary constructiveness of its basic concepts made it eventually inacceptable to him.

It is against this background that the appearance of Jaspers' *Allgemeine Psychopathologie* has to be understood, in which phenomenology became the primary, though not the only, method

5. "Zur Phänomenologie und Morphologie der pathologischen Wahrnehmungstäuschungen," *Zeitschrift für Psychopathologie*, II (1914), 1–35, 121–43, 481–569.

of a comprehensive psychopathology. The fact that Jaspers did not even mention "pathopsychology" may be explained by his prime interest in pathology, rather than in psychology. More relevant is the fact that Jaspers deliberately started from the normal as the proper background for a description and understanding of the pathological, not from the pathological, as the pathopsychologists proclaimed.

In this connection one of the most stimulating and richest texts of this period that used the word "phenomenology" in its title deserves to be mentioned: T. K. Oesterreich's *Phänomenologie des Ich in ihren Grundproblemen* (1910), a book which, after a first part devoted to the psychology of the normal "I," dealt in its second part particularly with the pathological phenomena of ego-fission. However, this work can hardly be invoked as illustrating the significance of philosophical phenomenology for psychiatry. For one thing, the term "phenomenology" was never explained, and one can only infer that in the title of the book it stood for self-observation in the traditional sense. It is true that Oesterreich mentioned Husserl's *Logische Untersuchungen* frequently, though, in spite of general admiration for Husserl, he usually disagreed with him. More important is the fact that he never referred to Husserl's phenomenology as such. Under these circumstances, Oesterreich's work represents merely a last example of an independent phenomenology in the tradition of descriptive psychology, which as such was of considerable significance for psychopathology. But it cannot be invoked as a piece which illustrates the influence of the new phenomenological philosophy on psychopathology.[6]

[2] The Place of Jaspers' General Psychopathology

It is at this point that Jaspers' *Allgemeine Psychopathologie* of 1913 has to be mentioned as the first major landmark on the way to a phenomenological psychopathology in touch with phenomenological philosophy. Not that Jaspers simply transformed psychopathology into a phenomenological enterprise. His major objective was to provide a synthesis of all the insights in the field, based on a clear methodology distinguishing the major methods employed. It was in the framework of this

6. See also Maria Oesterreich, *Traugott Konstantin Oesterreich* (Stuttgart: Fromanns, 1954), pp. 61–78.

methodological reorganization that the psychological part of psychopathology was clearly set apart from its non-psychological aspects. Within this new pathology Jaspers also separated the study of the subjective phenomena as experienced by the patients from the study of other psychological data. But the fact that impressed the readers of this text most was that a systematic and detailed section on phenomenology headed this psychopathology. This fact alone may account for the impression that Jaspers' psychopathology was nothing but phenomenology. But there were additional reasons for this impression, including his references to the writings of philosophical phenomenologists. In any case it cannot be denied that this text proved to be the decisive event in the rise of phenomenological psychopathology. It will be considered as such in the present chapter. The full meaning of the work in its relation to phenomenological philosophy will be discussed in Part II, Chapter 6.

In the present context one ambitious and seemingly parallel attempt to relate psychopathology to the phenomenology of the twenties must not go unmentioned: the work of the Berlin psychiatrist Arthur Kronfeld, who had been for some time a member of the Heidelberg Clinic and whose important critical report on phenomenology in psychopathology of 1922 has been mentioned before (p. 92). At first sight his book on the essence of psychiatric knowledge,[7] of which only one volume appeared, may look like a massive attempt to introduce Husserlian phenomenology into psychiatry. For its Table of Contents listed such topics as "Prolegomena to a General Psychiatry as Rigorous Science," and "Foundations of the Phenomenology and Descriptive Theory of the Psychic," with several phenomenological subtitles. At the end of the first volume, Kronfeld outlined the phenomenological tasks in psychiatry and in particular the topic of "pathological intentionality" (p. 412). However, closer inspection reveals that he rejected Husserl's a priori grasp of essences, in favor of a descriptive phenomenology as a mere pre-science, for which Theodor Lipps served as the chief model. As such it was to give a "pure description of the psychic in its mode of being." Philosophically, Kronfeld considered himself a follower of Johann Jakob Fries, the psychology-oriented post-Kantian philosopher, who was interpreted in Göttingen by Leonard Nelson, Husserl's younger and highly critical colleague. Thus Kronfeld's connection with Husserl's phenomenology is at best tenuous. There is

7. *Das Wesen der psychiatrischen Erkenntnis* (Berlin: Springer, 1920).

little reference to Jaspers in his book, and there are indications of personal tensions between them.

[3] From Jaspers to Binswanger

As a psychopathologist Jaspers did not found a school. In fact, soon after having written his classic, he left psychopathology for psychology, which he considered a way station to philosophy. At this stage he became the leading spokesman for a new philosophy of existence that affected even some of the sections of later editions of the *General Psychopathology*.

None of those who entered the field of phenomenological psychopathology after Jaspers could fail to be affected by him. His influence was felt primarily by the members of the Heidelberg Clinic, of which Jaspers was a leading member.[8] The first member of the clinic whose work I will consider is Willy Mayer-Gross, who was characterized by Jaspers as the most "open-minded [*aufgescholossen*] for all scientific possibilities."

A. *Willy Mayer-Gross (1889–1961)*

Mayer-Gross is of particular interest to the Anglo-American world as the coauthor of a handbook on *Clinical Psychiatry* (jointly with the geneticist Michael Roth and the institution psychiatrist E. Slater), which, now in its third edition, has become a major text in the field.[9] On the surface it shows very few traces of phenomenology. However, the introduction, while admitting that "description of phenomenological aspects is not of primary interest in most schools of psychology today" pleads that "it is of the greatest value in understanding, if not the person, still some of the illnesses to which he is liable, and is a *sine qua non* for the diagnosis on which treatment is to be based." In the second edition of 1960, where, prior to the plea for a "multidimensional approach," "existential analysis" is listed as the last of six rival approaches, phenomenology is distinguished from the existentialist school, which is said to appeal to it illegitimately. "Phenomenology is a factual approach, based on the work of Jaspers, and differs from existentialism by seeking no

8. See Jaspers' sketch in his autobiography in *The Philosophy of Karl Jaspers*, ed. Paul Schilpp (LaSalle, Ill.: Open Court, 1957).

9. *Clinical Psychiatry*, 3d ed. (Baltimore, Md.: Williams & Wilkins, 1969).

aid from philosophical short-cuts" (p. 30). While here Mayer-Gross rejects existentialism as based on Heidegger's "pessimism," an exception is made for the work of "such serious and humane psychiatrists as L. Binswanger, V. von Gebsattel, and Erwin Straus." However, Mayer-Gross did not take any specific interest in Binswanger's phenomenological anthropology and *Daseinsanalyse*.

In view of these restrained, but still marked, pleas for a phenomenological approach, it is noteworthy that Mayer-Gross himself, especially during his early Heidelberg period before emigrating to England in 1933, had made significant contributions to phenomenological psychopathology, even though later on he became more interested in other parts of the field. Even more important is the fact that during this phase he was also in touch with philosophical phenomenology.

Thus his second publication, a contribution to Specht's *Zeitschrift für Pathopsychologie,* dealt with the "phenomenology of abnormal feelings of happiness," [10] which, in describing two types of happiness, also made use of the phenomenology of normal feelings as developed by Moritz Geiger. Thus, in distinguishing between rapture (*Glücksrausch*) and the (rapture-free) affect of happiness (*Glücksaffekt*), Mayer-Gross pointed out that while both were experienced in what Geiger had called "inward concentration" (*Innenkonzentration*), the former was turned on itself, as it were, and the latter had a tendency to radiate over the whole field of our consciousness.

Mayer-Gross's first book, on the "oneiroid form of experience," [11] dealing with states of dreamlike confusion (*Verwirrtheit*) based on autobiographical accounts was, according to Kurt Schneider, the first attempt of a phenomenological exploration and even a new establishment (*Neuaufstellung*) of symptom complexes (such as incompleteness, restlessness, uncertainty of fulfillment). Here Mayer-Gross tried to go beyond a merely static phenomenology of elementary units in Jaspers' sense toward an understanding of nosological units. In developing this idea he referred repeatedly to Husserl's *Logical Investigations*. Also he described the oneiroid experience, distinguishing between act and content and pointing out its lack of fulfillment and closure.

10. "Zur Phänomenologie abnormer Glücksgefühle," *Zeitschrift für Pathopsychologie*, II (1914), 588–601.

11. *Selbstschilderungen der Verwirrtheit: Die oneiroide Erlebnisform* (Berlin: Springer, 1924).

Mayer-Gross's later phenomenological descriptions in connection with his work on schizophrenia were less pointed and technical. But even here the phenomenological ingredient was unmistakable, even though his interest in this aspect was less pronounced.[12]

B. *Hans W. Gruhle (1880–1958)*

Another member of the Heidelberg school around Jaspers, not to be omitted here, was Hans W. Gruhle. Gruhle's primary orientation was psychological. He had started out from Lipps and Stumpf, but he moved increasingly toward the Gestalt approach of Wertheimer, Koffka, Köhler, and Goldstein. One of the more skeptical members of the Heidelberg team, he at first put up considerable resistance against Jaspers' phenomenological leanings. However, in his major work, the *Verstehende Psychologie* (1948), which deals primarily with normal psychology, the first large section is entitled "Phänomenologie." Yet even here, and also in other works in which he discussed the applicability of phenomenology to psychopathology, Gruhle made it plain that this phenomenology had nothing to do with Husserl's *Wesensschau*.[13]

C. *Kurt Schneider (1887–1963)*

The phenomenological psychiatrist Kurt Schneider had originally no close links with the Heidelberg clinic until he took charge of it as director in 1946. He had received his main training in Tübingen and Cologne and had held previous academic positions in Cologne and Munich. Schneider's work in phenomenological psychopathology was largely based on the approach of Scheler, with whom he was closely associated during Scheler's Cologne period between 1921 and 1928, though he by no means followed him blindly, especially in the last phase of his philosophy. However, Schneider's earlier studies on the abnormalities of the emotional life were based almost completely on the distinctions made by Scheler in his books on ethics and on the phenomenology of sympathy and love. This is true particularly of

12. See, e.g., "Die Klinik der Schizophrenie," in *Handbuch der Geisteskrankheiten*, ed. O. Bumke (Berlin: Springer, 1932).

13. "Die psychologische Analyse eines Krankheitsbildes (Schizophrenie)," *Zeitschrift für die gesamte Neurologie und Psychiatrie*, CXXIII (1930), 479–84.

Schneider's study of the "strata of the emotional life and the structure of the states of depressions," [14] in which he dealt especially with the endogenous depressions. Here he utilized Scheler's distinction between four layers: the sensuous, the vital, the psychic, and the spiritual, omitting, however, the last, and distinguishing between "unmotivated" endogenous and purely reactive depressions. He located the former in the vital, the latter in the psychic layer. In this manner he also distinguished between two types of sadness, the vital and the psychic, which, however, can interact. Kronfeld considered this the first clinical application of phenomenology.[15]

In a subsequent larger study on "Pathopsychological Contributions toward the Psychological Phenomenology of Love and Sympathy," [16] Schneider explored disturbances of the sentiments, again on the basis of Scheler's earlier work, but augmented by some of Pfänder's and Jaspers' distinctions. Of particular interest here are the initial considerations of the relations between phenomenological psychology as a descriptive study of real experience and Husserl's universal pure and transcendental phenomenology, and Schneider's clear awareness of the special problems of such a phenomenology as applied to abnormal phenomena. But Schneider's main contribution is the concrete investigation of the abnormal modification of the phenomena which Scheler had distinguished. Schneider identified four such modifications: (1) weakening of love and sympathy down to the vanishing point; (2) "estrangement" (*Entfremdung*) of these emotions when they are experienced as no longer one's own; (3) failure to absorb the feeling of others because of immersion (*Versunkenheit*) in one's own feeling; and (4) intensification of one's feeling for others based on an increase in one's own feeling. (The last two distinctions would seem to be differences in explanation rather than in descriptive characteristics.) Another brief study of the "phenomenological psychology of inverted sexuality and erotic love" [17] pointed out the indispensableness of a study of "in-

14. "Die Schichtung des emotionalen Lebens und der Aufbau der Depressionzustände," *Zeitschrift für die gesamte Neurologie und Psychiatrie*, XLIX (1921), 281–86.

15. "Über neuere pathopsychische und phänomenologische Arbeiten," p. 449.

16. Pathopsychologische Beiträge zur phänomenologischen Psychologie von Liebe und Mitfühlen," *Zeitschrift für die gesamte Neurologie und Psychiatrie*, LXV (1921), 109–40.

17. "Bemerkungen zu einer phänomenologischen Psychologie der invertierten Sexualität und erotischen Liebe," *Zeitschrift für die gesamte Neurologie und Psychiatrie*, LXXI (1921), 346–51.

tentions" and directions for the understanding of sexual abnormalities and attempted to point out phenomenological differences between male and female attitudes (*Einstellungen*).

During an interview in 1962 Schneider intimated to me that he had become increasingly disillusioned with Scheler's "unscientific" kind of phenomenology. His influential text on clinical psychiatry, published in 1966, certainly no longer stressed phenomenology explicitly.[18] But implicitly it is still present, especially in the Appendix on the psychopathology of feelings and drives, which referred not only to the phenomenological psychology of Scheler but also to Stumpf, Pfänder, and even Nicolai Hartmann. However, Schneider did not care for the phenomenological anthropology of Binswanger. Nevertheless, he became greatly impressed and intrigued by Heidegger and the possible significance of his ideas for psychopathology. Thus, in a brief study about the relation of depression and *Dasein*,[19] dedicated to Heidegger on his sixtieth birthday, he credited him with having made such a study possible and asserted that the anxieties of the cyclothymic psychotic are not mere symptoms of psychosis but reveal the basic anxieties (*Urängste*) of man (for his soul, for his body, and for his life). Yet Schneider warned against a similar use of schizophrenic symptoms.

D. *Viktor von Weizsäcker (1886–1957)*

This may also be the proper place to record the role of a marginal but influential figure of the Heidelberg circle: Viktor von Weizsäcker. As a student of internal medicine, whose primary theoretical interest was in the physiology of the senses, he generally rejected phenomenology in its Husserlian as well as in its Heideggerian form. But he was strongly attracted by Scheler, especially by his later thought on biological philosophy.

Several aspects of his basic conception of the *Gestaltkreis* showed considerable convergence with phenomenological ideas and had at least a resonant effect on them. The idea of the *Gestaltkreis* itself, a term probably best rendered as "formative cycle," started from the observation that there is an interaction between animal perception and movement and that, especially

18. *Klinische Psychiatrie*, 7th ed. (Stuttgart: Thieme, 1966). English translation of the 5th ed., *Clinical Psychopathology* (New York: Grune & Stratton, 1959).

19. "Die Aufdeckung des Daseins durch die cyclothyme Depression," *Der Nervenarzt*, XXI (1950), 193 ff.

in the case of tactual perception, touch not only directs other perception but, conversely, this perception directs further touch. On a more general level this involved for Weizsäcker the (re-) introduction of the subject into objectivistic biology. Here von Weizsäcker's biology came closest to Husserlian phenomenology, much as he rejected it for reasons which at times reveal odd misunderstandings.

[4] The Place of Ludwig Binswanger and Erwin Straus

Toward the end of the twenties, phenomenology took a new turn. In philosophy this turn was released by the emergence of Martin Heidegger and his existential analytics in *Sein und Zeit* (1927). Its equivalent in psychopathology was the advent of the new "anthropology" of Ludwig Binswanger, Viktor von Gebsattel, and Erwin Straus. A significant landmark of the new trend was the beginning, in 1930, of the new journal *Der Nervenarzt,* which became the major outlet for the new phenomenological anthropology.

As in the case of Jaspers, I am reserving the detailed study of Binswanger's thought to a separate monographic chapter. In the present context the important thing is to block out his role in the context of phenomenological psychopathology. The decisive change here was the way in which Binswanger broke down the narrow boundaries of Jaspers' phenomenology, which had confined it to describing isolated subjective phenomena characteristic of the psychotic patient, leaving the study of the connections between them to two different approaches: understanding in the manner of Dilthey and, where intelligibility broke down, "scientific" explanation. Binswanger did not recognize these boundaries. To him there was no good reason for forbidding phenomenology to reach out beyond isolated phenomena, whose isolation was actually the result of artificial factors. Why should phenomenology refrain from describing the connections between successive elements of phenomenal experience? The way to achieve such understanding was through a study of the subjective "life-history." But there was also no good reason for sharply separating the connections that are intelligible from those that are merely causally explainable. Thus Binswanger had the courage to attack what to Jaspers seemed to be unintelligible in principle: the world of the schizophrenic. The main lever for such an understanding seemed to be the new approach opened up by Heidegger's analytics of human *Dasein*, although its philosophical objective had nothing to do with an understanding of human existence for its own sake, let alone the sake of psychopathic existence. But this did not prevent Binswanger from developing a full-fledged anthropology of human existence based on Heidegger's conception of *Dasein* as being-in-the-world.

This new anthropology, in the sense of a study of man in his normal and abnormal entirety as he experiences himself in relation to the world, became the main task of phenomenological psychopathology. In this new enterprise Binswanger was supported by three independent phenomenological psychopathologists, less committed to Heidegger's conception, to be sure, than himself: Viktor von Gebsattel, Eugène Minkowski, and Erwin Straus. Von Gebsattel's main philosophical inspiration came from Scheler's philosophical anthropology. In Erwin Straus's case, the new orientation had its root in his fight against the Pavlovian conception of man as a mechanism of reflexes, a misconception already prepared by Descartes's dualism; thus his main goal was to restore the unity of Man, phenomenology being the means to recapture it. In a similar sense this can also be said about the pioneer of phenomenological psychopathology in France, Eugène Minkowski, though he was little interested in anthropology as such and even less in Heidegger. These four will be studied in depth in Part II.

Among those who discovered very early the psychopathological potential of Heidegger's existential analytics, one more member of the Heidelberg school should not go unmentioned: Alfred Storch (1888–1962). During the twenties he published phenomenological studies in the Jaspers tradition, yet he actually went considerably beyond Jaspers. Thus Storch's first "phenomenological attempt,"[20] written in 1923 in response to Eugen Bleuler's request for a demonstration of the significance of phenomenology for psychiatry, is one of the most perceptive studies of the way in which the world of the schizophrenic and his self are given him in his own experience. Against the background of the phenomenology of the normal consciousness of reality as developed by Husserl and as found particularly in the early work of Hedwig Conrad-Martius, Storch demonstrated the fruitfulness of these descriptive accounts by showing, for instance, the way

20. "Bewusstseinsebenen und Wirklichkeitsbereiche in der Schizophrenie," *Zeitschrift für die gesamte Neurologie und Psychiatrie*, LXXXII (1923), 321–41.

in which consciousness and the sense of reality, in its independence of consciousness, become modified in psychotic experience. However, his major attempts to enter into the world of the schizophrenic were based on Heidegger's analytics of *Dasein* as being-in-the-world. Storch also believed that an understanding of archaic thinking as revealed by recent anthropology could aid our understanding of this world.[21] In this attempt Storch did not make use of C. G. Jung's frame of reference. But he did utilize sympathetically Freudian psychoanalysis, especially its pioneering psychotherapeutic efforts.

[5] Since Binswanger

Binswanger founded no school. He never was associated with any university. But his clinic in Kreuzlingen near Constance had the atmosphere of an intellectual and cultural center which attracted leading thinkers and radiated influences much more than any university "school" could have done. In fact, the universities themselves came more and more under Binswanger's spell. Most of these radiations went into Germany. In Zurich, where the Burghölzli Clinic remained the center of Swiss psychiatry, Eugen Bleuler, the authority on schizophrenia and one of Binswanger's teachers, was at least interested in the non-philosophical aspects of phenomenology.[22] Binswanger was even offered the opportunity of succeeding him in 1927. And Bleuler's son Manfred, his actual successor, became sympathetic even to the later *Daseinsanalyse*. The university psychiatrist who came most strongly under Binswanger's influence was probably Jakob Wyrsch in Bern. Medard Boss, who will be taken up separately, turned more directly to Heidegger.

The most important among Binswanger's Swiss followers was Roland Kuhn (b. 1912), associate director of the important public hospital in Münsterlingen (Thurgau), where between 1910 and 1912 Hermann Rorschach had conceived the first ideas for his celebrated psychodiagnostic tests. This fact accounts for

21. See especially "Die Welt der beginnenden Schizophrenie und die archaische Welt," in *Wege zur Welt und Existenz des Geisteskranken*, ed. W. von Baeyer and W. Bräutigam (Stuttgart: Hippokrates-Verlag, 1965), 19 ff.

22. See his forthright skeptical response ("*Korreferat*") to Binswanger's momentous "Referat" on Phänomenologie before the Swiss Society for Psychiatry in *Schweizer Archiv für Neurologie und Psychiatrie*, XII (1923), 330–31.

Kuhn's keen involvement in Rorschach studies, expressed especially in three articles in the *Monatsschrift für Psychiatrie*.[23] In introducing his original contributions about mask interpretations of the inkblots, Kuhn characterized his own method as "phenomenological" in its attempt to find out what is going on at the moment of the interpretations, how they are determined, and what they mean. This study also contains first references to Heidegger and Binswanger's *Daseinsanalyse*. But Kuhn does not claim for phenomenology Rorschach himself, who died too young to become acquainted with it, much as he seems to have turned away from earlier Freudian influences. However, Kuhn does see affinity between Rorschach's approach, Gestalt psychology, and Katz's color phenomenology. Kuhn has also published several case studies based on Binswanger's approach, one of which has been included in translation in the Rollo May volume on *Existence* as the final piece.[24] More recently Kuhn has given general expositions of *Daseinsanalyse* in Binswanger's sense, such as the monographic one in *Psychiatrie der Gegenwart*.[25] His interest in the significance of Pfänder's phenomenological psychology for psychiatry is noteworthy. It is also worth noting that Kuhn, who combines chemotherapy with psychotherapy, is the inventor of one of the most effective antidepressive drugs (Tofranil). But he stresses the need for psychotherapy all the same.

In Binswanger's own judgment, as he expressed it to me in an interview in 1962, the place where his work was being developed most creatively was the Heidelberg psychiatric clinic. Here in the fifties under the directorship of Walter von Baeyer, three younger men in particular carried on anthropological psychology in Binswanger's spirit, yet independently and imaginatively: Heinz Häfner, Karl Peter Kisker, and Hubert Tellenbach. While their output is by no means the result of teamwork, it shows enough common features to justify a joint introduction.

23. *Monatsschrift für Psychiatrie und Neurologie*, CIII (1940), 39–128; CVIII (1943), 1–57; CIX (1944), 168–270; also published in book form as *Die Maskendeutungen im Rorschachversuch*, 2d ed. (Basel: Karger, 1954). See also *Schweizer Archiv für Neurologie und Psychiatrie*, LIII (1944), 29–47.

24. "Mordversuch eines depressiven Fetischisten und Sodomisten an einer Dirne," *Monatsschrift für Psychiatrie und Neurologie*, CXVI (1948), 66–151. English translation by Ernest Angel, "The Attempted Murder of a Prostitute," in *Existence*, ed. Rollo May, Ernest Angel, Henri F. Ellenberger (New York: Basic Books, 1958), pp. 365–425.

25. "Daseinsanalyse und Psychiatrie," in *Psychiatrie der Gegenwart*, ed. H. W. Gruhle et al. (Berlin: Springer, 1963), I/II, 853–902.

Not only can these men draw on an unusually wide philosophical background, but they also all put philosophical phenomenology to much more intensive use in their pathological studies than has been done before. They have applied this approach in almost dovetailing fashion to the study of the psychopath, the schizophrenic, and the melancholic. And they have paid particular attention to an understanding of these abnormalities by attending to their beginning stages, the entrance field (*Vorfeld*) of the full disturbance. I shall back up these hints by at least a few specific illustrations without any pretense of condensing their findings into a few paragraphs.

Heinz Häfner (b. 1924), now at the University of Mannheim, is probably the one closest to Binswanger, as is shown by the latter's extended preface to Häfner's main monograph thus far.[26] As far as philosophical methodology is concerned, Häfner himself gives most explicit credit to Husserl's phenomenology as supplying the real foundations for psychopathological insight (p. 214). In particular he thinks that it can provide access (*Freilegung*) to the "horizon of psychopathological experience" (pp. 12–30) by leading us back to the pre-scientific life-world, by bracketing all restrictive interpretations, and by allowing us at the same time to grasp the essential structure of human existence. However, at this point Häfner wants us to return from mere essential insights to the facticity of empirical analysis of concrete forms of *Dasein* as represented in his psychopathological case material. In other words, Husserl provides the foundation for an empirical analysis of *Dasein* that uses the patterns of Heidegger and Binswanger. Häfner's main field of research is the controversial area of the psychopathological personality. Suffice it to mention what he considers to be the main yield of his analyses: namely, the discovery of an essential characteristic of the psychopathic form of *Dasein* which he calls *Fassade*—i.e., the kind of false front which the psychopath erects in his relation to himself and to others as his style of existence (p. 101).

Karl Peter Kisker (b. 1926), now at the University of Hannover, has used phenomenological philosophy in a new manner to deepen the understanding of the schizophrenic process. His philosophical foundation, aided by personal studies under Karl Löwith in Heidelberg, includes familiarity with the latest *Husserliana* publications. But he also shows unusual knowledge of the Anglo-American literature, including particularly Kurt Lew-

26. *Psychopathen: Daseinsanalytische Untersuchungen zur Struktur und Verlaufsgestalt von Psychopathien* (Berlin: Springer, 1961).

in's American production. He received his psychiatric training under Kurt Schneider, but his anthropological research was sponsored mostly by von Baeyer.

For Kisker phenomenological psychopathology has to be approached philosophically. It has to start from the life-world as made accessible by a transcendental reduction of our dogmatic beliefs (without commitment to Husserl's transcendental idealism) and by essential insights which allow us to vary the range of our experiences. But while Husserl's approach permits the proper grasp of the region for research (regional ontology), it is Heidegger's analytics which supplies the patterns for a first understanding (*Vorverstehen*) of this region. In psychopathology Binswanger has set the pace for such studies. However, Kisker does not accept Binswanger's utilization of Husserl's transcendental phenomenology, especially in his last studies of melancholia and mania. Kisker's attempt to penetrate into the world of the schizophrenic takes the form of empirical studies of the changes in his lived experience (*Erlebniswandel*).[27] These changes, with their abrupt breaks, begin in a preparatory field (*Vorfeld*), showing a characteristic de-differentiation or alienation, leading to such developed stages as segregation (*Auseinandersetzung*), incorporation (*Einordnung*), and articulation (*Ausgliederung*). All these situations can be symbolized by Lewinian topological diagrams, which help in making intelligible the autonomy of the psychopathic situation (*Psychonomie*).

Hubert Tellenbach (b. 1914) has made melancholia the main area of his phenomenological research, but lately he has also begun to explore the phenomenology of the epileptic. Having completed a study of philosophy in Kiel, he entered medicine and psychiatry in Munich. In his phenomenological anthropology he is perhaps closest to von Gebsattel [28] and, through him, to Heidegger. Tellenbach's goal is to show us the essential structures (*Wesensstrukturen*) of such worlds as that of the melancholic. The way to this goal leads through the empirical phenomenology advocated by Binswanger under the guidance of Wilhelm Szilasi.

Tellenbach's exploration of melancholia began with a detailed study of the change in the spatiality of the world of the melancholic (after what had been shown before about the

27. *Der Erlebniswandel des Schizophrenen: Ein psychopathologischer Beitrag zur Psychonomie schizophrener Grundsituationen* (Berlin: Springer, 1960).

28. See von Gebsattel's preface to *Die Melancholie* (Berlin: Springer, 1962).

change in its temporality by Minkowski, von Gebsattel, and Straus).[29] The main change observed was the loss of depth in the space of the melancholic. Later Tellenbach explored the phenomenology of the oral sense (smells and tastes) in melancholia. His main book thus far (which includes not only phenomenological typology but also studies of the intellectual history of the problem and pathogenic and clinical discussions) stresses such general essential characteristics as "*Inkludenz*" (i.e., the self-enclosure of the melancholic within boundaries) and *Remanenz* (i.e., the staying of the melancholic behind his own demands on himself). Tellenbach also conducts interesting studies about the "approaches" (*Vorfeld*) to melancholia—thus an extreme tendency to "orderliness" seems to be a characteristic pre-morbid trait.

The preceding sketch of some of the phenomenologically most interesting work of this young anthropological group in the Heidelberg clinic would be incomplete without a reference to its director, Walter von Baeyer (b. 1904).[30] His own anthropological contributions to psychiatry are less extensive than his other work in psychiatry and less phenomenologically committed. On the whole the influence of Buber and Binswanger is more conspicuous in his approach than that of Husserl and Heidegger. More recently he has taken particular interest in Paul Ricoeur's work on the voluntary and the involuntary. For von Baeyer anthropology differs from descriptive phenomenology inasmuch as it is a more comprehensive attempt to achieve maximum intelligibility of endogenous psychopathological phenomena. It requires an understanding of the total way in which the psychotic exists—not only of his subjective experience. Among von Baeyer's concrete studies in anthropology, the one on the concept of encounter among fellow-beings has proved to be unusually influential, distinguishing between different types of encounters and their failures, especially in the relation between doctor and patient.[31] The latest joint work by von Baeyer and Wanda von Baeyer-Katte is based on and permeated by phenomenological considerations.[32]

Heidelberg has also been the focus for related developments

29. "Die Räumlichkeit der Melancholischen," *Der Nervenarzt,* XXVII (1956), 12–18, 189–98.

30. See also *Festschrift,* in *Jahrbuch für Psychologie, Psychotherapie und medizinische Anthropologie,* XII (1964).

31. "Der Begriff der Begegnung in der Psychiatrie," *Der Nervenarzt,* XXVI (1955), 369–76.

32. *Angst* (Frankfurt am Main: Suhrkamp, 1971).

in the field of psychosomatic medicine. They include contributions to the phenomenology of the body and of social relationships, contributions that were inspired by Viktor von Weizsäcker's anthropology. Leading names are A. Auersperg, H. Christian, and W. Bräutigam. The work of Herbert Plügge, though not very voluminous, has struck me as unusually promising.[33] Thus, his studies on the sense of well-being (and "ill-being") as a neglected field in medicine have progressed considerably beyond the usual global phenomenology of the body to a more differentiated account of the experiences of specific body zones and organs in health and in sickness, especially in internal diseases and in heart disease. While Plügge considers himself self-taught as a phenomenologist, he gives special credit to O. F. Bollnow, von Gebsattel, Merleau-Ponty, Sartre, and Szilasi, but occasionally he also refers to Husserl and Heidegger.

To a lesser degree, similar interest in phenomenological anthropology has been noticeable in the psychiatric clinic at Freiburg in Breisgau, especially during the period when Wilhem Szilasi represented phenomenology in the philosophy department. Phenomenology is also fundamental to the work of Wolfgang Blankenburg, who has now moved to Heidelberg. His first study, a "contribution to the interpretation of terminal schizophrenic states," based on the detailed study of a senile patient,[34] is an ambitious attempt at phenomenological *Daseinsanalyse* which uses philosophical concepts in order to explore the spatial and temporal dimensions of the schizophrenic's world. Blankenburg aims here to widen our normal frames of understanding with a view to finding the essential structures (*eidos*) of the worlds of the psychotic.

Of even greater significance is his book on the loss of the sense of obviousness (*Selbstverständlichkeit*) in hebephrenic schizophrenia free from delusions.[35] Here on the basis of an independent conception of phenomenology, which however includes Husserl's *epochē*, Blankenburg offers phenomenological interpretations of characteristic features of certain types of schiz-

33. See, e.g., *Wohlbefinden und Missbefinden: Beiträge zu einer medizinischen Anthropologie* (Tübingen: Niemeyer, 1962). See also his *Vom Spielraum des Leibes* (Salzburg: Nihm, 1971).

34. "Daseinsanalytische Studie über einen Fall paranoider Schizophrenie," *Schweizer Archiv für Neurologie und Psychiatrie*, LXXX (1958), 9–105.

35. *Der Verlust der natürlichen Selbstverständlichkeit: Ein Beitrag zur Psychopathologie symptomarmer Schizophrenien* (Stuttgart: Enke, 1971).

ophrenic experience that turn out to be illuminating counterparts of Husserl's phenomenological reduction of the natural world. The result also throws light on the essential proportion between the sense of the obvious and its absence in amazement and doubt, a proportion that is missing in the world of the schizophrenic.

The phenomenological ingredients in the work of two psychiatrists who are not directly connected with the Heidelberg school, Jürg Zutt and C. Kulenkampff in Frankfurt, are also of considerable interest. Only occasionally will Zutt mention phenomenology. His real concern is anthropology, or what he calls "understanding anthropology" (*verstehende Anthropologie*).[36] Zutt speaks of anthropology as a study destined to overcome the dualistic division of the study of man into psychology and somatology. By calling it "understanding" (*verstehend*), he assigns it the task of penetrating (*durchschauen*) normal structures and, in the case of an understanding psychiatry, penetrating abnormalities and seeing them as disruptions (*Störungen*) of the normal. This means to him that abnormalities are deficiencies of man's full powers and particularly of his power to rise above the merely lived body (*gelebter Leib*) to the level of the spirit (*Geist*), which, following Romano Guardini, he considers to be the central characteristic of man. However, while his most systematic work, the "Versuch," is rich in suggestions, it is anything but a comprehensive system of such a psychiatry. Phenomenology is not mentioned by name in this work, and only rarely is it mentioned in Zutt's preparatory studies. But it is present, if only by way of references to Heidegger, Sartre, or Binswanger. More important, Zutt's studies contain concrete phenomenological observations of considerable interest. Thus his, and incidentally C. Kulenkampff's, use of Sartre's phenomenology of the glance in connection with the study of the world of the psychotic and especially the schizophrenic is noteworthy; however, this does not commit Zutt to Sartre's interpretation of the glance as an attack on the other's freedom rather than as "the most revealing and beautiful expression of man" ("Versuch," p. 809).

Even more original is Zutt's interest in the different ways in which man can be related to his lived body as both supporting and supported (*tragend-getragen*). Here too the related studies of Kulenkampff about the phenomenon of stance (*Stand*) and

36. See especially *Auf dem Wege zu einer anthropologischen Psychiatrie, Gesammelte Aufsätze* (Berlin: Springer), 1963; and "Versuch einer verstehenden Anthropologie" in *Psychiatrie der Gegenwart,* I/II, 763–852.

loss of stance (*Standverlust*) are phenomenologically and psychopathologically illuminating. Zutt's concepts of the settings of human being (*Daseinsordnungen*) in their relation to space, as expressed in dwelling, a phenomenon taken up previously by Heidegger, and of other such orders have proved to be an aid to anthropological understanding.

Gerhard Bosch (b. 1918), a student of Zutt's, has used a "phenomenologico-anthropological approach" to the study of autistic children based on an analysis of their speech.[37] This approach, aimed at a better understanding of the constitution of the world of the autistic child, uses as its philosophical frame of reference Husserl's constitutive phenomenology of the world, and particularly the social world, as well as Binswanger's and Zutt's more specialized studies. Bosch describes particularly the autistic defect in the possibilities of encountering others and constituting a common world with them. In Tübingen, W. Th. Winkler, trained in the school of Robert Gaupp and Ernst Kretschmer, has developed the idea of a "dynamic phenomenology" that aims at a study of pathological transformations neglected in previous "static" phenomenology.[38] It is illustrated by the concept of ego-*anachoresis* (ego-withdrawal), which Winkler developed together with Heinz Häfner, as a phenomenon accounting for schizophrenic dissociation from intolerable parts of experience.

[6] Phenomenology in Dutch Psychiatry

Phenomenology has had a remarkable impact on Dutch psychopathology and psychiatry, as it has on Dutch psychology. While a good deal of the pertinent literature is accessible only to students with a good command of the Dutch language, enough of it is also available in German and French for representative sampling.

The leading figure among this group was H. C. Rümke (1893–1968) in Utrecht. Other important names are those of E. A. D. E. Carp, Janse de Jonge, J. H. Van der Berg, and L. Van der Horst.

37. *Der frühkindliche Autismus: Eine klinische und phänomenologisch-anthropologische Untersuchung am Leitfaden der Sprache* (Berlin: Springer, 1962).

38. "Dynamische Phänomenologie der Schizophrenien als Weg zur gezielten Psychotherapie," *Zeitschrift für Psychotherapie und Medizinische Psychologie*, VII (1957), 192–204.

Rümke became known first by a monograph on the phenomenology of the feeling of happiness.[39] It made use of Willy Mayer-Gross's earlier study but went considerably beyond it by analyzing happiness as a state of consciousness in all its aspects, paying special attention to the ways in which it is experienced, e.g., what is in the foreground and background of the experience. A phenomenological analysis of its genesis distinguished "responsive happiness" feelings (reactive) from "autochthonous" ones, for example those derived from states of intoxication. Scheler referred to this study as congenial to his in the Preface to the third edition of his *Formalismus,* although Rümke had not mentioned Scheler.

Rümke has increasingly become a leading spokesman of phenomenology in psychiatry even on the international scene,[40] but without claiming to monopolize the field. In his later work he made active use of Binswanger's anthropology and of its French ramifications from Minkowski to Sartre. However, a recent collection of Rümke's later essays, now accessible also in German,[41] has made clear the limits of his involvement, by calling it, after the title of the initial lecture, "A Flourishing Psychiatry in Danger." While Rümke wanted to encourage the enrichment which psychiatry had experienced, thanks to phenomenology as well as to psychoanalysis, psychosomatics, etc. (all more or less interested in salvaging the subjective aspects of psychic life), he saw dangers in the lack of coordination between these flourishing innovations, the loss of scientific standards, and particularly the temptation to drop the demands of "objectivity." In other words, Rümke was concerned about the proper integration of the new developments into the framework of "scientific psychology."

In the case of phenomenology, he distinguished at least three types—the phenomenology of Jaspers based on empathy, Husserl's phenomenology based on *Wesensschau,* and Binswanger's phenomenological anthropology—which all wanted to go beyond the mere description of the phenomena in an attempt to understand them. Rümke believed with Binswanger that this kind of phenomenology existed in hidden form even in psy-

39. *Zur Phänomenologie und Klinik des Glücksgefühls* (Berlin: Springer, 1924).

40. See, e.g., his paper on "Phenomenological and Descriptive Aspects of Psychiatry," at the *Third World Congress of Psychiatry in Montreal,* I (1961), 16–25.

41. *Eine blühende Psychiatrie in Gefahr,* ed. and trans. by Walter von Baeyer (Berlin: Springer, 1967).

choanalysis (pp. 47–48). In pleading the case of phenomenology together with that of other new developments, Rümke did not claim for it any special degree of certainty: it shared in the mere probability of all empirical research. But he believed in its indispensability among the foundations of psychiatry.

Rümke's concrete contributions to phenomenological psychology and psychopathology did not stop with his study of happiness. They ranged from his survey of the phenomena of compulsion, through more detailed studies of the attitudes of opening up and closing up, to a particularly rich study under the explicit title "The Phenomenological Aspect of Affective Contact." An example of his flair for overlooked and original phenomena were his studies about the aversion to one's own nose.

J. H. Van den Berg, who holds a chair in "psychology and phenomenological psychopathology," has become known in the Anglo-American world through the earliest, and in many ways still the simplest and clearest, introduction to phenomenological psychiatry.[42] While this work brings out the differences between phenomenological psychiatry and psychoanalysis, it does not go into the philosophical foundations, except for a brief last historical section, too brief for a real understanding of this aspect.

Later, Van den Berg introduced the idea of a "historical psychology" dealing with the changing nature of man, which he called "metabletica." This conception may at first sight seem to be a denial of the phenomenological idea of a permanent essence. In fact, in this work Van den Berg does not even mention phenomenology by name. However, quite apart from the fact that even under Sartre's phenomenological existentialism, man has a nature determined by his choices, it may well be maintained that for Van den Berg change is part of the phenomenological essence of man.[43]

The most voluminous contribution to this new Dutch psychiatry is the two-volume work on anthropological psychiatry by L. Van der Horst, produced in cooperation with four other Dutch psychiatrists (A. A. Boon, Joh. Booij, P. The. Hugenholtz, and

42. *A Phenomenological Approach to Psychiatry* (Springfield, Ill.: Charles Thomas, 1955).

43. Some discussion of the subject can now be found in *Metabletica van de materie* (Nijkerk: Callenbach, 1968), translated in *Humanitas* VII (1971), 274–90, esp. 284–85. See also *Metabletica* or *Leer der Veranderingen* (Nijkerk: Callenbach, 1956). English translation, *The Changing Nature of Man: Introduction to a Historical Psychology of Man* (New York: Delta Books, 1961). For a "Bibliography of Selected Works to Date," see *Humanitas* VII (1971), 411–12.

van der Leeuw).[44] However, this work does not supply anything like a planned system. The first volume deals with various aspects of "general psychiatry," the second ("Special Psychiatry") mostly with selected "marginal psychoses" (*Randpsychosen*), i.e., psychoses marginal to schizophrenia. The emphasis is on anthropology, not on phenomenology as such. This anthropology is contrasted with biological anthropology and aims at a total view of man as an "existing" being. Phenomenology is mentioned frequently as the main methodological foundation, with occasional references to Brentano, Husserl, Scheler, Heidegger, and Binswanger.

[7] Phenomenology in French Psychiatry: Henri Ey (b. 1900)

Phenomenology in French psychiatry seems to be on the rise, though its present role must not be overestimated. French psychopathology, highlighted by such names as Janet, Charcot, Bernheim, and Babinski, has always paid considerable attention to the subjective aspects of mental pathology, even though it has kept generally within the framework of medical science. The first significant change came with the advent of psychoanalysis, which, in Freud's case, was itself indebted to Charcot and to the Nancy school. Not much later, phenomenology secured its first foothold in French psychiatry through Eugène Minkowski, who during the First World War had settled in France, having come there from his native Poland via Germany and Bleuler's Zurich. In his phenomenology he reflected mostly the psychological ideas of Scheler. But what recommended Minkowski's new phenomenology to the French was his even stronger attachment to, and phenomenological interpretation of, Bergson's work. An important event in this first phase was the founding in 1925 of the group *L'Evolution psychiatrique* with its impressive new journal by the same name, which began in 1929. As a rallying point for the new currents, it gave primary emphasis to psychoanalysis, as represented by its chief editor A. Hesnard, before he became interested in phenomenology. But the most important figure in the naturalization of phenomenology in France became Henri Ey, who, after World War II, jointly with Minkowski, revived *L'Evolution psychia-*

44. *Anthropologische Psychiatrie* (Amsterdam: Van Holkema and Wagendorf, 1946).

trique. Minkowski will be the subject of a separate study in Part II; Hesnard will be discussed in connection with the infiltration of phenomenology into psychoanalysis. Henri Ey (b. 1901), who had his roots in non-psychoanalytic psychiatry and who has adopted psychoanalysis only eclectically, seems to fit best into the framework of the present chapter.

Yet Ey is not a mere eclectic. The way in which he assimilated other approaches, particularly phenomenology, shows him to be a creative user of the new motifs. The degree to which he has done so in the case of phenomenology justifies the claim that thus far his is the most thorough and original utilization of phenomenological philosophy in French psychiatry.[45]

Ey's own contribution to psychiatric research and systematization rests on an unusual familiarity with the philosophical literature, even with the original German texts, much as he usually relies on the leading French phenomenologists as his guides, especially in the cases of Husserl and Heidegger. It is worth noting that his interest in the work of the Germans has been reciprocated by them to the extent that he is the only French contributor (writing in French) to lead off the section on general conceptions and philosophical basic questions in a recent handbook of contemporary psychiatry,[46] and that his book on consciousness, in a translation by K. P. Kisker, has been included in the series of *Phänomenologisch-Psychologische Forschungen*, where it follows the translation of Merleau-Ponty's *Phenomenology of Perception*.

The importance of Ey's contribution is also attested by his leading roles in French and international psychiatry. As head of a section of one of the larger French clinics near Paris (Bonneval), he made it a center of major conferences. He also is general secretary of the new world conferences for psychiatry.

Apparently his interest in phenomenology has developed only gradually. Since his first studies on the concept of "automatism" (*L'Evolution psychiatrique* [1932]), which do not yet mention phenomenology, his main objective has been the syste-

45. I am glad that in my estimate as an outsider I have the support of a highly qualified psychiatrist, Karl Peter Kisker, as expressed in his preface to the German translation of Ey's book on consciousness (*Das Bewusstsein* [Berlin: de Gruyter, 1967], p. xxiv).

46. "Esquisse d'une conception organi-dynamique de la structure, de la nosographie et de l'étiopathologenie des maladies mentales," in *Psychiatrie der Gegenwart*, I/II, 720–62. English translation in E. Straus, M. Natanson, and H. Ey, *Psychiatry and Philosophy* (New York: Springer, 1969), pp. 111–61.

matic development and support of a unifying theory of psychopathology along evolutionary lines, which he calls "organo-dynamic." Its model is the conception of the British neurologist Hughlings Jackson, who also profoundly influenced Kurt Goldstein. By calling this theory "organic," Ey wants to bring out the hierarchical structure of the organism with its organic infrastructure and psychic superstructure; by calling it "dynamic," he wants to point at the processes of an evolution in which the organism structures, but also "de-structures" itself. In the light of this conception mental diseases appear as "deficit" processes which break down the normal structures while maintaining a reduced level of organization. In such cases consciousness may sink off to the level of the subconscious and the imaginary, which can best be understood from a study of dream and sleep.

In itself this conception does not imply any phenomenology. But in order to grasp mental diseases as organizations with a unifying, peculiar "counter-sense" as distinguished from mere collections of symptoms, caused mechanically by lesions, and from mere statistical deviations from a mean, a phenomenological analysis is needed which has to explore particularly the change in intersubjective relations between the patient and other subjects, his being in the world (*Dasein*) and his sense of reality and irreality.[47]

The growing role of phenomenology in Ey's work can best be traced in his most ambitious project, a series of loosely connected psychiatric studies, beginning in 1948, of which three volumes have appeared thus far.[48] Their purpose is to lay the groundwork for a "natural history of insanity (*folie*)." Of the eight studies of the first volume only the last, devoted to "the dream, 'primordial fact' of psychopathology," shows in its initial investigation of "hypnic dissolution" explicit traces of phenomenology. Here Ey makes ample use of Sartre's phenomenological studies of the imagination (*L'Imaginaire*), and the study of the structure of the dream begins with a "phenomenological analysis," again based on Sartre, followed first by a dynamic structural analysis and then by a discussion of explanatory theories.

The phenomenological ingredient becomes much more pronounced in the third and biggest volume (780 pages), published in 1953, whose eight studies deal with the structure of the acute

47. *Ibid*, especially the "deuxième thèse (phénoménologique)," pp. 734 ff.; Eng. trans., pp. 128 ff.

48. *Etudes psychiatriques*. Vol. I (Paris: Desclée de Brouwer, 1948; 2d ed., 1952). Vol. II (1950; 2d ed., 1957). Vol. III (1954; 2d ed., 1960).

psychoses and the "de-structuration" of consciousness. Most of these studies contain phenomenological and existential sections referring specifically to Husserl and Binswanger. Of particular interest are the studies of mania (#21), melancholia (#22), delirious fits and hallucinatory psychoses (#23), and epilepsy (#26). But the main invasion of phenomenology occurs in the concluding study of consciousness (#27). It opens with the following sentences:

> There are words which scare us. Of course we do not escape from this fear even now that consciousness appears to be at the center of the abnormal mental life, as it is in the center of existence, not as a word without sense or as a deus ex machina but as that fundamental structure of the lived reality which is a reality too . . . (III, 653).

It is as a means to meet this "scare" that Ey seems to be calling for the aid of phenomenology. Having surveyed the phenomenological findings about the loss of structure in the acute psychoses, he now approaches the general structure of consciousness, beginning with some observations on the philosophical problem. Even here Ey reaffirms his final goal as a reintegration of consciousness and the brain processes. But first he pays close attention to the philosophic contribution to the study of consciousness and devotes a long footnote of several pages to Husserl's and Heidegger's phenomenology of consciousness (III, 701 ff.).

This first, somewhat hesitant, study explains why Ey, prior to preparing another volume of his *Etudes,* found it necessary to devote an independent book to the subject of consciousness, which may well remain his most important contribution, at least to phenomenological psychopathology.[49]

The four parts of this book deal with conscious being (*être conscient*) in general—a term, incidentally, which in his second edition Ey would have liked to replace by "conscious becoming" (*devenir conscient*)—with the field of consciousness, with the self, and with the unconscious. The latter part is the briefest; it was supplemented by an important fifth part in the second edition. Without any pretense of abstracting this unusually rich work, I shall concentrate on its phenomenological features.

The introductory part begins with a chapter which ostensibly tries to define consciousness. It immediately turns to Husserl's and Sartre's conceptions. In characterizing consciousness as intentional, Ey refers to Brentano and Husserl, but also to the

49. *La Conscience* (Paris: PUF, 1963; 2d ed., 1968).

gestaltists, and to Merleau-Ponty. After a first survey of the levels of consciousness from animal forms to moral conscience, Ey defines conscious being as the having (*disposer*) of a personal model for the world (p. 39) which includes two interrelated dimensions: actualized lived experience (*le vécu*) and a personality or self at the center. The structure so defined is then compared briefly with four philosophical conceptions. William James and Henri Bergson are given four pages each, followed by eighteen pages on "*La Phénoménologie.*" The twelve-page discussion of Husserl pays detailed attention to transcendental phenomenology with special tributes to Ricoeur's and Merleau-Ponty's interpretations; here Ey acknowledges his rare good fortune in having found through the latter a chance for linking phenomenology with the needs of scientific psychology. Heidegger is given less space (six pages), and here de Waehlens is Ey's main guide. Having thus taken account of the philosophical contribution, Ey announces his own approach, via the "royal road of psychopathology," a plan which renews the early unfulfilled promise of Wilhelm Specht's pathopsychology (see above p. 93).

Accordingly, the second part of the book, devoted to the field of consciousness, begins with a sketch of its "phenomenological psychopathology," leading from the de-structuring of the field in sleep and dream through various stages of dreamlike confusion, and through delirious and hallucinatory stages to depersonalized and manic-depressive deformations. On the basis of this scale of de-structuration, Ey now builds a "phenomenology of the field of consciousness in its lived actuality," using Husserl and Gurwitsch as his corroborating aids. Three levels of the field can thus be distinguished: (1) the soil or infrastructure with a "vertical" dimension of wakeness (*vigilance*), (2) a well-constituted level allowing for facultative movement in the normal, awake subject, and (3) the level of the selective organization by a free self. These two phenomenological chapters are followed by one of a hundred pages dealing with the neurobiology of the conscious field, which tries to establish an isomorphism of the two fields reminiscent of Wolfgang Köhler's similar attempt.

The third part turns to the personality or the self at the center of the field. Again Ey begins with a chapter of phenomenological psychopathology, describing the progressive de-structuration of the self from mere "alterations" in (1) the psychopathic (characteropathic) and (2) neurotic (hysterical) self, to "alienations," where the self becomes another person, as (3) the schizophrenic self, which identifies with a different person, whereas the (4) demented self in its disorganization no longer even owns a world. This chapter is followed by one on the structure of the normal self and its self-structuring, with an extensive critical review of major theories about the genesis of the person. Then Ey gives what he calls a phenomenology of the ego making itself into a person, in which he explores its "ontogenesis" as subject of knowledge, as constituting his world, as composing his personality, and as autonomous character, and "the dynamic structure of the ego" with its values, its capacity to include its body, its language, and its reason, and finally its historicity. At the end, the reciprocal relation between the self and the field of consciousness is reassessed. In these sections there are relatively few references to other phenomenologists. However, Ey uses Sartre's discussion of the ego as his point of departure, although he by no means agrees with his view about its "transcendence."

In the fourth part Ey finally turns to the unconscious. For his start from the conscious does not imply that he rejects the conception of the unconscious. Nor does he reject Freudian psychoanalysis, in spite of many reservations which make him say, "I am a psychoanalyst and I am not a psychoanalyst." Actually his discussions in this chapter are merely preliminary. On the whole, he sees the unconscious as simply the obverse of the conscious and in fact its indispensable counterpart. But relatively little phenomenology enters this chapter. However, Ey refers to Merleau-Ponty, Ricoeur, and de Waelhens as participants in an "exciting and excited" debate (*passionante et passionée*) with the psychoanalysts in 1960, which has not yet been published. Apparently, Ey will return to the subject in a future volume of his *Etudes*. To some extent he already has—in the fifth part that he added to the second edition on the "conscious becoming" (*devenir conscient*). But his immediate concern is a detailed exploration of hallucinations that is about to appear in a large, new book.

In spite of Ey's increased use of phenomenology, one must not overlook the fact that for him it is only one of several approaches in psychiatry. Thus his treatise on psychiatry, which in its introductory chapter discusses phenomenology at the very end, giving it much credit, warns against the danger of neglecting the "determinism" of sickness. Nevertheless, Ey's studies embody the most sustained use thus far of philosophical phenomenology in French psychiatry. Not all of his interpretations of this phenomenology are hardly always correct, and his original analyses are not necessarily final. But his example is bound to strengthen the phenomenological trend in psychiatry, even beyond France.

An interesting development in French phenomenological psychopathology, as distinct from psychoanalysis, is indicated in a study of neurosis and psychosis by a Belgian psychiatrist, Dr. P. Demoulins, prefaced by A. de Waelhens.[50] Philosophically, the work is based mainly on Sartre's conception of phenomenology and existentialism, incorporating also the ideas of Henri Ey, which include, for example, his use of the dream as a clue for basic distinctions between neurosis and psychosis.

[8] Phenomenology in Italian Psychiatry

One might expect considerable interest in phenomenological psychopathology in Italy, especially in view of the remarkable and renewed surge of Italian interest in phenomenology, not only existentialism. There is clear proof of Ludwig Binswanger's impact in the fact that Danilo Cargnello, of the Psychiatric Hospital of Sondrio, has assembled the first almost complete bibliography of Binswanger's writings. Frankl's logotherapy also has attracted a following.

These few sentences are at best an installment of what in all probability is already a much vaster story. As an indication I can only point to the phenomenological ingredients in Roberto Assagioli's *Psychosynthesis*.[51] As in many other parts of this book, I can only hope that others who are better informed will feel the incentive to fill the gaps.

[9] Phenomenology in Hispano-American Psychiatry

Although at the moment I see no chance for exploring this field myself, let alone for guiding others, I must give at least a hint about the role of phenomenology, or rather of phenomenological existentialism, in Spanish psychiatry and particularly in the so-called school of Barcelona.

50. *Névrose et psychose: Essai de psychopathologie phénoménologique* (Louvain: Nauwelaerts, 1967).

51. *Psychosynthesis* (New York: Hobbs, Dorman, 1965).

The leading names here are Ramon Sarró, J. J. Lopez Ibor, and P. Lain Entralgo. A significant title is that of Ibor's *Vital Anxiety* (*Angustia vital*) (1952), which is stimulated largely by Ortega, Scheler, and Heidegger.

According to Sarró, in spite of the inadequate acquaintance of the Spanish psychotherapists with Husserl's phenomenology and Heidegger's ontology, the existential-anthropological tendency predominates in the Spanish universities.[52] The situation seems to be similar in Latin America, but thus far without outstanding productive achievements.[53]

[10] Phenomenology in British Psychopathology: R. D. Laing (b. 1927)

Until recently, there was little evidence of phenomenological influence in British psychiatry. As we have seen, Mayer-Gross, whose text on *Clinical Psychiatry* was such an unusual success, made only a very cautious plea for phenomenology. However, interest in Jaspers led at least to a translation of his *General Psychopathology* by a Manchester team.

The main foreign import was psychoanalysis, introduced effectively by Ernest Jones. Then came existentialism. It is in the wake of existentialism in its Sartrean form with its plea for existential psychoanalysis that interest in a new kind of phenomenological psychopathology seems to be taking root.

Perhaps the most promising case of creative assimilation of phenomenological themes combined with original phenomenological investigations is that of a London psychiatrist associated with the Tavistock Institute of Human Relations, Ronald D. Laing, who, together with D. G. Cooper as Director, started an Institute for Phenomenological Studies. Laing's versatile mind also includes cultural politics and daring poetry.

"It is to the existential tradition that I acknowledge my main intellectual indebtedness" [54]—this clear statement of Laing's is backed up by the mention of Kierkegaard, Jaspers, Heidegger, Sartre, Binswanger, and Tillich. But there are also occasional references to Minkowski, who provided the motto for Laing's first book, and to Merleau-Ponty, Medard Boss, and other phe-

52. *Handbuch der Neurosenlehre und Psychotherapie*, ed. V. Frankl et al. (Munich: Urban & Schwarzenberg, 1959), I, 138.
53. Teodoro Binder, "Nichtanalytische Therapie," *ibid.*, I, 220–25.
54. *The Divided Self* (Chicago: Quadrangle Books, 1960), p. 9.

nomenological existentialists. However, thus far the names of Husserl and Scheler figure only in passing in Laing's later studies of intersubjectivity.[55] Clearly, Laing's main interest in phenomenological philosophy focuses on Sartre, to whose later thought Laing, in cooperation with D. G. Cooper, has devoted a monographic study preceded by a French foreword by Sartre himself. In this foreword Sartre not only commends this condensation of his own work of the 1950–60 decade (badly needed indeed!) as a "very clear and very fruitful exposé of my thought," but also voices his support for Laing's approach to mental disease.[56] But regardless of such generous credits, Laing is right in asserting that his studies are not "a direct application of any established existential philosophy."

This is true even of his first book, a "study of sanity and madness," in which he describes his primary goal as a "science of persons" as distinguished from a study of organisms—i.e., of complexes of things with "It-processes." [57] This goal calls for an "existential-phenomenological account." Such an account has to explore the nature of a person's experience of the world and of himself with a view to relating all his particular experiences to his "being-in-the-world," very much in the spirit of Heidegger and Binswanger. But it should also be pointed out that Laing pays tribute to Freud, whom he sees as "the greatest psychopathologist" (p. 24), though he believes that Freud's theory needs replacing. In fact, Laing thinks that while psychoanalysis includes an "intra-phenomenological level" which is valid, its "extra-phenomenological level" depends for its validity on the soundness of its intra-phenomenological foundations.[58] Laing even admits the need for an extra-phenomenological extension of phenomenology in the case of psychotic phenomena, pointing out that the world of the psychotic can be reached only by "phenomenological inference" (p. 14). A more serious defect of Freudian psychoanalysis, as Laing sees it, is its neglect of the social factors. Thus, in many ways his social phenomenology parallels the interpersonal psychiatry of Harry Stack Sullivan.

However, Laing has moved far beyond such merely theoretical considerations. In "going as directly as possible to the pa-

55. *Interpersonal Perception, A Theory and a Method of Research* (New York: Springer, 1960). See also *The Politics of Experience* (New York: Pantheon Books, 1967).

56. *Reason and Violence* (New York: Humanities Press, 1964).

57. *Divided Self,* p. 21.

58. *The Self and Others* (Chicago: Quadrangle Books, 1962), pp. 14–16.

tients themselves and keeping to a minimum the discussion of the historical, theoretical, and practical issues raised particularly vis à vis psychiatry and psychoanalysis,"[59] Laing has pointed out some new and significant phenomena in both the individual and the interpersonal range of psychopathology. Thus Laing describes as the basis of his attempt to understand the schizophrenic person what he calls "ontological insecurity," the anxiety over such events as "engulfment" of one's identity, of "implosion by an encroaching world" or "petrifaction," a condition which he finds particularly well described in Sartre's *Being and Nothingness*. Laing also investigates the unembodied self as a common variation to the embodied self. The basic split in the schizophrenic personality severs the self from its body (p. 191).

But even more original and promising are some of Laing's phenomenological observations in the interpersonal range between the self and others and particularly in the dyadic relation between two selves. Here he has paid particular attention to the significance of perspectives on the self, developed especially in his study of *Interpersonal Perception*, written jointly with H. Phillipson and A. R. Lee. This conception, clearly stimulated by Sartre's phenomenology of the perspectives of one's own body, introduces not only perspectives of the self but also such additional phenomena as "meta-perspectives" (i.e., perspectives on someone else's perspectives of a person, e.g., one's own view of the other's view of oneself), "meta-metaperspectives," and so on, ad infinitum, in a way which at times indicates an almost idiosyncratic fascination with the reiterative possibilities of language. This provides Laing with a highly differentiated tool for exploring interpersonal understandings and misunderstandings. It yields him in particular the concept of a spiral of reciprocal perspectives, a concept which reminds us of Alfred Schutz's concept of the reciprocity of perspectives as basic for the social relationship, but going considerably beyond it by adding the meta-perspectives and the possibility of infinite reflections of these perspectives. As Laing sees such spirals develop, particularly in cases of distrust,[60] he even believes that their study can help us in coping with international misunderstanding.

Together with A. Esterson, Laing has also made impressive use of this approach in the first of a projected series of case studies of the schizophrenic family.[61] It attempts to show that

59. *Divided Self*, p. 16.
60. *Interpersonal Perception* (New York: Springer, 1966).
61. *Sanity, Madness, and the Family* (New York: Basic Books, 1964).

"the experience and behavior of the schizophrenics is much more socially intelligible than has come to be supposed by most psychiatrists." In fact the authors express the belief "that the shift of point of view that these descriptions both embody and demand has an historical significance no less radical than the shift from a demonological to a clinical viewpoint three hundred years ago" (p. 13). What this shift actually involves is the study of the mutual perspectives of the members of a family on the basis of separate and joint intensive interviews, resulting in their juxtaposition in parallel columns which show the contradiction of perspectives as a basic source for the rise of so-called schizophrenia in cultural contexts. However, it should not be overlooked that thus far the authors avoid far-reaching interpretations of the new data of this social phenomenology, even though in other areas Laing's claims can be quite extravagant.

[11] Conclusions

AGAIN, the total picture resulting from the preceding survey supplies no sufficient basis for sweeping claims. In the wider context of today's psychiatry, the phenomenological trend is only one of many, and it is by no means the strongest one, especially at a time when chemotherapy is revolutionizing psychiatric practice. Nevertheless, the fastest-growing edge of applied, if not all, phenomenology may still be in psychopathology, rather than in present psychology. Certainly the flow of new concrete studies in this area has not yet subsided. Also, phenomenological philosophy has been put to much more specific use here than in other fields, such as sociology. This does not mean that it can supply the answer to an understanding of the phenomena. But it has provided the tools for major breakthroughs in the understanding of psychoses which before seemed utterly incomprehensible.

4 / Phenomenology in Psychoanalysis

A SEPARATE CHAPTER on the relations between phenomenology and psychoanalysis calls for an explanation. To begin with, the attempt to separate psychoanalysis from psychopathology and psychiatry may well be questioned. Although psychoanalysis originated as a new and very different approach to these fields, it may still be considered as merely a "school" within them rather than a completely separate enterprise. However, psychoanalysis has certainly developed into much more: it has led to the development of a new type of general psychology with a dynamic theory of personality. One could even think of psychoanalysis as a new unifying link and bridge between normal and abnormal psychology. Without making or subscribing to such ambitious claims, I would maintain simply that psychoanalysis is a new approach that is sufficiently different from its predecessors to justify separate discussion. But it should be understood that this is not meant as an attempt to cut psychoanalysis off from the two fields on which it has had such a profound impact.

However, there is an additional reason for a separate treatment of the relation between psychoanalysis and phenomenology. For this relation poses some very special problems. The basic one is that at first sight phenomenology, conceived as the study of consciousness as immediately given, and psychoanalysis, the study of the unconscious as inferred on the basis of highly sophisticated techniques in the form of constructive hypotheses, seem to have nothing in common. Even worse, when phenomenology is interpreted as a philosophy which confines the universe to the world of consciousness, and psychoanalysis is interpreted as one which sees in consciousness only a powerless by-product of irrational forces, the two would seem to be incompatible. Thus there is a need for much more careful investigation of the mutual relationship in the manner of Paul Ricoeur's searching essay on Freud.

But this is only part of the problem, though it is the part which, especially in the beginning, has been in the foreground. At least equally and ultimately even more important was the assumption that not only the conscious but even the unconscious mental life has purposes or meanings and has to be understood in terms of these meanings rather than physico-chemical causes. The recognition of these meanings committed the practice of psychoanalysis to a kind of broadened mentalism and finalism. This emphasis was closely related to the practical origins and ultimate objectives of psychoanalysis as a therapeutic enterprise which was anything but fatalistic. In fact by striving to raise the unconscious into consciousness and thus to redirect the blind forces of the unconscious into more rational channels, psychoanalytic therapy gave consciousness a privileged status. It expressed itself, for instance, in the growing importance assigned to the ego and its functions by the later Freud as well as by his orthodox followers.

Finally, there is the whole problem of scientific verification. In trying to verify what seem at times to be highly speculative hypotheses, even psychoanalysis has to confirm its anticipations by the kind of evidence in which the insight of the subject is indispensable. Not only for therapeutic purposes but as a decisive test of the correctness of the analysis, the patient has to accept the analyst's interpretation which at the start may have been completely inaccessible and unacceptable to him. This too means an appeal to consciousness. What it adds up to is that psychoanalysis in its actual development cannot dispense with consciousness as the beginning and end for its probe of the unconscious.

How far has phenomenology as the systematic study of the essential structures of consciousness in all its forms been able to help psychoanalysis in this enterprise? The present chapter will supply at least some of the historical answers. The picture as it will emerge will show that, on the whole, during the German phase the psychoanalytic and the phenomenological movements hardly made any contact. All the more striking is the contrast with the situation during the French phase, when the two not only became engaged in dialogue but seemed to come close to merging. A comprehensive picture of the relationships between phenomenology and psychoanalysis up to the present moment would be in itself an assignment for a whole book. For the ramifications of the Psychoanalytic Movement are at the moment at least as wide and complex as those of the Phenomenological Movement. What I propose to do, and what still seems to be very much needed, is to offer chiefly an account of the historic relations between the two independent Austrian-based movements once their peripheries had begun to intersect.

I shall begin with the few extant facts about the attitude of the classic pychoanalysts toward phenomenology, and shall follow with a discussion of some of their more interested successors. I shall also try to assemble some data about the early phenomenological reaction to psychoanalysis. This will provide the background for a discussion of two men whose work represented the first significant encounters of the two approaches: Paul Schilder and Ludwig Binswanger, who will be discussed in greater detail in Part II.

[1] Freud and Phenomenology

It is not surprising that it took some time before the two young movements, which started almost simultaneously (Husserl's *Logical Investigations* appeared in 1900–1901, Freud's *Interpretation of Dreams* in 1901), had grown sufficiently to make even superficial contact.

One has to be aware from the very start of Freud's outspoken aversion to all philosophy in the academic sense, which would clearly include a philosopher like Husserl, who was generally considered an anti-psychologist. It was therefore to be expected that Husserl did not figure in any of Freud's published writings.[1]

1. However, the term *Phänomenologie* occurs twice in Freud's last work, the London fragment of the *Abriss der Psychoanalyse* of 1938 (*Gesammelte Werke* [Frankfurt: Fischer, 1960–68], XVII, 78–79), this work hereafter referred to as *GW*. English translation, *Complete Works*, 24 vols. (New York: Macmillan, 1964), XVIII, 155–57. Here Freud records the "insight" that "normal and abnormal phenomena which we observe, i.e., phenomenology, require a description from the standpoint of 'dynamics' and 'economics' (the quantitative distribution of libido)" (my translation). Seemingly not much more is involved than Brentano's division of psychology into a descriptive and a genetic branch, the later called "Ätiologie" (etiology) by Freud. But the descriptive branch is clearly one with a difference, since Freud's phenomenology includes even

But it must not be overlooked that Freud was in contact with two contemporary philosopher-psychologists who were also of considerable importance in the early days of phenomenology: Franz Brentano and Theodor Lipps, the former the philosophic awakener of Husserl; the latter, though initially one of the targets of Husserl's attack on psychologism, later a supporter, on friendly terms with Husserl, who in turn assimilated some of Lipps's ideas into phenomenology. Lipps, with his analytic psychology, was furthermore the teacher of most of the members of the older phenomenological movement, such as Pfänder.

The question of the extent to which Freud's personal contacts with Brentano in the early seventies, during his medical studies in Vienna, left any traces on psychoanalysis has been discussed cautiously by James R. Barclay, after reviewing some of the chronological facts recovered by Philip Merlan.[2] But in view of Freud's conspicuous silence,[3] it can no longer be established whether the eight points of agreement which Barclay finds between Brentano's and Freud's views in psychology were the result of direct or indirect influence from Brentano on Freud. However, granting some traces of Brentano's concept of intentionality in Freud's thinking, it must not be overlooked that Brentano, after a careful study of the philosophical debate about the unconscious from Thomas Aquinas to Eduard von Hartmann, had vetoed the whole conception as scientifically unsound.[4] Thus, if Freud knew the *Psychologie* at all, it is not surprising that he never referred to it.

All the more important for Freud was the encouragement he received intellectually, if not personally, from his reading in Theodor Lipps, particularly *Grundtatsachen des Seelenlebens*

---

dynamic drives and the economy of their distribution. In the following chapter about "psychic qualities," Freud also makes it clear that his phenomenology of the psychic (psychische *Phänomenologie*) is to deal not only with the conscious but with the various forms of the unconscious.

I am indebted to Dr. Alexandre Métraux for the identification of several pertinent texts in Freud's writings.

2. "Franz Brentano and Sigmund Freud," *Journal of Existentialism*, V (1964), 1–33.

3. Barclay seems to have overlooked the one explicit reference to Brentano's book of riddles, *Aenigmatias* (1878), where Freud adds a contemporary pun on Brentano's name in a footnote to *Jokes and Their Relations to the Unconscious* (*GW*, VI, 31 n; Eng. trans. VIII, 32 n); Freud, however, does not reveal anything about his personal or intellectual relations with Brentano, especially the fact that he had attended five of his courses.

4. *Psychologie vom empirischen Standpunkt* (Leipzig: Duncker & Humblot, 1874; rev. ed., Leipzig: Meiner, 1924), Book II, chap. 2.

(1883), in which according to Ernest Jones [5] Freud had marked a passage about the unconscious as the basis for the conscious, and in *Komik und Humor* (1898). Thus in his study on *Jokes and Their Relations to the Unconscious* (1905), Freud gave Lipps lavish credit for giving him "the courage and capacity to undertake this work" (*GW*, VI, 5; Eng. trans., VIII, 1 n.) because of his plea for the unconscious (*GW*, VI, 164–65; Eng. trans., VIII, 147–48). Lipps's role in the seventh chapter of the *Interpretation of Dreams* is even more important. Here, in introducing the concept of the unconscious, Freud referred particularly to Lipps's lecture delivered at the Third International Congress at Munich in 1896 (which Freud could hardly have attended) and his "forceful statement that the unconscious is less *a* psychological problem than *the* problem of psychology" (*GW*, III, 616; Eng. trans., V, 611). That the study of the *Grundtatsachen* was of considerable importance for Freud in working out his basic theories is also attested in a letter to Wilhelm Fliess from Aussee (August 26, 1898, Nos. 94 and 95), where he referred to Lipps as the one "whom I suspect to be the best mind among present-day philosophical writers."

It is also not without interest that as late as 1938 in his London fragments Freud referred to Lipps twice.[6] True, Lipps's conception of the unconscious could not yet meet Freud's needs, though Lipps's dynamic conception of the unconscious as psychic energy was certainly in line with Freud's energetics. However, it must be realized that Lipps's theory of the subconscious was more of a program than an actual achievement; most of his developed psychology dealt with the consciously accessible and was more descriptive (in the pre-phenomenological sense) than explanatory. This defect accounts to some extent for a penetrating study of the unconscious by Moritz Geiger, one of Lipps's erstwhile students and a later associate of Husserl.[7]

What all this evidence amounts to is that, though Freud was bound to have heard about phenomenology and Husserl through such associates as Binswanger and Schilder, he did not find enough in it for more sustained study.

5. Ernest Jones, *Life and Work of Sigmund Freud* (New York: Basic Books, 1953), I, 149.

6. *GW*, XVII, 80, 147; Eng. trans., XXIII, 158, 286: "A German philosopher, Theodor Lipps, has proclaimed with the greatest precision that the psychic is in itself unconscious, the unconscious is the truly psychic."

7. "Fragment über das Unbewusste," *Jahrbuch für Philosophie und phänomenologische Forschung*, IV (1921); see also my book *The Phenomenological Movement* (The Hague: Nijhoff, 1965), pp. 216 ff.

[2] Carl Gustav Jung and Phenomenology

There is also no evidence of any deeper interest in phenomenology as a philosophical movement on the part of C. G. Jung. It is true that the term "phenomenology" occurs in a number of his writings and even in titles of essays and chapters of larger publications. But I am not aware that Jung had any connections with members of the Phenomenological Movement or even with phenomenological psychologists. In fact, Jung's most characteristic conceptions, such as that of the collective unconscious, hardly lend themselves to phenomenological verifications.

Nevertheless, Jung's repeated references to phenomenology are worth collecting and examining. For instance, in a lecture of 1928 on psychological typology, republished in the Appendix of his *Psychological Types,* he speaks of a "psychische Phänomenologie" (p. 573) as the proper foundation for his psychological typology.[8] This phenomenology is to be based in turn on a "clinical phenomenology" or symptomatology. By analytic methods we are to proceed from these symptoms to the "phenomena," i.e., the "complexes" in back of the symptoms. Thus psychological phenomenology is really the study of the unconscious complexes inferred from the manifest symptoms, an assignment hardly reconcilable with the usual conception of phenomenological psychology.

Later, in an essay of 1936 ("Über den Archetypus") Jung contrasted his own position to that of a "theory" not based on phenomenology. Specifically, he charged Freud with such excessive theory without phenomenological foundations, a theory which is left "hanging in mid-air . . . lacking knowledge of general phenomenology." In his own case Jung found such foundations in Pierre Janet, William James (*Varieties of Religious Experience*), and Theodore Flournoy.[9] Also, in his 1937 Terry Lectures at Yale on "Psychology and Religion," Jung introduced himself as an empiricist who "adheres as such to the phenomenological standpoint":

8. *Psychologische Typen, GW* (Zurich: Rascher, 1960), VI, 571 ff.; this part of the German work has not yet been translated.

9. C. G. Jung, *The Archetypes and the Collective Unconscious,* in *The Collected Works of C. G. Jung,* trans. R. F. C. Hull (Princeton, N. J.: Princeton University Press, 1959), Vol. IX, Part 1, pp. 54–56.

> I restrict myself to the observations of phenomena and I eschew any metaphysical or philosophical considerations. . . . The methodological standpoint which I represent is exclusively phenomenological, that is it is concerned with occurrences, events, experiences—in a word, with facts.[10]

The latter sentence makes it plain that Jung's phenomenology coincides for him with natural science, comparable with zoology, which deals with the "phenomenon" of the elephant or such "phenomenological groups" as anthropodes.

A similar position is expressed in the lecture of 1945 (revised 1948), "On the Phenomenology of the Spirit in Fairy Tales" (*Zur Phänomenologie des Geistes in Märchen*, originally *Zur Psychologie des Märchens*), where in the beginning Jung stressed the essentially "phenomenological standpoint of modern psychology" in contrast to a science which "meddles with questions of substance." [11] Such a phenomenology is to include the description and ordering of the events, followed by an examination of the regularity of living behavior. It does not exclude belief, conviction, and experiences of certainty. But it lacks all means to prove their "validity in the scientific sense."

This last phrase suggests that Jung did distinguish between phenomenology and natural science and also that he came close to a phenomenological attitude. But there is still no indication of a real link with phenomenological philosophy. Jung's use of the term "phenomenology" suggests that he used it merely as a communicative device, in response to its growing popularity.[12]

[3] Alfred Adler and Phenomenology

There is even less evidence of interest in phenomenology in the writings of Alfred Adler. But this should not be interpreted as more than indifference on the part of a therapist who was not primarily interested in finding a new philosophical framework for his practice. The need to do so arose only gradually.

10. *Zur Psychologie Westlicher und Östlicher Religion, GW*, XI, 2–3; Eng. trans., XI, 5, 6.

11. *Collected Works*, Vol. IX, Part 1, pp. 207–54.

12. In this connection it is interesting that the English version of *Aion* (*Collected Works*, Vol. IX, Part 2) replaced the subtitle "*Untersuchungen zur Symbolgeschichte*" with "Researches on the Phenomenology of the Self," to which Jung specifically agreed.

It is therefore not surprising that, after the transplantation of individual psychology to the United States, Adler's followers showed a pronounced and even increasing interest in bringing out parallels and possible points of contact not only with other psychological approaches but also with phenomenology and existentialism. Thus since 1957, the *Journal of Individual Psychology*, according to the statement on its cover, has been "devoted to a holistic, phenomenological, field-theoretical and socially oriented approach to psychology and related fields" (although no interpretation of these terms is given in the text). However, since 1959 several articles have tried to bring out specific connections between Alfred Adler's views and those of various phenomenological existentialists.[13] In 1961 the journal published the "Symposium on Phenomenological Conceptions of Personality," in which C. H. Patterson, F. P. Kilpatrick, Abraham Luchins, Richard Jessor, and Ted Landsman participated, and which was arranged by the American Psychological Association in 1960.[14]

[4] Freud's Followers

A. *Ludwig Binswanger and Paul Schilder*

On the whole, Freud's most faithful followers did not show any more interest in phenomenology than did their master. However, at least two, Ludwig Binswanger and Paul Schilder, made major attempts at bridgebuilding. The significance of these attempts merits the special studies of their work in Part II.

How far did these pioneers succeed in establishing a real rapprochement between psychoanalysis and phenomenology? The evidence is far from clear. In the case of Binswanger, in spite of his continued affection for Freud, phenomenology increasingly took the place of psychoanalysis to the extent of absorbing it. In Schilder's case, references to phenomenology diminished, especially during his American period. The task of

13. Wilson Van Dusen, "Adler and Existence Analysis," and "The Ontology of Adlerian Psychodynamics," *Journal of Individual Psychology*, XV (1959), 100–11, 143–56. See also Wilson Van Dusen and Heinz L. Ansbacher, "Adler and Binswanger on Schizophrenia," *Journal of Individual Psychology*, XVI (1960), 77–80; "The Phenomenology of Schizophrenic Existence," *Journal of Individual Psychology*, XVII (1961), 80–92.

14. *Journal of Individual Psychology*, XVII (1961), 4–38.

bringing about a more lasting connection was left to the French and American phases of both movements.

However, two other members of Freud's narrower circle took at least a belated interest in phenomenology: Paul Federn and Heinz Hartmann. There were special reasons for this. Both Federn and Hartmann had a stake in the increasing role of the ego within the Freudian triad of id, ego, and superego, a development which in Freud's own case led to the famous formula at the end of the thirty-first of the *New Introductory Lectures on Psychoanalysis:* "Where id was, there shall ego be." Anna Freud, too, had given the ego a major place among the mechanisms of defense. This was bound to arouse interest in a phenomenology of the ego.

B. *Paul Federn*

Paul Federn (1871–1950) belonged to Freud's intimate circle. And although he went far beyond Freud by applying psychoanalysis not only to neurotics but by introducing it into the treatment of psychotics, he always believed himself to be in line with Freud, even in the development of his ego-psychology. Only in his last American years did he seem to have realized how far he had gone beyond the master's ideas.[15] Federn was definitely aware of phenomenology as a movement, if only on the basis of his references to the "ego-psychology" of Eugène Minkowski and Paul Schilder, "the most courageous and intuitive of all." [16] Federn himself based his ego-psychology on three definitions of the ego—descriptive, phenomenological, and metapsychological. He understood "phenomenological" to be the same as "subjectively descriptive" in terms of feeling, knowing, and apprehending. His phenomenological definition of the ego stated: "The ego is felt and known by the individual as a lasting or recurring continuity of the body and mental life in respect of time, space, and causality, and is felt and apprehended by him as a unity." [17]

Federn's chief example of such a phenomenological description can be found in his 1949 lecture at the Veterans' Administration Hospital in Topeka, Kansas. Here he claimed "phenomenological evidence" for the "bodily and mental ego, ego

15. Eduardo Weiss, "Paul Federn," in *Psychoanalytic Pioneers,* ed. Franz Alexander et al. (New York: Basic Books, 1966), p. 157.

16. *Ego-Psychology and the Psychoses* (New York: Basic Books, 1952), p. 222.

17. "The Awakening of the Ego in Dreams," *ibid.*, p. 94.

boundaries, ego complex, and ego feelings as giving us new insight into the essence of the ego" (p. 213), always stressing that this is not just a matter of theory or construction but of "phenomenological experience" (p. 221). While these descriptions rarely go beyond assertions, their originality merits further clarification and verification. Thus his study of "orthriogenesis," the process by which in normal awakening the ego reoccupies its boundaries in everyday life (a process for which Federn also uses the orthodox term "cathexis") is a particularly good example of Federn's phenomenology (pp. 90–92, 98). Federn's ideas about psychosis as sickness of the ego have been put to therapeutic tests in the work of Gertrud Schwing.[18]

C. *Heinz Hartmann*

Considerable references to phenomenology and even to Husserl occur also in the writings of Heinz Hartmann, the main promoter of the psychoanalytic ego-concept, who had worked in the field of psychology together with Paul Schilder.[19] In his German publications in the twenties, he had referred to Dilthey's "phenomenological psychology" and mentioned Husserl's theory of signs and signals from the *Logical Investigations*, but without expressing much interest in these studies. However, in his early German work on the foundations of psychoanalysis,[20] in a chapter on "Understanding and Explanation," he explicitly related the psychoanalytic enterprise to phenomenological psychology, chiefly in Jaspers' sense. Yet he expressed preference for the term "descriptive psychology" in order to avoid "confusion with Husserl's phenomenology" (p. 374). As to Jaspers' phenomenology, "psychoanalysis affirms that phenomenological research is only one condition, though an essential one, for the fulfillment of its task" (*ibid.*)—which is pretty much what Jaspers himself claimed: "Its results, when they are firmly established, may also be used in psychoanalytic research."

One might look on the whole development of ego-psychology as a return from hypothetical constructions, as in the case of

18. *A Way to the Soul of the Mentally Ill*, trans. Rudolf Ekstein and Bernard H. Hall (New York: International Universities Press, 1954).

19. "Zur Klinik und Psychologie der Amentia," *Archiv für die gesamte Neurologie und Psychiatrie*, XCII (1924), 531–76.

20. "Verstehen und Erklären," in *Die Grundlagen der Psychoanalyse* (Leipzig: Thieme, 1927). An English version of this chapter is included in *Essays in Ego-Psychology* (New York: International Universities Press, 1964), pp. 369–403.

the superego and the id, to the level of experiential description. However, neither Anna Freud nor Hartmann in his *Ego Psychology and the Problem of Adaptation* (1939) stressed this angle, as did Schilder and Federn.

[5] German Phenomenology

As to Husserl, there is again no evidence of serious interest in psychoanalysis until very late in his life.[21] But this late evidence is sufficient to show that his conception of phenomenology as the science of pure consciousness by no means involved a denial of the unconscious or permanent disinterest in it. For instance, in one of the last completed sections of the *Krisis*, in discussing the tasks of a phenomenological psychology and in speaking about the consciousness of the horizon of consciousness, Husserl mentioned not only what is unconscious in the sense of remaining in the unnoticed background, but the unconscious intentionality of depth consciousness ("with whose theories we do not identify, however"), mentioning specifically the repressed (*verdrängt*) affects of love, humiliation, and *ressentiment* as legitimate topics for phenomenological psychology, to be treated by the method of reduction.[22] There is also a more explicit text by Eugen Fink in the Appendix of this volume prepared in 1936 for the completion of *Krisis* (*Husserliana* VI, 473 ff.). This text does not reject the concept of the unconscious but merely argues that it cannot be tackled successfully before a thorough study of the phenomena of consciousness, since phe-

21. There is, however, one piece of biographical evidence about a personal contact between Husserl and a phenomenologically interested Dutch psychoanalyst, Johannes Van der Hoop, who was apparently Husserl's host during the Amsterdam lectures of 1928 and visited him again later during the year in Freiburg (W. R. Boyce Gibson, *Diary*, October 19, 1928, *Journal of the British Society for Phenomenology*, II [1971], 71).

Van der Hoop's books do not mention his personal contacts with Husserl and express thanks only to Heidegger, Heinz Hartmann, and H. C. Rümke. But the preface of *Conscious Orientation: A Study of Personality Types in Relation to Neurosis and Psychosis* (London: Kegan Paul, 1939) also states that "my encounter with phenomenology through Husserl and Heidegger has been of very great assistance to me. My attempt . . . must be regarded as a phenomenological investigation" (p. ix). In the "Philosophical Commentary" (Part III) toward the end of the book he also states that "Phenomenology is indispensable to psychoanalysis" though "fruitful only if supported by psychoanalytic observation" (p. 272).

22. *Krisis*, §69 (*Husserliana* VI, 240).

nomenologically the subconscious is founded on the conscious, not vice versa. Thus the phenomenological naïveté of the present theory of the unconscious could be overcome by means of "intentional analysis."

The first phenomenologist to take a serious interest in psychoanalysis was Max Scheler—another sign of his characteristic flair for new developments in philosophy, the sciences, and life in general. In fact, in his first major phenomenological book on sympathy and love (1913), Scheler devoted some twenty pages specifically to a discussion of Freud's "naturalistic or ontogenetic theory of love," as far as it was developed at that stage.[23] And he came back to it even in his later writings. From the very start Scheler accepted the facts established by Freud, especially those about early childhood sexuality, and stressed their importance. He was critical, however, of the theory built upon them, particularly the obscurity of some of Freud's basic concepts such as libido, the inadequacy of such interpretations of culture as those based on the sublimations of libido, and in general Freud's monistic explanation by the libido alone, a monism later abandoned by Freud himself. Even so, Scheler predicted that psychoanalysis would eventually be able to achieve a real understanding of personal destiny. In this connection it is worth mentioning that Scheler did express agreement with Freud's first American disciple, the Harvard psychiatrist James J. Putnam, whose version he called philosophically much more adequate.

On the whole, then, German philosophical phenomenology made only passing and superficial contact with psychoanalysis. As far as one can determine, the reason for this failure was clearly not hostility, but a difference in interests. Certainly, the field of consciousness seemed to offer greater challenges and rewards than an area of scientific research which was still as controversial as that of the unconscious.

[6] The French Scene

One of the striking differences between the German and the French phases of phenomenology is the different attitude toward psychoanalysis. Compared with the merely in-

23. *Zur Phänomenologie und Theorie der Sympathiegefühle und von Liebe und Hass* (Halle: Niemeyer, 1913), pp. 203–6, 226–43. English translation by Peter Heath, *The Nature of Sympathy* (New Haven, Conn.: Yale University Press, 1954), pp. 177–79, 196–212.

cidental late remarks of Husserl, the digressions of Scheler, and the total silence of Heidegger's own writings, psychoanalysis has been a major topic for the French phenomenologists, with the possible exception of Gabriel Marcel. Alphonse de Waelhens, in an essay containing some original phenomenological observations on the phenomenology of sexuality, has suggested that this feature is related to the distinctive interest of the French phenomenologists in the (lived) body, language, and the elimination of the dualism of consciousness and mechanical organism.[24] Whatever the explanation may be, French phenomenology has certainly given psychoanalysis much more of a hand than has previous phenomenology. How far has it taken it?

At first psychoanalysis in France seems to have been as detached from philosophy and phenomenology as were Freud himself and his immediate followers in Austria and Germany. Sartre's interest since the days of his studies in Berlin (1933)—especially his development of an existential psychoanalysis—does not seem to have made any lasting impression on the active psychoanalysts. Nor do the studies of his friend Jean Hyppolite on the significance of Hegel's phenomenology for psychoanalysis seem to have had much of an effect, except in the case of Jacques Lacan. Only Merleau-Ponty's discussions, incidental though they were in his writings, reached the psychoanalysts, and especially Angelo Louis Hesnard. At this point the psychoanalysts became seriously interested even in Husserl.

The major figure in the assimilation of phenomenology by the French psychoanalysts was clearly Hesnard. He will therefore be the main representative of this trend in the present discussion. However, other names must not go unmentioned, although no comparable study can be offered. They include Daniel Lagache and Jacques Lacan. Among the Belgians A. Vergote is of special interest, along with de Waelhens.

A. *Angelo Louis Hesnard (1886–1969)*

Perhaps the most remarkable thing about "Dr. Hesnard" is that he was both one of Freud's early pioneers in France and later the chief advocate of Merleau-Ponty's phenomenology and its application to psychoanalysis. Less closely related to Freud personally than one of the better known and philosophically less interested of Freud's protagonists, Marie Bonaparte, he was

24. "Phénoménologie et psychanalyse," in *Existence et Signification* (Louvain: Nauwelaerts, 1958), 191–211.

nevertheless with Louis Régis the coauthor of the first French work on psychoanalysis;[25] Freud acknowledged this in an appreciative letter to Hesnard (implying, however, that Hesnard had not yet done justice to his doctrine of symbolism).

As to Merleau-Ponty, Hesnard gave him credit for having "completely rethought Husserl, bringing to him not only a clearness essentially characteristic of the French spirit, but a personal follow-up of critical studies in neurophysiology and psychopathology which are of the greatest interest to psychiatrists."[26] What was of special interest to Hesnard in Merleau-Ponty's phenomenology was its concept of pre-reflective consciousness and its emphases on the close bonds of consciousness with the body and the world. Because of Hesnard's interest in Merleau-Ponty's phenomenology, he invited him to write a preface for his book on Freud. Merleau-Ponty accepted and the text that resulted is actually much more than a mere introduction to Freud's own work and its impact.[27] For one of Hesnard's theses, which also throws light on the invitation, was that

> Freud, by his discoveries, had opened the way for a new philosophy and . . . his doctrine and method are neighbors of a concrete philosophy whose relatively recent success is considerable: phenomenology (p. 308).

The book itself, in addition to giving a condensed account of Freud's main teachings and a selective survey of the history and spread of psychoanalysis in various parts of the world, discusses in its last and largest section the significance of psychoanalysis for other fields. It is here that, in the chapter on psychoanalysis and philosophy, the relation of phenomenology and psychoanalysis is central and the idea of a "phenomenological psychoanalysis" is presented. In fact, Hesnard calls Freud, because of his search for the meaning of all our acts, a phenomenologist *avant la lettre* (p. 313). For phenomenology can offer to psychoanalysis an enlarged concept of consciousness, which includes the "latent or implicit" and thus can do justice even to the unconscious. More specifically, it promises a new concept of reason which can incorporate the irrational, an in-

25. *La Psycho-analyse des névroses et des psychoses* (Paris: Alcan, 1914).

26. *Apport de la phénoménologie à la psychiatrie contemporaine* (Paris: Masson, 1959), p. 5.

27. *L'Oeuvre de Freud et son importance pour le monde moderne* (Paris: Payot, 1960).

tegration of sexuality as part of the lived body, a critique of psychological objectivism, and a basic role for intersubjectivity.

However, Hesnard's most extensive and systematic treatment of the phenomenological contribution to psychoanalysis is contained in his report to the congress of French neurologists and psychiatrists held in Tours in 1959, which matches the report on psychoanalysis that he had given thirty-six years earlier at Besançon. It begins with a general exposition of phenomenology in the spirit of Merleau-Ponty, stressing the concept of consciousness as intentionality engaging man in his world. Its application to neuropsychiatry yields a better understanding of cerebral lesions, of lesional psychoses, and finally of neuroses. The third and largest part discusses psychiatric applications, dealing first with psychosis in general, then with its classic types, and finally taking up psychotherapeutic applications. In this context Hesnard also gives some of his own interpretations of the psychoses, based on the idea that mental disease is an existential disease,[28] and that its main feature is the disturbance of the *inter*subjective bond, which results in its replacement by an *intra*subjective world.

Of course, the significance of phenomenology to psychoanalysis is here only a subsidiary theme. It is clear that Hesnard, as President of the French Psychoanalytic Society, has not changed his fundamental allegiance to psychoanalysis. But Hesnard's 1959 report also expresses his conviction, and tries to implement it, that phenomenology can support and develop psychoanalytic conceptions and theories by utilizing Merleau-Ponty's approach (see esp. pp. 39 ff.).

As to the main stumbling block, the concept of the unconscious, Hesnard believes that phenomenology, which rejects the term "unconscious" as "practically convenient, but ambiguous" and dispensable, offers an equivalent in that of a latent and implicit consciousness. From the other side, in Hesnard's view, such psychoanalysts as Lacan, in their emphasis on the latent and implicit workings of language, come closest to the phenomenological position (p. 15). The chances for a phenomenological interpretation in the style of Merleau-Ponty are even stronger in the case of such concepts as regression, repression, sublimation, etc. Finally, in a suggestive footnote Hesnard states that many such concepts "gain" by being conceived and expressed from a phenomenological angle. In fact, the relation with

28. *Apport de la phénoménologie à la psychiatrie contemporaine*, p. 40.

other beings, whose knowledge is essential for the psychiatrist, can be understood only from the angle of phenomenological intersubjectivity (p. 41 n.).

One would, however, be mistaken to see Hesnard as merely a chronicler and an interpreter of the impact of phenomenology on psychoanalysis. He himself, having been an active worker in the field long before he underwent the phenomenological influence, has also contributed to its application. A good example is his use of Merleau-Ponty's phenomenology in his study of the world of "morbid consciousness." [29] Here he sees in the morbid world a variation of the normal world as presented by Merleau-Ponty, comparable to the world of the child and the world of the primitive. It is a world fragmented because of the patient's inability for unified organization, which deeply affects his mode of existence in the world. In this light "all mental sickness is existential sickness." Hesnard sees the neurotic person as a subject who is no longer capable of maintaining an authentic intersubjective bond with other people, the psychotic patient as one who out of the debris of his normal world constructs a fictitious world, an intrasubjective world, as Hesnard calls it. On this basis Hesnard tries to give interpretations of specific forms of neuroses as special forms of disturbances in man's relations to the world.

A particularly instructive attempt on the part of Hesnard to integrate psychoanalysis with phenomenology is his book *Psychoanalysis of the Human Bond.* Actually, it is an effort to utilize phenomenology to fill what Hesnard considers a major gap in psychoanalysis: its failure to do justice to interpersonal relations. While Freud's theory of identification with others plays an important part in these relations, it does not account for what Hesnard considers the foundation for social acts, the "anonymous intersubjectivity" which he finds in Merleau-Ponty's *phenomenology* of social behavior.

B. *Daniel Lagache*

The psychoanalytic theories of Daniel Lagache, especially those about the structure of the ego, its different types, and their relations among each other, lend themselves to phenomenological interpretation in the sense of Husserl's developed

29. See "Nature de la Conscience: Conscience normale et conscience morbide," (*L'Evolution psychiatrique* [1959], pp. 353–82; see also *L'Oeuvre de Freud,* pp. 322 ff.).

"egology." While Lagache has not stressed this connection, he is aware of phenomenology as a potential aid to his development of the Freudian scheme. Thus, in discussing some of the extravagances of psychoanalysis, he appeals to phenomenology as the best guardrail, and asks:

> Inasmuch as we spoke of phenomenological attitude rather than of clinical attitude, isn't our methodological consciousness indebted to the philosophers and the psychologists? [30]

C. *Jacques Lacan (b. 1901)*

It is not easy to pin down the role of as non-systematic a writer as Jacques Lacan in the context of the phenomenology of psychoanalysis. However, his extraordinary personal influence makes it imperative at least to mention him.

On the basis of his writings, now collected in a 912-page volume,[31] one might well come to the conclusion that at present phenomenology has little, if any, explicit significance for his version of Freudian psychoanalysis. Certainly, his references to phenomenology seem to have decreased and become more guarded, as he identifies with the ostensibly anti-phenomenological philosophy of structuralism. But it cannot be overlooked that in his earlier writings, also included in the latest collection, there are repeated appeals to phenomenology. Thus, in an essay of 1936 ("Au delà du 'Principe de Réalisme,'" pp. 73–92), the primary contribution of the "Freudian revolution" against associationism appears to be its "phenomenological description of psychoanalytic experience" by means of the free association as expressed in linguistic form (p. 82). Apparently, Lacan decided not to continue along this line after the war (p. 69). But even his later writings contain occasional references to phenomenology and show that he is aware of Husserl as well as Sartre and Merleau-Ponty (see, e.g., pp. 160 ff.), though he is often quite critical of them. In the systematic index to the volume (by Jacques-Alain Miller), no reference to phenomenology or existentialism as such occurs. This should not make one think that there are no implicit traces of the original phenomenological impulse. Thus Lacan's theory of symbolism, which

30. "Psychoanalyse et psychologie," *L'Evolution psychiatrique* (1956), p. 264. See also "Voisinage de la philosophie et de la psychanalyse," *Encyclopédie française,* Vol. XIX, *Philosophie et religion,* 19.26.10–19.26.15.

31. *Ecrits* (Paris: Edition du Seuil, 1966).

refers chiefly to de Saussure's linguistics with its distinction between what signifies and what is signified and asserts the primacy of the former over the latter, seems to be closely related to Merleau-Ponty's explicit phenomenology of language.

D. *Antoine Vergote*

The one who seems to have gone farthest in claiming the phenomenological character of Freudian psychoanalysis is the Belgian Antoine Vergote.[32] He argues that Freud had discovered that the psychic is defined by meaning, and that this meaning is dynamic and historic. Before even knowing it by name, he had thus put the phenomenological method—which consists in letting the phenomena speak as they are in themselves—into action (p. 38). Vergote particularly applies this method to Freud's interpretation of dreams, as an attempt to understand the meaning of the manifestations of the unconscious, which is essentially "effective and dynamic intentionality of forces."

Obviously, this kind of phenomenology goes considerably beyond a merely descriptive version and is in its very definition oriented more toward Heidegger's hermeneutic phenomenology than Husserl's. In fact, Vergote himself, while stressing the parallel, does not want to identify Freud's approach with Husserl's (pp. 58–59).

All these attempts at rapprochement do not add up to a complete phenomenologization of psychoanalysis. Nor is there any certainty that they will in the future. But there are indications that, as both movements spread, their territories will increasingly overlap. And there would seem to be definite promise that, as psychoanalysis tries to deepen its foundations and buttress them by a return to experience, it will find a useful ally in a phenomenology which has deepened and widened its conception of consciousness. But it would be fatal for both if such an alliance were to lead to a sacrifice of their distinctive natures. Ricoeur is right: phenomenology has to remain faithful to its demand for intuitive verification and essential insight. And psychoanalysis can hardly shed the boldness of its interpretative hypotheses; it must probe into the darkness of the unconscious without abandoning its identity.

32. "L'Intérêt philosophique de la psychologie freudienne," *Archives de philosophie*, XXI (1958), 26–59.

5 / The American Scene: Beginnings

THE RATIONALE for the present chapter may seem to be based merely on practical considerations of local interest. There is some justification for this impression. This chapter is indeed meant to serve the American world from which and for which this book is primarily designed as an orientation. But there is also this much of an objective reason for such a local focus: What has recently happened in the United States by way of an outburst of interest and activity in the field of phenomenological and existential psychology and psychiatry is enough of a "phenomenon" to call for separate attention, regardless of its permanent significance.

To obtain a comprehensive view, let alone a critical one, of the lush growth of these new disciplines on American shores would be a forbidding assignment. There is so much in quantity, and yet thus far so little that stands out by its scope and quality, that it would be impossible to be exhaustive and very difficult to be selective. Yet I hope to offer more than a random sample. What I shall attempt is to point out some of the landmarks, to give some clues for understanding the new trends, and to provide the materials for their comparative evaluation.

The chief milestone in the development of American phenomenological and existential psychology and psychiatry was the publication in 1958 of the volume, *Existence: A New Dimension in Psychiatry and Psychology* (note the order) edited by Rollo May, Ernest Angel, and Henri F. Ellenberger. Prior to it there had been only sporadic spurts of what was mostly grassroots phenomenology, with eclectic loans from the scant sources then available in translation from the German and French philosophical and psychological world. The main living connection with these European roots was Paul Tillich. With the appearance of May's volume the climate changed rapidly. But I shall offer no more than samples from this current history. My main goal will be to present the period before *Existence* in an effort to bring out some of the more original American contributions.

[1] General Orientation

It has been suggested that there is absolutely no connection between the latest burgeoning of phenomenology among American psychologists and psychiatrists and the philosophical tradition of phenomenology. There is certainly good reason for questioning premature claims based on the mere occurrence of the label, particularly as far as the relation to Husserlian phenomenology is concerned. On the other hand, it would be strange if there were no legitimate basis whatsoever for the common use of the term in the post-Husserlian era, especially if phenomenology is taken in the wider sense. But only careful studies can establish the facts of the case.

From the very start I would like to confront one major criticism of the American developments, voiced particularly by Binswanger and Roland Kuhn: that of a lack of background knowledge and understanding of the European antecedents, particularly of Husserl and Heidegger, on the part of the new American enthusiasts.[1] Unfortunately there is a good deal of truth to this objection, although many excuses could be given, beginning with the unavailability of good translations in a country where, realistically, knowledge of the pertinent languages and access to the literature cannot be expected. But granting these weaknesses in terms of continuity with the traditions, there could be also some phenomenological virtue in a fresh start, in "going to the things"—provided one arrives there and arrives there more fully and more quickly than one's predecessors. How far have the American phenomenological existentialists succeeded in doing so?

1. See, e.g., *Psychiatrie der Gegenwart*, ed. H. W. Gruhle et al. (Berlin: Springer, 1963), I/II, 897.

[2] Pacemakers: William James and Gordon Allport

Any attempt to understand the rise of an indigenous American phenomenology would have to analyze the soil for the new seed. This could be a vast and somewhat speculative enterprise. Instead, I shall merely evoke the names of two of the pacemakers of phenomenological psychology: William James in the nineteenth century and Gordon Allport in the twentieth.

That William James has a particularly strong claim to be included among the ancestors of phenomenology, and not only in America, has been asserted almost too often and too sweepingly. Several studies, most fully and critically that of the Dutch psychologist Johannes Linschoten, have shown phenomenological motifs in James's psychological work.[2] There is even good evidence of a limited influence on James by Franz Brentano. On the other hand, it must not be overlooked that the term "phenomenology" never occurs in James's writings, and also that James's name is conspicuously absent from the writings of the new American phenomenological psychologists. All that I shall claim here is that the spirit of James's bold and open-minded psychology helped to create a climate in which phenomenology could take root among American psychologists.

The situation is of course very different in the case of Gordon Allport, who was fully aware of the growth of the Phenomenological Movement both in philosophy and psychology. But while he aided and abetted phenomenology and existentialism from their tender beginnings, he can certainly not be claimed fully by either of them. While they owe him much in the way of a hearing and of encouragement, phenomenology has at best added new material for his own hospitable synthesis.

2. *Auf dem Wege zu Einer Phänomenologischen Psychologie: Die Psychologie von William James* (Berlin: de Gruyter, 1961). English edition by A. Giorgi, *On the Way Toward a Phenomenological Psychology: The Psychology of William James* (Pittsburgh, Pa.: Duquesne University Press, 1970). Among more general attempts to present William James as a protophenomenologist, see Bruce Wilshire, *William James and Phenomenology* (Bloomington, Ind.: Indiana University Press, 1968); John Wild, *The Radical Empiricism of William James* (New York: Doubleday, 1969); James M. Edie, "William James and Phenomenology," *Review of Metaphysics*, XXIII (1970), 481–526; and H. Spiegelberg, "What William James Knew about Edmund Husserl: On the Credibility of Pitkin's Testimony," *Life-World and Consciousness: Essays for Aron Gurwitsch*, ed. L. E. Embree (Evanston, Ill.: Northwestern University Press, 1972), pp. 407–22.

Allport's initial contact with phenomenology took place from the peripheral vantage points of the Berlin school (Gestalt) and the Hamburg of William Stern, where he studied in 1922–23. He saw them through sympathetic eyes, but nevertheless those of an independent and selective outsider. Allport's own cautious, but determined plea for the use of personal documents in the study of personality [3] shows the importance he attached to the subjective phenomena as seen by the experiencing subject. And his bold attempt in 1943 to rehabilitate the discredited ego in contemporary psychology had at least strong phenomenological undertones.[4] In his programmatic Terry Lectures, in distinguishing between a Lockian and a Leibnizian tradition in psychology, he mentioned phenomenology specifically as an important branch of the Leibnizian tradition with its emphasis on the person as a source of acts.[5] But he also made it clear that it can claim only equal rights with the Lockian tradition. As a pluralistic synthesizer, Allport can at best be considered a philo-phenomenologist, anxious to restore the lost balance in psychology.

[3] Donald Snygg (1904–1967) as a Phenomenological Pioneer

THE FIRST OUTSPOKEN PLEA for a new phenomenological psychology in America came in 1941 in an article by Donald Snygg entitled "The Need for a Phenomenological System of Psychology" in the *Psychological Review*, XLVIII, 404–24. It was followed in 1949 by the joint text of Snygg and Arthur W. Combs, *Individual Behavior: A New Frame of Reference for Psychology*, in which the new "phenomenological approach," also called "a personal approach," was more fully developed.

What was this new approach? Its most outspoken expression may still be Snygg's postulate of 1941: "Behavior is completely determined by and pertinent to the phenomenological field of the behaving organism." [6] Phenomenology, therefore, consists pri-

3. *The Use of Personal Documents in Psychological Science* (New York: SSRC, 1942).

4. "The Ego in Contemporary Psychology," Presidential Address before the American Psychological Association (1943), republished in *Personality and Social Encounter* (Boston: Beacon Press, 1960), pp. 71 ff.

5. *Becoming: Basic Considerations for a Psychology of Personality.* (New Haven, Conn.: Yale University Press, 1953), pp. 12 ff.

6. *The Phenomenological Problem*, ed. Alfred E. Kuenzli (New York: Harper, 1959), p. 12.

marily in the exploration of the phenomenal field of the individual, including his phenomenal self.

The seemingly independent rise of this new conception of phenomenology calls for some explanation. For ostensibly it has no roots in any preceding American psychology, let alone in phenomenological philosophy. I am indebted to Snygg for a remarkably full and clear account of the genesis of his conception in a letter from which I shall select the most pertinent items. On the negative side, he made it plain that, while he was aware of Brentano and Husserl as early as 1933, he had no direct knowledge of their works and was certainly not influenced by them in formulating his phenomenological program. However, in 1929 he learned about Gestalt psychology through Wolfgang Köhler. His own work led him to see the importance of the perceptual field for behavior, even before he had come across Kurt Koffka's distinction between the "geographical" and the "psychological" environment. The term "phenomenological" did not enter Snygg's thinking until one of his Toronto teachers, William Line, told him that he was using a phenomenological approach, which led to his first use of the term in his Ph.D. thesis of 1935. From then on the crucial importance of the phenomenal field as the "frame of reference" for the individual's behavior, with the phenomenal self at its center, acquired increasing importance in Snygg's studies of animal and human motivation. In 1945 Snygg began collaborating with Arthur W. Combs, who had worked with Carl Rogers,[7] and together they published *Individual Behavior* as the first sustained development of the new "phenomenological approach."[8] The Foreword of the book credits Freud and his followers with the first impetus in the new direction.

This genealogy of Snygg's phenomenology does not take us back directly to any philosophical sources. However, it must not be overlooked that some of Snygg's psychological inspirers were

7. See also Combs's "Phenomenological Concepts in Nondirective Therapy," *Journal of Consulting Psychology,* XII (1948), 197–267, where non-directive is an equivalent term for "phenomenological" or client-centered therapy (p. 207).

8. *Individual Behavior: A New Frame of Reference for Psychology* (New York: Harper, 1949; 2d ed., 1959). Incidentally, in the second edition of 1959, Combs as sole reviser of the book, gave it the subtitle, "A Perceptual Approach to Behavior," and announced: "In this book we will not use the term 'Phenomenological,' but we shall occasionally use the term 'phenomenal field,' only because this synonym will serve to avoid repetition." No clear reason for the avoidance of "phenomenology" and the demotion of "phenomenal" to second place is given. One may suspect the wish to avoid philosophical entanglement.

not innocent of phenomenological philosophy. This is true in particular of Wolfgang Köhler, who, apart from his own interest in phenomenology, both in its psychology and philosophy, had developed his own version of it, as was shown in Chapter 2. This is even more true of Kurt Koffka. As to William Line, the Canadian psychologist who first suggested to Snygg that he was doing phenomenology, one might suspect that he reflected the widespread interest of Canadian psychologists in European phenomenology—Robert MacLeod, the student of David Katz, is an example.

However, it is obvious that these stimuli were at best indirect and corroborative. The primary and ultimately more important factor reflected the growth of the new approach out of the concrete needs of psychological research and practice. In Snygg's case it is particularly instructive to observe how behavioristic his original approach was. His main concern was to make individual predictions; only later did the needs of counseling, teacher education, and therapy add further weight to the case for the exploration of the phenomenal field.

On the other hand, it must be admitted that thus far the concrete yield of the new program, even in terms of the promised predictions of individual behavior, is not yet impressive. Also, it must be realized that the method to be used in the exploration of the phenomenal field of other subjects was characterized as analogical inference, a method which in its indirectness is of course anything but phenomenological in the original sense.

Nevertheless, Snygg's plea for phenomenology as the necessary complement of behaviorism remains a landmark in the establishment of an indigenous phenomenology in America. But for a more influential and promising development, one has to turn to Carl Rogers and his school.

[4] Phenomenology in the Client-Centered Approach of Carl Rogers (b. 1902)

At first sight it may seem far-fetched to claim Carl Rogers for phenomenology. Indeed, Rogers' interest in phenomenology was late and slow in developing. Nevertheless, in his recent role as one of the two representatives of phenomenology at the symposium on "Behaviorism and Phenomenology" at Rice University in 1964, Rogers took the side of phenomenology as the main ingredient for the "third force" in psychology, between behaviorism and psychoanalysis.[9] Thus the main questions in the present context are: How different is Rogers' phenomenology from its traditional forms? How far is it indebted to philosophical phenomenology?

In what follows I shall first trace the rise of phenomenological terms and conceptions in Rogers' development. Then I shall try to determine the relation of this conception to other phenomenological forces. Finally, I shall discuss the phenomenological character of Rogers' non-directive therapy.

A. *The Entrance of Phenomenology into Rogers' Psychology*

As Rogers himself has made amply clear, his primary interest in psychology was clinical therapy. Theory became important to him only as the new method, which was developed in coping with concrete situations, called for a supporting theory.

Accordingly, Rogers' first books contain no references to any philosophical theory, let alone phenomenology. In particular the new method of non-directive therapy first developed in *Counseling and Therapy* (1940) does not even speak of the phenomenal field. *Client-Centered Therapy* (1951) is the first of Rogers' major works in which the term "phenomenological" appears, not only with reference to Snygg's and Combs's enterprise but in a retrospective characterization of his own work. The main reason for this new interpretation is apparently this insight: "The essential point about the therapeutic process is that the way the client perceives the objects in his phenomenal field—his experiences, his feelings, his self, other persons, his environment—undergoes change in the direction of increased differentiation." [10]

But beyond this indication of the importance of the phenomenal field, there is still no explicit characterization of phenomenology as Rogers understands it. References to phenomenology increase in Rogers' later writings, though they remain incidental.[11]

9. "Toward a Science of the Person," in *Behaviorism and Phenomenology: Contrasting Bases for Modern Psychology,* ed. T. W. Wann (Chicago: University of Chicago Press, 1965).

10. *Client-Centered Therapy* (Boston: Houghton Mifflin, 1951), p. 142.

11. See, e.g., *Psychotherapy and Personality Change* (Chicago: University of Chicago Press, 1967), where the findings about changes in the relation between self-concepts and ideal concepts after client-centered counseling are characterized in Chapter 5 as "phenomenological" (p. 9), and the question of "how to make the best use of phenomenological data"

Rogers' contribution to Sigmund Koch's *Psychology: A Study of a Science,* Vol. III, "A Theory of Therapy, Personality, and Interpersonal Relationships as Developed in the Client-Centered Framework" [12] contains his most ambitious theoretical formulation thus far of the theory underlying client-centered therapy. Here Rogers, in referring to phenomenology, envisions that "the discovery and development of a contextual basis for this theory in some form of existential philosophy will continue. The general orientation of philosophical phenomenology is also likely to continue to have its influence in this respect" (p. 250). This prognosis implies that philosophical phenomenology is an important adjunct to client-centered therapy. But Rogers' most outspoken identification with phenomenology is still his statement for the Rice Symposium of 1964. It remains to be seen in what sense this new phenomenology fits into the phenomenological tradition.

B. *Rogers' Way to Phenomenology*

There is no shortage of autobiographical accounts of Rogers' own development, of the evolution of his new therapy and of the theory with which subsequently he underpinned it. But he has made no explicit statement about the growth of his interest in phenomenology. There is also no record of his study of the phenomenological psychologists or philosophers. There is only his tribute to Kierkegaard and Martin Buber, with whose work he "became acquainted at the insistence of some of his 'theological' students at Chicago who were taking work with me." [13] There is no evidence and little likelihood of personal contacts with representatives of the Phenomenological Movement. Thus, as far as Rogers' phenomenology can be considered phenomenological in any of the established senses, this is clearly a case of a spontaneous parallel, later confirmed by the discovery of corroborating agreements.

It must be realized that Rogers' initial interest was in clinical work with children, particularly during his twelve years in Roch-

---

is discussed in the concluding chapter (p. 429). The important essays collected under the title *On Becoming a Person: A Therapist's View of Psychotherapy* (Boston: Houghton Mifflin, 1961), particularly those in Chapters 5 and 6, are characterized as belonging to a "phenomenological, existential, person-centered trend" (p. 125).

12. (New York: McGraw-Hill, 1962).

13. *On Becoming a Person,* p. 199.

ester, New York. These years not only taught him the defects of a narrow psychoanalytic and coercive approach but also showed him the significance of considering the client's perspective. His first book, *The Clinical Treatment of the Problem Child* (1939), which was primarily a survey of the various ways of understanding the child and of treating his problems, was seemingly quite neutral, but special attention was given to the so-called "relationship therapy" developed especially by Fred Allen and Jessie Taft, who were part of a Philadelphia group inspired by the emancipated Freudian Otto Rank. Rank, known chiefly for his will therapy, had actually a much more philosophical background than Freud; however, it did not include phenomenology. What was most important for Rogers was the Philadelphians' "respect for the integrity and capacity of each person," a therapy which he characterized as more emotional than intellectual, and which was based on a new relationship between social worker and parent in an atmosphere which expressed acceptance, avoided criticism, and tried to lead to "clarification of feeling" and "acceptance of self."

In retrospect it becomes clear how much the practical ideas of the Philadelphia group contributed to Rogers' move toward a phenomenological position. But it was only in *Counseling and Psychotherapy* (1942), the fruit of his Ohio years, that Rogers began to formulate his own approach. Now counseling became the main lever of therapy. In contrast to advice-giving, counsel, as Rogers sees it, is based on the hypothesis that "a definitely structured, permissive relationship allows the client to gain an understanding of himself to a degree which enables him to take positive steps in the light of this new orientation." Counseling, then, is to aim at insight into, recognition of, and acceptance of self. It is achieved through a reorganization of the perceptual field in which the counselor sees new relationships previously overlooked.

This emphasis on the need for insight makes counseling a much more cognitive affair than before. But even more important is the beginning of the emphasis on the need for paying attention to the perceptual field of the client: it increased when non-directive therapy became client-centered therapy. As the negative name suggested, non-directive therapy still remained largely on the outside of the client and tried by its permissiveness to act as a catalyst in developing the counselor's insight. "Centering" on the client does not only suggest a more active role on the part of the counselor; it also means that the counselor has to make the client the focus of his attention.[14] Before, his role was interpreted as passive, "staying out of the client's way." Now he is "to assume insofar as he is able the internal frame of reference of the client, to perceive the world as the client sees it, to perceive the client himself as he is seen by himself, to lay aside all perceptions from the external frame of reference while doing so, and to communicate something of this empathic understanding to the client" (p. 29). The counselor has to "gain the center of [the client's] perceptual field, seeing through the client's eyes" (p. 32), which proves to be a rather difficult assignment. What becomes particularly important is the study of the therapeutic relationship as experienced by the client (pp. 65 ff.).

The process of therapy is then described in terms of changes in the client's perception of himself: first, in the direction of increasing "self-acceptance," and, second, in the sense of "increased differentiation in the perceptual field," which now is, for the first time, identified with the phenomenal field. Such differentiation means the "separating out and bringing into figure any significant perceptual element which has heretofore been unrecognized" (p. 145). In this context Rogers also refers for the first time to Snygg's and Combs's "phenomenological viewpoint" (p. 146). Actually, Combs had started as a student of Rogers', but Rogers felt that the new phenomenological psychology of *Individual Behavior* that Combs had developed with Snygg had gone too far (as he said in an interview with me in 1955) in making the phenomenal view all-important. Rogers' final theory of personality and behavior states even more explicitly that the phenomenal field is an essential part of the structure of the person; it is the world to which the individual reacts, in this sense "reality." This makes it clear why Rogers took an intense interest in the description of the phenomenal world, though thus far only as it was described by the client himself. Thus the phenomenological world was not only the main causal factor for man's behavior but was also the main point of attack for the therapeutic process.

At this stage one might think that the introduction of the phenomenological motif is nothing but a loan from Snygg via Combs. But this would be an oversimplification. Rogers had moved toward such a conception before, but now he made a much more systematic use of it in therapy, assigning the thera-

14. *Client-Centered Therapy* (Boston: Houghton Mifflin, 1951), p. 27.

pist the task of being a phenomenologist entering into the patient's phenomenal frame of reference.

But Rogers' "phenomenology" did not stop with the adoption of the idea of the phenomenal field by client-centered therapy. Rogers has not only continued to develop his theory but also has given increasing attention to the enrichment of its methodological and conceptual framework. Its most complete form can be found in his statement for the Koch volume (see above, p. 150).

The last piece of monumental research undertaken by Rogers and a large staff of collaborators at the University of Wisconsin under the title *The Therapeutic Relationship* involves what may well seem to be a supreme test for client-centered therapy, its application to psychotics and specifically to schizophrenics.[15] Ostensibly, this sober and painstaking piece of research contains no explicit reference to phenomenology; in fact, it has all the earmarks of an attempt to determine the results of the approach through objective measurements. However, what is so measured is actually the impact of the "subjective" or phenomenal factors on therapy. The underlying hypothesis, obviously based on some experiential evidence, is that certain factors in the therapist's attitude, when perceived as such by the client or patient, make the decisive difference for the therapeutic change in him. These factors are what Rogers calls (1) congruence in the therapist, i.e., consonance between his experience and behavior, (2) accuracy of "empathy," and (3) unconditional positive regard. In fact, it is not so much the presence of these factors but the client's perspective of them—i.e., what R. D. Laing would call the client's metaperspective of the therapist's perspective—that is effective. Phenomenologically, perhaps the most interesting of these factors is what Rogers calls "empathy." For what is involved here is the therapist's understanding not merely of the client's feelings but of his inner world.

Another significant aspect of the therapeutic relationship is that congruency requires increased attention of the therapist to his own feelings and his own phenomenal world. This becomes specially significant in the extreme cases of the withdrawn schizophrenic, where non-directive therapy simply cannot break the ice of catatonic silence. Here the therapist himself has to start the process by communicating to the patient some of his own experience with regard to the situation and the patient. To this

15. *Therapeutic Relationship and Its Impact: A Study in Psychotherapy with Schizophrenics*, ed. Carl Rogers et al. (Madison, Wis.: University of Wisconsin Press, 1967).

extent one might say that such a theory is no longer exclusively client-centered but bi-centered, or bipolar, consisting in an effort to explore two phenomenal worlds and having them interact for the benefit of the client. What now seems important is that the client becomes aware of the phenomenal world of the therapist as one which includes him, giving him the sense of being understood, being no longer alone.

In this context it is significant that among his many collaborators Rogers specifically mentions Eugene T. Gendlin as the one who not only has initiated the program but "has contributed a basic theoretical framework upon which a number of our process measures have been built" (p. xviii). Gendlin, whose contributions Rogers had recognized also in his publications after *Client-Centered Therapy,* seems to be the philosopher-psychologist through whom Rogers made a second and much more direct contact with phenomenology than he had through Snygg and Combs. As a student of Richard P. McKeon, with his ecumenical orientation, Gendlin was particularly open to phenomenological ideas. Apparently, Gendlin's share was strongest in the development of Rogers' concept of the self as a process of experiencing.[16]

Gendlin's main attempt to build a bridge from philosophy to the psychotherapy of Carl Rogers and thus to provide new foundations for his emerging theory of personality was a book called *Experiencing and the Creation of Meaning* (1962).[17] In the

16. See *On Becoming a Person* (Boston: Houghton Mifflin, 1961), pp. 128 ff.; *Behaviorism and Phenomenology* (Chicago: University of Chicago Press, 1964), pp. 109, 126 ff.; Eugene T. Gendlin, "A Theory of Personality Change," in *Symposium on Personality Change,* ed. Philip Worchel (New York: Wiley, 1964), p. 110 n.

I am particuarly indebted to Professor Gendlin for the following paragraph from a personal letter of April 9, 1970.

> Rogers' basic problem in *Client-Centered Therapy* and, as he stated it himself, later in Sigmund Koch, ed., *Psychology: A Study of a Science* (Vol. 3, p. 184 f.) was how to think about, and measure, "congruence" of "self" and "organism," the basic conceptions of his theory. If the basic concept was the congruence or divergence between organism and self, how could one talk phenomenologically about it? Rogers already had the wish to proceed phenomenologically, but it seemed impossible to speak phenomenologically of the congruence between what one would be aware of and what, by definition, one was unaware of. He felt stuck with a basically non-phenomenological conception. He wanted to be, but wasn't phenomenological.—My contribution was to formulate the theory along phenomenological lines. . . . Rather than viewing "congruence" as a comparison between content-of-awareness and content-of-organism, I reformulated it as the *manner* of the experiencing process, thus conscious and observable.

17. *Experiencing and the Creation of Meaning* (Glencoe, Ill.: Free Press, 1962).

present context its subtitle, "A Philosophical and Psychological Approach to the Subjective," is perhaps even more important than the main title. For its problem is to find a proper support for the new role of "the phenomenon of subjectivity," as Rogers himself had called it in the Koch volume, which forms the starting point for Gendlin's study. Here Rogers had deplored the inadequacy of logical positivism and had reached out for an "existentialist orientation." [18] Gendlin's main objective is to provide the basis for such a reorientation that can bridge the gap between the two schools and between the objective and the subjective. Part of this attempt consists in his reinterpretation of the term "experience" in the sense of what is directly felt, of "experiencing" in contrast to the contents of such experiencing.[19] On the other hand "meanings," symbols, or concepts are by no means minimized. Their "creation" is not the only form in which they occur, but novel meaning is of particular significance for the therapeutic process and change. In fact it is the interaction between experiencing and conceptualization which is an essential part of this process, in which (non-directive) therapy can give a helping hand.

In developing this new frame Gendlin's main emphasis is "existential." Phenomenology is simply the method for handling the subjective existential aspect of the living process. It is this increasing reflection on the approach rather than on its material contributions which may account for Gendlin's stronger interest in phenomenology and in phenomenological philosophy as such. From this point it is instructive to watch how his initial philosophical chapter, which uses Dewey's concept of experience as its point of departure, leads him to an intensive study of phenomenological philosophers in an appendix of the book. But Gendlin leaves no doubt about the fact that to him, and not only to the interested reader, Husserl, Sartre, and Merleau-Ponty are his most important supports. Specifically, he credits Husserl (*Logische Untersuchungen*) for his plea for wordless (pre-predicative) thought, Sartre for his views about the "implicit meaningfulness of feeling," and Merleau-Ponty for the roles of feeling in meaning.

But ultimately it is not labels that count. It is characteristic

18. Rogers, "Theory of Therapy, Personality, and Interpersonal Relationships," in Koch, *Psychology*, III, 251; Gendlin, *Experiencing and the Creation of Meaning*, p. 48.

19. Rogers, "Theory of Therapy, Personality, and Interpersonal Relationships," III, 242 ff.

that Gendlin in his constructive appraisal at the end of Moustakas' volume on *Existential Child Therapy* interprets phenomenological existentialism as an approach which "aims to explicate directly what we concretely are, live and experience" (p. 233) as "experiential theory" and "experiential psychotherapy" [20] (p. 246). Its main function is to integrate experiencing and conceptual reflection in a creative exchange.

C. *The Place of Phenomenology in Rogers' Psychology*

To claim all of Rogers' psychology for phenomenology would clearly stretch one's classifications to the breaking point. Not only did Rogers adopt the label only late and incidentally, but it is also rather obvious that he never tried to practice phenomenology consciously. At best one can say that in retrospect he acknowledged that his approach had considerable affinity with that of the phenomenologists as he understood them. As he himself put it in his autobiography:

> I was surprised to find, about 1951 [i.e., the publishing date of *Client-Centered Therapy*] that the direction of my thinking and the central aspects of my therapeutic work could justifiably be labeled existential and phenomenological. It seems odd for an American psychologist to be in such strange company. Today these are significant influences on our profession.[21]

It may also be asserted that he consciously took over phenomenological stimulations and contributions first from Snygg and Combs and later from Gendlin. What phenomenology meant for him was the rehabilitation of the subjective experience.

But this must not make one overlook the fact that Rogers was increasingly concerned about the objective and "scientific" verification and measuring of his subjective findings. In this sense it may be claimed that Rogers was at least as much an objectivist as a phenomenological subjectivist. But it is necessary to study more closely what his objective verification involved. For instance, change in personality is measured less on the basis of actual behavior than of standardized preferences as exemplified by Stephenson's Q-sorts. In this sense Rogers' objective

20. *Existential Child Therapy*, ed. Clark Moustakas (New York: Basic Books, 1966).

21. *A History of Psychology in Autobiography*, ed. E. G. Boring and G. Lindzey (New York: Appleton-Century-Crofts, 1967), V, 378.

measurement means only the correlation of one type of subjective experience of change with another (preference choice).

To Rogers phenomenology served as a methodological ally. In turn Rogers' increasing recognition of phenomenology was one of the important factors in its naturalization in America and its reception into active research.

[5] American Phenomenology in the Fifties

Perhaps the best picture of the state of indigenous American phenomenology, free from philosophical infiltration, can be obtained from Kuenzli's anthology,[22] which begins with Snygg's article of 1941 on the need for a phenomenological system of psychology. In this volume phenomenology, which is never explicitly defined, seems to consist in the study of the "phenomenological field," the "phenomenal self," and related topics. Kurt Lewin is the name most frequently mentioned. However, what constitutes the "problem" of this phenomenology is not explicitly stated; but presumably it concerns the adequacy of such an approach. The volume includes five papers on the self by Combs, Carl Rogers, Victor Raimy, Lawrence K. Frank (1939), and Saul Rosenzweig, and five about social psychology ("The Self and Others") by R. B. MacLeod, Hadley Cantril, Theodore M. Newcomb, Carl Rogers, and Abraham S. Luchins. Of the three papers by discussants, one by Brewster Smith challenges the extreme position according to which the study of the phenomenal field is not only necessary but sufficient for psychological prediction; it is followed by a rejoinder from Snygg and Combs and a final paper by Jessor pleading the compatibility of phenomenological and non-phenomenological psychology.

Such a psychology has every right to exist on its own, even if it is no more able to make good on its promise of better prediction than the usual stimulus-response psychology. But it should not be forgotten that this psychology has historical roots in a phenomenological philosophy. Renewed contact with it should benefit its further development.[23]

22. *The Phenomenological Problem*, ed. Alfred E. Kuenzli (New York: Harper, 1959).

23. See my essay, "The Relevance of Phenomenological Philosophy for Psychology," pp. 219–41, in *Phenomenology and Existentialism*, ed. E. N. Lee and Maurice Mandelebaum (Baltimore, Md.: Johns Hopkins Press, 1967).

[6] Rollo May (b. 1907)

A. *The Role of Phenomenology in May's Existential Psychology*

At the moment the most influential native American spokesman for an existential phenomenology may well be Rollo May. Not only by his own writings, but by bringing together a considerable group of American psychologists and philosophers sympathetic to existential and phenomenological psychology and psychiatry, has he prepared the climate for a new approach to phenomenological psychology, both creative and critical.

While Rollo May's interest in existential thought goes back to his very first publications, his emphasis on phenomenology as such is relatively recent. Even in the anthology on *Existence*, of which Rollo May served as the main editor, his own introductory contribution hardly mentions "phenomenology." It enters merely in the layout of the two sections of translations, where Part II is entitled "Phenomenology," Part III, "Existential Analysis." This division is apparently based on a distinction developed by May's psychiatric contributor Henry F. Ellenberger. May's interpretation of this distinction became fully clear from his presentation of phenomenology at the Cincinnati Symposium of 1959 on Existential Psychology as "the first stage in the existential therapeutic movement," which he characterized as a "helpful breakthrough for many of us."

May did not discuss phenomenology explicitly until the first Lexington Conference on "Phenomenology: Pure and Applied," where, actually at the request of Erwin Straus, he spoke about "The Phenomenological Bases of Psychotherapy." [24] Here May, without attempting to develop his conception, assigned it the task of bridging the gap between theory and psychotherapy while also providing a new basis for the best insights in Freudian psychoanalysis through a better understanding of the fundamental nature of man, transference, and the unconscious.

24. *Phenomenology: Pure and Applied*, ed. Erwin Straus (Pittsburgh, Pa.: Duquesne University Press, 1964), pp. 166–84; republished with slight changes as "A Phenomenological Approach to Psychotherapy," in *Psychology and the Human Dilemma* (New York: Van Nostrand Reinhold, 1966), pp. 111–27.

B. *May's Way to Phenomenology*

This is not the place for an intellectual biography of a living author such as May. At best we can attempt to find the reasons why existential phenomenology met some of his personal, and in particular his intellectual, needs.

May began his early adulthood as an artist in Europe and has never abandoned his interest in artistic creativity.[25] But it is significant that early in his life he took part in Alfred Adler's summer school on the Semmering Pass.[26] But, clearly, May did not accept Adler without reservation. In discussing the theory of anxiety in the context of Adler's theory of inferiority, May spoke of Adler's oversimplifications and generalities.[27] In the years after 1933, May made contact with two of the leading refugee scholars from Germany: Kurt Goldstein and Paul Tillich. Goldstein acquainted him not only with his organismic theory and his idea of self-actualization but also with his view of anxiety as a catastrophic reaction of the organism. Tillich, whose courses at Union Theological Seminary May attended regularly, gave him his first access to existential thought, to Kierkegaard, and to Heidegger.

In the thirties May began his psychological work as a counselor who, judging from his first book on *The Art of Counseling*, had adopted on the whole the approach of liberal theology. His first major work on *The Meaning of Anxiety* (1950), based in part on his personal experience as a victim of tuberculosis, saw anxiety as both the problem of the age and the basic symptom of neurosis. On the whole this was a descriptive study with a keen sense for the varieties of the experience. It ranges from Spinoza via Pascal to Kierkegaard. May questions biologists, psychiatrists, and sociologists as well as philosophers. But Heidegger hardly enters and is seen merely through the perspective of Tillich. In mentioning the existentialist movement (p. 29), May does not yet give the impression of identifying with it. A rich collection of case studies follows. Freud and Kierkegaard emerge

25. "The Nature of Creativity," in *Creativity and Its Cultivation*, ed. H. H. Anderson (New York: Harper Row, 1959), pp. 55–68.

26. See the reference to "the humble and penetrating wisdom of Alfred Adler, with whom I have had the privilege of studying, associating, and discussing intimately." *The Art of Counseling* (Nashville, Tenn.: Abingdon, 1939), pp. 7 ff.

27. *The Meaning of Anxiety* (New York: Ronald, 1950), p. 135.

as those with the deepest insight into anxiety. The question of how to meet anxiety leads to the question of the development of the self (p. 232), to which anxiety is intimately related.

Accordingly, *Man's Search for Himself* (1953) is the title of May's first work to carry an independent message. It contains May's pre-existentialist attempt to meet the problem stated in the title. The point of departure of this search is "our predicament," which, apart from loneliness and anxiety, is characterized by five losses. Of these, the most significant are the loss of the center of values in our society, the loss of the sense of self, and the loss of the sense of tragedy. May's solution is chiefly the rediscovery of selfhood culminating in creative self-consciousness.

May's close contact with the new European existential psychology and philosophy seems to have begun around this time—i.e., in 1954, four years later before the appearance of *Existence.* The volume itself did not pretend to do more than give better access to the European schools. Nevertheless, May's first essay, "The Origins and Significance of the Existential Movement in Psychology," claimed the superiority of the new approach over that of Freud in deepening "the understanding of man on the deeper and broader level," uniting science and ontology. May's second essay, "Contributions of Existential Psychotherapy," revealed his own adoption and assimilation of some of the new conceptions. This becomes particularly clear in his interpretation of what he considered to be the main insights of existential ontology. They include being and non-being, anxiety, being-in-the-world, the three modes of world as seen by Binswanger, time and history, and finally implications for psychotherapeutic technique.

The essays that May has written since 1951 have been collected in a book entitled *Psychology and the Human Dilemma* (1967), which interprets man's "dilemma" as his capacity to experience himself as both subject and object at the same time. (This actually turns out to be not a dilemma in the technical sense but a "dialectical" relationship between two indispensable approaches.) In singling out three valuable emphases of the existential movement, he begins with "the new way of seeing the reality of the patient called phenomenology," tracing it back to Husserl and characterizing it as "essentially and in its simplest terms the endeavor to take the phenomenon as given without asking at once for its causal explanation."

Love and Will (1969), May's latest book, is perhaps his most original, outspoken, and constructive in therapeutic and cultural respects. It is another question how far this work should be put to the credit of his phenomenology, which, as a matter of fact, is hardly mentioned by name. However, especially in his climactic Chapter IX, he does try to relate intentionality to phenomenology in the sense of Brentano, Husserl, and Heidegger. But his conception of intentionality, as expressed in his main definition ("the structure which gives meaning to experience"), apart from being far from clear and consistent throughout the book, has little if anything to do with the phenomenological tradition, in spite of May's seeming quotations based on secondary sources, which may account for some of the misunderstandings. His puzzling distinction between "intentionality" and "intention" becomes somewhat clearer in the light of his dependence upon Paul Tillich. Tillich had first developed this distinction in his *Systematic Theology,* written shortly before *The Courage to Be,* from which May quotes at the end of his chapter.[28] In the latter book Tillich made the terminological recommendation of using "intentionality" in contrast to "vitality" and as a substitute for the discredited term "spirituality." Although in *Systematic Theology* Tillich had wisely avoided any claims to a phenomenological precedent for this use, in *The Courage to Be* (p. 81), less wisely, he referred sweepingly to "the medieval philosophers" as parallels.

C. *Some Phenomenological Themes*

May's own existential psychology contains a number of motifs that are of phenomenological interest, some of them dating back to his pre-existential period. I am thinking here particularly of his conception of the self, which differs significantly from that of Snygg and Rogers and comes out most clearly in his interpretation of "existence." How little such existential philosophers as Heidegger and Sartre make of the personal I-consciousness is generally overlooked. For May, existence is experienced most explicitly in the "I-am" experience, the act of contact with and acceptance of the fact that "I am." [29] In fact, he sees in this the basis for the solution of a person's problems and for ego-development.

28. Paul Tillich, *Systematic Theology* (Chicago: University of Chicago Press, 1951), I, 181 ff., *The Courage to Be* (New Haven, Conn.: Yale University Press, 1952).

29. *Existence*, ed. Rollo May, Ernest Angel, Henri F. Ellenberger (New York: Basic Books, 1958), pp. 43 ff.

May has developed this theme even more fully in his contribution to the Cincinnati Symposium of 1959 [30] in which he gives the following characteristics of the self as self: (1) centeredness; (2) self-affirmation as the need to preserve centeredness; (3) the need and opportunity to step beyond centeredness and to participate; (4) awareness of centeredness; (5) self-consciousness as the human form of centeredness; and (6) anxiety.

These characteristics deserve comment.

1. The centeredness of the self was an increasingly important theme in the anthropology of Paul Tillich, to whom May feels so deeply indebted. Yet "the principle of centeredness" appears explicitly only in the third volume of Tillich's *Systematic Theology* (1963). There is no point in raising the question of priority. But the concept is certainly not a mere loan on May's part. The real question is that of the exact meaning of the term "centeredness."

2. The need to preserve centeredness leads to an original interpretation of mental sickness, namely, as an attempt to preserve centeredness by retrenchment. This interpretation is clearly related to Kurt Goldstein's view of anxiety as a catastrophic response.

3. The need to reach out seems related to the concept of intentionality and existentialist transcendence.

4. The emphasis on awareness, as distinguished from self-consciousness, is indicative of May's attempt to assimilate the Freudian conception of the unconscious which, he has warned, must not be neglected.

5. May sees in self-consciousness the unique chance and task of man, which has to be supported in therapy.

6. What is most characteristic of May is perhaps his Kierkegaardian emphasis on the essential connection between selfhood and anxiety as the sense of the possibility of non-being and even self-destruction. This is what he also calls the tragic nature of human existence, something which he feels is prematurely denied by the optimistic views of human nature that are represented in Rogers' belief in the powers of the human self. This emphasis on the tragic and even the demonic sides of human nature is a distinctive feature of May's semi-theological view of man. Yet even in these features May sees a new possibility for human dignity. Thus he finds in the tragedy of Oedipus the King only one part of the Oedipus symbol, which must be matched by

30. "Existential Bases of Psychotherapy," *Existential Psychology* (New York: Random House, 1961), pp. 75 ff.

the reconciliation in the second Oedipus tragedy, in which evil becomes a blessing.

Obviously, phenomenology is not May's primary interest. His main concern is a new existential view of man capable of supporting a therapy that can strengthen the self in facing the anxieties of life, and particularly of modern life. This seemed to be the promise of the new existential thought initiated by Kierkegaard, Tillich, and Goldstein. Binswanger was to May the one who had come farthest in fulfilling the promises of the new existential psychology. And Binswanger was at the same time the main guide to phenomenology, the major tool of his *Daseinsanalyse*.

[7] *Existence (1958)*

THE PUBLICATION in 1958 of the 446-page volume, *Existence: A New Dimension in Psychiatry and Psychology*, under the joint editorship of Rollo May, Ernest Angel, and Henri F. Ellenberger may be considered the most important event in the development of American phenomenological existentialism. It offered for the first time a representative selection in translation from the new European literature. But the three introductory chapters, two by May and one by Ellenberger, a native of Switzerland, amounting to more than a quarter of the volume, were at least of equal importance.

Actually, the initiative for the volume came not from Rollo May but from Ernest Angel, a psychologist and coeditor of Basic Books, who was chiefly interested in the translations and who, together, with Ellenberger, decided on the selections. Rollo May acted only as the coordinator and also consulted Paul Tillich on the whole project.

May's two introductory chapters presented the new movement in the light of his own original approach. Ellenberger's "Clinical Introduction to Psychiatric Phenomenology," based on a more European perspective, de-emphasized the ties with philosophical phenomenology. But at the same time Ellenberger tried to distinguish between several kinds of psychiatric phenomenology such as descriptive phenomenology, genetic-structural phenomenology (Minkowski), and "categorical phenomenology" (Ellenberger's own contribution). Existential analysis was presented as more comprehensive than these phenomenologies and also as therapeutically oriented.

The translations were divided into two halves, entitled "Phenomenology" and "Existential Analysis" respectively. The first group of some sixty pages began with a case study in schizophrenia by Minkowski, who, in the dedication of the volume, was cited as "the pioneer of phenomenological psychiatry." This piece was followed by a lecture of Erwin Straus of 1948 and an article by von Gebsattel (on the world of the compulsive) of 1938. The second group, which filled more than half of the volume, consisted of three texts by Binswanger, called in the dedication "explorer in existential analysis," and one by Roland Kuhn; the first is a Binswanger article of 1946, explaining the research trend (*Forschungsrichtung*) of *Daseinsanalyse* in psychiatry.[31] It is followed by two of Binswanger's case studies on schizophrenia and Kuhn's paper on the case of a manic-depressive. The implication of the division into the two groups seemed to be that phenomenology is a less-developed phase of existential analysis. But it does not become clear that Binswanger had done his major work in phenomenology before he had begun his existential phase—prior to the entry of Minkowski, Straus, and Gebsattel into the field. The selections made good sense as illustrations. But in the light of the material surveyed in Part II of this book, beginning with Jaspers, *Existence* obviously failed to give an adequate idea of the range of the new movement. More important in the present context is the fact that there was a certain tendency to minimize the "confusing interference of philosophy into the field of psychiatry" (p. 92). Thus Husserl's role is minimized and Scheler is not even mentioned.

[8] Since *Existence*

The appearance of the Rollo May volume signaled the beginning of a new wave of phenomenological and existential activity. Perhaps the most characteristic symptom was the almost simultaneous birth of several existentially oriented magazines, usually connected with new societies which hold more or less regular meetings with lectures and discussions. All of them prefer existential to phenomenological labels. No matter what name takes precedence in the American consciousness, the two are certainly closely connected, if not identified.

31. The translation of the title as "The Existential Analysis School of Thought" is misleading.

However, what is the significance of the explosion and particularly the value of the new production within and without these new organizations? The *Journal of Existential Psychiatry*, started in 1960 by Jordan Scher in Chicago, was backed by an imposing roster of names on its editorial board, both American and foreign, and by an "ontoanalytic" association. In 1964 it was converted into a more philosophical *Journal of Existentialism* under new editors.[32] The first issue, preceded by "Prolegomena" which proclaim a belief in man as being more than a "mechanical or statistical abstract," began with a paper by Viktor Frankl ("Beyond Self-Actualization"), who figures frequently among its contributors, as do Minkowski, Binswanger, Medard Boss, and others, who appear in translated texts. However, no definite pattern can be perceived in these pieces nor in those of the increasing number of American contributors. Phenomenology is mentioned only incidentally. Nor does there seem to be any explicit attempt to clarify the meaning of Scher's new term "ontoanalysis."

The *Review of Existential Psychology and Psychiatry* technically began one year later (1961). But it was preceded by a journal *Existential Inquiries* that was started in 1959 in mimeographed form by Rollo May. Later it was published by Duquesne University Press, with Adrian Van Kaam as its first editor. The editorial board largely overlapped with that of the *Journal of Existential Psychiatry*. Behind the *Review* stands the *American Association for Existential Psychology and Psychiatry*, which began with a conference in New York in 1959, followed by a symposium on existential psychology at the Annual Convention of the American Psychological Association in Cincinnati, at which Abraham Maslow and Gordon Allport took prominent parts.[33] Since then the *Review* has published contributions by such leading Europeans as Frankl, Paul Tillich, J. J. Buytendijk, Gabriel Marcel, Helmut Plessner, and Medard Boss, as well as by Americans like Carl Rogers.

Whereas previously the emphasis has been on existential motifs, with phenomenology mentioned only as a method of existentialism, phenomenological titles and contributions have lately been on the increase.

32. In 1966 Scher started a new journal, *Existential Psychiatry*, apparently along the original lines of the earlier *Journal of Existential Psychiatry*.

33. These papers have since been published under the title *Existential Psychology* (see above, n. 30).

The American Journal of Psychoanalysis, the main outlet of the Karen Horney secession from the main American psychoanalytic organization, has recently opened up its columns increasingly to existentialism and has published symposia with Paul Tillich and Rollo May as participants. In fact, its main editor Horace Kelman has published two installments of a paper entitled "A Phenomenological Approach to Dream Interpretation" (XXV [1965], 188–202; XXVII [1968], 75–94).

The growing interest in *Individual Psychology*, chief organ of the American Adlerites, has been mentioned previously (Chapter 4). What would be more important than journal publication would clearly be the production of books by new American authors who would make sustained use of the phenomenological and existential approach. However, thus far the output is still on a limited scale.

Apparently, it was Abraham Maslow who coined the phase "Third Force Psychology" for a new type of psychology other than behaviorism and psychoanalysis. It includes phenomenology as one of the many sub-movements that range from the New-Freudians to such "personologists" as H. A. Murray. As far as a specific program is concerned, a volume of essays by Maslow himself perhaps has been the most influential.[34] He attached special importance to the existentialists, much as he deplored some of their intricacies and vaguenesses. He also saw that "existentialism rests on phenomenology; i.e., it uses personal, subjective experience as the foundation upon which abstract knowledge is built."

As to his own psychology of being (not related to the frequent emphasis on ontology), it was to a large extent a development of Kurt Goldstein's conception of self-actualization. Such self-actualization manifests itself particularly in what Maslow called "peak-experiences." It is in this connection that he referred repeatedly to a phenomenological approach, but without making it exclusive and without engaging in detailed description and analysis (pp. 92 ff.).

Maslow also has been the leading spirit of a new movement called "Humanistic Psychology," supported by a growing association and publishing a *Journal of Humanistic Psychology*. Erich Fromm, Kurt Goldstein, Karen Horney, and Gordon Allport were invoked as some of its inspirers, though they do not figure among the contributors. However, Maslow himself, Charlotte Buehler,

34. *Toward a Psychology of Being* (New York: Van Nostrand, 1962), pp. ix, 9.

James Bugental, Carl Rogers, and many others not only appear on the masthead of the *Journal* but are represented on its pages. "Existential Psychology" and "Phenomenological Psychology" are mentioned as congenial attempts to "open up the vast and crucial inner life of man." But as such they do not play a conspicuous part in the multifaceted activities of the "Third Force." Thus, in the collective volume *Challenges of Humanistic Psychology*, phenomenology in the philosophical sense of Husserl figures only in the contributions by Colin Wilson.[35]

James Bugental's *The Search for Authenticity* [36] is meant as an existential analytic approach to psychotherapy. It is an attempt to combine a "humanistic psychology" with existentialism, without much explicit transatlantic borrowing. However, the view of human existence here presented is anything but easy-going. It stresses the essentially tragic side of human existence, as did Rollo May. Phenomenology is mentioned in passing, in the characterization of humanistic psychology as both valuing meaning and based on human "validation." It is equally implicit in the existential approach as the "phenomenological root" of such a psychology (p. 18). But while many of the phases of the analytic therapy (which makes ample use of Freudian suggestions, particularly the "ontogonic" phase meant to rebuild existence) can be related to phenomenology, especially through Bugental's stress on "awareness," there is in this therapeutically oriented book no attempt to develop an explicit phenomenology of authenticity. By this term Bugental understands primarily being-in-the-world in accord with the givenness of man's nature and of the world (p. 32)—hardly a conception that would be acceptable to Heidegger or Binswanger.

Joseph Lyons in his *Psychology and the Measure of Man* [37] offers a "phenomenological approach" to clinical problems. The goal is "a true science of man" as a person, not as an "impersonal Other." However, this well-written essay, dealing also with such topics as "Situation and Encounter," is on the whole mostly metaphenomenology, discussing critically and sympathetically previous work in the field. Thus, under the heading "the intentional subject," Lyons discusses the role of the clinical therapist as partner with his client, using the term "intentionality" in a highly

35. Colin Wilson, "Existential Psychology: A Novelist's Approach," in *Challenges of Humanistic Psychology*, ed. James Bugental (New York: McGraw-Hill, 1967), pp. 69–78.

36. *The Search for Authenticity: An Existential-Analytic Approach* (New York: Holt, Rinehart & Winston, 1965).

37. (Glencoe, Ill.: Free Press, 1963).

personal sense (p. 225). On the whole, this is a phenomenology dealing with the clinical psychologist, not with phenomenological psychology as such.

Adrian van Kaam, a native Dutchman, has done a great deal to establish phenomenological psychology, not only at Duquesne University but generally in the American academic world, particularly through his editorial enterprises. However, these by no means exhaust his energies. Trained in Holland, he did as his doctoral dissertation at Western Reserve University a "Phenomenal Analysis: Exemplified by a Study of the Experience of 'Really Feeling Understood'" under the partial supervision of Kurt Goldstein, Abraham Maslow, and Carl Rogers. It now figures as the main illustration of applied phenomenology in his book on *Existential Foundations of Psychology* (1966).

Ostensibly, this book keeps away from phenomenological philosophy. As far as psychology is concerned, it is a treatise *about* existential psychology, as the author conceives of it, rather than a sample of it. It stresses its "anthropological" component. The later chapters deal with "anthropological phenomenology," in which van Kaam distinguishes several subdivisions. Considering phenomenology primarily as a mode of "anthropological" existence or an attitude, he believes that the phenomenological method should be the foundation for the study of all human behavior and stresses the perspective nature of all experience.

Obviously, this is not yet more than a beginning. It will probably take much more time and effort before the new European ingredients have been critically absorbed and integrated into the mainstream of the American tradition. And it will take even more time before original and large-scale systematic work can be expected. Meanwhile, the following words by a sympathetic Dutch observer may be worth pondering:

> If the followers of Sullivan, those of phenomenological anthropology and of psychoanalysis should manage to meet on common ground, the collaboration not yet accomplished between them would open up to them ways to new important insights.[38]

38. Translated from H. C. Rümke, "Aspects of the Schizophrenia Problem" (1963) in *Eine blühende Psychiatrie in Gefahr* (Berlin: Springer, 1967), p. 226.

PART II

Studies on Major Figures in Phenomenological Psychology and Psychiatry

Introduction

THE FOLLOWING TEN CHAPTERS were written as independent studies. Their sequence is neither strictly chronological nor systematic. The Jaspers chapter leads off because of his pioneering role in the development of phenomenological psychiatry. The next four chapters (Binswanger, Minkowski, von Gebsattel and Straus) deal with four phenomenological anthropologists, who formed a loose alliance. Buytendijk (Chapter 11) is a relatively independent figure. The arrangement of the remaining four studies reflects Goldstein's affinity to Buytendijk, and the concern of Schilder, Boss, and Frankl with various forms of psychoanalysis.

Even the structure of each study is not exactly symmetrical. But generally the attempt has been made to determine comparatively the subject's relation to philosophical phenomenology, his conception of phenomenology, and some of his most original uses of it.

6 / Karl Jaspers (1883–1969): Introducing Phenomenology into Psychopathology

[1] Jaspers' Place in the History of Phenomenological Psychopathology

No student of the development of phenomenological psychopathology would think of contesting Jaspers' historic role in initiating a new phenomenological trend in this field. The strange thing is that Jaspers himself did not think of himself as a phenomenologist, even as far as psychopathology was concerned.[1] Yet there can be little question about the fact that objectively phenomenology could not have achieved the position in psychopathology which it now holds without Jaspers' pioneering. It also would be hard to deny that around 1912, when Jaspers wrote his article, "The Phenomenological Trend in Psychopathology," he considered himself an active supporter of this trend (*Forschungsrichtung*). Historically, it would therefore be impossible to suppress his part in the development of phenomenological psychopathology.

However, since Jaspers' relation to phenomenology and to phenomenological philosophy in particular is at the very least an

1. Thus in the 4th edition of the *Allgemeine Psychopathologie* (Berlin: Springer, 1946), p. 42 (hereafter abbreviated as *AP*), and again in the preface to the 7th edition (Berlin: Springer, 1959), he protests specifically against the misinterpretation of this book as "the major work of the phenomenological trend." In fact, on the occasion of an extended interview in April, 1962, which put me in his special debt, he made a point of dissociating himself not only from phenomenology as a philosophy but from the new phenomenological psychopathology. The 7th edition of *AP* has been translated into English by J. Hoenig and Marian W. Hamilton, *General Psychopathology* (Chicago: University of Chicago Press, 1963).

ambivalent one, I shall attempt first to establish the main facts of this relationship. Next, I shall try to determine the connections between psychopathology and Jaspers' philosophy and to study the rise of phenomenology within this psychopathology. A discussion of Jaspers' conception of the phenomenological method will be followed by some illustrations of its use in psychopathology. This scheme should make it possible to assess the real significance of phenomenology for Jaspers' psychopathology.

[2] Jaspers' Relation to the Phenomenological Movement

Any attempt to relate Jaspers' psychopathology to the Phenomenological Movement should begin by recording the chronological facts, and especially Jaspers' own perspective of these facts.[2]

Jaspers himself states that it was not until 1909 that he became aware of Husserl, clearly by reading his *Logische Untersuchungen.*[3] What impressed him about Husserl's "phenomenology" was, in ascending order, its usability for the description of the experiences of the mentally ill, the discipline of Husserl's thinking, his conquest of psychologism, and his insistence on the clarification of unnoticed assumptions:

> I found confirmed what was already at work in me: the urge to the things themselves [*Drang zu den Sachen selbst*]. In a world full of prejudices, schematisms, conventions, this was at the time like a liberation. Husserl made the comparatively strongest impression on me. True, I did not consider his phenomenological method a philosophical procedure, but as he himself had considered it at first, as descriptive psychology. I used it as such, gave such descriptions in psychopathology, and formulated the method in its principles for use in psychopathology . . .[4]

2. Only after the completion of my manuscript did I receive a copy of Oswald O. Schrag's *Existence, Existenz and Transcendence: The Philosophy of Karl Jaspers* (Pittsburgh, Pa.: Duquesne University Press, 1971); the fifth chapter ("Jaspers and Phenomenology") contains a generally perceptive and judicious discussion of Jaspers' relations to Husserl and Heidegger.

3. "Mein Weg zur Philosophie" (1951), in *Rechenschaft und Ausblick* (Munich: Piper, 1958), p. 386.

4. *Ibid.* About the genesis of this work, see also the "Nachwort zu meiner Philosophie," in *Philosophie*, 3d ed. (Heidelberg: Springer, 1955), I, xv–lv.

However, only Jaspers' fourth publication, his "Analysis of Hallucination" (1911), refers to Husserl explicitly in several places, not only by commending the second volume of his *Logische Untersuchungen,* and especially its fifth investigation (on intentionality) as "the clearest and most unobjectionable expression" of the proper interpretation of perception, but by adding that his own "summary analysis of perception, which neglects important distinctions, had its point of departure in Husserl's investigations." Other references show Jaspers' acquaintance with the details of these analyses.[5]

But the most explicit testimony to the appeal of Husserl's phenomenology for Jaspers is his article of 1912 on the phenomenological trend in psychopathology. Here, after showing the need for an independent phenomenology within psychopathology as an indispensable preparation for explanatory theory, he acknowledged that:

> in the area of psychological research E. Husserl has taken the decisive step toward a systematic phenomenology, after the ground had been prepared by Brentano and his school and by Theodore Lipps (*GSzP,* p. 316).

A footnote on the same page mentioning earlier independent psychopathological studies by Kandinsky, Oesterreich, and Hacker, refers to his own articles on hallucinations as examples of this approach. But Jaspers then adds that there is not yet a generally acknowledged trend of research (*Forschungsrichtung*) deliberately preparing the ground for the tasks of psychopathology.[6] The final appeal of the article is not for a fundamental reform but for a further spread of the phenomenological attitude among psychiatrists.

Jaspers sent reprints of these two studies to Husserl and received from him a very laudatory acknowledgment. However, by this time Jaspers had also seen Husserl's programmatic article on "Philosophy as a Rigorous Science" (1910), which he had read with admiration for its single-mindedness, but with indignation at its "perversion" of philosophy by the attempt to transform it

5. "Zur Analyse der Trugwahrnehmungen," in *Zeitschrift für die gesamte Neurologie und Psychiatrie,* VI (1911), 469; also in *Gesammelte Schriften zur Psychopathologie,* 7th ed. (Berlin: Springer, 1963), p. 198 (hereafter abbreviated as *GSzP*). See also *AP,* Part I, chap. 1, §1d.

6. "Die phänomenologische Forschungsrichtung," *GSzP,* p. 316.

into science.[7] Then, in 1913, the year in which both the first volume of Husserl's yearbook with his own *Ideas toward a Pure Phenomenology* and Jaspers' *General Psychopathology* appeared, there was a first personal encounter in Göttingen that resulted from Husserl's special invitation to Jaspers, who happened to be visiting a common friend. As Jaspers described the scene, Husserl's attempt to embrace Jaspers as one of his disciples repelled him, in spite of Husserl's compliments for his expert practice of phenomenology in his writings. But what seems to have disillusioned Jaspers even more was Husserl's disregard for Schelling, as being a philosopher of no serious importance. A later visit to Husserl in Freiburg in 1921 clearly did not change anything in Jaspers' estimate of Husserl; he continued to see him as a likeable scholar but not a great philosopher.[8]

However, the most important document for assessing Jaspers' relation to phenomenology remains his *General Psychopathology* of 1913. One must realize that the primary purpose of this work was that it serve as an introduction to psychopathological thinking for students who in the more traditional texts had been given, on the whole, a mere summary of findings, more or less organized and dogmatically presented. To Jaspers, the proper subject matter of psychopathology was "the actual conscious psychic events" (p. 2). His intention was for his book to be "general" in the sense of aiming at an essential grasp of the subject (*Wesenserfassung*) rather than at a collection of all the results of psychopathology (p. 33). Accordingly, methodological reflections and, especially in the later editions, philosophical considerations abound in the actual development of the book.

In the present context the main consideration concerns the place of phenomenology in the general pattern of this work. In the first and longest of the seven chapters of the original book,

7. *Rechenschaft und Ausblick,* p. 386. See also the "Nachwort zu meiner Philosophie" on Jaspers' "disgust" (*Widerwillen*) about Husserl's article:

> For here, in the sharpness of thinking and consistent reasoning, the philosophy which was essential to me was once more repudiated. The essay became for me a revelation. For I fathomed, as I believed, that here most pointedly the place had been reached where, because of the claim to rigorous science, everything that could be called philosophy in the high sense of this word had come to an end. Insofar as Husserl was a professor of philosophy, he seemed to me to have committed a betrayal of philosophy in the most naïve and pretentious manner" (p. xvii; my translation).

8. Some of the above information is based on a conversation that I had with Jaspers in April, 1962.

the term "phenomenology" is added in parentheses after its main title ("The Subjective Phenomena of the Abnormal Psychic Life"). "Phenomenology" had already been characterized in the Introduction in the section on methodology (p. 4). In the chapter itself only the first footnote refers to Husserl:

> Initially Husserl uses the term for "descriptive psychology" of the phenomena of consciousness, in which sense it applies to our investigations, but later he uses it for essential insight [*Wesensschau*], in which we do not engage.

Thus, even at this stage, Jaspers identified only with a part of Husserl's phenomenology, in fact a part already transcended by its author, who as early as 1903 had repudiated as misleading the label "descriptive psychology." In the actual development of his chapter, however, Jaspers makes ample use of Husserl's general analysis of consciousness with its pattern of intentional acts referring to intentional objects.

In the nine editions of the work with their extensive revisions, the phenomenological chapter has grown considerably, but it does not seem to have changed its basic character or position, though it now has become a subdivision of the first of six parts about the "Separate Elements [*Einzeltatbestände*] of the Life of the Soul."

It may be worth mentioning that there is no explicit reference to phenomenology in Jaspers' proto-existentialist *Psychologie der Weltanschauungen* (1919). But his brilliant biographical case study of Strindberg and Van Gogh (1922) includes an explicit "phenomenological inventory" (p. 53) of Strindberg's "consciousness of objects" (*Gegenstandsbewusstsein*), pp. 49 ff.[9] However, in Jaspers' almost complete turn to philosophy, his interest in Husserlian phenomenology had practically disappeared. When he uses the term at all, as in the section on the will in the second volume of his *Philosophie,* it becomes clear that phenomenological description is incapable of grasping the real essence of the will. Jaspers came back to the subject only in connection with the interrogation conducted by some of the contributors to the Karl Jaspers volume of Paul Schilpp's Library of Living Philosophers, who tried to explore the reduced role of phenomenology in the existential "elucidations" of his *Philosophie.* But by now Jaspers opposed explicitly any merger of phenomenology and existential

9. "Strindberg und van Gogh," in *Arbeiten zer augewandten Psychiatrie* (Bern: Bircher, 1927).

thought. He even spoke of the "radical difference" between phenomenology of consciousness and elucidation of existence.[10]

In fact, my own more direct information makes it clear that in his last perspective Jaspers minimized the role of Husserlian phenomenology to such an extent that he no longer assigned to it a decisive role for his own development, even in psychopathology.

This raises the question of whether other members of the Phenomenological Movement had any significance for the development of Jaspers' psychopathology. Jaspers mentioned explicitly such descriptive psychologists as Theodor Lipps and his school (*GSzP*, p. 316), as well as members of the congenial Würzburg school like Oswald Külpe and August Messer. But the only members of the "older movement" in Göttingen and Munich who were singled out were Moritz Geiger (whom he knew personally), for his special contributions to the phenomenological psychology of feeling (*AP*, p. 328; Eng. trans., p. 108), and Wilhelm Schapp, for his phenomenology of perception (*AP*, p. 197; Eng. trans., p. 108). Max Scheler, whose genius Jaspers recognized, but whose personality did not appeal to him, was given specific credit for his phenomenology of *ressentiment* (*AP*, p. 270; Eng. trans., p. 325) and his phenomenology of sympathy.

Most intriguing is Jaspers' relation to Heidegger, again an original thinker whose philosophical power attracted Jaspers, especially in the beginning, but whom he rejected all the more strongly on the basis of his political record and its moral implications. In the present context, the decisive fact is that, when Heidegger emerged, Jaspers' interest in psychopathology and its phenomenology had already become secondary. Hence Heidegger was mentioned only once in the later editions of the *Psychopathologie*, and that only in connection with his ontology of man, an ontology whose claim to ultimate knowledge Jaspers considered incompatible with true philosophy. In the only place where Jaspers dealt with Heidegger's phenomenological ontology explicitly, i.e., in an exchange with the theologian, Rudolf Bultmann in 1953,[11] his main objection to it was that it "operated scientifically, phenomenologically, objectively" and resulted in a "non-committal phenomenological knowledge, and by the same

10. Paul Schilpp, *Philosophy of Karl Jaspers* (LaSalle, Ill.: Open Court, 1957), p. 819. German edition (Stuttgart: Kohlhammer, 1957), p. 813.

11. *Die Frage der Entmythologisierung* (Munich: Piper, 1954), p. 12. English translation, *Myth and Christianity* (New York: Noonday Press, 1958), p. 8.

token, a learnable, usable knowledge that is a perversion of philosophy" (p. 9). Yet Jaspers admitted that "psychiatrists employ Heidegger's existential categories for certain types of illness, both chronic and acute, often not without success."

Philosophically, the Phenomenological Movement as such was clearly a matter of indifference to Jaspers. But even so, phenomenology remained for him one, if not the basic, method of his psychopathology. Just how important was it? Before this question can be answered, it will be important to understand Jaspers' psychopathological enterprise in the total context of his thought.

[3] Jaspers' Conception of Philosophy and Its Relation to the Science of Psychopathology

The attempt to show the significance of philosophical phenomenology for psychology and psychopathology requires in Jaspers' case a preliminary clarification of his views about the relation between philosophy and psychopathology. For Jaspers' interpretation of this relation was certainly peculiar, based as it was on his very special conception of the relation between philosophy and science.

This relation must be understood in the light of Jaspers' conception of philosophy, which is anything but conventional. In fact, Jaspers himself made it clear that philosophy had nothing to do with what went by this name in the German universities of the time, although he acknowledged the example of the "great philosophers" such as Spinoza, his first philosophical guide. But among his contemporaries he acknowledged only one genuine philosopher, the sociologist Max Weber. He justified his own intrusion into academic philosophy, on which he had never planned at the start, as an attempt to revive genuine philosophy, in contrast especially to the so-called scientific philosophy of its major exponent in Heidelberg, the Neo-Kantian Heinrich Rickert and to Edmund Husserl, the advocate of philosophy as a "rigorous science." [12]

> When the consciousness became dominant in me that in our time there was no genuine philosophy in the universities, I thought that in the face of such a vacuum even the weak had the right to bear witness for philosophy and to say what it was and what it could be, even if he could not produce a philosophy himself. Not

12. *Rechenschaft und Ausblick*, p. 394.

> until then, when I was close to forty, did I make philosophy the task of my life.

What then, is this philosophy in Jaspers' sense, if it is not a science? Jaspers' full answer can be found only in what is still his largest, central, and favorite philosophical work, his three-volume *Philosophie* (1932). But he has reflected on it independently before and after. To try to condense the result of his efforts into a compact formula would be foolhardy. Some of his formulations, however, are at least good guides to the kind of understanding that is needed in this context. I choose the ones in his essay *Über meine Philosophie* (1941), in *Rechenschaft und Ausblick,* and in particular the statement, "Philosophy is practice, but a unique kind of practice." Philosophical meditation is thus a "performatory" act in which I "approach Being and myself, not an unconcerned thinking, in which I am occupied with an object without being involved" (pp. 401–2). Thus philosophy is no longer a theoretical enterprise. Its chief mission is to awaken, to appeal, to bring about the realization of true existence in the world. To this extent and in this sense Jaspers' primary concern in philosophy was to influence existence, though, as the *Philosophie* shows, not human existence in isolation, but existence in relation to "transcendence," i.e., that which lies beyond existence.

But what is the relation of this new enterprise to science? Is it anti-scientific? By no means. Even though Jaspers believed that philosophy and science have entirely different objectives, he held that, especially today, they need one another. In particular, philosophy, which deals with what cannot be known objectively, presupposes the exploration of what is knowable. Even though philosophy is more than science, it can only be achieved by way of the sciences. "Through the free mastery of the sciences I am to become free for what is more than science, but can become clear only by way of them."

But this general interest in science as the indispensable access to a non-scientific philosophy does not yet account for Jaspers' stake in psychopathology. At first sight there may be only biographical reasons for this. His autobiographical writings do not state explicitly why it was medical science rather than any other study that he chose when he "wanted to know what reality is," why he sought it in laboratories and hospitals rather than in the study of law, his earlier choice (p. 385). Nor did he say explicitly why he chose psychiatry as his field of specialization. But his preference for it as a way to psychology was clearly determined by his interest in man as more than an object of somatic pathology. It was here, in psychiatry, that he hoped to find out what science could tell him about the basic facts of human existence.

[4] The Rise of Phenomenology in Jaspers' Psychopathology

How seriously Jaspers took science can be gathered from his preoccupation with methods as well as with results, even before he had taken up psychiatry. But it was in psychiatry that his methodological interest became dominant. In this most ambitious and problematic field of medical research and practice Jaspers was soon struck by the confusion of approaches and theories, and on the whole by "baseless talk" (*grundloses Gerede*). "There did not seem to be a unifying common scientific psychiatry for all researchers." [13] The choice was between "brain mythology" and the "mythology of psychoanalysis." [14]

Jaspers' very first psychopathological studies revealed his concern for method. His second publication, on paranoiac jealousy, written after his dissertation on nostalgia and crime of 1910, was meant as a "contribution to the question of 'either development of personality or process.'" Here he tried to develop two basic approaches to the psychopathological material, self-transposal or empathic understanding of the phenomena in their connection and succession on the one hand, and the merely causal explanation of an unintelligible "process" on the other (*GSzP*, p. 113). Yet, he began with the statement:

> . . . we do not want to lose the sense of the inexhaustibility and the enigma of each mentally sick human being, which we ought to keep in the face of the seemingly most trivial cases (*GSzP*, p. 85).

Jaspers' characteristic impatience with the state of psychiatry is perhaps best revealed by his critical report on methods of intelligence testing and the concept of dementia, which also expresses his typical rejection of a "ready-made" system as "intolerable" (*GSzP*, p. 142 ff., esp. p. 191).

It was at this point that Jaspers became actively interested in the possibilities of phenomenology, and specifically Husserl's use

13. "Autobiographie," in Schilpp, *Philosophy of Karl Jaspers*, p. 17; German ed., p. 11.

14. *Rechenschaft und Ausblick*, p. 409.

of it in the *Logische Untersuchungen*, as shown in his own studies of illusions and paranoic ideas (*Wahn*). They were followed by his programmatic article on the phenomenological trend in psychiatry. Then came the invitation of his Heidelberg colleague, K. Wilmanns, and the publisher Springer to prepare a comprehensive general psychopathology, to which Jaspers responded not without hesitation but with enthusiasm. For he realized that this enterprise would give him the chance for a reconstruction of psychopathology along new lines. As we have already noted, he saw his main task not only in the arrangement of the facts but even more in the development of true medical thinking. Hence the new synthesis was not to result in another textbook or encyclopedic handbook. The goal was to provide conceptual clarification of what was known, how it was known, and what was not known. All methods were to be considered, but the emphasis was to be on two new methods to which Jaspers gave priority, phenomenology and what he called *verstehende Psychologie*, perhaps best rendered as interpretive psychology, a method for which he had received his main inspiration from Wilhelm Dilthey, the pioneer spokesman of the *Geisteswissenschaften*. In a special article on causal and intelligible connections between fate (*Schicksal*) and psychosis in dementia praecox he had already tried to separate these two methods. Here the relation between the two is stated as follows:

> To put before us [*vergegenwärtigen*], delimit, describe, and order them is the task of phenomenology, to comprehend psychic connections convincingly is the entirely different task of interpretive psychology.[15]

Nevertheless, both these methods were for Jaspers parts of what he called "subjective psychology," in contradistinction to "objective psychology" or *Leistungspsychologie*, which was based on the more traditional methods.

Little purpose would be served by reporting on details of the *Allgemeine Psychopathologie*, especially now that it is accessible in translation. What matters here is only the place of phenomenology in the wider context of Jaspers' system of psychopathological knowledge of man. First of all, it has to be stressed that the purpose of the entire book, especially in its later editions, was not restricted to supplying methodologically clarified knowledge of

15. "Kansale und verständliche," in *Zusammenhänge zwischen Schicksal und Psychose bei der Dementia praecox (Schizophrenie)*, *GSzP*, pp. 329–422.

psychopathological disturbances. Its real subject matter and target was man himself in his sickness, insofar as the sickness is psychologically conditioned (*AP*, p. 6; Eng. trans., p. 7). However, man is the kind of being of which no complete knowledge is possible. In fact, as Jaspers saw it, man as such can never be objectified. This existential aspect of man is what becomes more prominent in the later sections of this book. It is therefore not surprising that in retrospect Jaspers designated as the moving force in his book his philosophical interest in man. Insight into the inexhaustibility and "infinity" of each single individual man, including sick man, was what Jaspers expected even from the medical practitioner.

But this philosophical and existential understanding of man has as its foil such sciences of man as psychopathology. And it is as one of its scientific methods that phenomenology enters into the exploration of what is explorable scientifically about man. This phenomenology has obviously nothing to do with philosophy and especially not with the philosophy of human existence.

Actually the chapter on phenomenology, consisting of 85 out of a total of 718 pages in the fourth edition, is not only the first of fourteen chapters (the last two parts being no longer subdivided into chapters) but also the longest. The other chapters deal with a study of objective performance (*Leistungspsychologie*), somatic expression, etc.

What, then, are we to make of Jaspers' emphatic denials that this psychopathology was phenomenological? It is certainly true that it is not phenomenological in its entirety or even in the majority of its content. On the other hand, one has to consider that Jaspers limited phenomenology to the study of the isolated elements of the psychic life. If one includes the whole range of subjective phenomena in their interconnection, then the entire second part of the book, with its four chapters of interpretive psychology (113 pages, amounting to more than one-fourth of the total text), would also have to be considered as phenomenological. In fact Jaspers himself admitted that phenomenology was represented in most of the other chapters (*AP*, p. 40; Eng. trans., p. 47). What is even more important, the phenomenological sections are not only first but basic for the entire work; a reversal of this order would be out of the question. Moreover, Jaspers' emphasis on methodology made the phenomenological sections stand out much more clearly than they had in other works of introspective psychology and psychopathology. Finally, the phenomenological character of the work was its most original feature at the time. It is thus not surprising that the *Allgemeine Psychopathologie* was hailed as the first major achievement of phenomenology in psychopathology. Historically, it remains so to this day. But even systematically it contains so much phenomenology that it is not irrelevant for our perspective in this book. However, in order to prove this point one has to take account of Jaspers' conception of phenomenology.

[5] Jaspers' Conception of Phenomenology

It is important to realize that Jaspers did not simply borrow his version of phenomenology from others—and certainly not from any philosopher.

In the article of 1912 on the phenomenological trend in psychopathology its task had been described as *Vergegenwärtigung* (i.e., literally "presentification," or better, "putting before us")—clarifying, demarcation, and ordering of the psychological phenomena.[16] What are to be put before us, limited, and distinguished are the psychic occurrences in others, notably the patients. What is meant by these procedures?

1. "Presentification" (*Vergegenwärtigung*) is certainly not a primary component of the phenomenological method as envisaged, for example, by Husserl, although he may mention it in connection with the intuitive fulfillment of our intentions or in "experiments" in freely varying imagination. What, then, is *Vergegenwärtigung*? While Jaspers does not make any attempt to describe it explicitly, it is plain that what is involved is not a perceptual experience but rather an imaginative procedure.

> Since we can never perceive the psychical phenomena in others directly, as we can physical phenomena, it can only be a matter of empathic understanding [*verstehen*], to which we can be directed by enumerating in each case a series of external characteristics of the psychic situation; by enumerating the conditions under which it occurs, by visual analogies, and by symbolization or by a kind of suggestive presentation. In this attempt the personal accounts [*Selbstschilderungen*] of the patients, which we can elicit and examine in personal conversation, can help us. We can develop these most fully and clearly, whereas those in written form composed by the patients themselves, while often richer in content, have simply to be accepted. Clearly, whoever has experienced the

16. *GSzP*, pp. 315 ff. Almost the same formulation can be found in *AP*, pp. 22 ff., 46; Eng. trans., pp. 25 ff., 54.

occurrence himself, has the best chance of finding the appropriate description (*AP*, p. 47; Eng. trans., p. 55).

Thus it is obviously not what is given in immediate intuition which forms the starting point for the phenomenological psychopathologist. His material has to be obtained indirectly and even then it is given only to his presenting imagination. This it has in common with the directly given of "introspective" phenomenology —its intuitive content.

2. "Demarcation" (*Begrenzung*): While Jaspers does not tell us in detail what is involved in this procedure, he seems to have in mind the sorting out of groups of phenomena that belong together and the assignment of special terms to them. This procedure, which is at least related to concept formation in the customary sense, is certainly not peculiar to philosophical phenomenology and is not stressed in its methodology, much as the distinction of essentially different forms of the phenomena is one of its characteristic features.

3. "Description" (*Beschreibung*): Where the similarity with philosophical phenomenology is most pronounced is in Jaspers' stress on the need for description based on systematic categories, comparisons, demonstration of similarity, and arrangements in series (*AP*, p. 47 n; Eng. trans., p. 55 n).

Jaspers denied that his phenomenology included *Wesensschau* in Husserl's sense. He certainly avoided this term. But this does not mean that he avoided the thing meant. Thus, when stressing that phenomenology immerses itself in individual cases, Jaspers added that it also teaches us what is universal for many cases (*AP*, p. 48; Eng. trans., p. 56). Later in the book, when he explored the psychic life in its entirety and considered man in general, he even used the expression *eidos* of man, a term which Husserl had reintroduced for the general essences, for that which can be approached through all its particular forms (eidology as distinguished from typology [*AP*, pp. 517 ff.; Eng. trans., p. 617]). This indicates that phenomenology supplies at least one of the bases for such a study of the universal essence of man, even though it does not stress it. However, the real test of *Wesensschau* will be a consideration of the question of how far Jaspers' phenomenological descriptions actually avoided essential insight in Husserl's sense.

There is seemingly one further limitation to Jaspers' phenomenology: In restricting it to the study of the elements of the psychic life (*Einzeltatbestände*), Jaspers barred it from any consideration of connections between them, leaving the study of the intelligible connections to interpretive psychology, and that of the unintelligible or merely causal ones to explanatory psychology. What accounts for this sharp division between the study of the elements and that of the connections, and specifically between phenomenology and interpretive psychology? Interpretive psychology was a method which Jaspers had discovered independently and apparently even before he had come in touch with Husserl's phenomenology. At least this is what a footnote in *Allgemeine Psychopathologie* (p. 250; Eng. trans., p. 301) suggests. Through Max Weber's studies of 1903–6 Jaspers had become acquainted with the tradition of the *Geisteswissenschaften,* although he did not meet Weber personally until 1909. We know, too, that he was also indebted to Georg Simmel and especially to Dilthey's famous essays of 1894 about descriptive analytic psychology. He applied this method for the first time in 1913, in an essay on causal and understandable connections between fate and psychosis. Thus the two methods, phenomenology and *verstehen,* had clearly separate origins in Jaspers' mind. Jaspers also assigned different functions to them. Phenomenology was to give us access to the subjective ingredients of psychopathological life. *Verstehende Psychologie* was to provide access to connections which might occur not only among subjective but also among objective facts. It was to show us how one phase of these facts issues genetically from the other.

Thus at first sight phenomenology and *verstehende Psychologie* may seem to have to do with very different problems. But that must not make us overlook the overlap. For what is *verstehen* in Jaspers' sense? Its main tool is again *self-transposal,* as it was in the case of the phenomenology of the elements. Besides, in some parts of Jaspers' discussion of understanding, it becomes quite clear that for him there is such a thing as phenomenological understanding or static understanding based on the personal accounts of the patients (*AP,* p. 255; Eng. trans., p. 301).

Jaspers' distinction between phenomenology and *verstehende Psychologie* is therefore not as rigid as it might seem at first sight. Both of them are based on empathic self-transposal; the only difference is that in the first case we only put ourselves into isolated or static phases of a psychic event, while in the second case we also put ourselves into the linkage between one and the other. This is hardly a difference in principle.

There is also this additional reason for thinking of *verstehen* as a phenomenological operation: In one place (*AP,* p. 252; Eng.

trans., p. 303) Jaspers points out that we can understand only the ideal types of intelligible connections, not single individual connections directly. If this is true, then "understanding psychology" moves even closer to the understanding of essences in Husserl's sense than does the phenomenology of particulars.

To this extent it seems that Jaspers' own phenomenology already contained the germ of a much wider application, even though his insistence on the absolute disjunction between empathic *verstehen* and causal explanation excluded phenomenology from the field accessible only to such explanation, specifically the field of the psychoses.

[6] Illustrations of Phenomenology from Jaspers' Psychopathology

It is not enough to study Jaspers' theoretical interpretation of phenomenology. Only through an examination of his practice of it can his conception be fully understood.

Actually, this practice preceded his theoretical reflections. His article concerning the analysis of hallucinations (*Trugwahrnehmungen*), "*Leibhaftigkeit und Realitätsurteil*" (1911), is of particular interest as an important phenomenological case study which preceded the more elaborate analyses of the first chapter of *Allgemeine Psychopathologie*. It was Jaspers' most explicit application of Husserl's analyses of perception from the *Logische Untersuchungen*.

These studies reappear in a new context in the first chapter of *Allgemeine Psychopathologie* (pp. 78–90; Eng. trans., pp. 93–108), a chapter which is dedicated to the "subjective phenomena of the diseased psychic life" and is subdivided into two sections, the first on the single phenomenon, the second on the "ensemble" of phenomena. The examination of the single phenomena had in the first edition merely four subdivisions (on object-consciousness, on personality-consciousness, on feelings and states of feeling, and on drives and will). Later, four subdivisions were added, dealing with spatial and temporal experience, body-consciousness, reality-consciousness, and reflective phenomena, respectively. Even then, Jaspers made no claim that this scheme was final. The second section, dealing with the ensemble of phenomena, was also changed in the second edition. One subsection was eliminated, and the additional subsections included attention and its fluctuations, sleep and hypnosis, psychotic changes of consciousness, and fantasied connections. Each section is preceded by general psychological remarks of considerable phenomenological interest, though all are given in small print, as a background for the description of the abnormal phenomena.

Basic for these phenomenological studies is the fundamental phenomenon (*Urphänomen*) of the correlation of subject and object, or of the ego and its contents. This reflects, of course, the familiar phenomenological view of the intentional structure of consciousness. It permits Jaspers to divide the field into the "objective" and the "subjective" aspects of consciousness, not only normal but abnormal. There is also a special study of ego-consciousness, in its normal and abnormal modifications. In the present context it may be best to illustrate Jaspers' approach by a brief look at his account of the consciousness of objects and of the consciousness of the ego.

A. *Object-Consciousness*

Jaspers provides a wide array of types of object-consciousness, in which, against the background of a briefly outlined normal psychology, the dimensions of abnormal variations are outlined and illustrated by concrete case material. It may be worthwhile to look more closely at some of these, all the more since Jaspers had developed some of the basic distinctions in his earliest casework.

1. Normal perception lends itself to pathological variation as far as the intensity of sensations (e.g., color intensity), quality (e.g., color substitutions), and synesthesias are concerned.

2. Perception may also show abnormal characters in the form of a general alienation of the perceived world by novel characters or by the breakup of this world into fragments.

However, the major modifications occur in the areas of illusions, hallucinations, and pseudohallucinations. Jaspers restricts illusions to deceptive perceptions based on transformations of genuine perception, induced either by inattention, by such affects as fright, or by "paridolic" modifications of perception through fantasy, modifications which may, for instance, read some meaning into the shape of clouds, etc. By contrast, genuine hallucinations are completely new and unrelated to previous perceptions. What distinguishes them from mere representations is the character of fullbodiedness (*Leibhaftigkeit*), as distinguished from a mere picture likeness (*Bildhaftigkeit*), which is also characterized as "objective" or being felt as present. It should be pointed out that, unlike the way the term is used in Husserl, *Leibhaftig-*

keit can also occur when we do not see the object but have the distinct feeling that something or someone stands directly behind us, a sensation which may of course be quite erroneous. Jaspers insists that there is no gradual transition but a "phenomenological abyss" between the *Leibhaftigkeit* and *Bildhaftigkeit.* Mere picture character can be found in the pseudohallucinations first discovered by the psychiatrist Kandinsky, whom Jaspers sees as a forerunner of phenomenological psychopathology.

While these distinctions do not directly reflect any influence of philosophical phenomenology, they are at least supported by the parallel studies of Brentano and Husserl. However, the main phenomenological interest of Jaspers' distinctions derives from the descriptive richness and comprehensiveness of the development which is characteristic for these parts of his psychopathology.

B. *Ego-Consciousness*

It is against the background of a brief characterization of five major features of ego-consciousness in general that Jaspers outlines the modes of their transformation in abnormal experience. Thus the consciousness of ego can be lost completely; actually the illustrations Jaspers introduces suggest merely that the ego no longer has a sense of its own reality (as in the "cogito ergo sum") or that it becomes detached from its own activities when these seem to be controlled from the outside. According to Jaspers, the ego's sense of unity can be modified by a strange doubling of experiences without a duplication of the ego itself; two series of experiences seem to be taking place side by side. The identification with previous phases of the ego may break down in the sense that the present ego no longer acknowledges its identity with that of its previous stages. The separation from the outside world facing the patient may vanish to the extent that he identifies with animate and inanimate objects far beyond his own body. Under "consciousness of personality," such modifications as imputing false urges to oneself, changes in the feeling of experience, and instability in maintaining one's role are mentioned. Hallucination and similar abnormal experiences may result in new personalities splitting off in the form of separate impersonations.

While Jaspers usually discovers traces of such modifications of ego-consciousness in normal experience and uses them as aids in making these modifications intelligible before introducing case material, he admits in places that we are "hardly capable" of visualizing such phenomena as imposed thought (*Gedankenmachen*) or draining of thought (*Gedankenabzug*) as modifications of the active life of the ego.

[7] The Significance of Phenomenology for Jaspers' Psychopathology

What, then, has phenomenology contributed to the development of Jaspers' psychopathology? To what extent would his psychopathology have been possible without phenomenology? Jaspers himself, in retrospect, has gone so far as to say that his work would not have taken a different course if he had never known Husserl. Even if one does not take such a disclaimer at face value, it cannot be ignored. The references to Husserl, especially in Jaspers' early works, are not numerous enough to show a decisive influence of Husserl's ideas on Jaspers. But they are there. And it is clear that at that time Jaspers was anxious to identify them specifically.

A sober estimate of the significance of phenomenology for Jaspers at the decisive pre-philosophical phase of his work might be derived from the following considerations: When Jaspers discovered that psychopathology had to be rebuilt, and actually to be rebuilt on a phenomenological foundation, he found that no such foundation yet existed. So, in his early studies he inevitably attempted to assemble it piecemeal, by himself. It was only natural that he would look for parallel efforts in other areas, especially in psychology, where the most congenial work was clearly that of Brentano and the early Husserl. He also found similar aids in Theodor Lipps and Oswald Külpe; however, the scheme that proved most valuable was the pattern of intentionality and the parallelism of act and content.

There would be little point in trying to determine how far the patterns thus suggested actually stimulated Jaspers' concrete research. The brief sketches of a more psychological nature, especially the ones in *Allgemeine Psychopathologie* which precede the psychopathological main text, often suggest that Jaspers did not want to claim originality for his phenomenological psychology. What seems to me defensible, all the same, is that among the parallel psychopathological work of which Jaspers was aware, the phenomenology of Brentano and the early Husserl and especially their conception of intentionality, was most congenial. Knowledge of these enterprises acted at least as a confirmation, perhaps even as a reinforcement, for Jaspers' own independent work. Jaspers' phenomenology might indeed have been developed without Brentano and Husserl, but it would probably not have developed as quickly and confidently as it did, had their example not strengthened his hand.

But there are more significant aspects to the place of phenomenology in Jaspers' *Allgemeine Psychopathologie.* This new classic gave phenomenology a strategic place in the foundation of the new science. Thus it not only became an entering wedge for all phenomenology but a testimony to the philosophical phenomenology of Husserl. The result was clear enough: Jaspers' psychopathology not only stood out as the most impressive demonstration of the place and opportunity given to phenomenology in psychopathology, but it also opened the gates for much more sweeping invasions. Such is the story which now has to be unfolded.

Jaspers may not have thought of himself as a psychopathological phenomenologist. But neither did Franz Brentano nor Carl Stumpf think of themselves as phenomenologists, although Husserl's phenomenology would not have been possible without them. In this sense, Jaspers could well be considered as the Brentano of phenomenological psychopathology.

7 / Ludwig Binswanger (1881–1966): Phenomenological Anthropology (*Daseinsanalyse*)

[1] General Orientation

No apologies are needed for claiming Ludwig Binswanger as a proponent, in fact as a protagonist, of phenomenology in psychopathology. It was characteristic of his affirmative, outreaching mind that he did not insist on being different from other thinkers and movements. Though he tested everything, he held on to what he considered good. This did not make him an easy joiner (in contrast to many of his colleagues); he consistently avoided going on editorial boards, particularly those of organizations whose standards he distrusted. Instead, he was always eager and ready to have others meet him on his own ground, especially the unique and hospitable ground of his Bellevue Sanatorium in Kreuzlingen.

But while Binswanger never refused the phenomenological label, it certainly did not describe the whole range of his interests and his work. The most appropriate title for his contribution is still the untranslatable [1] term *Daseinsanalyse*, which according to Roland Kuhn was first suggested by Jakob Wyrsch but was adopted by Binswanger himself in the forties. Binswanger was thinking of the phrase "phenomenological anthropology," [2]

1. I call it untranslatable because it is too closely connected with Heidegger's conception of human existence to be safely rendered by the vague term "existential analysis."

2. See, e.g., the title of Volume I of his collected essays, *Zur phänomenologischer Anthropologie*, and also "Über die daseinsanalytische Forschungsrichtung in der Psychiatrie," in *Ausgewähle Vorträge und Aufsätze* (Bern: Francke, 1942–55), I, 190–217 (reprinted in *Existence*, ed. Rollo May, Ernest Angel, and Henri F. Ellenberger [New York: Basic Books, 1958], pp. 191–213).

and in the present context that may be preferable as a less mystifying label for his enterprise.

Binswanger contrasts such a *phenomenological* anthropology with *philosophical* anthropology; the former does not claim to determine the essence of man as a whole but confines itself to phenomenological experience—i.e., how human *Dasein* is concretely experienced. It is this aspect of Binswanger's work that will be presented here, an aspect which, especially in the Anglo-American world, has not yet been sufficiently brought out. While it is true that Binswanger's work is not merely applied phenomenology, its most important part remains the phenomenological strand; never once does he seriously question the rights of phenomenology.[3]

[2] Binswanger's Concerns

> Above all, let us hold fast onto what it means to be a man.
>
> Kierkegaard, *Concluding Unscientific Postscript*

The Kierkegaard motto of this section was chosen by Binswanger himself for his breakthrough essay on "Dream and Existence" (1930), which contained the first demonstration of the new *Daseinsanalyse* in a field previously explored mostly by Freudian psychoanalysis.[4] There can be little doubt that this motto reveals the central concern of Binswanger's entire work and life. Binswanger was first and foremost a psychiatrist identifying with psychiatry as a science. But he was a psychiatrist with a difference, in fact with many differences. Perhaps the primary one was that for him psychiatry was not merely a matter of treating the insane, the psychotic, and the neurotic, but a personal encounter between physician and patient as human beings. For Binswanger, psychiatry required the understanding

3. The impression that Binswanger stood apart from phenomenology is promoted not only by the layout of Rollo May's *Existence,* where Binswanger figures as the chief exhibit of Part III (Existential Analysis) in contrast to Part II (Phenomenology), but by Henri Ellenberger's introduction (pp. 120 ff.), which contrasts "existential analysis" with "phenomenology" and is based on a narrow and questionable interpretation of the latter.

4. "Dream and Existence" (1930), in *Being-in-the-World,* trans. Jacob Needleman (New York: Basic Books, 1963). The origin of this motto is not given on the *Ausgewählte Vorträge;* the motto itself is omitted entirely in Needleman's translation. It can be found in the translation by W. Lowrie (Princeton, N. J.: Princeton University Press, 1944), p. 177.

of man in his entirety, with his normal as well as his abnormal variations. For such an understanding of man Binswanger turned, notably in his first book, to general psychology. But he soon came to realize that the typical "naturalistic" psychology of the day, treating man as a subject-less facet of objective "nature" ("naturalism") knew little of him in his concrete existence, and that the psychologists, in contrast to the psychopathologists, did not even care to do so. To make up for this vacuum, more was needed than the kind of excursions into phenomenological psychology in small print that could be found in the phenomenological parts of Jaspers' psychopathology. The only place where Binswanger could hope to find such insights was in philosophy. The story of Binswanger's attempt to understand man in health as well as in sickness can therefore be appreciated only in the light of his use and development of the suggestions which he had found in the main philosophies, classic and contemporary, and which culminated in his own understanding of *Dasein* through a "phenomenology of love." To understand Binswanger's search calls for a developmental approach, a life history, which has been mostly ignored in previous accounts.

But before attempting it, at least one other interest of Binswanger's must not be forgotten, as it has been too frequently: his concern for the status and future of psychiatry as a science. For Binswanger was anything but anti-scientific, much as he fought the narrowness of a merely naturalistic science which could not accommodate the total phenomenon of man. In fact, Binswanger literally suffered under the lack of such a supporting science. Perhaps the best expression of this subsidiary concern can be found in the title of the second volume of his collected essays, *Concerning the Problematics of Psychiatric Research and the Problem of Psychiatry.* Regardless of one's view of Binswanger's achievements, the fact that he wanted to contribute to converting psychiatry into a more rigorous science makes his effort congenial to the spirit of Husserl's enterprise.

[3] The Genesis of Phenomenological Anthropology

A minimum of biographical information is indispensable as background for an understanding of the philosophical ideas which have stimulated and permeated Binswanger's work. While he did not care to prepare anything like an autobiography (even at the age of 81 when I had a chance to ask him about it in conversation, he told me that he was much more interested in the future—i.e., in his unfinished research on the problem of delusion [*Wahn*]), his works contain sufficient incidental information to piece together a meaningful account of his intellectual odyssey.[5] To this I have been able to add a few items based on my one memorable encounter with him in 1962.

The external facts are relatively uncomplicated and undramatic. Born into a family transplanted from Germany into Switzerland after 1848 with a tradition in psychiatry going back to his grandfather, Ludwig, the founder of the Bellevue Sanatorium in Kreuzlingen, Binswanger had attended the humanistic Gymnasium in German Konstanz nearby and the Kantonsschule in Swiss Schaffhausen, where, in addition to a classical education, he was exposed to Kant. He studied medicine exclusively, at Lausanne, Jena, and Heidelberg, and never attended philosophical courses. He served his internship at the Burghölzli, the leading Swiss psychiatric clinic in Zurich, under Eugen Bleuler, the trail-blazing explorer of schizophrenia, who had been the first university psychiatrist to respond to Freud's revolution but who was disinterested in philosophy. Binswanger worked first under Bleuler's assistant, Carl Gustav Jung, who brought about the momentous first meeting between Sigmund Freud and Binswanger in Vienna. Although Binswanger had a chance for a university career and (according to Roland Kuhn) received specific offers to the Burghölzi and as Bleuler's successor at the University of Zurich, he preferred to assume the directorship of

5. Principal sources in print include:

Prefaces: in *Grundformen und Erkenntnis menschlichen Daseins* (Zurich: Niehans, 1941), pp. 13–18; 3d ed. (Munich: Reinhardt, 1962), pp. 11–17 (especially important). *Ausgewählte Vorträge und Aufsätze* (Bern: Francke, 1947), I, 7–11; II (1955), 7–39.

Recollections of Encounters: Erinnerungen an Freud (Bern: Francke, 1956). English translation, *Sigmund Freud: Reminiscences of a Friendship* (New York: Grune & Stratton, 1957). "Mein Weg zu Freud," in *Der Mensch in der Psychiatrie* (Pfullingen: Neske, 1957). "Dank an Husserl," in *Edmund Husserl, 1859–1959*, ed. H. L. Van Breda (The Hague: Nijhoff, 1959), pp. 64–72. "Die Philosophie Wilhelm Szilasis und die psychiatrische Forschung," in *Beitrage zur Philosophie und Wissenschaft* (Bern: Francke, 1960), pp. 29–40.

Letters (published thus far): to Erwin Straus, in *Conditio Humana: Erwin W. Straus on His 75th Birthday,* ed. W. von Bayer and R. M. Griffiths (New York: Springer, 1966), pp. 1–2.

Histories: Zur Geschichte der Heilanstalt Bellevue in Kreuzlingen (Privately printed, 1959). See especially pp. 28–38.

Diaries: 16 vols. for the period after 1912; not yet accessible.

the Bellevue. He soon converted this sanatorium into an international meeting ground and unique cultural center, not only for psychiatrists, but for psychologists, philosophers, scholars, and artists, of whom his and his wife's guest books contain a remarkable record. Binswanger himself published a sample in the form of Edmund Husserl's entry of August 15, 1923. Other visitors included such philosophers, mostly phenomenological, as Pfänder (1922), the first to come, Max Scheler, Heidegger (who came twice), Wilhelm Szilasi, Ernst Cassirer, Martin Buber, and others. The visitor who probably meant the most to Binswanger was Sigmund Freud, who visited the Bellevue in 1912.

The personal and literary encounters with many of these visitors have had considerable importance for the development of Binswanger's thought. In fact, Binswanger, in his touching responsiveness and gratitude for contributions from others, may easily have overestimated them. For Binswanger was no mere eclectic and syncretizer. On the contrary, while open to all new ideas, he responded to them in a highly specific and creative manner. The best way to show this is to indicate how these influences fitted in with the development of his phenomenological anthropology. But first it is important to take account of what was probably the major challenge, if not the continuing theme, in this development: the encounter with Sigmund Freud's psychoanalysis.

A. *The Challenge of Freud*

Binswanger made it clear that his search for an understanding of man was determined decisively by his persistent struggle (*Ringen*) with Freud. The encounter with Freud may seem at first sight to have been an accident based upon Binswanger's apprenticeship under Bleuler and Jung at a time when both were under the spell of Freud's early discoveries. But the fact that Freud's impact on Binswanger lasted through his entire life indicates that it was much more than an accidental stimulation. Freud presented to him a fundamental challenge not only for psychiatry as a science, but for Binswanger's whole understanding of man. The problem was how to assimilate Freud's thinking into an adequate anthropological framework, which the preceding psychiatry, even that of Jaspers, could not provide. Although in fact Binswanger remained ambivalent to Freud's thought, this ambivalence did not interfere with their personal friendship, which was based chiefly on Binswanger's moving admiration and love for Freud as a person.

Binswanger himself has distinguished five stages in his approach to Freud. The first was one of mere learning, listening, reading, and reporting; it began with Binswanger's first report on psychoanalysis and clinical psychiatry and was marked by several publications in psychoanalytical journals. During this early stage Binswanger acted as President of the Zurich Psychoanalytic Society (1910) and though prevented from presiding, maintained an association with a "new group" founded in 1919. Freud himself, in his *History of the Psychoanalytic Movement*, referred to Binswanger's Kreuzlingen as one of two institutions which had opened their doors to psychoanalysis. But apparently, even this period was not free from skeptical reservations. It yielded to the second stage of full acceptance, but only after a period of testing. The third stage, apparently not completely separated in time, was that of determining the place of psychoanalysis in psychiatry; to Binswanger this was primarily a "methodological or epistemological problem." Now he tried to find a place for Freud's innovations in the framework of general, or better, philosophical psychology. The absence of such a psychology was one explanation for Binswanger's interest in phenomenology as an alternative to Freud's own constructions, which Binswanger could not accept sight unseen. Binswanger's major effort in this direction was the first volume of his *Allgemeine Psychologie*, which he dedicated to his "teachers," Eugen Bleuler and Sigmund Freud. Yet he found himself unable to complete it by a second volume, which would have dealt with the basic concepts of Freud's system. He did try to assimilate the Freudian method to that of phenomenological experience in an essay of 1926.[6] On the whole, however, this stage ended in failure; abandoned manuscripts piled up in Binswanger's drawers. He explained this failure by his involvement in the new methods of Husserl and Heidegger, which did not allow him to go to the roots of Freud's conceptions and theories of the psyche and of human nature.

The fourth stage culminated in Binswanger's address on the occasion of Freud's eightieth birthday in 1939. It showed Binswanger at the farthest remove from Freud. Now that he had developed his own anthropology on Heideggerian foundations,

6. "Erfahren, Verstehen und Deuten in der Psychoanalyse," *Ausgewählte Vorträge*, II, 67 ff.

Freud's "naturalism," in the shape of his conception of man as *homo natura,* i.e., as being definable completely in terms of the natural sciences, proved in its one-sidedness to be inacceptable to Binswanger. Yet even at this stage Binswanger claimed a certain support of his position from a conversation with Freud at their last meeting at the Semmering Pass in 1927, when Freud suddenly admitted: "Yes! The spirit is everything. . . . Mankind has always known that it possesses spirit. I had to show it that there are also drives." Binswanger still hoped that he could accommodate Freud's man within the larger frame of his own comprehensive anthropology.

However, a last, fifth stage allowed Binswanger to come to an even more positive final appraisal of Freud's anthropology. It was at this point that he discovered that Freud's conception of nature was really much deeper than that of scientific naturalism, nature being something which Freud approached with a sense of awe.

What then was the real significance of Freud for the genesis of Binswanger's phenomenological anthropology? One way of interpreting it may be in terms of his relationship to the phenomenological psychopathology of Jaspers. This phenomenology, as we saw, gave only a partial account of mental sickness. For Jaspers the field of psychopathology remained sharply divided into those phenomena which were fully intelligible and those which were at best causally explainable. From the very start, i.e., in his essay of 1920 on "Psychoanalysis and Clinical Psychiatry" (*Ausgewählte Vorträge,* II, 40 ff.), Binswanger never accepted this dichotomy, much as he admired Jaspers with his characteristic generosity for what he had achieved by introducing Dilthey's *verstehen* into psychopathology. The promise Freud held for Binswanger was that of a new unifying conception of human nature which allowed him to account for what at first sight seemed like unintelligible phenomena, an interpretation that found meanings, in the sense of a teleology, in seemingly meaningless behavior. To Binswanger, Freud offered the best chance thus far for understanding what it means to be a man.

What was missing in Freud were chiefly two things: (1) a defensible methodology, justifying this kind of interpretation scientifically on psychological and philosophical grounds: this was the promise of Husserl's phenomenology; (2) a less one-sided, more comprehensive anthropology: this was the promise of Heidegger's *Daseinsanalytik.* It remained to be seen how far Husserl and Heidegger fulfilled these promises and how far Binswanger succeeded in completing the house of a new psychiatry above the basement of Freud's new psychoanalysis.

The story of this philosophical supplementation of Freud's psychoanalysis can best be traced by dividing Binswanger's philosophical development into four phases:

1. The Pre-Phenomenological Phase: Kant and Natorp
2. The First Husserlian Phase
3. The Heideggerian Phase
4. The Second Husserlian Phase

B. *Binswanger's Philosophical Development*

1. The Pre-Phenomenological Phase: Kant and Natorp

Binswanger's attempt to integrate Freud's discovery into a philosophy of man began by a search for the proper psychological frame. Binswanger had entered the world of philosophy through the "shaking, even revolutioning" (*aufrüttelende, ja aufwühlende*) early encounter with Kant's *Critique of Pure Reason*, while still in Gymnasium.[7] The obvious point of departure for him, therefore, was Neo-Kantianism, and specifically the Neo-Kantian conception of scientific psychology. Here it was Paul Natorp, who, in his *General Psychology According to the Critical Method*, seemed to offer solid hope. To Natorp psychology was the science of the subjective, in contrast to the nonpsychological sciences based on the method of objectification (*Objektivierung*). This meant that the data of psychology could be secured only by the opposite method, that of subjectification (*Subjektivierung*), which required a peculiar "reconstruction" starting from the objective data; mere description of the immediate data would not do. The result was that Natorp's psychology acknowledged contents of consciousness (*Bewusstseinsinhalte*), to be described by a peculiar phenomenology, but denied the existence of corresponding acts. Also, the ego, much as Natorp insisted contrary to the early Husserl on its indispensability, was not a matter of direct experience but something to be assumed as a necessary postulate. In the long run this approach to the subjective could not satisfy Binswanger's longing for the concreteness of direct experience. Actually, it seems to have been Natorp's own critical discussion of Brentano's and Husserl's descriptive enterprises which stirred up Binswanger

7. "Die Philosophie Wilhelm Szilasis," p. 29.

so deeply that he was led to their own writings. Hence it is not surprising that Binswanger's first major work took the form of another *General Psychology,* which used Natorp's own title but promised no more than an introduction to its problems. This was the book in which Binswanger fought his solitary way with the texts from Neo-Kantianism to the descriptive phenomenology represented by Brentano and the early Husserl. However, his move from Neo-Kantianism must not be interpreted as a complete abandonment of his Kantian start. Nor was this necessary in view of Husserl's increasing rapprochement to Kant, mediated to a large extent by his personal ties with Natorp. But Binswanger's transcendentalism means something quite different from Natorp's or Husserl's. What he preserved was the search for the "a priori" foundations in the very structure of man's being which make concrete experience, and ultimately *Dasein,* possible.

2. The First Husserlian Phase

Binswanger's best account of his approach to phenomenology took the form of a posthumous tribute to Husserl in 1959. It was in 1922, according to Binswanger, when his study of Brentano and Husserl had finally removed his "naturalistic cataract," that he not only published the first volume of his introduction to the problems of general psychology, but presented to the Swiss Society for Psychiatry his report on phenomenology. For all practical purposes this report amounted to his open, though by no means indiscriminating, espousal of the new trend. At that time Binswanger had not yet been in touch with any of the leaders of the Phenomenological Movement in philosophy. He met the first one around Easter, 1923: Alexander Pfänder:

> Pfänder has played an important role in my own philosophical or better phenomenological career. For he was the first live phenomenologist on whom I laid eyes, probably around 1922. Previously I had picked up everything from reading, even my Zurich lecture on phenomenology. I still see him before me, as I met him at the Konstanz station and asked him whether he approved of my lecture, whereupon he reassured me with his characteristic delicate smile, adding that it was perfectly permissible to develop phenomenology from the artistic angle as I had done it in the lecture.[8]

8. From a letter written to me by Binswanger in 1962 (my translation). Pfänder repeated this estimate in a letter of May 25, 1925, after

This meeting was apparently arranged by Dr. Alfred Schwenninger, a former Pfänder student and at the time an assistant at the Psychiatrische Landesanstalt close to Reichenau Constance, where since 1920 Pfänder had visited frequently during the spring, and where, according to Binswanger's diaries, they met and had discussions. Schwenninger also arranged the first meeting between Binswanger and Husserl a year later on the Reichenau, which was followed by Husserl's visit at Kreuzlingen, where Husserl not only gave a lecture about phenomenology, but left an entry in Binswanger's guest book pointing out that the way to a true psychology required a return to the childlike naïveté of an elementary study of consciousness.[9] It would seem that this prescription, along with the "overpowering lecture Husserl gave," left a permanent mark on Binswanger's further phenomenological development. As he put it, Husserl gave him a solid foundation for his own work without committing him to Natorp's problematic reconstruction of the subjective, opening up new dimensions for a descriptive approach with a much richer content than Brentano's brief sketch of intentionality. For, as Binswanger saw it, Husserl's analysis of intentionality, by showing the link between the subjective act and the intentional object to which it was directed, effectively bridged the gap between subject and object, a gap that was for Binswanger the "cancer of psychology and philosophy."

It may be well to illustrate Binswanger's first phenomenological phase by a closer look at his *Introduction to the Problems of General Psychology*, which he never repudiated, although he moved far beyond it. Meant as a kind of prolegomena for an examination of the foundations for psychoanalysis, it consists in a painstaking examination of the basic concepts of classical and contemporary psychology as pertinent to the work of Bleuler and Freud. After a first chapter, discussing the naturalistic accounts of the psychic, a second one reviews alternative characterizations of it, beginning with Leibniz and culminating in the comparative accounts of Natorp, Bergson, and Husserl. Husserl's answer proves to be the one most adequate, though it is by no

---

receiving a reprint of his Zurich lecture. He also suggested that Binswanger develop his sketches of a "phenomenology of schizophrenia." The exchange of altogether fourteen letters between Binswanger and Pfänder, to which Dr. Wolfgang Binswanger gave me generous access, contains similar suggestions and culminates with Binswanger's unsuccessful attempt to consult Pfänder in Munich in 1929. Pfänder's subsequent series of illnesses seems to have prevented later contacts.

9. See "Dank an Husserl," p. 65. See also below, p. 365.

means perfect. In a third chapter the non-naturalistic account of the psychic is developed by a study of the concepts of function and act. With the problem of subjectivity as the point of departure, the account of intentionality by Brentano and Husserl proves to be the most helpful foundation for an empirical exploration of the psychic and a development of the Kantian approach. A final chapter, clearly needed for a development of a concrete psychology and psychiatry on the way toward psychoanalysis, takes up the problems of the alter ego and of personality. Here Scheler, with his phenomenological account of the perception of other selves, emerges as the most helpful guide. To conclude, Binswanger develops his concepts of person and personality. But there is no clear picture of what lies ahead, and one can well understand Freud's puzzlement, expressed in his letters, as to how all this would contribute toward a better understanding of the unconscious.

More explicit, and in many ways even more important, was Binswanger's testimony for phenomenology in his *Referat* of 1922 (matched by a sympathetic but reserved discussion [*Korreferat*] of Eugen Bleuler). Contrasting phenomenology first with "natural science" (in the sense of the physical and biological sciences), Binswanger stressed its use of a special kind of intuiting (*Anschauung*) other than sense experience. He also illustrated Husserl's essential intuition (*Wesensschau*) by a discussion of the artist's grasp of the essential nature of his subject, in a special section referring to Flaubert, Franz Marc and van Gogh. Here he characterized the fundamental principle of the phenomenological method as analysis confined to what can be found in consciousness, showing, however, that much more is given than what is generally believed. As "criteria" for distinguishing essential insight from merely factual experience, Binswanger's account refers to the suspension of the belief in reality, the "bracketing," i.e., the phenomenological reduction, and to the abstraction from individual cases. Finally, some of the implications of this phenomenology for psychopathology are spelled out, particularly with regard to Bleuler's conception of autism, a phenomenon into which phenomenology can try to enter by means of self-projection (*einleben*) based on the otherwise puzzling accounts of the patients themselves. Then, on the basis of examples, the essential nature of the disturbance can be grasped and described. In the spirit of such a report, Binswanger did not yet identify with phenomenology and even voiced some critical reservations. But although he was undecided as to how far phenomenology could be reconciled with scientific psychiatry, there could be no doubt that Binswanger saw in phenomenology the future of psychiatry.

Another result of this early phase was Binswanger's paper on "Lebensfunktion und innere Lebensgeschichte" (1927). It developed a new and important conception of the inner life history as the basis for the interpretation of such disturbances as hysteria, which was related not to functional disorders in the organism but to desires and other conscious experiences. Binswanger developed the new concept largely on the basis of Scheler's phenomenology, although he also called on Pfänder's "decisive" clarification of the concept of motivation.

Thus far, Binswanger had found phenomenology to be merely a workable tool for achieving a better understanding of pathological phenomena that formerly had seemed to defy such an attempt. But he had still a long way to go before he could answer philosophically the challenge of Freud.

3. The Heideggerian Phase

The appearance of Heidegger's *Sein und Zeit,* i.e. its first installment in 1927, meant a second turn for Binswanger.[10] However, it did not mean a turning away from Husserl. For Binswanger, Heidegger had simply added another dimension to Husserl's phenomenology, in fact one which now enabled him to develop his own anthropology as the basis for what he was to call *Daseinsanalyse.* Binswanger himself admitted later that his interpretation and utilization of Heidegger's enterprise for a new anthropology was based on a misunderstanding but, in fact, a "productive," misunderstanding, as Hans Kunz had called it before, of Heidegger's *Daseinsanalytik,* the attempt to use the ontological structure of human existence as the privileged access to an interpretation of the meaning of Being as such. But the incompleteness and later abandonment of Heidegger's attempt did more than invite the misunderstanding of *Sein und Zeit* as anthropology, as proved in Heidegger's role in the rise of existentialism as a philosophical movement. What Heidegger did provide in passing became a nucleus for a new and creative interpretation of the experience of human being (*existenzielle* or ontic analysis, as distinguished from *existentiale* or ontological analysis).

10. *Ibid.*, p. 66.

Again, Binswanger's first contact with Heidegger, his fellow alumnus of the Gymnasium at Constance, was through reading. A first personal encounter took place on the occasion of a lecture of Heidegger's in Frankfurt in 1929, which Binswanger attended. But the entire history of their personal relations cannot yet be written, although a correspondence of some thirty-five fascinating pieces, to which Dr. Wolfgang Binswanger has given me access, provides a solid foundation for it. It includes several meetings in Freiburg, Constance, Kreuzlingen, and Amriswil, where Heidegger was present at Binswanger's 85th birthday shortly before Binswanger's final illness. The present context calls only for a preliminary appraisal of Heidegger's impact on Binswanger's philosophical development.

Heidegger's contribution to Binswanger's thought was based almost completely on his first publications, though Binswanger continued to read the later ones as well. Actually what Binswanger took out of *Being and Time* were mostly motifs from the first section, the preparatory analysis of everyday existence. The most important of these was the characterization of human existence as being-in-the-world. By the link of the intentional directedness of consciousness, this fundamental structure did more than mend what Binswanger had called the cancerous split between subject and object. Now, the intentional object developed into a full world, and consciousness developed into *Dasein,* which comprised more than merely consciousness and "transcended" into this world. Other motifs taken from Heidegger's hermeneutics of *Dasein* included the existentialia of "worldliness," spatiality, facticity, thrownness (*Geworfenheit*), fallenness, and, most specifically, "care" (*Sorge*). Only comparatively little of the "fundamental analysis" of *Dasein* in Heidegger's second section seems to have permeated Binswanger's creative interpretation; notably the existentialia of temporality and historicity. But the topics of being-toward-death, guilt, and conscience hardly figure in Binswanger's use of the text.

The new anthropology based on the utilization of Heidegger's being-in-the-world found first expression in a lecture on "Dream and Existence" of 1930. Modes of existence such as falling and rising were pointed out, primarily in dreaming existence. Heraclitus was invoked as the first anthropologist who had distinguished between the many individual worlds (*Eigenwelt*) of the dream and the one common world of awakenness, thus making the dimension of worldliness part of the structure of man himself.

But the main psychopathological fruit of Binswanger's new approach were three studies of 1931–32 on the flight of ideas (*Ideenflucht*) as displayed in manic states. In many ways these studies represent the most concrete and sustained demonstrations of the new anthropological approach to psychopathology.

But although Heidegger's *Daseinsanalytik* was useful for Binswanger's new anthropology, it was not adequate. Thus Binswanger's largest and philosophically central work, the *Grundformen und Erkenntnis menschlichen Daseins,* is for all practical purposes an antithesis to Heidegger in the form of a "phenomenology of love," a love, which, as Binswanger put it in one place, had been left freezing in the cold outside of Heidegger's picture of human existence. Heidegger's failure to include the social dimension in his analytics except for the brief treatment of coexistence in the preparatory study of everyday existence (where the impersonal "man" appeared as a major form of inauthentic existence) obviously could not satisfy Binswanger, the warm-hearted advocate of a new type of psychiatry based on the loving encounter between doctor and patient. This frustrated need had been partially fulfilled by the early phenomenological study written by Heidegger's emancipated student Karl Löwith on *The Individual in the Role of Fellow Man,* in its relation to a *Mitwelt,* though even the being-together (*miteinander-sein*) of this study did not yet provide an adequate place for Binswanger's love.[11] Perhaps more important in this respect was the role of Martin Buber, a frequent guest in Kreuzlingen (four times), who, while not a phenomenologist in the narrower sense, was certainly deeply interested in the existential approach to his basic experience, the dialogue between I and Thou.

The result for Binswanger was a work which claimed to be more than a mere methodological introduction to the problems of psychology, i.e., not a second edition of his first book, which he seems to have contemplated at the beginning. Even the title "Anthropological Foundations of Psychological Knowledge," which Binswanger had considered, appeared misleading in its close link with objectivistic psychology. The actual dual title *Grundformen und Erkenntnis menschlichen Daseins,* i.e., literally, "Basic Forms and Cognition of Human Dasein," (with its odd combination of the subjective and the objective genitive)

11. *Das Individuum in der Rolle des Mitmenschen* (Tübingen: Mohr, 1928; repr. 1969).

indicates that the primary objective was to present a new phenomenological anthropology of basic forms of human existence; the justification of this anthropology by a new kind of knowledge (*Daseinserkenntnis*) occupies only the second part. The three chapters of the first part explore the being-together (*miteinandersein*) of me and you, subdivided into we-hood (*Wirheit*) in dual loving and in the participation of friendship; the mere being together of an impersonal "one" with an impersonal other in plurality, based on the way in which we take one another in our social dealings, which Binswanger finds strikingly expressed in phrases such as "taking someone by his word," or "by the hand," or, worst, "by the ear"; and finally, the togetherness of one's relation to oneself in the singular mode, e.g., in self-love in relation to one's own private world (*Eigenwelt*).

All this amounts to a kind of reversal of Heidegger's supposed anthropology of care (which was never Heidegger's real objective). But this does not mean that Binswanger denied "care," even in the new anthropological (existential) frame. Now, however, care seems to be a derivative, if not a defective, mode of the authentic social existence in loving we-hood.

The second part of the book deals with our knowledge of this human *Dasein*, i.e., with its epistemology. An account of this type of knowledge had better be postponed here until a fuller consideration of Binswanger's conception of phenomenology has been presented. Suffice it to point out here that the main function of Binswanger's love or sense of encounter in we-hood is to overcome the conflict between love and care. As this Hegelian synthesis "unfolds," it draws on all kinds of sources, from philosophy through literature. The main guides to this "phenomenology of love" are Goethe and Dilthey. After an account of their accounts of our knowledge of human *Dasein*, Binswanger continues:

> Since then we have received the gift of a new method which permits us to see Dasein in itself and from itself [*aus ihm selbst und von ihm selbst her*] and to describe it. This method is the phenomenology of Husserl. Only on this foundation was it possible to interpret *Dasein* ontologically and anthropologically and to explicate its structure as that being in which there is essentially the possibility of understanding being.[12]

The path to this new understanding was Husserl's enlarged conception of *Anschauung*, as already prepared in the "crystal

12. *Grundformen*, p. 702.

clearness of his *Logische Untersuchungen*," which had removed the "positivistic cataract."

It is therefore not surprising that in his "Thanks to Husserl," written some twenty years after Husserl's death, Binswanger acknowledged that his debt to him was more significant and permanent than the one to Heidegger. But, as we shall see, in 1959 he had additional reasons for this reappraisal.

There is relatively little explicit discussion of psychopathology and psychoanalysis in *Grundformen.* This work was primarily Binswanger's supreme effort to develop his own anthropology, which he had missed in Heidegger. It is certainly not an easy work despite, perhaps even because, Binswanger tried so hard to relate his ideas to the tradition both in philosophy and in literature—a fact which, added to his attempt to match Heidegger's language, hardly contributes to its intelligibility. But the book still does credit to Binswanger as a self-taught student of philosophy and a humanist.

However, Binswanger had not given up psychiatry. These were the years of the five remarkable case studies in schizophrenia that followed his earlier work with manic depressives. These classic examples of *Daseinsanalyse,* especially the cases of Ellen West and Lola Voss, contain concrete descriptions of the worlds in which these patients lived. They also led to some new general insights into schizophrenic existence as a special way of "being-in-the-world." But they did so mostly in a static manner, describing the "being," rather than its becoming.

4. The Second Husserlian Phase

Even during the Heideggerian phase, Binswanger had never turned away from Husserl, though it was clear that Husserl could not provide him with an anthropology. This Heidegger could do, though Binswanger found it necessary to put the pattern upside down, as it were, by giving love a place of primacy over care, as the authentic form of existence, and by putting social existence over the private existence of the isolated exister in his *Jemeinigkeit* (being-each-his-own). But now Husserl assumed a new significance for Binswanger. In order to understand it, one has first to take account of his encounter with another phenomenological philosopher, Wilhelm Szilasi.

Szilasi, an unusual philosopher with a background in science (chemistry), but also keenly interested in psychiatry, equally at home in Husserl and Heidegger and trying to find a new synthesis between their enterprises, entered Binswanger's world in 1951 as a sympathetic critic of the concept of experience in Binswanger's *Daseinsanalyse*. Pointing out its incompleteness, he suggested that the most appropriate supplementation would lead through an assimilation of motifs in Husserl's later philosophy, which Binswanger had not yet utilized. Szilasi's concise, but by no means colorless, introduction to Husserl, given in his lectures at Freiburg, where he held pro tem Heidegger's and Husserl's chair between 1945 and 1962, became the main basis for Binswanger's last Husserl interpretation.[13] In addition, Binswanger's meetings with this new personal friend offered him constant professional counsel and support.

In 1960 Binswanger published a small volume on *Melancholia and Mania* with the subtitle "Phenomenological Studies." His last book on delusion, *Wahn* (1965), carried the subtitle "Contributions Toward Its Phenomenological and *Daseinsanalytic* Investigation." This prominent reappearance of the label "phenomenology" made one of his Heidelberg friends, K. P. Kisker, speak in a critical review of a "phenomenological turn" in Binswanger.[14] Binswanger himself was not only surprised at this characterization but insisted that his departure from *Daseinsanalyse* had been inspired by Heidegger, although he had moved on toward a part of Husserl's phenomenology that he had previously neglected, i.e., constitutive phenomenology. Recognizing that his earlier use of Husserl had remained restricted to what he had called descriptive phenomenology, Binswanger now had come to the conclusion that such static understanding of the psychotic modes of existing was not enough. It was also indispensable to attain access to the genesis of the psychotic worlds, i.e., to understand how these delusional worlds had become constituted. This new interest made Binswanger aware of Husserl's constitutive phenomenology, developed particularly in his *Formal and Transcendental Logic* of 1929. In studying the constitution of the world of the manic depressive, Binswanger tried to show how the normal constitution of the world as something which is presumed to continue ceases in the mode of existence of melancholic consciousness. In other words, Husserl's theory of transcendental constitution now became a clue to a compre-

13. *Einführung in die Phänomenologie Edmund Husserls* (Tübingen: Niemeyer, 1959). See also *Philosophical Review*, LXX (1961), 267–69.

14. *"Die phänomenologische Wendung L. B.'s," Jahrbuch für Psychologie, Psychotherapie und medizinischen Anthropologie*, VIII (1962), 142–53.

hension of the departures of the world of the psychotic from that of the normal person. Specifically, Binswanger utilized conceptions such as appresentation (beyond direct presentation), e.g., of the body or of others (developed by Husserl in the *Cartesian Meditations*) for understanding the deformation of the world of the manic in which such appresentation no longer occurred. Husserl's doctrine of the transcendental ego provided further guidelines. Thus the transformations of melancholia appeared in a changed constitution of time, its future and past dimensions. It is not surprising that much in the work of the octogenarian remained relatively sketchy. What is surprising is the boldness with which Binswanger now tried to show concretely how Husserl's conceptions could serve as frames of reference for the psychopathologist. In fact, Binswanger seriously suggested that in psychopathology Husserl's theory of the transcendental consciousness could take the place that the theory of the organism held in somatic medicine. This is indeed a startling claim and an amazing posthumous triumph for Husserl.

In his final book Binswanger even tried to demonstrate the way in which delusions are constituted by a peculiar constitutive dismantling (*Abbau*), a deficient mode of the normal constitutive synthesis in which our world is mounted (*Aufbau*), as it were.

The new "phenomenology of delusions (*Wahn*)" is an attempt to "describe and understand the shift (*Ver-rückung*)," a literalizing reinterpretation of the German word *verrückt* (in English, "mad," "deranged"), which goes with the change from the normal to the abnormal structure of the conscious world. Operating with the help of some of the basic concepts in Husserl's constitutive phenomenology as interpreted by Szilasi, Binswanger tried to convey a concrete idea of what is going wrong when these worlds are being constituted. But it must be realized that such understanding does not yet tell us *why* these defects in normal constitutions occur. How far this kind of genetic understanding can be added from other sources remains at this stage an open question. But Binswanger did not claim to have the final answer on any of these issues. His ambition in his last work was to lay a breach through which others might enter. Only in his concluding sentences did Binswanger hold out the prospect of a supplement to the descriptive phenomenology of the essence of delusion by an existential analysis, possibly a final return to the level of *Daseinsanalyse* on Heideggerian grounds.

[4] Binswanger's Conception of Phenomenology

Binswanger's allegiance to phenomenology as a method has been unqualified ever since he found his way to it from his Neo-Kantian start. But this does not mean that his conception of phenomenology has always been the same. He never claimed that his final conception differed substantially from that of others, especially Husserl's. In fact, he told American inquirers that the best way to an understanding of his *Daseinsanalyse* led through the study of Husserl and Heidegger. Nevertheless, in a researcher and thinker as original as Binswanger, phenomenology was bound to develop modifications, some of which deserve special discussion before their concrete import can be shown further on. For Binswanger, such "modes" of phenomenologizing consisted at times only in emphases and de-emphases, not all of them deliberate and explicit. Binswanger was not a methodologist interested in method for its own sake. His entire philosophizing was conducted in the service of his main human concerns.

In the light of these concerns, especially the one to "hold fast to what it means to be a man," Binswanger espoused phenomenology as the best approach to a deeper understanding of what went on in his patients through understanding the phenomena of the world in which they lived. This meant also a reconstruction of the science of psychiatry that was not restricted to phenomenology but had a phenomenological anthropology as its foundation.[15] For Binswanger a primary need in this reconstruction was its liberation from a false "naturalism" which he called the "naturalist," and at times also the "positivist," "cataract." It is not insignificant that Binswanger, after first speaking of a "natural science (*naturwissenschaftlich*) cataract" in his trailblazing *Referat* on phenomenology of 1922 (republished at the start of the first volume of his selected essays of 1947), amended the adjective in a footnote at the beginning of the second volume (1955) to read "naturalistic" (*naturalistisch*). Even without an explicit explanation of this amendment, it is plain that Binswanger's seeming rebellion against science was chiefly meant as a way to its reconstruction. "Naturalism" as here used is presumably identical with the kind of naturalism fought by Husserl in

15. *Ausgewählte Vorträge,* II, 295.

"Philosophy as a Rigorous Science," i.e., a natural science reducing all phenomena to objects of the physical and biological sciences. This was also the kind of naturalism professed, though not practiced, by Freud in his conception of man as *homo natura*. But for Binswanger such science did not coincide with science as such. The problem was to find new non-naturalistic foundations for it. The Neo-Kantian attempt of a "subjectivation" of psychology through "reconstruction" did not satisfy Binswanger. Nor did Dilthey or Jaspers. So he turned to phenomenology in its philosophical form.

In what follows I shall try to point out the main features of Binswanger's phenomenological approach. Let us first attempt to determine how far Binswanger accepted the basic features of such an approach. At the start, phenomenology was for Binswanger chiefly descriptive phenomenology. As such its main contribution was the light it shed on intentionality as the basic structure of the psychological world, a new phenomenon which could not be accounted for in terms of "naturalistic" science. For Binswanger the intentional directedness of our subjective acts to their objective content also provided a cure for the split between subject and object which he considered to have been one of the banes of science.

Binswanger's phenomenological description had as its basis the enormous range of phenomena which an intuitive experience freed from naturalistic or positivistic blinkers had opened up. This must not make one overlook the fact that Binswanger never abandoned some reservations against an "absolute intuitionism" which Natorp and later Szilasi had nourished in him.[16] What Binswanger seemed to object to was the assertion that pure consciousness is given "absolutely." This absolute certainty or "apodicticity" of Husserl's cogito meant to him a philosophical presupposition to which he could not subscribe. But this did not preclude "intuition" in the sense of *Anschauung* as the starting point of all knowledge, including psychological knowledge.

From this point of view the term "experience" (*Erfahrung*) was much more characteristic of Binswanger's main methodological commitment, but to him experience was to be understood in a wider and deeper sense than in common empiricism. As such it was even to comprise psychoanalytic experience, which in Binswanger's sense was by no means a matter of a mere

16. *"Dank an Husserl,"* p. 72.

transempirical hypothesis. In fact Binswanger later widened this concept to the extent of even admitting dream reports as parts of experience. It was Szilasi who, through his essay on the "Experiential Foundations of Binswanger's *Daseinsanalyse*" reinforced this self-interpretation of Binswanger, giving him the idea that there were new modes of experience neglected thus far but accessible in the light of his new approach.

Binswanger's conception of *analysis* as applied to the phenomena of *Dasein* also calls for some comment. Obviously differing from the meaning of analytics as introduced by Kant and taken over by Heidegger for his study of the ontological structures of human existence (*existentialia*), Binswanger's "analysis" does not seem to have any technical connotations. Its meaning can be gathered sufficiently from what he does in his case studies: an exploration, aspect by aspect, of the structures such as spatiality or temporality that are distinguishable in the worlds of the patients. Binswanger's analysis does not exclude; but instead it moves toward a comprehensive synthesis at the end.

What Binswanger had to say on phenomenological *description* is more significant. For he emphasized imagery and metaphor as indispensable for phenomenology. In fact, he went so far as to state that, in contrast to discursive and scientific language, they embody the authentic (*eigentliche*) language of phenomenology and *Daseinsanalyse*. Thus the seeming metaphors of falling and rising as applied to modes of existence are claimed to describe authentic experiences. Consequently, phenomenology does not require elaborate interpretations of dreams as being mere symbols for unconscious realities.[17] Dreams can speak for themselves. This bold claim clearly does not deny the facts of etymology. Analogical uses may be later than the literal ones, but they are nevertheless based on direct experiences.

Binswanger has no serious reservations against the next step of the phenomenological method, the move to general or essential insights (eidetic phenomenology). How important it is to base this step on a study of individual cases in depth is impressively illustrated by Binswanger's great case studies on schizophrenia, where the comprehensive essential insights were formulated only in an introduction written much later.

A related concept in Binswanger's approach is that of the a priori. It is clearly more than a part of his Kantian heritage. Actually, his use of the philosophically imposing, but scientifi-

17. "Daseinsanalyse und Psychiatrie," in *Ausgewählte Vorträge*, II, 289–91.

cally suspect, label was somewhat unorthodox if not solecistic. Thus, when he spoke of the a priori structures of *Dasein,* he had in mind the basic structures of human existence that pervade all its empirical modifications. When he referred to Heidegger's a priori clearing (*Freilegung*) of *Dasein* he seemed to be referring to the method rather than to the goal, the "cleared" fundamental framework of all existence. Apparently Binswanger used "a priori" almost as a synonym for "transcendental," which to him also designated the basic structures that make all experience possible.

But this does not mean that Binswanger's a priori implies some general and necessary propositions not capable of, or in need of, any verification. These propositions are not simply to be taken for granted but are to be discovered and verified in phenomenological research. Thus, for all practical purposes, Binswanger's a priori need not scare the less transcendentalist minds into believing that he had subordinated scientific research to philosophical dictates.

How far did Binswanger advance from descriptive to transcendental phenomenology in Husserl's sense? While even in his initial *Referat* of 1922 he did not suppress Husserl's method of suspending belief in existence or bracketing, Husserl's favorite terms "*epochē*" or "reduction" are almost conspicuous by absence for anyone familiar with Husserl's increasing insistence on this device as the *sine qua non* of his transcendental phenomenology. Whatever the meaning of this seeming omission may be, Binswanger was certainly not blind to the new gains which the later phases of Husserl's "transcendentalism" could bring for the phenomenological psychopathologist. Thus, during his second Husserlian phase he attempted a genetic phenomenology of psychotic delusions (*Wahn*), especially in manic and depressive states in which important concepts from Husserl's later writings played a major part. But even then reduction was not mentioned explicitly as a step which had to precede the study of the constitutive processes in health and in sickness. This whole new dimension in Binswanger's work remained unarticulated, and the utilization of Husserl's more specific distinctions between active and passive constitution, as worked out especially in *Erfahrung und Urteil,* is missing.

It may be more important to inquire into Binswanger's use of Heidegger's addition to the phenomenological approach, "hermeneutics." With all his ambivalent admiration for Heidegger, Binswanger never seems to have discussed this particular feature of Heidegger's analytics explicitly. Its best equivalent may be his more general consideration of the problem of *verstehen,* which, especially through Jaspers, had become such a central concern for psychopathology. It also was of major significance to Binswanger in his attempt not only to understand the psychoses but to clarify and justify basic insights in Freudian psychoanalysis. From the very start, Binswanger never accepted the dichotomy of intelligible and merely explainable connections between the elements that Jaspers had explored in his phenomenology; Binswanger rejected any rigid division between neurotic and psychotic disturbances. To Binswanger intuitive understanding even of the world of the psychotic was possible through a study of his inner life history, using as much subjective material as was available but interpreting it in a more imaginative way. Thus in 1930, in a review article of a book by Erwin Straus, who still believed that in special situations experience could be emptied and deprived of meaning, Binswanger insisted that in the light of Heidegger's insights there were no completely meaningless experiences, since all are integral parts of the structure of being-in-the-world. This clearly calls for a kind of interpretation which goes considerably beyond mere recording, however phenomenologically widened. As to the nature of such interpretation (*Deuten*), Binswanger as late as 1955 gave only tentative suggestions, such as the existence of a phenomenological self-evidence which could accompany even the relation between the symbol and the symbolized in psychoanalysis.[18]

A potentially more original operation is involved in Binswanger's attempt to justify the new phenomenology of love that he developed in his work on the fundamental forms of *Dasein.* For here he appealed to a special type of "knowledge of *Dasein*" (*Daseinserkenntnis*) which, for instance, revealed dual "wehood" as more basic than isolated selfhood:

> In contrast to objective knowledge, which can merely "build cognitive walls around love," knowledge of *Dasein* is to find its ground and foundation in the being together of me and you.[19]

This is the initial statement which Binswanger puts at the head of the introduction of Part II of his book, repeating it al-

18. *Ausgewählte Vorträge,* II, 15. Actually, Heidegger, orally and in his letters, kept urging Binswanger to write a "hermeneutics of exploration," which Binswanger never attempted.

19. *Grundformen,* p. 21.

most literally from the introduction of Part I. To assess the full import of this claim, and, even more, to present Binswanger's justification in a nutshell is beyond the scope of the present account, which is concerned only with its phenomenological aspects. In this perspective it is important that not only "objective" scientific knowledge was rejected as a possible way toward love as the fundamental form of *Dasein;* even phenomenology in the sense of Husserl's essential insight (*Wesensschau*) was disqualified. Strangely, Scheler, who often stressed love as the foundation for our knowledge of values, did not figure in this context.

Binswanger's knowledge of *Dasein* starts from (the experience of) a loving togetherness in which we must be totally engaged, an encounter involving a we-experience, in which we are rooted in our own being, yet from which we "vault beyond" (*Überschwung*) our own *Dasein.*[20] One implication is that without a full realization and acceptance of the basic experience knowledge of loving we-hood is impossible. The reference to "vaulting beyond" is combined with an appeal to a loving imagination (*Einbildungskraft*), i.e., literally, the power of inbuilding through which we can build love into ourselves. In the further development of this part, additional clues to Binswanger's new method of loving, imaginative cognition emerge. At first sight there seems to be a conflict between Binswanger's identifying love and his interpretation of Heidegger's isolating care (*Sorge*). But his cognition of *Dasein* promises a synthesis of both. All this is stated in terms so permeated by Hegelian language that only a much fuller account could supply as much real clarity as this conception allows. In the present context the main question is how far the "unfolding" of this new mode relates it to other forms of knowledge, especially phenomenological knowledge. This is what Binswanger tries to achieve in a final long chapter in which he also attempts to assess its epistemological "truth." First Kant and Hegel are considered. Then Binswanger compares his own solution with the phenomenologies of Goethe (!) and Husserl and the existential analytics of Heidegger. Congenial though they are, Binswanger does not claim that they

20. The German text says: "frag-, ja sprachlose Seinsfülle, wirhaft gläubiges Feststehen im Sein, reiner Überschwung" (*Grundformen,* p. 490). Such a telescoped, almost untranslatable characterization can at best be considered as an attempt to evoke the experience rather than to describe it.

coincide. Husserl's method, which respects the phenomena above everything, remains a model (p. 642). But his phenomenological "ideation" still differs from Binswanger's loving imagination. In *Daseinserkenntnis* Binswanger finds an imaginative realization of essential insight, where the knower is no longer a nonparticipant observer (p. 450); such knowledge cannot be attained by effort, but comes—and here Binswanger uses a late Heideggerian expression—as a favor or grace. It is incompatible with the phenomenological reduction or suspension of belief. At this point Binswanger turns to Dilthey's peculiar life knowledge as basic, especially for history. Eventually, Binswanger's *Daseinserkenntnis*, with all its congeniality to these methods, emerges as something *sui generis*. Yet in the end Binswanger pays another tribute to Husserl's phenomenology as the method without which he never could have developed his own.

Is this method of *Daseinserkenntnis* itself phenomenological? Clearly Binswanger himself thought so in making it the epistemological foundation of his phenomenology of love. Whether or not this claim can be honored largely depends, of course, on one's standards of phenomenological "rigor." What has to be faced, however, is that Binswanger, in spite of all his efforts, has to call for an initial surrender to we-hood which makes all subsequent phenomenological re-examination of his claims problematical.

[5] Some Basic Conceptions of Binswanger's Phenomenological Anthropology

Clearly, in the case of an applied phenomenologist it is much more relevant to pay attention to what he does than what he says about phenomenology. Chances are that his own theory of what he does is even less fitted to what he is actually doing than in the case of the pure phenomenologist.

What makes this task more difficult in Binswanger's case is the very abundance of available illustrations. To meet this difficulty I shall select samples of Binswanger's phenomenologizing from various phases of his development, beginning with the Freudian theme of the unconscious. These samples will be followed by a discussion of the significance of Binswanger's approach to psychopathology, psychiatry, and psychotherapy.

A. *The Phenomenology of the Unconscious*

Perhaps the major theoretical obstacle to the acceptance of Freud's psychoanalysis has been his advocacy of the unconscious. Scientific psychology and psychiatry found it difficult to accommodate such an unobservable among their data and were apt to look upon it as pure speculation. But there were philosophers who had partially and reluctantly recognized it, especially Leibniz, Herbart, and Schopenhauer and Eduard von Hartmann, who were most outspoken. However, only one contemporary philosopher-psychologist was openly invoked by Freud: Theodor Lipps, although even Lipps did not go much beyond pointing out the central importance of the psychic unconscious.

Binswanger shared the uneasiness of most psychologists and philosophers about the status of the unconscious in science, though he never questioned its existence. His initial concern for its philosophical vindication was clearly related to this uneasiness. The key to a solution as he envisaged it lay in a better phenomenology of consciousness. As he put it: "Only he to whom the structure of consciousness is unknown talks most of the unconscious." Then he added the following footnote:

> Of course by saying this I do not mean to deny the facts of psychoanalysis, hypnosis, etc., but only its psychological interpretation up to now. At the time when Freud formulated his brilliant (*genial*) conceptions, the structure of consciousness was actually not yet widely known. It has become known to us especially through Brentano, Husserl, Natorp, Meinong, Scheler, Hönigswald. We agree completely with Husserl when he says that the so-called unconscious "is anything but a phenomenological nothing, but itself a marginal mode [*Grenzmodus*] of consciousness" (*Formal and Transcendental Logic*, p. 280).[21]

Binswanger's full solution might have been expected from the never-completed second volume of his early *Introduction to the Problems of General Psychology.* This also was Freud's hope, when he received Volume I with Binswanger's dedication. But the 1926 essay on "Experience, Understanding, and Interpretation" contains at least the general line of Binswanger's vindication of the psychoanalytic unconscious on phenomenological grounds.

Binswanger's startling claim was that it was Freud who for

21. *Schweizer Archiv für Neurologie und Psychiatrie,* XXVIII (1932), 236.

the first time had based the study of man on experience.[22] What Binswanger wanted to show was that Freud's interpretation (*Deuten*) was really not a mere theory but had its basis in experience. In fact Binswanger believed that it was our direct experience of the life of other persons, rather than the guesswork of inferential interpretations based merely on protocols (*hermeneutische Erfahrung*) that allowed us to interpret their dreams (II, 71). Thus the direct perception of the way in which the patient reported his dreams, his stopping, pausing, etc., was the basis of all interpretation, even when it went beyond the immediately experienced. As far as *Verstehen* was concerned, this too, as Binswanger saw it, was possible only on the basis of direct experience, a concept expanded by Freud into depths not previously probed and in fact not admitted even in Freud's theoretical conception of the human person.

But the inferences of Freud's method certainly exceeded the range of this widened experience and thus constituted a composite of direct experience and transempirical or hypothetical reasoning. However, even the hermeneutic understanding that transcends experience can be converted into experience, especially in the practice of psychoanalysis, where interpretations are verified by the patient. Eventually, the psychoanalytic interpretation can be understood as "quasi-experience."

But if the unconscious is now accessible to phenomenological experience, what about its structure as laid out in Freud's dynamic trinity of the ego, the superego, and the id, all of which can be at least partially unconscious? Binswanger discussed these entities briefly in a special section on *Daseinsanalyse* and Psychoanalysis in the Case of Ellen West.[23] Here Binswanger opposes any interpretations of such agencies as separate persons which would require for each one worlds of their own. At least in the case of the id this would be impossible. Yet Binswanger does not deny the right and the need for a scientific hypothesis of an impersonal id. It is just that for him a hypothetical inference to such an entity can be justified directly not on phenomenological grounds but only on the grounds of explanatory science, which is compatible with, but at best complementary to, phenomenological *Daseinsanalyse*. Binswanger's main rejection of such an explanation concerns a conception of man ac-

22. *Ausgewählte Vorträge*, II, 68.
23. *Schizophrenie* (Pfullingen: Neske, 1957), pp. 149 ff. Translated in *Existence*, pp. 314 ff.

cording to which he is nothing but "natural man" and is ignored as *Dasein* or being-in-the-world with freedom and love.

B. *Dasein as Being-in-the-World*

The decisive step in the development of Binswanger's *Daseinsanalyse* as a distinctive approach was clearly the adoption of Heidegger's conception of *Dasein* to replace the Husserlian concept of consciousness, which was never quite adequate anyhow in the mind of a Freudian who was also interested in the unconscious. What is more significant, in the light of the new conception, is that even Husserl's concept of intentionality now moved into the background.

The difficulties of rendering the German *Dasein* satisfactorily are so well known that they need not be restated here. The crux of the matter is that Heidegger has loaded the harmless German word *Dasein,* and especially the element of "*Da*" (there), which is neither here (*hier*) nor there (*dort*), with so many new connotations that not only a literal rendering but also a complete substitution is apt to break down under this load. An artificial word like "there-being," coined by William J. Richardson, at least gives warning of this difficulty. "Existence," especially in quotes, might do if properly interpreted, but the use of the untranslated German *Dasein* is still the safest way to give notice of the new connotations.

These connotations are what really matter. Heidegger's analysis explicated *Dasein* as a being in relation to an entire world, not merely in relation to specific intentional objects, and particularly to the world of daily use with its utensils (*Zeug*). It was this concept of the surrounding world of the living subject which became so fruitful to Binswanger in his attempts to interpret the context for the phenomena of his patients. It also gave him an alternative to the sterile confrontation between subjectivism and objectivism and the "split" between subject and object. Now world and self appeared as correlatives in symbiosis. *Dasein* itself was for Binswanger no mere static "being." It involved a way of moving in a world. Especially in his analyses of dreams, Binswanger showed different ways of living and moving in a characteristic space. Thus there are rising and falling, skipping, sliding, or jumping as styles of existing, exemplified most strikingly in the manic form of *Dasein.* Special forms of such movements can be found in Binswanger's studies of "failures of *Dasein*" (*missglücktes Dasein*). This term itself was taken over from Szilasi. But Binswanger gave ultimate credit to Heidegger's concept of *Verfallensein* and even dedicated his studies of three such modes of failure to Heidegger.

The first one of these is *Verstiegenheit* (literally, to have lost one's path in climbing a mountain): [24] the victim has maneuvered himself into a position from which he can no longer extricate himself. Characteristic is the disproportion between the height of the goals aspired to and the level accessible through experience. A prime example is Ibsen's master builder Solness, who builds structures which he can no longer climb, until he falls to his death. Other failures are *Verschrobenheit* (screwiness), where our meanings get mixed up, and *Manieriertheit* (mannerism), where, because of our inability to reach our own self, we seek support in an impersonal model.

The most important implication of the new conception was that for a real understanding of a person, and particularly a mentally sick person, one had to study primarily his world, not his organism or personality in itself set apart from his world. For Binswanger, self and world are correlative concepts—the self without its world is truncated; the world without its focus, the self, is no world.

Actually, Binswanger even spoke of several such worlds for the same person: the *Umwelt,* his non-personal environment; the *Mitwelt,* his social relations to others; and the *Eigenwelt,* his private world. In some cases he also distinguished between the ethereal world and the tomb world (the Case of Ellen West) or the fate world (*Schicksalswelt*). But what these terms stand for are clearly not separate worlds but regions within the comprehensive world of the person.

Binswanger's worlds can be analyzed according to several dimensions. This does not mean that in all his studies Binswanger followed the same pattern of analysis. His approach seems to depend on the nature of the case in question. In most cases he pays special attention to the characteristic kind of "worldliness" or articulation of the world, its temporal and its spatial structures. He may begin with a topography of several sub-worlds (the ethereal, the tomb world, and the world of praxis, as in the Case of Ellen West) and explore the role that death plays for

24. This term occurs as early as 1916 in Pfänder's *Zur Psychologie der Gesinnungen* as a characteristic of the "super-real" or "transcendent" sentiments and, generally, types of mental processes. Recently, Roland Kuhn has established that Binswanger was very familiar with and appreciative of this text.

this candidate for future suicide. He may begin with the relation of home world (*Heimat*) and "eternity," exploring the place of the dual, the plural, and the single mode of *Dasein* in the life of a highly autistic type (Jürg Zund), or with the role of the dominating theme of dreadfulness (*das Fürchterliche*) following its significance for temporalization, spatialization, and "materiality" in the patient's world (Lola Voss) or, more specifically, with the role of the terror of a primal scene in its development into a full-scale delusion affecting all the other areas of the *Dasein* (Suzanne Urban). Thus *Daseinsanalyse* puts a number of basic categories at the disposal of the analyst, but does not prescribe any rigid sequence in their application.

To illustrate some of these categories: *Spatiality* in the world of *Dasein* is expressed often in the form of a verb (*Räumlichung*) that conveys the way in which, in our projection of our world (*Weltentwurf*), we assign room to the various items that occupy such space. The problem of spatiality occupied Binswanger especially in the early period of his *Daseinsanalyse,* e.g., in his essay on the problem of space in psychopathology and in the studies on the flight of ideas. The spaces of our natural world are subdivided into the oriented human space and the homogeneous space of science, the tuned space (*gestimmter Raum*) created by architecture and the spaces in nature which have their peculiar characteristic moods. There is the esthetic space in works of the representational arts, as well as in music; and there is the narrowed space related to the threat of the dreadful, as in the Case of Lola Voss.

Temporality is a dimension to which Binswanger seemed to attach increasing importance, also as part of the projection of our work (*Zeitigung*). It is illustrated particularly in the Case of Ellen West, whose different "worlds" display different kinds of time. Her ethereal or dream world shows a fantasy-based inauthentic future, her world of the tomb the predominance of the inauthentic past in which nothing new can happen, her world of practice a disintegration of time (falling apart).

There is relatively little need to exemplify such figurative expressions as illumination and coloration, and Binswanger himself seems to make relatively little use of them in his major case studies. That the world of the optimist is rosy, cloudless, shining, or bright, that of the pessimist, dark or nightlike may seem obvious enough. "Materiality" of consistency is described in such terms as lightness or heaviness, volatility, lack of contours. Softness and malleability apply particularly to the manic form of existence.

C. *The Phenomenology of Love: Being-beyond-the-World*

Binswanger leaves no doubt that he considers his most important contribution to a phenomenological anthropology to be his new interpretation of love. Its chief development can be found in *Grundformen und Erkenntnis menschlichen Daseins*. The need for such a phenomenology was particularly urgent for him in view of his dissatisfaction with Freud's anthropology, in which the Eros with its libido figured so prominently. But Freud's "naturalistic" love did not and could not satisfy Binswanger's conception of man as a whole, and of the full human phenomenon of love.

No such help was to be expected from Husserl, whose phenomenological interests at best mentioned but did not explore the emotional range. One might wonder why Scheler's and Pfänder's discussions did not prove more important to Binswanger. But Scheler's attempt to link up love with the movement toward higher value would have had little to offer to Binswanger, who showed no interest in the philosophy of value. Nor were Pfänder's sentiments, with their centrifugal and centripetal flow, of much value to Binswanger's diagnosis of *Dasein*.

However, one must realize from the very start that what Binswanger had in mind when he developed his phenomenology of love was not the phenomenon discussed by those who consider love a one-sided act which may or may not be reciprocated by the beloved. For reasons never stated explicitly, Binswanger concentrated on the social love between one and another as a primary relation between an I and a Thou, or more specifically as a we-relationship between the two. Consequently, his analysis cannot claim to throw phenomenological light on anything but this special relationship, manifested by mutual love and resulting in solidarity, the being with one another of me and you (*Miteinandersein von Mir und Dir*) or we-hood (*Wirheit*). In fact, Binswanger assumes, though on the basis of the previous discussions of such phenomenologists as Scheler, that I and thou are secondary derivations from the primary we (the dual mode of *Dasein*). It occurs in two forms: the loving being-me-and-you, and the friendly being-with-each-other in sharing. It is absent, however, in the case of mere being-with (*Mitsein*), as it occurs in trivial interpersonal dealings and contacts.

Now the counterpart, and in this sense the basis, of Binswanger's phenomenology of love was always Heidegger's interpretation of *Dasein* as essentially care (*Sorge*). Binswanger, interested in this phenomenon only as an interpretation of human life, not as an access to the structure of *Dasein,* not only expressed the need of supplementing this interpretation by the explicit addition of love but also claimed its primacy. Compared with love, care is merely a defective type of being. Yet the basic framework for the new hermeneutics of love remained Heideggerian; so is much of the language. But there are differences in the approach as well. Most conspicuous is the constant appeal to poetic evidence, drawn mostly from Goethe and Robert and Elizabeth Browning.

Binswanger characterizes love in this sense first by its spatiality, its attitude toward space: love, as distinguished from power, which contends over space, is best expressed in the embrace, which implies the mutual yielding of space based on the boundless we-of-love.[25] Such often figurative and mystifying accounts should preferably be expressed in the more sober language of concrete descriptions. Sharing of the space, as opposed to the displacement not only in Cartesian space but also in care, may best describe it. The language of "encounter" may come closest to it.

Love has also a characteristic temporality, a timelessness which Binswanger relates to eternity, as distinguished from perpetuity. It means not infinite duration but a certain indifference to the flux of time according to past, present, and future, very much in contrast to the temporal concerns of care. In contrast to Heidegger's interpretation of *Dasein* as essentially each-his-own in solitary confinement, Binswanger sees in love a dual mode of being. (The special grammatical "number" called "dual" in Greek, is to Binswanger a striking expression of this special mode of *Dasein.*) In love *Dasein* is what we ourselves are, not what each one is for himself (*Jemeinigkeit*); it is "us-ness" (*Unsrigkeit*). It is also characterized by a special at-homeness (*Heimatlichkeit*) of the lovers with one another, not in physical space, but in a space which is "everywhere" and "nowhere." In contrast to Heidegger's care in its confinement to this world in its finiteness, love steps beyond the finite world of *Dasein* by

25. *Grundformen,* p. 26.

vaulting beyond (*Überschwung*) into transspatiality (*Überräumlichung*), transtemporality (*Überzeitigung*), and transhistoricity (*Übergeschichtlichkeit*). This is what is involved in what Binswanger means by characterizing love not only as being-in-the-world but as being-beyond-the-world (*über-die-Welt-hinaus-sein*). It takes us beyond the world of one's own self to the world of we-hood. The being-beyond-the-world is therefore a being not in an absolute beyond, especially not a supernatural beyond, but merely in a social beyond of our individual private worlds in the "eternal now" (*ewiger Augenblick*) of love. Obviously, much of the ecstatic language of these characterizations cannot be taken literally. Its function can at best be evocative, a means of appealing to experiences which have still to be awakened by a peculiar kind of description that runs ahead of the immediately accessible.

D. Daseinsanalyse *of Schizophrenia*

For Binswanger *Daseinsanalyse* is not a mere psychiatric enterprise that applies primarily to neuroses. On the contrary, he wants to offer an analysis of all *Dasein*, comprising the normal as well as the abnormal range, and seeing in the abnormal not a fundamentally different phenomenon but a modification of *Dasein* as such. However, he also believes that such understanding allows us to achieve a real grasp not only of the neurotic but also of the psychotic range (as far as this distinction still has any validity). It abolishes in particular the distinction between the intelligible and the completely unintelligible regions among the psychological phenomena.

Psychoanalysis started as a new approach to the extreme form of neuroticism, e.g., hysteria. For a long time it did not attack the psychotic. The emphasis was on ambulatory treatment, not on work in the kind of institutional setup in which psychoses could be treated. But Binswanger in his sanatorium was much more ambitious. And his final target was clearly a better understanding of the most pronounced psychoses, such as schizophrenia, so labeled first at the Zurich Burghölzli by Eugen Bleuler, and the manic-depressive psychoses. To both he devoted major studies, beginning with the *Daseinsanalyse* of mania, then turning to schizophrenia, and finally returning to the manic-depressive illnesses, but now with the new tools of Husserl's constitutional phenomenology.

Perhaps the best way of illustrating what *Daseinsanalyse* can do for an understanding of schizophrenia is to show how far it has been able to throw light on one of its facets, the so-called "autism" of Eugen Bleuler.

The five major case studies united in Binswanger's book on *Schizophrenia* were written from 1945 to 1953, during the period of pure *Daseinsanalyse*, though in retrospect Binswanger pointed out the continuing significance of the Husserlian phenomenology of essences, especially for the fifth study (Susanne Urban) in which the essence of the terrifying (*Schreckliches*) plays a central role. Besides, the Introduction of *Schizophrenie* (1957) showed an even more pronounced return to Husserl in the final evaluation of these cases: Schizophrenia is now interpreted as a form of disruption of the Husserlian "presumption" that experience will continue in the same style of constitution as in past experience.

Accordingly, schizophrenia could now be characterized by

(1) the breaking apart of the consistency of natural experience leading to attempts at arbitrary interference and eventual failures;

(2) the splitting up of experience into rigid alternatives;

(3) attempts at covering-up (*Deckung*) of the intolerable alternatives;

(4) attrition (*Aufgeriebenwerden*) by these tensions, resulting in resignation and withdrawal and eventually in delusions (*Wahn*).

Binswanger believed that this analysis enabled him to break down the "cardinal symptom" of schizophrenia, "autism." But he did not claim that this analysis was valid for all forms of schizophrenia. In particular, it did not yet account for the concrete form of the paranoid ideas (delusions) in schizophrenia.

E. *Phenomenology of Mania and Melancholia*

First Binswanger applied his new anthropological method to a characteristic symptom of mania, i.e., the flight of ideas. Here Binswanger pays primary attention to the world of the person involved in the flight of ideas (*ideenflüchtiger Mensch*). Two detailed cases of an "orderly" flight of ideas are followed by one that illustrates disorderly (*ungeordnete*) flight. In the first case there is still a unity of theme behind the jumpiness of expression. This is lacking in the second case, one of complete confusion (*Verwirrtheit*). Here *Dasein* is characterized by more than skipping—namely, by a dancelike cyclonic movement, inspired by a festive joy of life and a general optimism. Time has shrunk to a mere present, and no real history is experienced, although there is a characteristic coming-back to the same basic theme. Binswanger also explores the peculiar place of the ego in these changed worlds of the manics. The underlying frame for most of these interpretations of the flight of ideas was Heidegger's analytics of *Dasein*. But this did not prevent Binswanger from occasionally calling on Husserl as well as on other philosophers, not all of them connected closely with the Phenomenological Movement. There are also occasional hints about the significance of this new type of understanding for Freud's psychoanalysis.

Binswanger's return to mania and melancholia (a term which he preferred to the vague "depression") in his second Husserlian phase is explained by the insufficiency of a mere *Daseinsanalyse* of the world of the patient. What is missing in the latter phase is the account of the constitution of these worlds, i.e., of the factors which determine their structures. In order to supply it, Binswanger now tried to utilize some of the key concepts of Husserl's later transcendental phenomenology, such as his concept of appresentation and his egology, as interpreted by Szilasi. The underlying idea is that in the psychoses the constitutions of the normal world can no longer take place. Thus the texture of the manic world is characteristically loosened. In melancholia the normal constitution of the world becomes loose in such a way that the motifs of suffering and guilt take control. Here self-reproaches are based on a reversal of the time constitution. Protention is extended to the past ("if only I had . . ."). On the other hand the ego loses in fullness and range of possibilities. The guiding themes are narrowed to the self and its losses.

It is different in the manic phase, which is primarily directed toward others. Failures of the constitution of the alter ego are characteristic. They can be understood in the light of Husserl's concept of appresentation of the other person. Here the other is no longer fully constituted but is possibly seen only as a mere thing. Furthermore, the "antinomic" structure of the manic-depressive existence can be understood as a malfunction of the pure ego which finds itself caught helplessly, unable to perform its normal constitutions. This leads to a distemper (*Verstimmung*), which in melancholia implies anxiety and anguish (*Qual*) and in mania signifies flight from the task of control. Thus the root of the manic-depressive psychosis consists in a weakness of the pure ego. Regardless of whether there is room for such a possibility in Husserl's doctrine of the pure ego, this concept certainly is compatible with recent attempts to enrich Freudian psychoanalysis by the concept of ego-strength (Anna Freud, Heinz Hartmann, and others).

F. *Phenomenological* Daseinsanalyse, *Psychiatry, and Therapy*

Considering the fact that Binswanger was for most of his life the director of a mental sanatorium and, except for occasional lectures, never associated with a university or research organization, one might well expect the chief interest of *Daseinsanalyse* to be therapeutic. All the more disturbing, if not shocking, has it been to some of his students and critics that Binswanger saw limits to therapy and that in the Case of Ellen West, for example, he looked upon her eventual suicide as a kind of liberation and answer to an insoluble conflict.

What one has to realize first is that Binswanger himself was explicit about the fact that *Daseinsanalyse,* in contrast to psychoanalysis, was not primarily a therapeutic but a scientific enterprise. Whatever significance it may have had for psychiatry and particularly for clinical psychiatry was only secondary and incidental. In fact, Binswanger did not lay claim to any special therapeutic method. As a therapist he was an eclectic, using traditional methods with a clear realization of their limitations. In the beginning he tried out strict psychoanalytic techniques on Freudian lines. Only later did he come to realize the limits of Freudian therapy, though he never abandoned it. At least in one case (*Singultus*) he successfully used "intervention by direct action." Like his friend Roland Kuhn, the inventor of the antidepressant Tofranil, he was also not opposed to medication.

The fact that Binswanger did not claim a distinctive and developed therapy based on *Daseinsanalyse* did not mean that such a therapy could not develop eventually. For he did believe that *Daseinsanalyse* had significance for therapy, and he even gave the following guidelines for it:

1. *Daseinsanalyse* understands the life history of the patient, not in the light of a theory but as a modification of being-in-the-world.

2. It lets the patient experience how he has lost his way and like the mountain guide tries to lead him back and restore him to the common world, re-establishing communication.

3. It treats the patient neither as a mere object nor as mere

patient but as an existence or as fellow man. Therapy means encounter as opposed to mere contact. Freud's transference is really such an encounter.[26]

4. It understands dreams not by interpretation but by a direct reading as a being-in-the-world. It can thus reveal to the patient his way of being-in-the-world and set him free for his real possibilities. All this takes place on levels where there is no distinction between conscious and subconscious experience.

5. It uses additional psychotherapeutic methods as means to open to the patient an understanding of human being which allows him to find the way back from the neurotic or psychotic way of being to the free disposal of his own normal possibilities.

But Binswanger was concerned not only about the therapeutic side of psychiatry. He was at least as seriously interested in its theoretical aspects and specifically in its status as a science. Just like Jaspers, he was in search of a solid foundation for this enterprise in its ambivalent position between mere biology and the humanities (the sphere of *Geist*). Binswanger did not claim that there was a clear and simple solution to the question of the status and unity of psychiatry. But he thought there was at least a key to such a solution. And he believed it could be found in the philosophical foundations of this science, notably in phenomenology.

Phenomenology implies that psychiatry has to be based on experience, though a special kind of experience. This experience has to begin with the experience of man preceding psychopathology and the distinction between normal and abnormal. The foundations for such an understanding of man can be derived from Heidegger's analytics of *Dasein,* despite that fact that his analytics ultimately has ontological objectives rather than anthropological ones. The anthropological use of analytics allows us to develop an empirical *Daseinsanalyse.* In Binswanger's view this *Daseinsanalyse,* properly developed, contains all the important concepts needed for the foundation and understanding of pathological as well as normal existence. Thus the science of man as mentally sick presupposes *Daseinsanalytik* just as pathology presupposes general biology, *Daseinsanalytik* being understood as insight into the a priori structure or *Seinsverfassung* of human being in general. On this ground floor rests *Daseinsanalyse* as the empirical-phenomenological investigation of defi-

26. Here Binswanger joins with the idea of Martin Buber's friend Hans Trüb: i.e., cure through encounter (*Heilung durch Begegnung*).

nite modes or *Gestalten* of *Dasein*. Therapy forms a second story above pathology.

[6] The Role of Phenomenology in Binswanger's Anthropology

What, then, is the place of phenomenology and particularly phenomenological philosophy in Binswanger's *Daseinsanalyse*? Ever since he had sought an adequate foundation for Freud's theory, philosophy had been the hope, and phenomenology the decisive guide, in this search, even to the extent of diverting him from the straight course of orthodox psychoanalysis.

To this extent philosophical phenomenology was indeed the indispensable ingredient in the development of *Daseinsanalyse*, quite different from its role in Jaspers' psychopathology, as Binswanger saw it. But this "influence" must not be exaggerated. It does not mean that *Daseinsanalyse* stands and falls with the validity of Husserl's or Heidegger's philosophies. Quite apart from the fact that Binswanger modified Heidegger's implicit anthropology significantly, he not only applied his *Daseinsanalyse* but put it to the test of more painstaking case studies than any other existential psychologist or psychoanalyst had done, especially in the studies on the flight of ideas, in the five schizophrenia studies, and in the studies on melancholia and mania.

Daseinsanalyse would have been impossible without phenomenological philosophy. But its validity does not depend on it.

[7] Toward an Appraisal of Binswanger's Phenomenological Anthropology

A full-scale appraisal of Binswanger's phenomenological anthropology, let alone his entire work, on the basis of a chapter in the present context, would not make sense. Only a monograph prepared by an expert, not only in philosophy but in the many fields which Binswanger combined, could do justice to such a many-sided achievement.

Binswanger's work has been severely criticized both from the philosophical and the psychiatric point of view. Heidegger has repudiated Binswanger's use of his philosophy. Jaspers, while acknowledging some of Binswanger's special investigations, rejected his major objective and achievement. Freud did not want any of it.

In order to do Binswanger even a minimum of justice, one has to realize that he considered himself a pioneer, not a system builder bent on rivaling Kräpelin or even Jaspers. His goal was to lay breaches into the walls that surrounded the secret of the mentally sick. The new weapons he used were psychoanalysis, phenomenology, and existential analytics. The remarkable and unique thing about him was his pioneering spirit, enhanced by unlimited ambition, the readiness to try, to learn from others, to be in the wrong, but never to give up. Hence the output of his efforts would not be a system; at best it would be a prolegomena. But in his major books he did achieve genuine beginnings on which others could build. The following he had, even without a chance of building an academic school, is ample proof for this appraisal.

This productive echo must not make one repress some of the doubts about the permanent value of a work which shows so much of the personal imprint of its creator. Speaking first about the philosophical foundations of Binswanger's anthropology: With all its self-taught erudition his scholarship remained limited and was apt to lead to misunderstandings, though productive misunderstandings, as in the case of Heidegger. But just how productive were they? In this regard his major philosophical work, the *Grundformen und Erkenntnis menschlichen Daseins,* conceived as an attempt to supplement, if not replace, Heidegger's anthropology, shows all the charms and limitations of Binswanger's enthusiastic approach. Enthralled by the idea that love is the superior counterpart of Heidegger's care, that it can "conquer everything," as it were, he took its superiority, its unproblematic sublimity so much for granted that he did not even give a descriptive analysis of its basic structure. And the final epistemology of *Daseinserkenntnis* loses itself in the forest of philosophical and literary testimonies which are his main guides, without confronting the basic philosophical challenges.

On the whole, Binswanger's use of phenomenology in his philosophy and also in his psychological and psychopathological work was as suggestive and imaginative as it was often incomplete. While he picked out new and significant phenomena e.g., "taking by one's weak side," the description often remained sketchy, relying on the suggestiveness of linguistic expressions. The careful check of his generalizations by imaginative variation also seems to be lacking. His highly figurative, if not high-flown, imagery as such may be inevitable and even indispensable. But too often its concrete significance for the phenomenon in question remains unclarified. For instance, it remains unclear just what "rising" and "falling" in a dream amount to. Here Binswanger's descriptions are often merely ostensive or pointing in the direction of the phenomena, without exploring them in all their dimensions as intentional structures.

But there would be little point in continuing with such a list of doubts and reservations. Suffice it to indicate that Binswanger's achievements must not be considered as permanent conquests. They are at best footholds, bridgeheads in a new world. Binswanger himself did not claim more. In this sense he was chiefly a trail-blazer for a new approach in phenomenological psychopathology, and there is little doubt that thus far he is *the* major one. Certainly, for better or worse, none of his potential rivals in this enterprise has made so much use of philosophical phenomenology.

8 / Eugène Minkowski (b. 1885): Phenomenology of the Lived (*Vécu*)

[1] Minkowski's Place in Phenomenological Psychiatry

When in his Sorbonne lectures of 1949 Merleau-Ponty lined up the pioneers of phenomenology in France,[1] his first "witness among us" was Minkowski, not only as the sole example of the influence of Husserl and Heidegger—a debatable point—but as a prime advocate of both phenomenology and existential analysis. The significance of Minkowski's contribution to French psychiatry is further attested by his role as one of the leading cofounders and editors-in-chief, together with Henri Ey, of *L'Evolution psychiatrique,* perhaps the major French psychopathological journal of today. But Minkowski's leadership in the development of the phenomenological approach to psychopathology has had international significance as well. It was in Zurich in 1922 that he presented his classical case of distortions of "lived time" immediately after Ludwig Binswanger's historic *Referat* on phenomenology. There was therefore ample justification for Rollo May to dedicate the volume on *Existence* to both Minkowski and Binswanger and to begin the selections under "Phenomenology" with Minkowski's nuclear case study.[2]

But Minkowski's real significance in the rise of phenomeno-

1. "Les Sciences de l'homme et la phénoménologie," *Cours de Sorbonne* (Paris, 1961), p. 5. English translation by John Wild, "Phenomenology and the Sciences of Man," in *The Primacy of Perception* (Evanston, Ill.: Northwestern University Press, 1964), p. 47.

2. "Findings in a Case of Schizophrenic Depression," in *Existence,* ed. Rollo May, Ernest Angel, Henri F. Ellenberger (New York: Basic Books, 1958), pp. 127–38.

logical psychiatry cannot be measured by such testimonies. What matters is the role of phenomenology in his own work. More specifically: What are Minkowski's contributions to and modifications of phenomenology, especially with regard to its new role in the French area? To understand and answer such a question, it is necessary to look first at Minkowski's basic objectives both in psychiatry and beyond it.

[2] Minkowski's Primary Concerns

The concluding considerations in Minkowski's *Traité de psychopathologie*[3] are entitled "On the Road of a Human Life" (Sur le chemin d'une vie humaine), and its final section carries the title "Human Life, the Primary Datum" (La Vie humaine donnée première). The Preface of the book states Minkowski's view of the purpose of psychopathology simply: "Psychopathology seeks to approach more and more human being [*l'Etre humain*], and it is this approach [*cheminement*] which matters above all" (p. xix). The final goal is to study and present in profile the "essential phenomena of our existence" (p. 738). In this sense, Minkowski's final goal is also a new anthropology. But he is not interested in developing a system of anthropology, not even in Binswanger's sense. His concern is what is human (*l'humain*) rather than what is man. One gets the impression that he is more concerned about the approaches to these goals than about reaching them. For Minkowski, phenomenology was such an approach, and in fact one of paramount importance. "Toward" (*vers*) is a characteristic start of many of his essays, especially of the brilliant vignettes in his "cosmology."

How far are these goals ever spelled out concretely? The dynamic, Bergsonian terms in which Minkowski thinks preclude any static formula. Is it at least possible to obtain a more definite idea of the quality of the "human" that he has in mind? An essential part of its connotation is determined by its opposite, the inhuman. Minkowski, who was a witness and near-victim of one of man's worst "inhumanities to man" during the Nazi occupation of Paris, makes the point that, whereas man can become inhuman, other living beings, especially animals, cannot be unanimal-like.

Apart from this clearly moral view, there is also a more

3. *Traité de psychopathologie* (Paris: PUF, 1968).

theoretical side to Minkowski's conception of the human. It is determined by his opposition to the merely quantitative, abstract, and in this sense scientific or prosaic, aspect and by his stress on the qualitative, concrete, and "poetic" aspect of human life in its fullness. Against the "scientific barbarism" of a merely quantitative science, which is expressed in its victory over the living experience of time and space, Minkowski feels a "boiling" (*gronder*) sense of revolt. What he wants in particular is to "reconquer our right over lived time." [4]

> We want neither to deny nor to renounce, nor to destroy nor to go back: thus we would once again give proof of barbarism. Hence the wish to return back cannot mean anything else for us but one thing: to resume contact with life and with what is "natural" and primitive in it, return to the first source from which springs not only science but also all the other manifestations of spiritual life, to study again the essential relationships which can be found originally, before science has modeled it after its fashion, between the different phenomena of which life is composed, to see whether we cannot extract from them something other than science does, without thereby plunging either into primitive naturism nor a mysticism which is often just as remote from nature as is science, a mysticism which also "rationalizes" in its imagery to which it resorts. We want to look "without instruments," and say what we see. Contrary to appearances, this is, incidentally, a pretty difficult assignment.
>
> This is how in our days have been born the phenomenology of Husserl and the philosophy of Bergson. The first has made it its goals to study and to describe the phenomena which compose life without letting itself be guided or limited in its research by any premises, whatever their origin and whatever their apparent legitimacy. The second has with an admirable boldness set up intuition against intelligence, the living against death, time against space. These two currents have not failed to exert a profound influence over the entire contemporary thought. The reason is that they corresponded to a real and profound need of our being (p. 3; my translation).

In what sense and to what extent can Minkowski be considered a phenomenologist? In his own perspective he certainly was one, increasingly. To some extent this allegiance can be demonstrated by the titles of some of his major writings. Its

4. *Le Temps vécu: Etudes phénoménologiques et psychopathologiques* (Paris: D'Artrey, 1933; 2d pr., Neuchâtel: Delachaux & Niestlé, 1968), p. 3. English translation by Nancy Metzel, *Lived Time* (Evanston, Ill.: Northwestern University Press, 1970).

clearest expression can be found in the subtitle of his "phenomenological studies" on *Lived Time* (*Le Temps vécu*), in many of his briefer pieces published in the *Recherches philosophiques* and later collected in *Vers une cosmologie*, and in other scattered articles. Most explicit among them is perhaps his paper on "Phénoménologie et analyse existentielle," in *L' Evolution psychiatrique*, XII (1948). But the most telling statement can be found in the Preface to his final *Traité de psychopathologie*, in which he espouses the "phenomenological method" from the very start (p. xvii). This does not mean that for Minkowski psychopathology is to be studied exclusively by phenomenological means. For he still distinguishes the clinical aspects from the purely phenomenological ones. But there is no question that phenomenology always has priority in his own work. Does this subjective adherence to phenomenology prove that Minkowski's phenomenology coincides with that of other phenomenologists, or even phenomenological psychiatrists? Before answering this question, one has to consider Minkowski's relations with other phenomenologists, beginning with Husserl.

Husserl is hardly mentioned in any of Minkowski's writings, and if so it is only with regard to his early pre-transcendental writings. For Minkowski he figures at best as one of the inspirers of Max Scheler, who is Minkowski's prime phenomenologist. Heidegger too is rarely invoked; he interests Minkowski less in his own right than as a major inspiration for his friend Binswanger. It would appear that Minkowski, as one of the senior French phenomenologists, has received relatively little from such younger converts as Sartre, Merleau-Ponty, or even Marcel. Characteristically, in Minkowski's view, the major French phenomenologist is the Henri Bergson of *Les Données immédiates de la conscience* (Time and Free Will). This does not mean that all of Bergson's writings, especially his metaphysical ones such as *Matière et mémoire* should be considered as phenomenology. Nevertheless, the basic Bergson is for Minkowski a natural ally of Scheler's and Husserl's.

This suggests that Minkowski is not a phenomenologist in any technical sense. His prime allegiance belongs to the phenomena of live experience, which he tries to track down directly with an awakened sensitivity. What other phenomenologists have seen and recorded independently is to him at best stimulation or corroboration, but never evidence that is sufficient enough to be considered as established. In this respect he differs significantly from Binswanger, who fell back on Husserl's or Heidegger's findings.

Much of this characteristic flavor of Minkowski's phenomenology is also reflected in his style. Although never aiming at an all-embracing system, he is not opposed to systematic treatises and writes with a peculiar flair for the particular as the proper point of departure for insights of a more essential nature. Perhaps his most characteristic writings are the autobiographical vignettes (*esquisses*) in which, starting from a certain phrase of ordinary language, he dwells (*se pencher*) on some of its overlooked, deeper connotations. To this extent ordinary language is actually a major tool of his phenomenology. So is metaphor as the most effective means of describing and recapturing the elusive nature of lived experience. His best allies in this enterprise are the poets. But poetry is not enough. It takes the sensitiveness and perspective of a Minkowski to see its full significance for an understanding of "the human."

[3] Minkowski's Way to Phenomenology

Minkowski discovered phenomenology in passing, as it were, while carrying on his medical studies. Born in Poland, he had studied in Warsaw, Paris, and especially in Munich. But his main interest even in those days was in philosophy. This interest got him involved first in physiological psychology, where he felt "like a traveler in the desert," as can be gathered from his first publications in German, beginning with his 1909 dissertation in biochemistry. During his three years in Munich before the outbreak of the First World War, he attended some of the lectures of Pfänder and Moritz Geiger (as he informed me in a personal letter).

The first major breakthrough for him was the simultaneous discovery of two books: Scheler's *Zur Phänomenologie und Theorie der Sympathiegefühle* and Bergson's *Les Données immédiates de la conscience*. These works gave him "a taste of phenomenological psychology at its most concrete."[5] Minkowski never met Scheler personally. Later on, however, when he had established himself in France, he did have considerable personal contact with Bergson. He saw Husserl only once, on the occasion

5. "Phénoménologie et analyse existentielle en psychopathologie," *L'Evolution psychiatrique*, XIII, no. 4 (1948), 142 ff.

of his Sorbonne lectures in 1929, without being impressed. The major personal link with the new phenomenology came through Ludwig Binswanger, during the brief period when Minkowski studied under Eugen Bleuler in Zurich before moving on to France, where he served in the French Army. Apparently, his personal links with the French phenomenological philosophers, from Marcel to Ricoeur, have been few. Minkowski's lack of contact with Sartre, for whom he has little use, seems purposeful. This does not mean that Minkowski is not aware of and informed about the French and German phenomenologists. There is at least evidence that he studied Husserl's *Logische Untersuchungen,* though it is doubtful that he read much more of him. Nor has he taken much direct interest in Heidegger's production.

At least as important as Minkowski's literary encounter with Scheler and Bergson was his meeting with the melancholic patient with whom he lived in such close contact that he became aware of what was the central difference in his world: the distortion of his sense of time. It was the discovery made in this classic case which showed him the relevance of Bergson's "phenomenology" of time. This discovery led to his first explicitly phenomenological study of 1923,[6] which in 1933 became part of his most influential book, *Le Temps vécu.*

In 1927 Minkowski published another major study, on schizophrenia. It did not mention phenomenology explicitly but appealed to Bergson's "immediate data of consciousness" as the basis for a new interpretation of the fundamental problem in schizophrenia and as a substitute for Bleuler's concept of autism: the loss of vital contact with reality. He introduced this idea as follows:

> Hasn't one of the greatest contemporary philosophers, H. Bergson, reminded us once more that a whole side of our life, and not the most unimportant one, has escaped our discursive thought entirely? The immediate data of consciousness, the most essential ones, belong to this order of facts. They are irrational. This is no reason why they are not parts of our life. There is no reason whatsoever to sacrifice them to the spirit of precision. On the contrary, one ought to catch them alive. Psychology, hitherto a desert country, scorched by the excessively hot rays of exact science, will

6. "Etude psychologique et analyse phenomenologique d'un cas de melancolie schizophrénique," *Journal de psychologie normale et pathologique* XX (1923), 543–58. English translation by Barbara Bliss, "Findings in a Case of Schizophrenic Depression," in *Existence,* pp. 127–38.

then perhaps be transformed into green and fertile prairies and finally approach life.[7]

The period of Minkowski's explicitly phenomenological studies reached its first climax in the thirties. Quite apart from *Le Temps vécu,* the subtitles of several of his essays during this period include the word "phenomenological." Some of the most perceptive and original ones were collected in the "philosophical fragments" which in 1936 appeared under the title *Vers une cosmologie.* This new cosmology widened Minkowski's perspective from the human in man alone (anthropology) to the human, and in particular the poetic, aspect of the entire universe. But Minkowski never followed them up by anything like a systematic outline of such a philosophical cosmology. In fact, his production during the following decades seemed to consist entirely of a stream of incidental, suggestive, and often brilliant observations scattered over a variety of conferences and journals. But out of this profusion the plan of some kind of a synthesis developed, partly in response to Louis Lavelle's (apparently provoked) invitation of 1939 to Minkowski to contribute a volume to *Logos,* his collection of treatises in various fields of philosophy. It took Minkowski more than two decades to conclude, if not to complete it; its publication shortly after his eightieth year constitutes a fitting climax to his life's work.

At first glance the *Traité* has the appearance of being Minkowski's magnum opus. It is certainly his largest work; but it is not a systematic whole. One might suspect that during the turbulent period in which Minkowski worked on it, the task grew beyond the grasp of his versatile hands. Thus, at the end of the preface, he credits Dr. Denise Ozon for having given "form and substance" to the book by suggesting that it be organized into chapters and sub-chapters, an organization which he himself no longer had the courage to impose on the manuscript. Even so the book has no clear plan and is not free from duplications, especially in the discussions of phenomenology. All the same, it represents a considerable enrichment of Minkowski's achievement. In particular its original designation for young philosophers leads to a special emphasis on the role of phenomenological philosophy for psychopathology. Besides, the book stresses the psychological aspects of psychopathology. Thus, a brief preview

7. *La Schizophrénie: Psychopathologie des schizoïdes et des schizophrènes* (Paris: Payot, 1927; 2d ed., Paris: Desclée de Brouwer, 1953), p. 65.

of this work, which otherwise is not likely to be accessible to Anglo-American readers, may be useful.

The more than 750 pages of the treatise are divided into three books, followed by some "final considerations." The first book goes by the title of "Foundations and Orientation of Contemporary Psychopathology." Book II is subdivided into two parts, one dealing with affectivity, the second, which starts with a section explicitly called "Phenomenology," with expression. Book III on "New Approaches and Evolution of Its Predecessors" starts with a chapter on phenomeno-structural analysis, which opens with a discussion of Minkowski's central case of schizophrenic melancholia. Chapter V contrasts the different approaches to psychopathology, restating Binswanger's conception of the phenomenological method and also taking up its relation to psychoanalysis. The "Final Considerations" concern the road (*chemin*) of human life, dealing with some psychopathic phenomena and ending with observations about human life as the primary datum.

[4] Minkowski's Conception of Phenomenology

Minkowski is not a theoretician. Hence he never wrote a study specifically on phenomenology and phenomenological method. His main ambition clearly is to demonstrate phenomenology; but this does not prevent him from reflecting about it. Such reflections can be found all the way from his first phenomenological studies to his final treatise. And there can be little question about the fact that he identifies increasingly with the phenomenological approach without denying the legitimacy of other methods in psychopathology.

Little purpose would be served by examining all his formulations chronologically. Suffice it to mention his first explicit statement on the occasion of his presentation of his central case at Zurich in 1922, where he distinguished between "psychological" and "phenomenological" findings. The psychological findings consisted of a clinical account of the case in the usual medical terminology of delusions and hallucinations; the phenomenological findings involved "a deeper understanding of the nature of the pathological phenomenon itself by asking, for instance, what is a delusion?" By way of comparing his own experience with that of the patient, Minkowski noticed that the latter was incapable of extrapolating from his present experience to the future, and that hence the patient's entire experience of time was different from his own. "Phenomenology" in this sense was therefore an attempt to penetrate to the basic phenomena that could make the merely psychological phenomena intelligible.

Minkowski's most explicit and valid statements about phenomenology can be found in the *Traité* of 1966. Although it deals with other material as well, and although only a few portions are labeled specifically as phenomenological, the approach permeates the whole book. Without claiming to have developed a special version of phenomenology, Minkowski makes it clear that for him phenomenology is largely a combination of Bergsonian and Schelerian elements. Its prime task is the study of the immediate data of consciousness, which are to serve as points of departure and as final authority. But it also attempts to determine what is essential and basic in these data. Its guiding principle is the closest possible approach to the phenomena.

Thus far it may appear as if Minkowski aims at nothing more than descriptive and essential (eidetic) phenomenology. It certainly is not Husserl's transcendental phenomenology as it evolved after his *Logische Untersuchungen.* Never does Minkowski mention any of the notorious phenomenological reductions. In fact, Minkowski's interpretation of phenomenology as offering us a closer contact with reality, if not with ultimate reality in the manner of Bergson's metaphysical intuition, makes a Husserlian interpretation close to impossible.

But this does not mean that Minkowski's phenomenology is nothing but a Bergsonian interpretation of early phenomenology. One addition to it is what he calls the "principle of double aspect," a theory that phenomenological analysis operates in two parallel directions. He calls the first the ideo-affective or ideo-emotive aspect, i.e., the aspect expressed in feelings that go with experiences such as suffering. The other, much more characteristic of Minkowski's research, is the phenomeno-structural or spatio-temporal aspect in the structure of time and space, as we experience and live them. At first sight these two aspects would seem related to the common distinction between act and content, or, in more Husserlian terms, between the noetic and the noematic. But, for one thing, Minkowski never refers to such distinctions based on analysis in terms of "intentionality." Besides, Minkowski's specific interest is restricted to phenomena of affectivity and of spatio-temporal features; it is not a general interpretation of conscious life in all its expressions.

What also must not be overlooked is that Minkowski always

acknowledges the limitations of the phenomenological approach. It can never supersede the exploration of the origins and causes of the phenomena. For phenomenology is unfit by definition to undertake it.[8] At this point clinical psychopathology has to take over from phenomenological psychopathology.[9]

This does not detract from Minkowski's basic attachment to phenomenology in his sense:

> The phenomenological method . . . while being a method of investigation, reaches beyond itself. It resounds in our general position in life. Being a phenomenologist does not reduce to doing phenomenology as one does astronomy, geology, etc. (p. xviii).

Further light on Minkowski's kind of phenomenology can be gained from his appraisals of the parallel enterprises of Jaspers and Binswanger.

Jaspers' phenomenology as developed in the first chapter of his *Allgemeine Psychopathologie* is to Minkowski not yet phenomenology proper. It does not present more than an enrichment of subjective symptomatology on the way to a better clinical diagnosis. In themselves the descriptions given by the patients are to Minkowski merely human documents (*documents humains*), not yet phenomenological data. For the latter purpose we need the kind of essential analysis which allows us to grasp the "basic source of trouble" (*trouble générateur*).[10]

Minkowski feels much closer to his friend Binswanger as far as phenomenology is concerned. Ostensibly, the only difference which Minkowski admits is his own emphasis on lived time in preference to the lived experiences and dimensions included in Binswanger's "worlds." [11] But there are clearly deeper differences, ultimately explained by the fact that to Binswanger, Husserl and Heidegger were essential foundations of his *Daseinsanalyse*. Minkowski's phenomenology claims no such foundations and remains largely noncommittal about their intrinsic and psychopathological value. As far as Husserl is concerned, Minkowski, as we have seen, had never advanced beyond his early work. As to Heidegger, Minkowski stated: "The Heideggerian conceptions —why not say it—haven't particularly attracted me at all. I have remained faithful to my beginnings, to the phenomenological

8. *Traité*, pp. 645 ff.

9. *La Schizophrénie*, pp. 19 ff.

10. *Traité*, pp. 55 ff. See also "Phénoménologie et analyse existentielle," pp. 140. ff.

11. *Traité*, p. 495.

method or at least to what I considered to be it; for here too we do not consider it all in the same way. . . . Personal differences enter . . ." (pp. 878 ff.). They certainly do between Binswanger, the devoted student of phenomenological philosophy, and Minkowski, for whom it serves at best as an inspiration for his own first-hand observations and discoveries.

Finally, a word is in order about the relation between Minkowski's phenomenology and psychoanalysis. In France the two fields have been close to each other from the very start—particularly since the group behind *L'Evolution psychiatrique* included psychoanalysts such as Hesnard from the journal's inception. Minkowski kept at a distance from this group, although he never repudiated it. To him the whole disjunction between the conscious and the subconscious seemed questionable, especially since Bergson as well as Husserl dealt only with the data of consciousness. To Minkowski one of the merits of the term "living" (*Le Temps vécu*) was that it undercut the whole issue and allowed him to be hospitable to both the conscious and the unconscious without taking sides with either one.[12]

[5] Phenomenology of Time

There is no shortage of possible illustrations for Minkowski's phenomenology in action. In fact, there are so many of them that it is very difficult to even list the areas he has covered. Such vignettes as those in *Vers une cosmologie* on "I Light a Lamp" ("J'allume la lampe") or "In Marching Ahead I Leave Behind Me Tracks on My Way" ("En avancant, je laisse derrière moi des traces sur mon chemin") could serve as examples. But these pieces do not add up to the comprehensive picture of the "cosmos" that Minkowski wants to achieve, and they have been relatively ineffective. However, more sustained applications of phenomenology can be found in Minkowski's work, especially in his exploration of time consciousness. The following pages attempt to show the way in which his phenomenological approach attacks such an assignment.

One might suspect that Minkowski's phenomenology of lived time is nothing but a loan from Bergson. Far apart from Minkowski's lavish tributes to Bergson, he incorporates so many

12. See "Approches phénoménologiques de l'existence (vues par un psychopathologie)," *L'Evolution psychiatrique*, XXVII, no. 4 (1962), 433–58. English translation in *Existential Psychiatry*, I (1966), 292–315.

of Bergson's ideas into his work that it could hardly be imagined without them. This is particularly true of the idea of the primacy of time over space. But this undeniable influence must not make one overlook the modifications of these motifs that are determined by Minkowski's own phenomenological perspective. To begin with, Minkowski speaks rarely, if ever, of pure "duration" (*durée pure*) as Bergson does; rather, he speaks of "pure time" (*temps*). The expression "lived time" (*temps vécu*) does not seem to occur in Bergson. Even the use of "lived" as a characteristic of what we experience can be found merely in the later parts of *Les Données immédiates*.[13] Also, Bergson's general *élan vital* becomes in Minkowski's phenomenology a "personal *élan*." Such terminological independence may not be significant by itself. But it indicates Minkowski's phenomenological preference for greater closeness to the personal experience of time rather than to the metaphysical intuition of "duration," "purity," and "vitality." In some places Minkowski even expresses reservations with regard to Bergson's later speculative and biological philosophy, especially his metaphysical intuition as far as it involves identification with the intuited reality. This is particularly true of Bergson's conception of creative evolution and some of the metaphysics expressed in his treatise on *Matière et mémoire*. Minkowski adopts those ideas of Bergson's which he can assimilate phenomenologically. In this sense Minkowski's phenomenology of time is Bergson stripped of his metaphysics and reduced to the pure data of consciousness.

No easy summary of Minkowski's phenomenological studies on time is possible, particularly in view of the fact that these studies did not develop in a systematic manner. All that makes sense in the present frame is a birds-eye view of the most phenomenological aspects. Of the two books of *Le Temps vécu*, the first is an "essay on the temporal structure of life," while the second, considerably longer, deals with the "spatio-temporal structure of mental disturbances." Book I begins with a chapter on becoming and the essential elements of "time-quality." It starts with the Bergsonian distinction between "abstract," measurable or spatialized time in its kaleidoscopic succession, and duration, now called "lived time," the major subject of the treatise. The first answer to the question about this lived time uses Bergson's phrase "fluid mass," but adds ". . . that mov-

13. See "La Pure durée et la durée vécue," in "Bergson et nous," special number, *Bulletin de la société française de philosophie*, LIII (1959), 239–41.

ing ocean, mysterious, grandiose, and powerful that I see around me, in me, in short everywhere when I meditate on time. It is becoming" (p. 16). Thus the following descriptions concentrate on the phenomenon of becoming (*devenir*), in an attempt to catch it as a pure phenomenon without the biological interpretation characteristic of Bergsonian thought. The subsequent considerations of the two major aspects of time lead to several more specific lived phenomena, such as "lived succession" and "lived continuity" (p. 27), that of the "now" (*maintenant*), to be distinguished from the phenomenon of the present, which is an unfolded, extended "now" (p. 32). Possibly even more significant is the phenomenon of the vital (*élan*) in Becoming, which "creates" the future (*avenir*). But this *élan* is also personal, i.e., for Minkowski it is identical with the phenomenon "*I* reach forward and thus realize something" (p. 39), a phenomenon which includes a personal and a super-personal aspect. The *élan* also involves the realization of a "work" (*oeuvre*). However, it is accompanied by a sense of limitation and loss in view of the opportunities cut off because of the concentration of the *élan* on the work. An additional group of phenomena concerns our contact with reality expressed through harmony with Becoming in a "lived synchrony," as experienced in contemplation and sympathy. At this point a first possibility for psychopathological use of these distinctions appears. For the personal *élan* proves to be related to schizoidism as described by Ernst Kretschmer, who had called the contact with reality "syntony." This makes it possible for Minkowski to see in the loss of vital contact with reality the basic disturbance in schizophrenia, which he had explored in his first book. "Loss of contact" also opens to Minkowski a deeper understanding of the basic disturbance involved in Bleuler's concept of "autism."

Another group of phenomena concerns our ways of "living" the future; the most outstanding ones are activity, expectation, desire, hope, prayer, and moral action. Death at the end of the human future presents us with an aspect which actually gives shape to the Becoming of our life. Finally, there is the past, whose phenomenology reveals a very different organization from that of the present, and the future, which is "amputated" from the living present (p. 155).

The second book of *Le Temps vécu* turns from the general phenomena to their significance for an understanding of mental disturbances. These studies do not add up to anything like a coherent pattern. They include the interpretation of Minkowski's classic case of schizophrenic melancholia, in which the patient has lost the dimension of the lived future. To pursue in detail how the phenomenological characters described in the first book function in the interpretation of psychopathological symptoms would make little sense. Suffice it to mention that such items as the basic disturbance in psychoses, schizophrenia, manic-depressive and other forms of depression, as well as in mental defectiveness, are examined in the light of the phenomenological studies of the first book. However, the final chapter of this part contains a very important supplement to the whole work in the shape of a foundation for a psychopathology of "lived space" (*espace vécu*). Here Minkowski breaks away from Bergson's demotion of space to a mere result of the distortion of duration by the geometrical intellect. Instead, Minkowski introduces the conception of lived space as the equal partner of lived time along with such sub-phenomena as "lived distance" and "spaciousness" (*ampleur*), all of which can undergo characteristic pathological modifications, such as hallucinations. However, as far as the problems of lived space are concerned, Minkowski defers largely to the equal or primary emphasis it has received in the thought of his friends Binswanger and Straus.

[6] Toward an Appraisal of Minkowski's Phenomenology

Few practitioners of phenomenology have written with as much personal involvement as Minkowski; yet it is surprising how little he uses existentialist phraseology. His sensitivity for neglected phenomena guided by casual observations of linguistic usage is unique. In this respect he has certainly demonstrated the potential of a fresh phenomenological approach based on a minimum of philosophical textual inspiration.

But such pioneering does not and cannot claim to result always in permanent and convincing insights. This is true even of some of the analyses of lived time, where Minkowski seems to shift from the investigation of lived time to the narrower study of time in human creative action, neglecting its merely passive aspects, when time is not a matter of active planning. On the whole, some of the essential insights that Minkowski asserts are presented without evidence of careful imaginative variations.

Minkowski is unusually frank in admitting that his perspective and his entire psychopathology are intensely personal. He also speaks not infrequently about the irrational character of the phenomena which he tries to explore. Such concessions, or rather his premature abandonment of a more interpersonal and less subjective verification of his findings, makes some of his work more vulnerable than it otherwise would be. Besides, Minkowski's primary dependence upon Bergson, rather than on phenomenology proper has to be considered. True, it is not a blind and uncritical dependence. It commits him only to Bergson's phenomenological insights. Nevertheless, Minkowski shares not only the beauties of Bergson's style but also some of his sweeping simplifications.

His is phenomenology at its most sensitive, but also at its most subjective. It has the virtues of pioneer research. But it calls for further cultivation by "permanent settlers," as it were.

9 / Viktor Emil von Gebsattel (b. 1883): Phenomenology in Medical Anthropology

[1] Von Gebsattel's Place in Phenomenology

Compared with Jaspers, Binswanger, Minkowski, or Straus, von Gebsattel hardly seems to deserve a special chapter in the present context. Certainly his literary output is no match for what his younger fellow phenomenologists have accomplished. His claim to our attention can only be based on the fact that he was the senior member of the inner circle of four phenomenological psychopathologists which included Binswanger, Minkowski, and Straus, and that they considered him an equal member and even the "most intuitive" among themselves. Such esteem is certainly a valid phenomenological credential, but it would be hard to demonstrate it here. Perhaps even more important are von Gebsattel's organizational achievements. He had a significant role in the founding and editing of a yearbook of psychology and psychotherapy which aimed to arouse interest in the new approach, the *Jahrbuch für Psychologie und Psychotherapie*. The original preface of the yearbook stated the goal of restoring to psychology the credit lost by "despiritualization" (*Entgeistigung*) and not replaced by the addition of depth psychology. The seventh volume (1960) added to the title the words "and medical anthropology." A new preface explained that the magazine was to be devoted to the "*totum humanum*, the whole man in his ontological scope as self, personality, and person, which is the subject of anthropology"; that it was focused on the fundamental structure of human *Dasein;* and that without a phenomenological and ontological *Wesensschau* of man, no understanding of him was possible. In this connection Binswanger and the Heidelberg and Frankfurt schools of psychiatry and internal medicine (Paul Christian, Herbert Plügge, and Walter Bräutigam) were specifically mentioned as congenial fellow workers.

Perhaps even more impressive now is the five-volume handbook of the theory of neuroses (1959–63), which von Gebsattel edited jointly with Viktor Frankl and J. H. Schultz, two collaborators with highly divergent outlooks. The major goal of this handbook was to present the most significant and valid findings in the field by surveying it from different points of view. No claim was made that the contributions represented the final word for such a science in the making. Phenomenology, while often invoked, e.g., by Ulrich Sonnemann and Viktor Frankl, was by no means the common denominator.

[2] Von Gebsattel's Relations to the Phenomenological Movement

Von Gebsattel's approach to phenomenology did not lead him directly into its main currents, although he was a witness to its beginnings. He first studied philosophy and psychology in Munich under Theodor Lipps, whose analytically descriptive psychology he exemplified in his Munich dissertation on the irradiation of feelings. This also got him in touch with Pfänder, who was at that time emancipating himself from Lipps, and who led him into the group of Munich phenomenologists who after 1907 were dominated by Max Scheler. In fact, von Gebsattel remained strongly attached to the Max Scheler of the Munich years, even in his later life.

But while von Gebsattel's starting point was the Munich circle, he was increasingly aware of other phenomenological trends. As a student von Gebsattel had met Husserl accidentally, as early as 1905, in Dilthey's house in Berlin, but he had had no further contacts with him.[1] Presumably, he had learned about Husserl's importance from the Munich circle, especially through Scheler. Yet no specific references to Husserl's ideas occur in von Gebsattel's writings, and only the term "*eidos*" (paired with the non-Husserlian "anti-*eidos*") is suggestive of him.

Von Gebsattel's relations with Heidegger are more direct. Ap-

1. This fact was stated in a personal communication to me from von Gebsattel.

parently in the years soon after the war Heidegger visited von Gebsattel, and later he even spoke, together with Binswanger, at von Gebsattel's seventy-fifth birthday. It is more difficult to determine the philosophical relations between the two. In his *Prolegomena*[2] there are references to "*Vorhandenheit*" (p. 41), to existence as the possibility to exist (p. 44), to anxiety as related to nothingness (p. 46), especially in a study on depersonalization of 1937; and similar borrowings appear elsewhere. But even such references do not prove that Heidegger's ideas—particularly his phenomenology, existential analytics, and ontology—have had any basic significance for von Gebsattel's anthropology. Thus the major philosophical influence on von Gebsattel clearly came from Scheler, beginning with his early phenomenology and terminating with his philosophical anthropology. Von Gebsattel's obituary to Scheler in the first volume of *Der Nervenarzt* is its clearest and most personal expression, particularly in its deploring of the loss of his anthropology, philosophy of religion, and metaphysics. But his main tribute concerned Scheler the phenomenologist, whose first pertinent contributions had actually appeared in a psychiatric journal (*Zeitschrift für Pathopsychologie*). Von Gebsattel credited Scheler chiefly for his idea of personalism, including his conception of the person as consisting essentially of acts. But von Gebsattel referred also to such specific items as Scheler's phenomenology of time experience which he considered essentially future-directed; strangely Husserl and Heidegger are not even mentioned in this context.

Much closer are the connections with his fellow psychiatrists, especially with the other members of the quadrumvirate. Among these, Straus figures perhaps even more frequently than Binswanger. But Minkowski's *Le Temps vécu* also has considerable importance for von Gebsattel. Equally significant are contacts with the Heidelberg medical group that formed around V. von Weizsäcker. The Vienna existentialists, especially Viktor Frankl, also made important contributions to von Gebsattel's views on the existential neuroses and their therapy. Here Igor Caruso is one of von Gebsattel's major followers, as is Eckart Wiesenhütter, his Würzburg assistant and helper. The volume *Werden und Handeln,* composed for von Gebsattel's eightieth birthday, is an impressive testimony to von Gebsattel's role.

2. *Prolegomena zu einer medizinischen Anthropologie* (Berlin: Springer, 1954).

[3] Von Gebsattel's Central Concern

Von Gebsattel's close to fifty publications consist mostly of short articles. Of his four books, the two major ones, which contain collections of detached pieces, are the following: the twenty selected essays which he edited himself in 1955 under the title of *Prolegomena zu einer medizinischen Anthropologie*, and the "contributions to a personal anthropology" which Wilhelm Josef Revers published in 1964 as *Imago Hominis*. While the articles in these volumes are grouped in subsections, they are not systematically connected. Nevertheless, the main titles of the books and especially the Preface to the *Prolegomena* state von Gebsattel's central theme: anthropology as seen from the medical perspective.

Why does von Gebsattel not offer more than "prolegomena"? Some of the explanation can be found in his peculiar conception of his theme. To von Gebsattel, anthropology is a fundamental doctrine of man's way of being (*menschliche Seinsart*) and of the "valid and comprehensive project of man's being" (*Seinsentwurf des Menschen*). Such a formulation indicates, almost in Heideggerian language, both the ambitiousness and the ambiguity of his enterprise. Actually, von Gebsattel believes that the time has not yet come for a philosophical or even a medical anthropology in the proper sense of the term. To von Gebsattel, Binswanger's "basic forms of human *Dasein*" are thus far the closest approach to it. But actually von Gebsattel seems to have serious and characteristic doubts as to whether man's being is not essentially unstabilized (Nietzsche) and ultimately a "secret," defying any final illumination. Meanwhile, it is at least possible to explore aspects of man's being. Scheler's "comprehensive structural analysis of man" is mentioned as a creditable exception to the general failure, though its ontological and phenomenological foundations are questioned.

The one-sidedness of present anthropology applies even to a medical anthropology which tries to see man in terms of sickness and health. Von Gebsattel's own attempt is to understand him in the light of a psychotherapy which tries to help the neurotic patient in particular toward a better understanding of his human being.

What aspects of human being stand out in this perspective?

For von Gebsattel, neurosis is essentially a blocking of becoming (*Werdenshemmung*). This means that man is primarily a being in the process of self-realization (*Selbstverwirklichung*), and with a special drive toward it. What is to be so realized is called the "persona." Its new meaning is that of a "personal center" (*personale Mitte*), expressed in the sentence "I am who am." Becoming, in this sense, is to be distinguished phenomenologically from mere evolution.

The most obvious question for an anthropological psychopathology is: How can sickness and perversions enter such a being? For neuroses are characterized as a disturbance in becoming. Can this defect, this tendency be understood at all? At this point, von Gebsattel introduces, or rather annexes, a concept popularized especially by Nietzsche—"nihilism"—claiming increasingly that there is actually a fundamental nihilistic trend in man. Von Gebsattel tries to derive it from the essential freedom of the person to deny as well as to affirm his being; yet he also calls it a "mystery."

It is therefore pertinent to point out that von Gebsattel's therapy is not a neutral enterprise related to a non-religious humanism. Von Gebsattel is a committed Christian, belonging to the group of German Catholics inspired by Scheler during his Catholic period and headed by Romano Guardini. Thus, in von Gebsattel, phenomenological and *Daseinsanalytik* or anthropological motifs receive their final interpretation and sanction from such religious categories as sin, sacrament, and salvation. Much of von Gebsattel's writing is related to purely homiletic religious concerns. But especially in the *Prolegomena* there is enough substance of importance even without this religious context and phraseology.

[4] The Role of Phenomenology in von Gebsattel's Anthropology

Von Gebsattel has always been considered one of the earliest advocates of phenomenology in psychiatry. This estimate seems to be confirmed by his own references to phenomenology, for instance in the Preface of his *Prolegomena*—though he makes little of this attachment and uses the term itself quite casually and only rarely in the titles of his essays. Thus it is all the more important to try to determine as far as possible the precise nature and function of phenomenology in von Gebsattel's work.[3]

Von Gebsattel is no theoretician, much less a theoretician of phenomenology. What he understands by it has to be derived from occasional remarks and from the context of its application. After the development of *Daseinsanalyse* there are noticeable shifts in that direction. There are occasions when von Gebsattel contrasts "casuistic phenomenology" with phenomenology itself,[4] and not unfrequently phenomenology is distinguished from interpretation, e.g., when he contrasts his view of becoming as the meaning of life with a theory of evolution that to him is a result of a reinterpretation.[5]

In his phenomenology of Eros and love, von Gebsattel tried, very much in the spirit of Scheler, to develop a comparative description of the essence of Eros and love between the sexes according to their different intent. Moreover, love itself was interpreted as a case of *Wesensschau*.[6] But in offering his findings concerning the phenomenology of fetishism, von Gebsattel ended with the statement that a purely descriptive analysis of this phenomenon and its ingenious interpretation was not enough and called for a theory of the formation of fetishes in order to make sense of this act, a sense which was to be found in its function as *Ersatz* for genuine love and even for sex. The same kind of theo-

3. In his Preface to the *Prolegomena*, he states that the following lectures and essays illustrate the "necessary rapprochements" (*Annäherung*) of phenomenological thinking and psychopathological experience to a fundamental theory (*Grundlehre*) of human existence. This would almost seem to imply that phenomenology is here chiefly an approach, one of two ways which lead toward, but do not or do not yet fuse with, anthropology. Von Gebsattel's earliest study on "Der Einzelne und der Zuschauer" (1913) contains a section of several pages, designated as "phenomenological," which is called "Concerning the Psychology of the Drive for Attention" (*Prolegomena*, pp. 246 ff.). Here von Gebsattel discusses the experienced difference in wearing a *Kutte* (cloak) in the case of the Cynics (Diogenes) and in the case of the saint (St. Francis). In 1925 von Gebsattel published an entire essay subtitled "Concerning the Phenomenology of Marital Union." A 1929 essay on fetishism is subdivided into a section entitled "Concerning Its Phenomenology" and another, "Concerning Its Theory."

References to phenomenology can also be found in von Gebsattel's writings since 1948, e.g., in "Aspects of Death" (*Prolegomena*, pp. 395 ff.), "Concerning the Psychopathology of Addiction" (p. 223), and "Daseinsanalytic and Anthropological Interpretation of Sexual Perversions" (p. 212), which contrasts casuistic phenomenology with theory.

4. *Prolegomena*, p. 213.

5. *Handbuch der Neurosenlehre und Psychotherapie*, 4 vols. (Munich: Urban & Schwarzenberg, 1959), III, 563.

6. *Prolegomena*, p. 152.

retical interpretation can be found in von Gebsattel's study of the world of the compulsive. *Daseinsanalyse* in the case of sexual perversions is introduced as "a new advance of theoretical thought" beyond "casuistic phenomenology."

However, no matter how widely von Gebsattel's implied conception of phenomenology is to be interpreted, it is clear that he is not satisfied with a mere description of the subjective data. He expects to obtain an understanding of their essential nature. More important, he wants to reach an understanding of their sense. And in trying to find such transphenomenal sense, he does not hesitate to use the phenomenologically suspect term "theory," although he would not commit himself to Freudian psychoanalysis or, for that matter, Jungian depth psychology with its persona-doctrine of the unconscious. However, he does express increasing interest in Binswanger's type of *Daseinsanalyse* as an interpretation of the modes of being-in-the-world.

[5] Von Gebsattel's Phenomenological Contributions

Von Gebsattel himself has divided his *Prolegomena einer medizinischen Anthropologie* into two parts: "Studies on Special Anthropology" and "Contributions to the Psychotherapy and Theory of the Neuroses." In *Imago Hominis* the second section, "Aspects of an Anthropologically Oriented Understanding in the Field of the Theory of Neuroses" offers studies of three neurotic attitudes (*Fehlhaltungen*) previously published in the *Handbuch*, Vol. II.

There is no systematic connection between these pieces. The following attempt to give a more concrete idea of von Gebsattel's phenomenological work will take samples from different areas of these studies.

A. *The World of the Compulsive and the Anancastic Attitude*

There is nothing fundamentally new about the study of compulsive ideas, even in descriptive phenomenology. Jaspers included illustrations of such behavior, some based on von Gebsattel's and Binswanger's earlier studies. What is new in the context of von Gebsattel's medical anthropology is the attempt to understand the entire world of the compulsive phenomenologically by incorporating it into an "anthropological-existential" framework. Von Gebsattel, after presenting three case studies, distinguishes two "sides" in this world: that of disturbance and disruption, and that of defense (*Abwehr*). Then he turns to an analysis of the anancastic person (*der zwangskranke Mensch*) in his world.

To von Gebsattel the foundation for compulsive ideas is an "anancastic phobia" characterized by depressive derealization and existential emptiness as "phobic background." On this basis the phobia leads to the constitution of a "counter-world" of nausea, horror, and terror (*Entsetzen*). The example of a phobia against dogs shows how *Dasein* can become dominated by the obsessive idea of impurity and a general anancastic phobia of dirt as an "anti-*eidos*."

New meanings to which he now has to react attach themselves to the world of the anancastic. The defense against this world is characterized by a disturbance of the ability to act, to start anything or to terminate it.[7] There is a characteristic disruption of temporal experience. Action becomes rigid and leads to the adoption of a ceremonial (*manie de précision*).

In addition to such an attempt to describe the world of the compulsive, von Gebsattel offers certain interpretations. For reasons not known in detail the movement of becoming within the personality of the anancastic has come to a stop; movement into the future has become blocked (p. 108) and he has become a helpless prey to disruptive powers. However, compulsory phenomena are to be seen against the background of a potentially intact, though powerless, personality. This offers the chance of a therapeutic reversal by removing the disturbance in the patient's becoming and by reversing the profile of importance (p. 117) within his world and thus his being-in-the-world.

B. *Depersonalization*

Of considerable interest and demonstrative value is von Gebsattel's treatment of depersonalization, especially since the field of ego-consciousness has an important place in von Gebsattel's picture of man and of the person (he also speaks of *Ichheit*, egohood). In fact, he believes that the decisive question not only in philosophy but in all serious neuroses is "*Who* am I?",[8] rather than Kant's question, "*What* is man?" Depersonalization is of

7. *Ibid.*, p. 104.
8. *Handbuch*, III, 540.

particular importance for the theory of melancholia and is often, but not always, associated with the experience of "existential emptiness." On the basis of protocols, von Gebsattel distinguishes five aspects of depersonalization:

(1) *"autopsychic":* the patients complain about loss of self-identity ("I am not myself, I am separated from my existence");

(2) *"allo-psychic":* the relation to others and in fact to everything outside seems dead;

(3) *"somatopsychic":* the body is no longer experienced as alive and one's own;

(4) the feeling of being split, no longer coinciding with oneself, of being other than oneself and even persecuting oneself;

(5) the feeling of being engulfed in an abyss (*Abgrund*).

"Critical interpretation" shows immediately the close connection between depersonalization and the derealization of the world of *Dasein*. For instance, what happens in melancholia is that our potentialities of becoming as existers in the world are put out of action (*ausschalten*). We can no longer encounter the world and hence no longer realize ourselves. Hence the double deficiency, particularly in our feeling of personal existence. Thus derealization and depersonalization form two aspects of one and the same disturbance in communication.

The phenomenon of depersonalization is apparently related to its opposite in a group of experiences that von Gebsattel calls *numinose Ersterlebnisse* (numinous prime experiences), among which the sudden discovery of one's own ego-hood plays a special part. Starting from a celebrated account of Jean Paul, von Gebsattel describes the case of a patient who had such an experience at the age of three. Von Gebsattel even expresses the belief that this happens typically as an encounter of ego and world when the child of three or four experiences a horror of cosmic loneliness. Von Gebsattel intimates that this kind of experience can counterbalance the depersonalization and derealization of the melancholic.[9]

C. *Addictions and Perversions*

One of von Gebsattel's special interests is the area of addictions, particularly the sexual perversions. In lining up a wide

9. "Numinose Ersterlebnisse," in *Rencontre / Encounter / Begegung* (Utrecht: Spectrum, 1957), pp. 168–80; also in *Imago Hominis* (Schweinfurt: Neues Forum, 1964), pp. 313–28.

variety of experiences centering descriptively around the drug addictions, von Gebsattel emphasized somatopsychic sensations as common to them. He also noted a characteristic indifference toward pain and even lust. An intensified feeling of oneself is important, though not decisive; there is always an overemphasis on the state of one's own *Dasein*. There is also indifference to achievement or loss, to all reason and measure. In fact the "violation of measure is the main stimulus of addictive behavior." [10] In general it aims at filling emptiness, but it does so in vain. For it antagonizes the drive to self-realization and cancels it (p. 227).

Thus addiction appears as an expression of a self-destructive "mania," opposed to man's drive to self-realization, a secret fraternizing with the abyss, which von Gebsattel relates to man's nature as a fallen creature. This general interpretation applies to all perversions, especially sexual perversions, to which von Gebsattel devotes considerable attention. Active and passive addiction to pain, onanism (in its pathological form), and Don Juanism are interpreted as various ways of enjoyment derived from destructiveness, which substitutes for failures of self-realization. There is much provocative and suggestive material in the descriptive phases of these studies. As to their interpretation, one may wonder how far they are slanted in the light of von Gebsattel's assumptions about man's basic fallenness and his nihilistic streak. In view of this doubt, it seems worth mentioning that a very different interpretation of sexual perversions has been offered by Medard Boss (at that time still greatly involved with the concept of *Daseinsanalyse*), according to which even the worst perversions still contain underneath an element of positive constructive love. Von Gebsattel has rejected this as a naïve oversimplification. Clearly this is an area where it is not easy to let the phenomena speak for themselves.

[6] Toward an Appraisal of von Gebsattel's Phenomenology

Von Gebsattel has failed to produce a single work which would demonstrate phenomenology as a distinctive, let alone a decisive, tool of psychiatry. But to expect such a work would be unfair. Von Gebsattel's primary goal was to develop

10. *Prolegomena*, p. 224.

not phenomenology but our understanding of man. Phenomenology meant for him a new approach to such an understanding—but not more than one among many. Using it, he has pioneered in its application to new areas, and has clarified it only incidentally. He has shown the powers of descriptive phenomenology, without giving elaborate descriptions, and has pointed out essential structures in the phenomena. He has even tried to interpret their meanings in the context of a personalistic anthropology inspired by Scheler. He has also absorbed some of the suggestions of *Daseinsanalyse* eclectically. All this forms part of an overarching therapeutic and at times even a religious and missionary framework. This frame does not interfere with its heuristic value. But without independent testing and developing it cannot claim full phenomenological validity.

10 / Erwin W. Straus (b. 1891): Phenomenological Rehabilitation of Man's Senses

[1] Straus's Place in the Phenomenological Movement

The youngest member of that "inner circle" of phenomenological anthropologists linked by personal friendships is particularly difficult to pin down. When in 1960 Binswanger characterized Erwin Straus jestingly as the cleverest of the quartet, since he always had new ideas, he also indicated the problem for any pigeonholing historian, especially one bold enough to attempt a biography of a man who does not choose to write his own.[1] Fortunately, the present context calls merely for an appraisal of the phenomenological aspects of Straus's work. Even such a limited project is not without its problems; but it is at least more feasible.

In attacking it I would like first to define Straus's place in the context of the Phenomenological Movement. Such an assessment can certainly not be made in terms of his academic associations. The remarkable thing is that from a relatively small and moving base Straus has secured an international stature which in turn has given distinction to his local stations.

Actually, Straus's relation with the Phenomenological Movement as such remained relatively undeveloped during his life on the Continent. Until his arrival in the United States in 1939, his emphasis was on concrete and original studies. He had no special links with any philosophical group. But he was one of the circle of philosophically and even phenomenologically oriented

1. However, he did assist me by checking on the accuracy of the factual information in this chapter and correcting some errors.

psychiatrists who in 1930 founded the journal *Der Nervenarzt*, to which he was a frequent contributor. In these early writings he mostly practiced, rather than preached, phenomenology. It was only in America, after he had established his final base of operations at the Veterans Hospital in Lexington, Kentucky, that he began to emphasize phenomenology as such, not only in his writings but as a common denominator for a new approach to psychiatry, psychology, and philosophy. This made Lexington and the Lexington Conferences which he initiated under the title of "Phenomenology Pure and Applied" one of the centers of phenomenology in the New World. But Straus never lost his roots in Europe. In this sense he was significant in the development of phenomenology not only as one of its practicing pioneers in America but as one of the most effective bridgebuilders across the Atlantic. Without Straus, phenomenological psychiatry in America would have remained mostly a promissory "intention" without live "fulfillment." In more than one sense he is today its most vital embodiment.

[2] Straus's Basic Concern

A BILINGUAL *Festschrift* for Straus's seventy-fifth birthday in 1966 carries the unexplained title *Conditio Humana*. Looking over Straus's books and articles, one might at first wonder how far this title expresses Straus's real concern. However, the phrase does occur climactically at the end of his most philosophical book-length essay on *Psychiatrie und Philosophie*, which appeared in 1963, in which a full discussion of the *conditio humana* is postulated as the basis for an understanding of the "destructions encountered on the ward." Straus credits psychoanalysis and *Daseinsanalyse* with having attempted such a discussion. But he adds that he considers it necessary to first investigate the "primal situation of man."

But if such understanding of the *conditio humana* is Straus's ultimate concern, this does not mean that it was his first objective. Straus started from and always returned to psychiatry. It was only in trying to understand the abnormal that he discovered increasingly that it was necessary to first understand the norm, a task which in turn required more knowledge than ordinary science could supply.

What, then, is this *conditio humana*? Clearly, it is not merely what the French glibly or resignedly call *la condition humaine*.

As Straus came to see it, the human situation is actually rooted in an even more basic situation "from which the human world grows." This conception of the human world as an integral, if not decisive part of the human condition is of such pivotal importance for Straus that the German edition of his major essays goes by the title of *Psychologie der menschlichen Welt*. For man's world is the actual key to man himself. In the Preface to this German edition, Straus stated that his interest in the relation between man and his world gradually widened to an attempt to understand man out of his world.[2] The search for the psychological possibility of this world led to the discovery of a whole "continent" of problems overlooked because of their closeness. "By way of an analytical reconstruction of human creation, we are led to an understanding of its creator, his achievements and failures." [3] This, as Straus sees it, is actually the task of "phenomenological psychology." Thus phenomenology, in Straus's sense, turns out to be the way to "explore human experience, revealing its depth and wealth, instead of reducing it." [4] How did phenomenology achieve this place in Straus's own work?

[3] The Role of Phenomenology in Straus's Work

The term "phenomenology" is certainly not conspicuous within the titles of Straus's publications. It was not until 1960 that it figured at the head of one of his essays, "The Phenomenology of Remembering," which was followed in 1962 by his "Phenomenology of Hallucinations." Even in 1966 he only reluctantly adopted the title *Phenomenological Psychology* for a collection of his selected papers in English; this was not surprising in view of the fact that only the First Part of this collection is made up of "Phenomenological Studies," as distinguished from the "Anthropological" and "Clinical Studies" of Parts II and III. Only since 1964, in connection with the announcements and publications of the Lexington Conferences, has Straus seemed to come out for phenomenology without reservations.

Actually, Straus's way to phenomenology deserves to be traced biographically. Not an easy name-dropper or a methodologist for methodology's sake, Straus has never been anxious to attach

2. *Psychologie der menschlichen Welt* (Berlin: Springer, 1960), p. vi.
3. *Ibid.*, p. vii.
4. *Phenomenological Psychology: Selected Papers*, trans. Erling Eng (New York: Basic Books, 1966).

labels to what he is doing. But he was aware of the Phenomenological Movement since the beginning of his university studies. Thus he attended the lectures in Munich of Pfänder and Geiger, many of the lectures in Göttingen of Reinach (and some of Husserl's), as well as the private lectures given by Scheler during the years of his academic eclipse. But he had no close personal contacts with any of these men at the time. He made real contact with Scheler only much later in Berlin, after he had read Straus's book, at Binswanger's suggestion, in Kreuzlingen. With Jaspers and Heidegger he had merely inconsequential encounters in the fifties.

Straus had serious reservations toward Husserl from the start, especially as far as the "transcendental reduction" was concerned.[5] This may well have kept Straus from committing himself explicitly to phenomenology in his earlier days. Besides, Husserl's attachment to Descartes, for Straus the ultimate source of Pavlov's theories, made him doubly suspect. Only after the appearance of Husserl's posthumous writings with their phenomenology of the *Lebenswelt* did Straus move closer to him. His own phenomenology has always been that of "going to the things" in the style of the early Munich and Göttingen phenomenologists. He found phenomenology especially alive in the work of his fellow psychiatrists Binswanger, von Gebsattel, and Minkowski, who have been his friends since the twenties.

References to this kind of phenomenology begin in Straus's monograph on *Essence and Process of Suggestion* (1925),[6] where Scheler is invoked explicitly (e.g., p. 54) and Husserl at least implicitly (with his distinction of *Kundgabe* and *Bedeutung* from *Logische Untersuchungen*, pp. 58 ff.).

However, a much more important motif in Straus's development is his struggle against the biological science of the Pavlov school with its mechanistic belief in the explanatory power of the conditioned reflex. Straus himself considers his lecture to a Berlin medical society, in which his critique of Pavlov was denounced as an assault on science itself, to have been a high point in this protest. This was apparently the start for Straus's first major work, *Vom Sinn der Sinne*, subtitled *Ein Beitrag zur Grundlegung der Psychologie*.[7] Its first part consisted in a detailed critique

5. *Ibid.*, p. xi.

6. *Wesen und Vorgang der Suggestion* (Berlin: Karger, 1925); republished in *Psychologie der menschlichen Welt*, pp. 17–70.

7. *Vom Sinn der Sinne* (Berlin: Springer, 1935; 2d ed., 1956). English translation by Jacob Needleman, *The Primary World of Senses: A Vindication* (Glencoe, Ill.: Free Press, 1963).

of the theory of the conditioned reflex. On the basis of this, Straus developed an approach to a new foundation of a psychological science for which the "primary world of the senses" would take the place of the misleading concept of meaningless stimuli. Clearly, this meant a new phenomenological approach to the phenomenal world. But even here the term "phenomenology" occurred only incidentally, in connection with such specific needs as that of a "phenomenological analysis of the concepts 'here,' 'there,' 'now,' and 'then' " (p. 66). This was also the period of two of Straus's most important essays on "The Forms of Spatiality" (1930) and "Lived Movement" (1935), which in *Phenomenological Psychology* head the six "phenomenological studies"; but they too never speak of "phenomenology."

By this time Straus had also made contact with Binswanger, who had not only absorbed Husserl's phenomenology but had already moved beyond him to Heidegger. The personal contact had been preceded by Straus's review of Binswanger's *Einführung* and began with a first meeting in Innsbruck at a medical congress,[8] after which Binswanger arranged a meeting of Swiss psychiatrists on Straus's book on suggestion and reviewed it himself. However, their close personal friendship should not make one overlook the important differences in views and perspectives that were even expressed in print. Binswanger objected to Straus's theory of the draining of meaning (*Sinnentzug*) as stated in his important book of 1930 on *Geschehnis und Erlebnis*. Here Straus maintained that there was a fundamental difference between meaningful *Erlebnis* (lived experience) and meaningless *Geschehnis* (event). He never accepted Binswanger's attempt to restore meaning even to the mere event through the encompassing conception of *Dasein*. But perhaps more important than such specific disagreements was a difference in approach. While Binswanger's phenomenology usually was based on the works of the phenomenological philosophers, whom he recognized as his masters, Straus always started afresh from the phenomena, at best stimulated by a quotation. Only rarely did he take note of phenomenological authorities.

An event that in Strausian terms looked at first merely like a senseless *Geschehnis* was the Nazi revolution, which disrupted his existence as a neurologist and psychiatrist in Berlin, where he also had been associated with the university. Straus came to the

8. See Binswanger's letter in *Conditio Humana: Erwin Straus on His 75th Birthday*, ed. W. von Baeyer and R. Griffiths (Berlin and New York: Springer, 1966), pp. 1 ff.

United States in 1938 first teaching psychology at Black Mountain College, then doing research at Johns Hopkins University, and later, in 1946, joining the Veterans Hospital in Lexington, Kentucky. The transition into the Anglo-American world has clearly affected the development of his thinking and writing. Thus, except for a short monograph *On Obsession* (1948), no major new book comparable to *Vom Sinn der Sinne* has appeared since he came to America. But in many ways the stream of articles which make up his English production since 1939 are in their variety phenomenologically much richer, and those essays that have been combined into the volume *Phenomenological Psychology* (1966) have crystallized into an impressive whole. However, Straus's German contribution to *Psychologie der Gegenwart* under the title *Psychiatrie und Philosophie*, now translated together with the contributions of Maurice Natanson and Henri Ey, comes closest to being a new book. It presents a sustained case for the indispensability of philosophy for psychiatry and, more specifically, the necessity of phenomenology for such a philosophy:

> If phenomenology is not the ultimate instrument of psychiatric theory, it is at least a powerful reminder that without philosophy psychiatry cannot make a lasting claim to knowledge. Conversely, to the extent that its cardinal insight is valid, phenomenological philosophy is a precious clue to the nature of consciousness in its normal as well as abnormal modalities.[9]

Straus demonstrates this by beginning with the problem of determining what is normal and abnormal as the basis for psychiatry. Abnormality, finding its primary expression in a breakdown of communication, leads back to a consideration of the nature of communication by reference to a common world, the visible world of the *Allon* (the Other). This in turn poses the basic philosophical question of the primary animal situation (*Ursituation*). In the light of his answer, Straus then interprets psychic abnormality as a disturbance of this primary situation.

This conception suddenly puts a heavy burden on philosophy. How does Straus discharge it? How far is his phenomenology able to help him in doing so? Answering this question requires first a clear idea of Straus's conception of phenomenology.

9. Erwin Straus, M. Natanson, H. Ey, *Psychiatry and Philosophy*, ed. M. Natanson (New York: Springer, 1969), p. ix.

[4] Straus's Conception of Phenomenology

Straus is no methodologist. The strength of his work is in the concrete practice of his implicit principles. But he does reflect on these at least incidentally. And he is intensely interested in their philosophical implications.

This applies also to his version of phenomenology. He has not written any special treatise dealing with phenomenology for its own sake, or even with the place of phenomenology in psychology and psychiatry, as did Binswanger, whom Straus invokes quite often when theoretical questions arise. But it is possible to determine his conception of phenomenology from incidental statements.

Thus Straus refers to what is "phenomenologically given" or to what can be found in the phenomena themselves. His study of the "Forms of Spatiality" claims to be based on "phenomenological analysis" of what we experience as opposed to clinical *Empirie* or experimental investigations. In his study of the sigh he calls for a "phenomenological analysis which respects the phenomena as they appear, accepts them at their face value, and resists the temptation to take them for coded signs which reveal their true meaning only after an intricate process of deciphering." Such an attitude confines us to the observable or "despised descriptive phenomena" as opposed to "dynamic hypotheses," including those dealing with the unconscious. This may well be the most explicit statement about phenomenology in all of Straus's writings.

Phenomenology, then, is primarily a descriptive method dealing with "pure" experience, as such opposed to hypothetical theory and to merely factual and experimental research. Specifically, it is opposed to the kind of reduction which Straus finds exemplified in Hobbes's interpretation of memory as decaying sense. Phenomenology can also yield insights into essential connections, a feature which comes out particularly in Straus's study of the "essence" (*Wesen*) of suggestion. But, as we have seen, Straus is opposed to the kind of reductions, especially the transcendental reduction, stressed increasingly by Husserl, which lead to an absolute consciousness as the fundamental stratum of all human experience. There is no absolute consciousness; there is only man in his experienced concreteness. Straus's phenomenology is essentially anthropological.

We have already noted Straus's adamant opposition to Husserl's Descartes, in whose non-phenomenological dualism he sees the root even for Pavlovian reflexology. For a merely material stimulus as an objective reality, in contrast to the merely subjective response, presupposes a Cartesian dichotomy of the phenomena of experience.

But not only does Straus reject Husserl's transcendental reduction; he also shows no interest in constitutive analyses. Straus's phenomenology, then, is a clear expression of the original descriptive phenomenology of the early Husserl and the Phenomenological Movement. But it belongs of course in a different setting. In the meantime *Daseinsanalyse* and existential psychology have entered the scene. And Straus does not ignore them. In fact the conception of different modes of being-in-the world is an important part of Straus's descriptions, especially those of pathological experiences. But this too is a descriptive rather than a hermeneutic feature.

Even more important is a consideration of more original features of Straus's method. Here special attention must be given to his conception of "historiology," a term which is basic to his book on *Vom Sinn der Sinne*, although it is not explicitly explained there. Such an explanation can be found, however, in the essay on "Shame as a Historiological Problem" (1933). What is involved here is "a deepened understanding of the phenomenon." Understanding it by way of historico-psychological categories means an understanding of the experiencer as a becoming being (*als ein Werdender*). As such, historiological understanding is opposed to psychoanalysis, which to Straus is mechanistic and even "solipsistic."

> Too long psychology has confined itself to analyzing the objective content of experience. . . . But only to an approach, which takes man as becoming in the debate [*Auseinandersetzung*] with his world, which furthermore takes into consideration the fundamental significance of temporality and historicity of experience can a phenomenon such as shame reveal itself completely.

The chief field for such a historiological psychology is the world of "sense." Thus the climactic last chapter of the book, the *Sense of the Senses*, is actually nothing but such a historiological interpretation of sensing and self-moving.

Straus does not claim explicitly that historiology is part of phenomenology. But there can be little doubt that historiological understanding is to be carried out within the framework of "phenomenological analysis." Nevertheless, phenomenology is not all-comprehensive. It is clear not only from Straus's practice but also from his explicit statements that, especially in psychiatry, there are rival approaches. Yet the phenomenological approach is basic for Straus's new psychology and psychiatry.

[5] Some Results—Concrete Studies in Phenomenology

> The knowledge sought [in these investigations] is not to make the world more controllable, but it is to open up the world; it wants to transform a silent world into one which speaks to us in a thousand places. The abundance and variety of the world in which we live is to become audible where it has been silent before.[10]

As the above motto shows, Straus's major concern is to *use* phenomenology, not to theorize about it. The fact that he has done so to an unusual degree makes it all the more difficult to select the kind of examples which can convey the richness of his harvest. What follows are therefore merely samples of his ways of using phenomenology. No attempt is made to give a panorama of Straus's new open world.

A. *The Salvaging of the Sensory World (Aesthesiology)*

In a mimeographed paper of 1950 on "The Existential Approach to Psychiatry," Straus expressed his own main project as follows:

> In my own work I have tried to "save" sensory experience from theoretical misinterpretation and then to apply the regained understanding of the norm to pathological manifestations.[11]

This almost Platonic program provides the best explanation for Straus's most striking contribution to concrete phenomenology, for which he has chosen the slightly mystifying term "aesthesiology" (which is clearly unconnected with its opposite term "anaesthesiology") and for which Straus gives credit to Helmut Plessner. The objective is clear enough: "to present sensory experience freed from traditional prejudices." That it has become

10. *Vom Sinn der Sinne,* p. 419 (my translation); Eng. trans., p. 399.
11. Unitarian Symposium No. 4, 1960, p. 5.

the victim of such prejudices is one of Straus's main charges. The source of these prejudices is modern science as supported by the philosophies of Galileo, Descartes, Hobbes, and Locke. Its dogma of the subjectivity of our sensations has prevented us from studying them for their own sakes in all their "sensory splendor."

The first task of aesthesiology is the phenomenological rehabilitation of the immediate sense experience. Only thus can the "axioms of daily life" be recovered "on which all intercourse of man with each other and with things is based," including even the very experience of the scientist. While not stated explicitly, these axioms seem to be the following:

1. The subject that experiences is not pure consciousness; it is an unrepeatable, actual, living creature who experiences events within the context of his personal life history; "reaching-out beyond oneself, thus attaining to the *Other* . . . [this] is the basic phenomenon of sensory experience." [12]

2. Sensory experience has the form of becoming in which every phase points to others, preceding and following it.

3. "The Other" (i.e., the world of my sensory experience, other than I, the *Allon*), is common to all the senses; yet each man perceives it specifically (by different modalities).

4. The reality of sensory experience is immediate.

5. Being-together and being-able-to-be-together are elementary facts in everyday life.

Yet these common axioms are not yet the most original part of the new phenomenology of the senses. Usually even phenomenologists do not pay much attention to the differences of the sense "modalities" and their ways of givenness.[13] What Straus is anxious to show is the whole "spectrum" of these modalities in their continuities and discontinuities. He demonstrates this by studying the differences between color and sound:

1. Colors as attributes cling to things; sounds are their detaching emissions.

2. Color is (relatively) constant; sound is transitory.

12. "Aesthesiology and Hallucinations," in *Existence*, ed. Rollo May, Ernest Angel, and Henri F. Ellenberger (New York: Basic Books, 1958), p. 147.

13. Though they are apparently not considered explicitly by Straus, the ones who have done the most in this direction are Hedwig Conrad-Martius, in her "Realontologie," *Jahrbuch für Philosophie und phänomenologische Forschung*, VI (1923), 159–333, and in *Husserl Festschrift* (Halle: Niemeyer, 1929), 339–70.

3. The temporality of color, i.e., its persistence, and of sound, i.e., its duration, differ.

4. Visible colors appear side by side within a horizon; sounds appear singly or in groups, with the ear synthesizing them.

5. The emptiness of color (darkness) differs from the emptiness of sound (silence).

6. Color appears at an ("aristocratic") distance; sound presses in on us.

7. In seeing (better, "looking") I move toward the visible. In hearing (listening) the sounds move at me.

8. The contact is even closer in touch, in which I am always touching and being touched in a reciprocal relationship.

9. The final spectrum of the senses arranges the modalities in a scale from the visible, via the audible, the touchable, what can be smelled and tasted, to pain, each one containing a special relationship between I and world ("Other"), as distinctive forms of communication between the two.

Against the background of this interpretation of normal sensations, hallucinations can be understood as characteristic distortions of our being-in-the-sensory-world. Alcoholic delirium, for example, is the de-stabilization of the essential stability of the seen. Similarly, the direction of sensation can change with involvement: feeling undergoes influences from the Other, which acquires "physiognomy," i.e., assumes the character of an action center. Thus "voices" of the schizophrenic press in like detached sounds. He also becomes the victim of "touch." In this light the schizophrenic is by no means withdrawn from reality but is immersed in an alien reality that is a variant of ordinary reality, paralyzing his action and cutting him off from normal communication.

B. *The Sense of Sensing (The Pathic vs. the Gnostic)*

The German and typically Strausian title of Straus's largest work, *Vom Sinn der Sinne,* plays on a double meaning of the word *Sinn,* which in his view did not lend itself sufficiently to literal translation. The wording of the English version, "The Primary World of [the] Senses," may be clearer as to one of Straus's objectives, the rehabilitation of the neglected world of the experienced senses, but it abandons the point of the original title, the use of the word *Sinn* in the sense of "meaning." For this is one of the main functions of the book: to show that the function of sensation has been completely misjudged in the consideration of the senses merely as tools of knowledge, as "gnostic" devices, and very poor ones at that. The burden of the book and of Straus's entire approach is to show that this is a fundamental misconception of what the senses are and what they are here for. For their chief function is not knowledge but communication between I and world, i.e., the Other, or the *Allon*. "Sensory experiencing [*Empfinden*] is not a form of knowing. It is neither a preliminary stage nor an inferior form of knowledge in comparison with its higher forms, perception, representation, thinking. . . ."[14]

In attacking the field of sensation, Straus makes it clear from the start that he is not concerned with the sense data. Leaning on the phenomenologically revived distinction between act and content, *Empfinden* (sensing) and *Empfundenes* (sense), he focuses on the act of sensing, while the sensed is chiefly a topic for aesthesiology. However, Straus is equally interested in the sensing subject, the who of the sensing act, for whom sensing is a way of his living being. In sensing, the subject is essentially involved, undergoing as well as doing, and in this sense "pathic." The German *spüren* as an equivalent of *empfinden* involves both tracking and suffering. Straus's exploration of the meaning of sensing begins with a critical examination of Pavlov's theory of conditioned reflexes, not as far as the evidence but as far as the interpretation is concerned. What Straus questions are its presuppositions and its adequacy for explaining inherent difficulties. The major charge is that Pavlov's theory implies the extermination (*Ausmerzung*) of the phenomenal world. To Pavlov the world consists merely of physical processes outside and inside the nervous system. Seeing is nothing but a stimulation of the retina (p. 41; Eng. trans., p. 41). This extermination especially hits the secondary qualities such as colors and sounds rather than vibration of light and air, although the secondary qualities have to be used even in identifying the primary qualities.

The second part of the book develops the real problem: What must sensing be if it can be a partner of conditioned reflexes? A study of the signals which mediate between the indifferent objective situation and the experienced situation reveals that the conditioned reflex cannot be interpreted as a mere mechanical relation; what are involved are ways of behaving (*Verhaltens-*

14. *Vom Sinn der Sinne,* p. 1 (my translation). Eng. trans. p. 4.

weisen) of animated (*beseelt*) beings (p. 111). The phenomenon of the signal, the phenomenon of nearness, the phenomenon of betweenness, require a fresh examination of the type of sensing which corresponds to them.

In the second edition of his book Straus has inserted a section under the provocative title, "Man Thinks, Not the Brain," which ostensibly is an attack on "objective psychology" and behaviorism, but actually contains further clarifications of the concept of signal (*Zeichen*) and stimulus. Besides, it shows that all these concepts make sense only in the context of the living being as a sensing whole.

But the really constructive discussions are contained in the last and largest part of the book, which contains the "historiological consideration of sensing and movement." Its burden is to show how sensing in combination with a new phenomenon, movement, functions in the historical becoming of man as a living being in his world.

In this "historic" scheme, which begins with the symbiotic understanding between men and animals in symbiosis, sensing is a form of sympathetic communication without speech, which belongs to a perspective being (p. 207; Eng. trans., p. 201). Here the term "communication" has of course a much wider connotation than in social philosophy, implying any kind of living connectedness between the ego and his world. Each sense represents a special kind of such connectedness. In intoxication and depersonalization this communication is interrupted.

Perhaps Straus's most original thesis is that of the unity and interdependence of sensing and moving. Dance, in which Straus has always shown a special interest, is a particularly good example of this union. But the motion here involved is not the inert motion of physics but the spontaneous "ensouled" self-movement of living beings. The characteristic qualities of sensing are related to the possibilities of approaching these beings or moving away from them (p. 242; Eng. trans., pp. 233 ff.). Spontaneous movement has no place in physics, which cannot even account for its appearance (p. 249; Eng. trans., pp. 242 ff.). It is essentially related to the now and here of an I and a then and there of its world. It has a "start" and a goal (p. 274; Eng. trans., pp. 260 ff.). Both moving and sensing take precedence over the physiological facts in contradiction to what epiphenomenalism asserts. Physicalism proves to be incompatible with these phenomena. In this sense even Gestalt psychology is still too epiphenomenalistic (p. 317; Eng. trans., p. 304).

C. *The Primal Animal Situation and Man's Upright Posture*

Considering Straus's conception of the sense of the senses, one might easily think that man and nature form a harmonious continuum without basic conflicts and major breaks. But this would certainly be a gross oversimplification. For Straus it would be much closer to the truth to think of man as the insurgent against pre-human nature.

Straus's anthropology is in fact a distinctive feature of his conception, which contrasts considerably with that of his friend Binswanger and indirectly with that of Heidegger. For an adequate appraisal of this difference, one has to pay some attention to Straus's critical dissents from the two.

They begin with Straus's distinction between lived experience (*Erlebnis*) and objective event (*Geschehnis*), the former endowed with meaning, the latter bereft of it, particularly after a catastrophic happening which deprives the *Erlebnis* of its meaning (*Sinnentzug*). Binswanger wrote a whole essay trying to show Straus the mistake of this sharp division. But, as Straus told me orally, he has not abandoned it.

To Binswanger the impossibility of a totally meaningless experience was actually an implication of his conception, taken over from Heidegger, of *Dasein* as being-in-the-world. This phrase occurs in Straus's earlier work too, though never to the extent that it does with Binswanger. But not until his treatise on *Psychiatry and Philosophy* did Straus state the extent and basis of his partial dissent from Heidegger. While realizing that Heidegger's ontological analytics of *Dasein* does not claim to be an anthropology, Straus found it objectively inadequate to take on this additional role. To begin with, Straus missed in Heidegger's analytics a place for life, for the body, for the "animalia" (p. 931; Eng. trans., p. 5). For Straus, even the name *Dasein* is unsuited to designate man, the living being. Besides, he found Heidegger's interpretation of nature as ready-at-hand (*vorhanden*) defective. In particular Heidegger had overlooked man's struggle with nature (p. 936; Eng. trans., p. 14). Hence, his being-in-the-world lacked "gravity" (p. 938; Eng. trans., p. 16). This critique of Heidegger's perspective on man's relation to nature indicates a basic difference between the perspectives of Straus and Heidegger-Binswanger. Heidegger's being-in-the-world signified to him familiarity, being alongside with the everyday world. In Binswanger the original "we-hood" implied a primary, loving union, at least with others.

This is definitely not Straus's perspective. As he has confirmed to me in a letter, since the middle fifties when he worked on the second edition of his book on *Vom Sinn der Sinne,* Straus increasingly has seen man's relation to the world as one of an I opposed to the world or, as he now calls it, the *Allon.* Even communication between an I and a you presupposes a common relation to such an *Allon.*

But we cannot set ourselves apart from this *Allon* without self-movement. And this self-movement begins with what Straus calls the primal animal situation (*animale Ursituation*), that of the animal getting up from the ground by opposing gravity and generally standing in a *here* as opposed to a *there.* On the basis of our common opposition to the *Allon,* communication between ego and alter ego can begin.

But the animal's primary situation is not yet identical with the upright posture. Man's erectness is more than the mere I-World opposition involved in getting up from the ground. Thus Straus discusses it separately in one of his most brilliant studies, "The Upright Posture," a revision and enlargement of an earlier German essay of 1949.[15]

The anatomical and physiological facts of the upright posture and its evolutionary derivation are of course an old theme of physical anthropology. What distinguishes Straus's approach is that he explores the present meaning of this posture for human existence. For it involves a specific attitude toward the world, in fact a special mode of being-in-the-world. "Human kinematics" (in contrast to kinematics in physics) begins with counteracting gravity by acquiring uprightness, which can be maintained only during awakeness (a phenomenon to which Straus has devoted additional studies). Standing is an activity needing attention and effort. It results in establishing distance, in fact three types of distance: (1) distance from the ground, which enables us to move freely, but which adds precarious maximum elevation to the safer distance from the ground of animals; (2) distance from things, which allows us to confront things and look at them from afar; (3) distance from our fellow men, which permits us to meet others "face to face" for various social relationships. The

15. "The Upright Posture," *Psychiatric Quarterly,* XXVI (1952), 529–61; *Monatsschrift für Psychiatrie und Neurologie,* CXVII (1949), Parts 4, 5, 6.

upright posture also allows us to walk, which is really a continually arrested falling forward. The significance of upright posture for the development of the hand and arm is explored, the hand now being available not only for "gnostic" touching but as the "tool of tools," the arms extending the body schema way beyond its anatomical space to whatever is within reach. Upright posture has significance too for the development of the features and functions of the human head, no longer directed primarily toward the ground; now "sight" becomes predominant over bite.

In later reflections on the upright posture [16] Straus, interpreting a verse from Goethe's *Faust,* has developed the idea that it enables man not only to see, as does the animal, but to intuit (*schauen*), to look out into infinity, and, no longer enslaved to immediate needs, to contemplate the things for their own sakes in their "whatness" (*So-sein, Eidos*). This is also the beginning of man's sense for the image (*Bild*) and the visual arts.

Straus's studies on the upright posture are the most highly integrated pieces of his phenomenological anthropology. But there are other equally original samples in his essays on "Man: The Questioning Being," on "Shame as a Historiological Problem," and on "The Sigh."

What should also not be overlooked in appraising Straus's emphasis on the unity of man as opposed to the Cartesian mind-body dualism is that this does not mean the kind of undifferentiated unity which seems to go with the picture of man as an embodied subject or incarnated consciousness, as has been advocated by French existential phenomenologists from Gabriel Marcel to Merleau-Ponty. Especially in some recent, in part experimental, studies of the expression of thinking,[17] Straus has shown that thinking involves the capacity of transposal from one's actual position to a merely imaginary one, something for which Straus has coined the term "excarnation," or "ekbasis." This capacity for excarnation, even if it does not involve a new dualism, shows that Straus's man is by no means a being in whom mind and body coincide. Man is an organism, but he is more than a mere organism—namely, a being with an I not tied to his body or to any particular fixed location within it.

16. "Zum Sehen geboren, zum Schauen bestellt," in *Werden und Handeln,* ed. E. Wiesenhutter (Stuttgart: Hippokrates, 1963), pp. 44–73.
17. "The Expression of Thinking," in James M. Edie, *Invitation to Phenomenology* (Chicago: Quadrangle Books, 1965), pp. 266–83.

D. *Psychopathology*

Considering the fact that Straus is a practicing psychiatrist with a background in neurology, it is surprising how few of his publications, especially those of larger scope, deal with pathology, and how many of them are devoted to normal psychology. This does not mean that Straus has deserted psychopathology; that he has not can best be seen from the "Clinical Studies" (Part III) of his selected papers in *Phenomenological Psychology*. But it does mean that in Straus's perspective little progress can be made in pathology without a fuller and broader understanding of the norm. In fact, pathology is to be developed against the background of the norm of our I-World relations, and all pathological phenomen are to be interpreted as breakdowns in the normal relationships between the I and the *Allon*. Straus does not actually offer a complete survey of such disturbances, but he supplies enough examples all the way from depersonalization to schizophrenia to show how such an understanding can work. His essays on "The Phenomenology of Hallucinations," "Disorders of Personal Time in Depressive States," "The Pathology of Compulsion," and "Pseudoreversibility of Catatonic Stupor" are his own major illustrations.

Straus tries to understand these pathological conditions by showing how in such situations the "axioms of everyday experience," which we normally take for granted, are in various ways undermined and abandoned. Thus, in the case of auditory hallucinations, the way in which ordinarily voices and speakers are conjoined is radically broken up: the schizophrenic hears only voices, no longer persons. Similar disruptions can occur in the tactile and even in the visual range. Phenomenology allows us to understand these phenomena as deformations of normal "modalities."

The same kind of deformation can be observed in the case of the time distortions typical in depressive states. Against the background of the phenomenological distinction between the individual time of our personal becoming, which may be fast or slow, and objective or cosmic time, it can be noted that in depressive states the personal time is distorted to the extent that the future becomes blocked, everything stands still, and there is no longer any continuity. All this can be understood as a deformation of our normal experience of time, uneven as it may be. With depression, even the relation to an objective cosmic time loses its sense.

Such examples can do no more than indicate how the pathological phenomena can become phenomenologically accessible as modifications of the normal "modalities" of our experience. Clearly, this involves a certain type of variation in the imagination. Of course we do not yet have anything like a causal understanding of why such disturbances take place and why they assume the particular form of a specific psychosis. Such an understanding is not what phenomenology ever promises. But it may yet provide the basis on which such insight may become possible, even if it has to adopt additional techniques such as those of dynamic analysis. For now, phenomenology can guide us to a fuller insight into what is going on in the patients' deranged minds.

[6] Straus as a Phenomenologist

In what sense and to what extent can Straus be classified as a phenomenologist? In his case such a question may seem to be pedantically incongruous. Certainly, his way of attacking his problems orally as well as in writing is something so spontaneous and imaginative that it defies pigeonholing. Compared with Binswanger and others, he shows little reverence for authority, phenomenological or otherwise. He may refer to others for occasional support, but more often he turns to them for critical dissent. His typical points of departure are the original phenomena which most others have overlooked. To this extent Straus is chiefly a pioneer. But he is also a rebel, ready to disagree with and to challenge the traditions, even those sanctioned by phenomenological authorities, including personal friends such as Binswanger.

There is also something unique about the style of his phenomenologizing, whether in live presentation or in writing. Challenging to the degree of abruptness, it may at times lack strict logical coherence. But it has all the charm and appeal of the sudden inspiration, the literary grace, and the humorous touch. In other words, few phenomenologists have combined so much of the artist with the scientist.

Straus's major concern is the recovery and rehabilitation of the phenomenal world of the senses in their pathic as well as in their gnostic aspects, regardless of "scientific" and philosophic prejudices of the Galilean-Cartesian tradition. It is in this protest against the restriction of the phenomenal world for purposes of philosophic certainty and technological control that his phenomenological orientation is most pronounced.

But his methods also show a good deal of continuity with the phenomenological tradition. There is not only the emphasis on fresh seeing and describing; but there is also the attempt to grasp the essence of the phenomena. Experimental and clinical evidence, while not eliminated, is called in mostly for demonstrative, corroborative, and supplementary purposes, as in Straus's "rheoscopic" laboratory for the study of expressions.

Although Straus's work would have been possible without the writings of Brentano, Husserl, Scheler, and Heidegger, they have inspired it as models and as dialectical challenges. Moreover, without the backdrop of philosophical phenomenology, Straus's work would not have stood out as plastically and provocatively.

Straus's major role has been that of an inspirer. His pioneering may not always have resulted in permanent insights. But what he has been able to work out under circumstances not always conducive to a coherent opus has done more to make phenomenology alive and to demonstrate its vitality than the more academic performances of the bigger names in its history. Even though his recognition in America has been limited, without him phenomenology in the New World would have remained mostly a second-hand affair without the original taste and spark he has added to it.

11 / Frederik Jacobus Johannes Buytendijk (b. 1887): Phenomenology in Biology

[1] Buytendijk's Place in the Phenomenological Movement

The central pioneer figure among phenomenologists in the Netherlands was and still is the biologist Buytendijk. No other phenomenologist can present equal credentials in biological science, either in research or in teaching. And few other biologists have moved as far into philosophy, and none into phenomenology, as he has without losing their base in scientific physiology. Yet these distinctions by no means exhaust the wide range of Buytendijk's interests and achievements, which include such fields as education and literature. His importance not only on the national but on the international level is enhanced by the fact that he is at home in German and French almost as well as he is in his native Dutch.

Thus in a sense Buytendijk transcends the boundaries of the present study of phenomenology in psychology and psychiatry. Actually, he started his work in animal biology, with all the credentials of the specialist. From there he moved gradually into psychology and anthropology, developing at the same time a universal conception of man. But the fact that psychology may well be considered his center of gravity is indicated by his long directorship of one of the largest psychological institutes on the Continent, at the University of Utrecht. The methodological link between all these interests, however, was Buytendijk's commitment to phenomenology.

[2] Buytendijk's Way into Phenomenology

Buytendijk's personal approach to phenomenology was derived from Max Scheler, the Scheler of the Cologne period, after 1920, with his growing interest in biology and philosophical anthropology. Apparently at his invitation, Buytendijk gave visiting lectures in Cologne between 1920 and 1923. In mentioning this fact, Buytendijk himself speaks about the admiration (*Verehrung*) Scheler aroused in him and Scheler's influence on his own thinking.[1] Thus, in recording Scheler's approach to *Wesensschau* as something to be constantly renewed for enrichment and deepening, Buytendijk reports Scheler's typical phrase *und auch das noch* (and then this too).[2] This does not mean, however, that Buytendijk accepted Scheler's views indiscriminately.[3]

Apparently, Buytendijk never made real personal contact with Husserl. He has indicated to me in personal conversation that Husserl's Amsterdam lectures on "Phenomenological Psychology" of 1928 failed to impress him. Clearly, Husserl's plea for a pure psychology and his growing transcendentalism had at the time little meaning for Buytendijk. And yet, Buytendijk became increasingly aware of Husserl's significance, not only for the whole movement but also for psychology in general.

Buytendijk was most outspoken about his awareness of Husserl on two later occasions: (1) at the Second Moosehart Symposium on *Emotions and Feeling* at the University of Chicago in 1948, where he not only announced the need for the phenomenological approach in animal psychology but cited as a primary example Husserl's conception of consciousness as intentional and meaningful, mentioning other phenomenologists from Scheler to Merleau-Ponty only in second place; (2) at the second international phenomenological symposium in Krefeld in 1956, where he delivered a major address on "The Significance of Husserl's Phenomenology for Present Psychology."[4] In this address, based already to a large extent on the Louvain publications of the

1. *Das Menschliche* (Stuttgart: Koehler, 1958), p. ix. See also Helmuth Plessner in *Rencontre / Encounter / Begegnung* (Utrecht: Spectrum, 1957), pp. 331 ff., about some of these encounters.

2. From personal conversations, supported by *Situations*, I (1955), 13.

3. *Pain*, trans. Eda O'Shiel (Chicago: University of Chicago Press, 1962), pp. 11 ff., 127, 140, 153.

4. *Husserl et la pensée moderne*, *Phaenomenologica* II (1959), 78–98.

Crisis of the European Sciences, Buytendijk credited Husserl with having broken the stranglehold of Cartesian dualism over psychology by his turn to consciousness as the mode of being of human subjectivity. He also interpreted the call "to the things" as implying both the unprejudiced non-metaphysical investigation of immediate experience and the attitude of standing back (*Distanz*) for the study of its meaning structures. By showing the relativity of natural science as founded on one particular type of perception, Husserl had also become for Buytendijk a liberator of psychology and the *Geisteswissenschaften.* In Buytendijk's view, standing back makes it possible to grasp the essentials of facts and events (p. 85) in a way which sees the questionable and even the enigmatic in the obvious. For in immediate experience much of the phenomena is hidden, as in the case of anxiety. This calls for the kind of understanding obtainable only through *Wesensschau* (p. 86) based on variation of the given either in experiment or in imagination (p. 89). Buytendijk finally tried to show the influence of Husserl's ideas about intentionality in concrete instances of psychological investigations. Thus Buytendijk increasingly gave Husserl credit for having developed the genuine phenomenological method which makes it possible to *understand* what was previously only *described* or *"explained."*

Heidegger's role in Buytendijk's writings is less conspicuous and was late in revealing itself. There seem to have been no personal contacts between the two. But Heidegger figures prominently in Buytendijk's phenomenology of the encounter (1951). With Binswanger he accepts Heidegger's conception of human *Dasein* as being-in-the-world, but thinks that care (*Sorge*) is more characteristic of the female than of the male mode of being-in-the-world. In short, in Buytendijk's phenomenology, Heidegger with his relative disinterest in the philosophy of life and of social existence has been largely a marginal stimulus in areas where his major concerns and his dissents from Husserl's phenomenology hardly matter.

Much more important for Buytendijk's thinking is the development of phenomenology in France. Among the new French phenomenologists, Gabriel Marcel is apparently closest to his concerns, especially in his studies on being and having. While Buytendijk has rejected Sartre's existentialism insofar as it implies the denial of objective values in Scheler's sense, and while he rarely if ever agrees with him, he discusses many of his ideas at length. For to Buytendijk too phenomenology is concerned with freedom in a situation. Sartre's ideas about consciousness and the emotions also are important to Buytendijk's phenomenological psychology. Likewise, he takes seriously Simone de Beauvoir's existential theory of the second sex, though he disagrees with some of her interpretations of the phenomena.

But Buytendijk's greatest affinity is clearly with Merleau-Ponty, who has reciprocated in some of his major writings. In view of their common interest in problems of life and behavior, such rapport needs little explanation. No wonder that in his preface to *Situations* (p. 12), Buytendijk stated that it is impossible to characterize pure (eidetic) psychology and what connects it with empirical psychology better than Merleau-Ponty had done; no wonder that in his book on *Woman* he subscribed to Merleau-Ponty's philosophical anthropology by quoting him repeatedly.

The extent of Buytendijk's relations to other applied phenomenologists in psychology and psychiatry is not without interest. No relationship seems to have existed between him and Jaspers, and even in the case of Binswanger no personal contacts are reported. But all the more impressive is the way in which Buytendijk expressed his affinity with Binswanger's position—not only in his estimate of Husserl's general significance for psychology [5] but in his dissent from Heidegger's diagnosis of *Dasein:*

> In unsurpassable manner Binswanger has further developed and overcome Heidegger's Fundamental Ontology by showing that *Dasein* is in itself loving encounter, openness [*Erschlossenheit*] of you for me and of me for you in the we.[6]

There are also strong personal ties between Buytendijk and von Gebsattel, who wrote the preface for the German edition of Buytendijk's book on *Woman,* and between Buytendijk and Minkowski, who did the same for the French edition of Buytendijk's book on *Attitudes and Movements.* Buytendijk's closeness in interests and approach to Erwin Straus is obvious, though there are differences in views.

But there is little point in continuing such a preliminary intellectual geography of Buytendijk's relation to his contemporaries, phenomenological or otherwise. I shall make an exception and mention only his relation to Romano Guardini. In the conversion of Buytendijk, the Dutch Calvinist, to Catholicism, Guardini's humanism had a major share. At the same time the many phenomenological motifs in Guardini's thought, stimulated but not

5. *Phaenomenologica* II (1959), 83.
6. *Das Menschliche,* p. 96.

dominated by Scheler, are relevant to the perspective of Buytendijk's later books.

[3] Buytendijk's Concerns

Buytendijk started out as a biologist and always remained one. But he is a biologist with a difference, which may well account for his becoming a psychologist and even a philosophical anthropologist. From the very start of his independent work, the psychology of animals had aroused his interest. His inaugural lecture in Groningen in 1925 made it clear that his basic concern was to understand the phenomena of life in such a way that the usual descriptive or explanatory approach would not and could not suffice. Buytendijk's original idea was that such an understanding of the meaning of life could be obtained by a study of animal action and expression. But he never implied that this was always possible, "Life is and remains a mystery," he wrote, quoting his physiology teacher Thomas Place in the Introduction to his academic speeches of 1961,[7] and he stressed this again in his book on *Woman*. But this did not keep him from trying to uncover as much of life as a widened and deepened science could.

However, the central phenomenon of life for Buytendijk is man—human life in the context of all life, and especially animal life. And in his concern for understanding the human (*Das Menschliche*) he wants to contribute to

> the rehabilitation of the great tradition of German anthropological meditation [*Besinnung*] which is still anchored in reverence [*Ehrfurcht*] before the human in all its manifestations and in the unconditional love for everything that bears the human face.[8]

It is Buytendijk's conviction that psychology has a special mission in the development of a new self-interpretation of man, for which Husserl's phenomenology has laid new foundations.[9] However, this emphasis on Buytendijk's ultimate interest in the human, in the deepening of his conception of man, including his religious concerns, must not make one overlook his stake in widening man's scope and liberating him. Buytendijk even has

7. *Academische Redevoeringen* (Utrecht: Dekker & Van de Vegt, 1961).
8. *Das Menschliche,* p. vii.
9. *Phaenomenologica* II (1959), 96 ff.

a sense for the *joie d'existence*, for the sensuous richness of life as expressed in play. His study of soccer (*le football*) is one of the more unusual, but all the more engaging, expressions of this interest.

[4] THE ROLE OF PHENOMENOLOGY IN BUYTENDIJK'S DEVELOPMENT

THE PROFESSIONAL BIOLOGY of his student days had little to offer Buytendijk in his real search. His own inaugural lecture in Amsterdam in 1914 on the "Energetic View of the Life Manifestations" contained merely "an echo of the perspective of his teacher Zwaardemaker supported by experiments and filled with vague speculations in natural philosophy." Even in 1917 Buytendijk did not go beyond the assertion that life was veiled in a mystery, of which we could at best lift a corner.

The tone is very different in his inaugural lecture at Groningen in 1925 about the understanding of the manifestations of life. Here there is no mention of energetics. Instead, Buytendijk emphasizes the "phenomenological method of understanding" in contrast to that of causal explanation.[10] Phenomenology is not yet mentioned by name, nor are any philosophical phenomenologists. But *verstehende* psychology is invoked as a major aid in the new enterprise. For this Buytendijk himself attributes "decisive importance" to his psychiatric-neurological education during the First World War, after which he taught general biology in Amsterdam, doing experimental work on animal behavior and writing a book on animal psychology. These were also the years during which he took up contact with philosophers such as Hans Driesch and Max Scheler in Cologne and with Viktor von Weizsäcker in Heidelberg. While Driesch's antimechanism was of course important for Buytendijk, his neovitalism left little trace in his thought.

By contrast, von Weizsäcker influenced him deeply. His concept of the *Gestaltkreis* as the cyclical unity of movement and perception can be found particularly in Buytendijk's most systematic work, that on attitudes and movements. So can von Weizsäcker's biological concept of subjectivity. In fact, Buytendijk refers to him as "my master" (*Lehrmeister*) who "has shown us that understanding of the human requires 'respect for the

10. See the brief autobiographical sketch at the end of *Mensch und Tier* (Hamburg: Rowohlt, 1958), pp. 26–28.

phenomena' and that 'flexible [*bewegliche*] mental participation' which makes it possible to combine discursive, scientifically secured knowledge into a plastically meaningful unity." [11] In this regard, von Weizsäcker reflected Scheler, to whom he was indebted for some of his basic ideas.[12] It was also through Scheler that Buytendijk came to know his later collaborator Helmuth Plessner, who had been a student of Husserl's in Göttingen and, before that, a student of Driesch's in Heidelberg.

Implicit references to phenomenology as the way to an understanding of the phenomena of life occur in several of Buytendijk's essays of the late twenties. An explicit one on the "phenomenological inspection" (*Betrachtung*) of the expressive movement of the face can be found in the study of 1929 on the essential difference between man and animal that appears in *Das Menschliche* (p. 49). But the main change was that Buytendijk came increasingly to see phenomenology as the most effective, if not the only possible, approach to an understanding of life and, as his horizon widened, to an understanding of man and his world. In the Preface to his Dutch addresses (1961), Buytendijk himself pointed out this "shift of accent" in the direction of "more outspoken orientation in the anthropological and phenomenological direction." Only since 1945 has Buytendijk seemed to identify completely with phenomenology to the extent of using the term in his literary titles and speaking of himself, or letting others speak of him, as a phenomenologist.

This shift in Buytendijk's methodological consciousness was closely related to the shift in his research interests, and his movement toward a new discipline was expressed outwardly in the change in his academic appointments. He began in the field of general biology, with emphasis on its physiological aspects. Studies in animal psychology led Buytendijk increasingly to the realization that any understanding of the animal psyche presupposed a study of human psychology and anthropology, rather than the other way around. Hence, in 1946 he became a professor of general psychology at Utrecht. Yet, after his retirement, he returned from the study of the "human reality" to the meeting of nature and spirit in psychosomatics, holding a lectureship in a new type of physiology for psychologists. Incidentally, Buytendijk also had visiting appointments in theoretical and comparative psychology at Nijmegen and Louvain.

11. *Das Menschliche*, p. 8.

12. See *Zwischen Medizin und Philosophie* (Göttingen: Vandenhoeck, 1957), pp. 12, 255.

[5] Buytendijk's Conception of Phenomenology

It is obvious that Buytendijk's interest in phenomenology was determined primarily by Scheler's theory and practice of it. But he has never been a blind follower of Scheler's, and his conception of phenomenology did not remain unchanged after Scheler's death. Thus the growth of phenomenology in France and Belgium, with which Buytendijk has been associated increasingly, has slanted his conception of phenomenology in the direction of existential thought. In connection with this new influence Buytendijk has also shown a much stronger interest in Husserl; it has probably been stimulated by his guest professorship at Louvain, the new center of Husserl studies, which has significantly changed the Husserl picture by giving access to his concept of the life-world. This was bound to attract a phenomenological biologist. Buytendijk's first formulations of phenomenology occur in an article on the interpretation of mimic expression,[13] which he wrote jointly with Helmuth Plessner. Of course, this article also reflects the views and influence of Plessner, who, partly as a result of his studies in Göttingen, had considerable reservations about Husserlian phenomenology.[14] In urging that any scientific investigation should start from the immediate phenomena of *Anschauung,* Buytendijk and Plessner wrote:

> It starts from the phenomena present in pre-problematic life and proceeds step by step through the features which belong to their manifestations [*Erscheinungen*] by way of elucidation of the inner structure and immanent description of the features which belong to the meaning [*Sinn*] to the conditions of the features which belong to the phenomena [themselves].

The method is thus carried from layer to layer and leads from the intuitive facts to the intuitable (*erschaubaren*) essences (*Wesenheiten*). It has to guard against letting the closeness to the phenomena be corrupted by theories about them, even if

13. "Die Deutung des mimischen Ausdrucks," *Philosophischer Anzeiger,* I (1925), 72–126.

14. "Bei Husserl in Göttingen," *Phänomenologica* IV (1959), 29–39; *Die Stufen des Organischen und der Mensch* (Berlin: deGruyter, 1928), p. v.

they contain ever so much scientific truth. Phenomenology must not lose itself in the delight of *Anschauung*. Though what is found phenomenologically does not admit of further explanation, philosophy as such has the task of pushing on toward the arch-phenomena (*Urphänomene*), which, to be sure, no longer yield to a purely phenomenological approach.[15]

For Buytendijk and Plessner phenomenology thus aimed at the discovery of the essences of such phenomena as mimic expressions as the start, but by no means the final destination, of scientific and philosophical knowledge. Its most important function is to prepare the ground for the study of the spontaneous behavior of animals and humans in its psychophysical neutrality, where it reveals an "original identity of intuitability and intelligibility." [16]

Buytendijk found increasing use for such a method in his studies of animal and human psychology. Later, when he had absorbed the new inspirations of existential phenomenology, especially in Merleau-Ponty, such conceptions as being-in-the-world, with its various modifications, the body as subject, and intentionality as productive function enriched not only the practice but the theory of his phenomenology.

This new conception became particularly explicit when in 1945 Buytendijk, in cooperation with other Dutch phenomenological psychologists, started the short-lived yearbook *Situation*. Here the goal of comprehending "man in his situation" was based on the "phenomenological method" that has its foundation in an "experience which precedes science, i.e., the *Lebenswelt*" (in the sense of Merleau-Ponty)[17] as a network of personal meanings. This does not imply an abandonment of "guarantees of exactness."

As means for achieving such exactness, Buytendijk suggests (1) the increase of the number of examined situations with their variations and the differences between them; (2) the practice, renewed in each case, of *Wesensschau* in the sense of Scheler; (3) the resort to existential anthropology and attention to new facts, e.g., of sociology, experimental psychology, and psychopathology, in order to direct attention to certain aspects of the phenomena; (4) structural analysis of the situation, the investigation of the indispensable conditions for the realization of what is essential. Yet, as Buytendijk himself puts it:

15. "Die Deutung des mimischen Ausdrucks," p. 77.
16. *Ibid.*, p. 84.
17. *Situations*, I (1955), p. 9.

Obviously such prescriptions do not add up to a new conception of phenomenology, let alone a foolproof method. The main proof has to be found in the concrete applications in the subsequent examples.[18]

[6] Applications

A. *Animal Psychology*

At first sight subhuman animal life may seem to be the least likely place for applying the phenomenological approach. Even if one should indulge in the kind of anthropomorphism which grants animals a manlike soul—which Buytendijk does not—the use of a method based on direct experience of what goes on in the animal psyche seems anything but safe. Certainly Buytendijk does not aid and abet the sentimental laymen's interpretations of "the mind of the dog," to which he has devoted a special book. But while acknowledging that animals are different from man, whose behavior is largely regulated by the "spirit," Buytendijk feels there is no good reason for denying that animals and men have common life experiences, or for studying, for instance, the "expressive movements" of animals, while guarding against the danger of "humanizing them." Buytendijk even considers it doubtful that animals perceive "things," or that buzzing bees or howling dogs experience any feelings or pain, in the way humans do. What he is looking for is an understanding of animal behavior which avoids both Watsonian behaviorism and mechanism on the one hand and a "psychologization of life à la Driesch" on the other, a concept that Buytendijk had tried but rejected after 1938.[19] What he does maintain, however, is that animal behavior has meaning, that it is animated by "intentions," and that it has its center in a "subject" that animates it. The basis for this view is not a merely speculative and unverifiable hypothesis but a plain phenomenological description of what a perceptive observer, not blinded by negativistic prejudices about the impossibility of "mental" events in animals, can immediately see when watching animal behavior. Such phenomenological understanding often requires experimental studies. Life may be ultimately a secret; but this must

18. *Ibid.*, p. 13.
19. *Wege zum Verständnis der Tiere* (Zurich: Niehans, 1938), p. 147.

not prevent us from trying to understand its manifest meanings as they present themselves to open-minded research.

Buytendijk's treatise on animal psychology is an even more explicit attempt to show that "phenomenological analysis" allows us to state the problems correctly and to elucidate the factual data.[20] It presents the animal as the subject of his behavior. As new and particularly striking cases the phenomena of rest and sleep and of animal knowledge are investigated. Thus a comparative analysis of rest in animal and in man reveals a phenomenological difference between rest which one "takes" and mere tranquillity (resting and being at rest). Resting is something which the organism does, like stirring; it has all the characteristics of an act. In man it is expressive of restoration of energies or preparation for action and is related to work as a personal task. This is not the case in animals, especially in lower animals.

B. *Human Movement*

Buytendijk's largest work, written underground during the Nazi occupation of the Netherlands, deals with "human attitudes and movements." [21] Actually, the subtitle "A Functional Study of Human Movement" and the Table of Contents make it clear that the more important of these two phenomena is movement, and that stationary attitudes are simply the starting positions of movements.

How to account for Buytendijk's fascination with this phenomenon in man? As a biologist watching man as a "phenomenon," he found in the succession of human behavior a characteristic, unified, and intriguing sequence of events. How is it possible to understand them? Is such understanding a matter of physiology or psychology? Does this task ultimately require something like a philosophical anthropology?

The field of human movement as self-movement pointedly poses the question of whether it can be handled by the science of mechanical motion or requires a very different teleological approach. As Buytendijk sees it, the physiology of movement can-

20. *Traité de psychologie animale* (Paris: PUF, 1952), p. xiii.

21. *Allgemeine Theorie der menschlichen Haltung und Bewegung* (Heidelberg: Springer, 1956). Dutch original, *Allgemeine theorie van de menschlijke honding und beweging* (Utrecht: Spectrum, 1948). French version, *Attitudes et mouvements* (Paris: Desclée de Brouwer, 1957).

not dispense with the concept of function and the meaning of such functions. His idea is that both can be assimilated by a new conception of behavior or comportment. Its basis is "a field of experience prior to the distinction between the physical and the psychic," or at least "a region where this distinction is inoperative." This immediate experience shows us the general characteristics of human and animal life as "being in the world as a living being and makes functionally intelligible the movements formed in the interaction between the individual and his vital field." Such formulations make it clear that for Buytendijk the bridge between physiology and psychology can be supplied by a phenomenological interpretation of being-in-the-world.

For a better understanding of this new approach it might be useful to achieve at least a birds-eye view of the range of topics taken up in this magnum opus of Buytendijk's, not yet accessible in English.

Part I develops the principles of a theory of movement based on the concept of function rather than process, showing the difference between movement in general and self-movement, pointing out the kind of space and time characteristic of self-movement, and discussing the system of human movement. Part II examines the basic human attitudes and movements, beginning with the stance (as a distribution of tensions), and continuing with a discussion of other bodily attitudes and of the human walk. Among sample reactions and achievements, Part III deals with reflexes, lid movements, the retracting of the hand, defense movements, the preservation of equilibrium, scratching, grasping, leaping, and throwing. Part IV takes up the non-action types of movement, i.e., expressive movements, from mere excitement to laughing and weeping. Part V follows the development of human movements from the prenatal stage to the movements learned later. The last part (VI) deals with the typology of human dynamics and examines the characteristic movements in youth and puberty, in man and woman, and in old age; it also deals with differences of movement in different constitutional types and finally with the problem of norms for movement. The book terminates in a discussion of bodily grace.

What precisely is the role of phenomenology in this vast enterprise? Actually Buytendijk does not display the word prominently, especially not in his titles. But the approach itself is all the more present in his actual analyses. For one thing, the entire book is an attempt to understand the essential nature of human movement in its various manifestations, much in the spirit of the phenomenology of Scheler, even though he does not figure prominently in the text. But there is also a much closer approach to phenomenology in Husserl's and Merleau-Ponty's sense in the emphasis on the need for studying the experience of the subject as basic for an understanding of human comportment. This sense of phenomenology is perhaps most explicit in the early section on self-movement. According to Buytendijk, it is impossible to grasp this by way of "analytic psychology" and "analytic physiology." Now, "what is physiological or psychological about the act of writing, speaking, marching, or laughing?" For Buytendijk, they have to be referred to

> a phenomenal world preceding the distinction between the physical and the psychic. This phenomenal plan is that of human existence as bodily presence to a world. . . . the theory of movements must be founded on an anthropology and consequently it cannot be a chapter of psychology or physiology. This foundation implies the phenomenological approach to the phenomena, aiming at the same time at the seizure of the human essence and of the essence of the attitudes and movements in question.[22]

Thus it is ultimately the phenomenon of existence as being-in-an-environing-world which emerges as the neutral ground to be studied by Buytendijk's functional approach. Human behavior is nothing but a form of this existence. Its focus is the human subject, which is expressed not only in movement proper but also in such manifestations as conditioned reflexes.

Buytendijk's latest book, thus far accessible only in Dutch, returns to his original beat in physiology. Here he tries to show that even in the vegetative life of man the "spiritual" plays a meaningful part along with blind necessity.[23] The book claims to be based on modern psychiatry and internal medicine as well as on "phenomenological reflection on the body." It deals with such modes of vegetative being as sleep, wakefulness, and fatigue, such states as hunger, thirst, lability, stability. It also returns to self-regulatory processes like posture and adds studies on body warmth, respiration, and circulation.

C. *Encounter*

"Encounter" has become almost the hallmark of Buytendijk's entire enterprise. Thus the book dedicated to him on his seventy-

22. *Ibid.*, p. 30. Translation mine, from the French version, p. 65.
23. *Prolegomena van een anthropologische fysiologie* (Utrecht: Spectrum, 1965).

fifth birthday in 1957, which has as its subtitle *Contributions toward a Human Psychology*, carries the word in its title in three languages: *Rencontre/ Encounter/ Begegnung*. More relevant in the present context is the fact that the only study that Buytendijk published under the title "Phenomenology" is his essay on the encounter.

However, Buytendijk was not the first to have made a study of this phenomenon. It was of central importance in Binswanger's conception of therapy as a human encounter between therapist and client, and is for him one of the fundamental forms (*Grundformen*) of human *Dasein* in its dual mode. There was also the influential, posthumous little book by Hans Trüb,[24] a psychotherapist who had moved from C. G. Jung to the I-Thou anthropology of Martin Buber, and W. von Baeyer's informative essay, mentioned in Chapter 3. What is new about Buytendijk's essay, which makes no claim to exhaust the subject, is that Buytendijk takes seriously the phenomenological approach to this situation: While he stresses that encounter is accessible only through the risk of active engagement "with all one's soul," he urges the bracketing of its reality in phenomenological reflection. In other words, the existential phenomena have no claim to be treated differently from other phenomena of phenomenology. But what is even more characteristic of Buytendijk's study is his attempt to put the human encounter into the wider biological and psychological framework with which he is familiar.

Buytendijk begins with perception as a form of encounter. For him sensation is not only a pathic communication, in the sense of Erwin Straus, but it is also part of a living encounter with the world in which consciousness is engaged, in the sense of Merleau-Ponty. Another early form of encounter is the primal play with a toy, involving aggressive movements and countermovements, first practiced by the baby in his relation with his mother. Then come the first human encounters of the child, in which the glance and especially the smile play leading roles.

However, Buytendijk is not satisfied with such a genealogy of encounter but also wants to give an "ontological" interpretation of it. The basic fact here is that man is present in his body in a way which Buytendijk finds elucidated by Heidegger's interpretation of "the god's" presence in a temple in his essay "Der Ursprung des Kunstwerks." Specifically, it is man's spirit

24. Hans Trüb, *Heilung aus der Begegung* (Stuttgart: Klett, 1951).

(*Geist*) which has to be present in his body to make encounter possible. But its presence has to be reciprocal if a real encounter is to take place; it is therefore rarely complete. On the basis of the spirit's presence in our body, and in that of the other, language and dialogue become possible as forms of encounter. Encounter is fully realized only in mutual communication. There are, of course, vast varieties of human encounter such as the love relationship between the sexes or the religious encounter.

D. *Pain*

Buytendijk's interest in pain and its meaning exceeds phenomenology in the strict sense. It is for him one of the areas where the specialization of the sciences has interfered with the study of a subject which intersects several artificial divisions.

His main study of pain, written while he was under pressure of arrest as a hostage by the Gestapo, does not call itself phenomenological. Only the last (fourth) part, i.e., not more than one-third of the book, on "Pain and Experience," is claimed to be phenomenological.[25] The first three parts, after an introductory exposition of the problems, deal with the physiology of pain, not only in the traditional but also in the new functional or phenomenological sense, and with pain in animal life, where Buytendijk is especially careful not to lapse into anthropomorphism.

As for the human experience of pain, Buytendijk does not see it as a mere feeling or a sensation, in the sense of Stumpf, much as he otherwise agrees with him. Even Scheler's associating of pain with the surface feelings seems inadequate. More significant to Buytendijk is an incidental observation by Husserl which sees pain as imbedded in the intentional experience of suffering. But this pattern has now to be seen in the context of the *Gestaltkreis* of movement and sensation, in the fact of being-moved (p. 115): "Pain is experiencing a performance of the organism [*Achelis*]."

There are two basic ways in which it is experienced: (1) by being struck suddenly, as expressed by an outcry, and (2) by suffering, as a state of being. To be struck is possible only for higher animals and man, when there is an attack on their psychophysical unity (p. 125). It has connection with self-consciousness; thus according to W. Preyer it is responsible for the child's recognition of his own body and self. The stage of

25. *Pain*, p. 93.

being afflicted (suffering) is not a mere passing event, but an adaptation ("bearing it"). Such suffering means a state of capitulation as compared with the restlessness and protest in being struck by pain. It disrupts the inner "vital" and psychic structure but does not attack personal existence. But once pain reaches the personal level, it can achieve existential meaning (p. 132). For a person can "live" what is painful (as an intentional object) through intentional acts. Thus the higher senses can experience pain as a distressing disturbance of a harmonious order within the outside world, and pain can thus become a distress call at the violation of order (p. 137) or a "painful insult." For painfulness ought to be distinguished from pain (p. 138). Pain can also become "somatized," through bodily pain such as heart pains (p. 139). The existential meaning of such personalized pain can be found in the personal answer to it, e.g., in surrender, which as such is still a personal act (p. 143). But it can also have a second significance, once self-control has been achieved, and one can express a heroic attitude. There is also the pain of birth pangs, whose meaning is the participation in the start of new life. Such participation is something objectively meaningful and points up the true meaning of pain in man (p. 159).

Clearly, such interpretations open new existential perspectives. It is another question whether they are phenomenologically compelling.

E. *Feminine Existence*

Buytendijk's book *Woman* is perhaps his most explicitly phenomenological study in its use of a fully developed method, although the subtitle calls it a "study in existential psychology" dealing with "woman's nature, appearance and *Dasein*." But even the Preface makes it clear that the whole book, in all three parts concerning the biological, the "appearance," and the female way of existence, is meant to be phenomenological.

One's first impression and suspicion may be that this book is merely an answer to the challenge of Simone de Beauvoir's *The Other Sex,* which Buytendijk actually calls the most important book written on the subject. But although perhaps no other author on the subject is more often discussed than she, it would be a mistake to think that Buytendijk's book is merely a male protest against her interpretation coming from a semi-existentialist with fewer credentials and greater partiality than hers! As a matter of fact, Buytendijk repeatedly shows considerable appreciation for and even agreement with de Beauvoir, rejecting only her Sartrean existentialism in its denial of all objective values, including those of activity. There is nothing anti-feminine about this book, although some may feel that it pays tribute to a suspect feminine "mystique" in the form of its plea for the "secret" of womanhood.

Buytendijk's interest in feminine existence and its phenomenology actually preceded de Beauvoir's book of 1949. For a long time Buytendijk had been interested in the difference between male and female movements in connection with his study of human self-movement, which actually seems to have been the nucleus of his full-fledged phenomenology of woman.

From the very start Buytendijk makes it clear that he does not consider woman as a creature completely separate from man, as some languages such as French and English seem to suggest. Woman is a "man." Her difference from the male is reflected in the different ways in which she exists in the world. As a foundation for this attempt, Buytendijk explores three aspects of woman: first, the biological, which is the task of anatomy and physiology on the one hand, and of scientific or objective psychology, including psychoanalysis, on the other hand. Even in this area phenomenology can help to establish the essential differences, e.g., between plant and animal, etc.[26] This is true also of the interpretation of psychological tests about differences, which have to consider the total situation (p. 129). In Part II, on the appearance of woman, the phenomenal aspect and expressive content of her body are explored as they manifest themselves in her shape, her face, her characteristic type of youthfulness, the greater symmetry of her two sides, and her voice. However, much of her appearance is relative and is formed by historical and social factors, "partly in answer to the male glance" (p. 198). As the culminating feature of woman's appearance, Buytendijk introduces the "mystery" of "interiority," expressed in her static relaxation as it can be observed in youthful feminine beauty and in the resignation of her old age.

But the most characteristic aspect of woman is her way of being-in-the-world and more specifically her bodily being-in-the-world, the body being the deepest ground for the difference in her relation to the world. This difference manifests itself in the specific "dynamics" of her behaving, her movements, and her

26. *Woman,* trans. Denis J. Barret (Glen Rock, N. J.: Newman Press, 1968).

way of handling things. The characteristic act in which she expresses herself is that of taking care of and being concerned about, which finds its purest expression in motherliness. Buytendijk takes the motto for this interpretation of the "dynamics" of female being from John Steinbeck's *Grapes of Wrath:* "Man, he lives in jerks. . . . Woman, it's all flow, like a stream, little eddies, little waterfalls, but the stream, it goes right on." Phenomenologically, the best way of studying this dynamic is to watch the different gait of women and men. Thus Buytendijk sees a different "intentionality" in the male step, with its accents at the end points, while the female gait shows no such stresses but is more evenly flowing and usually is made of smaller steps. However, the female mode of being is also expressed in gestures and in voice. Here the male intention tends toward the overcoming of opposition, whereas the characteristic "grace" of feminine movement expresses no such aggressiveness. There is in general something special about the original female world. To the boy the world consists of obstacles without intrinsic merit, whereas for the girl it includes values worth adapting to. Woman has her anchorage in being; her attitude is that of caring for, as opposed to working on, something; her activity shows an awareness of the concrete values to be conserved, of a participation in being. In this context Buytendijk expresses his agreement with Margaret Mead, for whom he shows a much higher appreciation than for Simone de Beauvoir. There is also a characteristic difference in woman's relationship to her own body, with which she lives much more closely than man. Finally, motherliness has to be considered not only as a biological possibility but as a way of being-in-the-world with others.

Thus Buytendijk's phenomenology of femininity seems to culminate in its implicit glorification. But though for Buytendijk femininity is the more complete realization of loving being-in-the-world, as it is for Ashley Montague, he does not express any explicit demotion of male being.

One may well wonder whether a man like Buytendijk can be qualified to develop a phenomenology of female existence. If phenomenology is based on immediate experience, man's knowledge of female experience is certainly at best indirect. In fact, Buytendijk himself admits that it is impossible for man to know the "special mode of her experiencing her own body" both in itself and in relation to the body of the other sex (e.g., in menstruation and in pregnancy). Such experiences are at least analogous to those of the male body, though Buytendijk does not discuss how these analogies can be put to use. But apart from this restriction, Buytendijk maintains that man and woman can very well understand each other, and that it is even possible for one sex to understand the other better than its own, as is often true in the case of the psychiatrist in relation to his patient. In order to understand another form of being, all that is required is that the other be included in one's own actuality. Such actualization can be achieved by participating with empathy. For Buytendijk, the criterion for the correctness of his own understanding of woman is that it illumines her being-in-the-world.

[7] The Contribution of Phenomenology to Buytendijk's Work

How much does phenomenology contribute to Buytendijk's results?

It was the goal of understanding the phenomenology of life which made it important for him to look for methods outside the traditional toolbox of the biologist. Even his experimental work, especially in animal psychology, was inspired by the guiding conceptions of his phenomenological philosophy, much as it remained subject to the verifying evidence of experimental confirmation and information.

Thus the idea of self-behaving, the clue to a new kind of teleological understanding of animal life, required the "introduction" of the subject into physiology. But while the immediate source for this concept is von Weizsäcker, its real justification can only be derived from the new defense of subjectivity in phenomenology and particularly in Husserl's later phenomenology of the *Lebenswelt*. Husserl also offered the concept of intentionality, which proved increasingly important for Buytendijk's understanding of animal as well as human behaving and its "sense."

Buytendijk's attempt to discover the essential differences between animal and human being depends implicitly and explicitly on his acceptance of the "eidetic" method, particularly Scheler's version of it. Neither induction nor deduction could justify it. Buytendijk's attempt to pin down this difference by distinguishing the different types of world in which animal and man live, the *Umwelt* and the *Welt*, is indebted not only to J. von Uexküll but to Scheler and is in line with the further developing of the concept of the experienced world through Heidegger and, in its final form, through Husserl's late conception of the *Lebenswelt.*

As Buytendijk moved into human psychology, especially into the phenomena of the encounter and into the problem of the difference between the sexes, he became increasingly interested in the Heidegger-Binswanger concepts of modes of being and being-in-the-world. In fact Binswanger's concept of love rather than Heidegger's *Sorge* proved to be most congenial to Buytendijk's final outlook.

In summation: Phenomenology supplied Buytendijk more and more with the tools for the treatment of his problems; he identified increasingly not only with phenomenological psychology but with phenomenology as a philosophical movement. His version of it has its roots in biological and empirical fact. What phenomenology has added is the soil and the atmosphere for the fuller development of his encompassing vision.

12 / Kurt Goldstein (1878–1965): A Rapprochement

[1] General Orientation

It is by no means clear that Kurt Goldstein should be included in an account of phenomenological psychology and psychiatry. Such an inclusion can be justified only after a cautious study of the available evidence. This evidence is interesting enough for its own sake and should be examined in any case. What is beyond question is Goldstein's increasing influence on the development of phenomenology, particularly during its French and American phases. Perhaps the clearest proof of this role is the inclusion of a translation of Goldstein's main work on the organism as the second volume in the Bibliothèque de Philosophie series of phenomenological works edited by Merleau-Ponty and Sartre, immediately between Ricoeur's translation of Husserl's *Ideas* and Heidegger's book on Kant. It was obviously Merleau-Ponty who had initiated the inclusion of Goldstein's work in the series. Aron Gurwitsch had called his attention to Goldstein during the thirties, when Gurwitsch was teaching in Paris. In fact, Gurwitsch is clearly the one who was and is chiefly responsible for establishing whatever relations there were between Goldstein, under whom he had studied in Frankfurt and whom he met again in America, and the Phenomenological Movement.

But this incontestable influence of Goldstein upon phenomenology does not yet justify drafting him into the Phenomenological Movement in however wide a sense one understands this phrase. For it is by no means definite that as independent a thinker as Goldstein underwent any significant influences from phenomenology. It is just possible that in his eyes the relationship was merely a parallel one. Thus our first task is to state the facts plainly, as far as they can still be established.

[2] Goldstein's Relation to the Phenomenological Movement

Goldstein never referred to himself as a phenomenologist. In his writings up to 1957 and especially in his major works he did not characterize any of his own studies as phenomenological. Only once, in 1957, did he refer to his concept of "existence" as "based on phenomenological observations," though he said nothing about what he meant by "phenomenological." [1] In his William James lectures of 1940 he also spoke of the "phenomenological differences" between anxiety and fear, calling this lecture (IV) in retrospect a "phenomenological analysis." [2] But on the whole he never went beyond expressing a sympathetic interest in phenomenological research, especially in its concrete forms.

However, in two rather late autobiographical publications, Goldstein discussed his relations to Husserl. Close to the end of his "Notes on the Development of My Concepts," he mentioned the "influence of philosophic ideas, particularly those of Kant, Ernst Cassirer and Edmund Husserl" (p. 13). Yet he did not specify these influences except in the case of Kant.

However, toward the end of his last publication, his autobiography of 1966,[3] he spoke at some length about his "presentiment" that his own "interpretation of patients may prove to be similar to the results of 'phenomenological analysis,' " a presentiment which had been confirmed by Aron Gurwitsch, Alfred Schutz, and Maurice Merleau-Ponty with regard to both the distinction between concrete and abstract attitudes and Husserl's concept of the life-world. However, beyond expressing his increasing interest in such parallels, Goldstein did not suggest

1. "Notes on the Development of My Concepts," *Journal of Individual Psychology*, XV (1959), 5–14, esp. 13.

2. *Human Nature in the Light of Psychopathology* (Cambridge, Mass.: Harvard University Press, 1940), p. 93. See also "The Structure of Anxiety," in *Progress in Clinical Psychology*, ed. L. E. Abt and B. F. Riess (New York: Grune & Stratton, 1957), II, 64.

3. Boring, G. E., and Lindzey, G., ed., *History of Psychology in Autobiography* (New York: Appleton-Century-Crofts, 1967), V, 145–66.

that he himself had been influenced by this realization, except in the sense of corroboration. When I had a chance to see Goldstein in New York in 1964, he even told me that he had never read any of Husserl's writings but had merely heard him once on the occasion of his Frankfurt lecture in 1932. He did express interest in Husserl's studies insofar as they were "concrete."

There were much closer ties between Goldstein and Max Scheler, and apparently even a personal friendship between Scheler and Goldstein's early collaborator Adhémar Gelb (1887–1936). Scheler referred to their studies on brain pathology repeatedly, especially in his work on the forms of knowledge.[4] Scheler in turn figures prominently in Goldstein's writings, especially in his main work *Der Aufbau des Organismus,* where he devotes nearly an entire chapter (IX in the German, XI in the English version) to Scheler.[5] But here he refers chiefly to Scheler's late views on philosophical anthropology and on the relation of life and "mind" (*Geist*), in which Goldstein was interested but from which he dissented. Scheler's specifically phenomenological work in his book on sympathy is mentioned only in Goldstein's contribution to the Buytendijk festschrift.

Surprisingly, Goldstein was much more positive in his printed statements about Heidegger, whom he had also heard only at a Frankfurt lecture. Thus in *Der Aufbau des Organismus* Heidegger figures in the company of Kierkegaard as one of the students of anxiety and fear. But his most explicit tribute to Heidegger can be found in the festschrift for Buytendijk (*Rencontre*) in which he discusses the "smile of the infant." This essay apparently was very important to Goldstein (see his Preface to second German edition of *Der Aufbau des Organismus,* p. xvi, where, in referring to the "phenomenological-ontological analysis" of our understanding of others, he quoted with apparent approval Binswanger's statement that Heidegger had made entire libraries obsolete by his method). Goldstein ended this essay with two quotations from Heidegger's *Sein und Zeit* on coexistence as independent confirmations of his own "biological" analysis.

At least one essay, written in 1950, shows that Goldstein

4. *Die Wissensformen und die Gesellschaft* (1925), in *Gesammelte Werke* (Berne: Francke, 1960), VIII, esp. 235 ff.

5. *Der Aufbau des Organismus* (The Hague: Nijhoff, 1934). English translation, with foreword by K. S. Lashley, *The Organism: A Holistic Approach to Biology Derived from Pathological Data in Man* (New York: American Book, 1939). New paperback edition (Boston: Beacon Press, 1964).

was aware of and took note of some of the psychological writings of the French existentialists.[6] Here Goldstein related his own views on emotion, especially on anxiety and joy, to those of Sartre in his *Esquisse d'une théorie des émotions*, expressing not only regard for, but far-reaching agreement with, Sartre's theory, relating it, however, to the organism rather than to "existence," and admitting the purposive character of the emotions, claimed by Sartre, as far as fear but not as far as anxiety, the "catastrophic reaction," was concerned.

Merleau-Ponty, when he visited the States in 1947, looked up Goldstein primarily for the purpose of making arrangements for the French translation of the organism book. Yet, Goldstein never seems to have referred to Merleau-Ponty in print, and orally, in my interview with him, he expressed considerable reservations about him.

In 1959 Goldstein commented on the fact that his concept of "existence" seemed to have a similarity with that underlying "existential psychiatry," but stressed

> that it did not develop in relation to the latter and that there are essential differences between the two. I agree with the existentialist concept insofar as I also deny that biological phenomena, particularly human existence, can be understood by application of the method of natural science. But I differ in the meaning of the term existence.[7]

On the whole, one must realize that Goldstein never claimed to be a philosopher or to be at home in philosophy as such. What he absorbed of its tradition and of its current developments was more or less incidental, and was derived mostly from personal contact and indirect information. His main source, even for Husserl and other phenomenologists, was his cousin Ernst Cassirer. Nevertheless, especially after he had developed his theory of organism and the holistic approach to it, he became increasingly interested in philosophy, to the extent of denying that there is a sharp division between science and philosophy.

But to the extent that he paid any explicit tribute to any contemporary philosopher, it was usually to Cassirer with his philosophy of symbolic forms. To be sure, Cassirer in turn was always sympathetic to Husserl, as Husserl was to Cassirer. It is also important to note Goldstein's personal closeness to Paul

6. "On Emotions: Considerations from the Organismic Point of View," *Journal of Psychology*, XXXI (1951), 37–49.
7. *Notes on the Development of My Concepts*, p. 13.

Tillich, which was mentioned by both men, spontaneously, in interviews I had with them.

Thus far, then, the case for reading phenomenology into Goldstein's self-interpretation is more than weak. Any claims beyond the solid facts that Goldstein was a strong influence upon many phenomenologists and that he sympathized with some of their concerns would need further evidence. Such evidence can come only from a closer examination of Goldstein's work for the kind of motifs which are at least parallel to those in phenomenology. In looking for such points of contact, we would do well to remind ourselves of the fact that it is the mark of a true phenomenologist not to be influenced by what other phenomenologists have said about a phenomenon, but to have reached the same insights directly from it. Any influences that aid this process are at best supplementary, if not immaterial. To what extent has this process been operating in Goldstein's case?

[3] Goldstein's Concerns

Goldstein was first and foremost a biologist and a physician with a professional base in neurology and pathology, notwithstanding his early interest, as a student, in philosophy.[8] The fact that from this base he moved closer and closer to philosophy and perhaps even to phenomenology was an instance of what happens when, to use Goldstein's own formulation, "we approach the material with as unbiased a method as possible, and allow ourselves to be guided by the material itself and employ that method which the factual material dictates." [9] In Goldstein's case, this material was the living organism, especially in its pathological processes, and it dictated the adoption of a "holistic approach." [10]

In the course of his studies on brain-injured soldiers during the First World War, Goldstein and his younger collaborator Adhémar Gelb had become increasingly impressed by the failures of "atomistic" biology, with its "fallacy" of isolation, to ob-

8. See *The Reach of Mind: Essays in Memory of Kurt Goldstein,* ed. Marianne L. Simmel (New York: Springer, 1968), pp. v ff.

9. *Language and Language Disturbances: Aphasic Symptoms and Their Significance for Medicine and Theory of Language* (New York: Grune & Stratton, 1948), p. xii. See also *Der Aufbau des Organismus,* pp. 346 ff.; Eng. trans., pp. 507 ff.

10. Goldstein does not seem to have related it to the philosophy of the inventor of the term "holism," Jan Smuts.

tain a genuine understanding of disturbances and of the remarkable adjustments of the organism to them. Understanding these, as Goldstein wanted to, was possible only if these isolated phenomena were seen in the context of the surrounding organism and the surrounding world with which they were in constant interaction. This seemed easy and simple enough in principle. But it conflicted with the usual interpretation of the scientific method as essentially "analytic." In fact, Goldstein did not mean to reject the analytic method in its entirety and stressed its importance at the level of initial observations. Where it became distorting and misleading was when it led, for example, to the kind of experiments where reflexes were studied in artificial isolation from the entire organism. Such isolation was apt to destroy the very object under investigation.

Thus Goldstein was led increasingly toward considerations of biological and general scientific methodology. Goldstein's book on the structure of the organism, the fruit of the early part of his exile from Germany in Holland, which may well have precipitated his metamorphosis, is actually a treatise on a new biological approach, leading from the problems of pathology, via general reflections about the organism and its theory, to a general theory of the essential nature (*Wesen*) of biological knowledge. But the work does not stop there. It moves on to more general philosophical considerations about life and "mind" (*Geist*), and about knowledge and action.

Some of the insights which Goldstein claimed in this context were the expressions of his genuine personal wisdom and humaneness. But there was nothing mystical or explicitly religious or theological about them. Individuality and freedom were his guiding stars in the moral and political world. Besides, Goldstein was no bland and easy-going eulogist of nature's harmonious unity. His sense for the discord of mutilation and suffering in the world of living beings was particularly acute because of his constant confrontation with some of its more distressing manifestations. He was particularly aware of the breakdown of organization and the failure of central controls that take place in "catastrophic" responses to a situation, such as those experienced in genuine anxiety. But Goldstein was also aware of the amazing powers of the organism to readjust to such catastrophic losses, if only by withdrawal to a more restricted range which it could still control by a redistribution of its reduced energies, thus restoring as much wholeness as the situation allowed.

Goldstein's universe is therefore neither perfectly meaningful nor meaningless. Its dominating feature is the interpenetration of these two aspects, the inextricable conflict between them. Yet for Goldstein there is no diabolical antagonism to meaning in the universe. It is easy to see how an outlook such as his would appeal to the vision of a philosopher of both sense and "non-sense" like Merleau-Ponty.

[4] Phenomenological Motifs in Goldstein's Theory

The only relevant task for the present study is to focus on some of the features in Goldstein's approach which come closest to phenomenology. In attacking the problem I do not want to repeat the more specific parallels already pointed out by Aron Gurwitsch concerning Goldstein's distinction between the concrete and the categorial attitude [11] and by Alfred Schutz on "Language and Language Disturbances and the Texture of Consciousness." [12] Instead, I shall concentrate on some more general features in the phenomenological methodology and examine the extent to which they have parallels in Goldstein's approach.

A. *Goldstein's Concept of "Phenomenon"*

There is of course nothing distinctively phenomenological about the use of the term "phenomenon." Even the positivists were fond of it. But for Comte or Mach it stood primarily for sense data. This is definitely not the case for Goldstein, who shows no particular affinity to the positivists in their preference for the mathematical physical sciences. A closer look not only at Goldstein's use of the term "phenomenon" but at his whole approach to what is immediately given shows that his concept is a distinctive one. It appears early in *Der Aufbau des Organismus,* where Goldstein states his three methodological postulates, the first of which reads: "Consider initially all the phenomena presented by the organism, giving no preference in the description to any special one" (p. 13; Eng. trans., p. 21). To Goldstein, the most striking violation of this principle was

11. "Gelb-Goldstein's Concept of 'Concrete' and 'Categorial' Attitude and the Phenomenology of Ideation," in *Studies in Phenomenology and Psychology* (Evanston, Ill.: Northwestern University Press, 1966), pp. 359–84.

12. *Collected Papers,* Vol. I, *The Problem of Social Reality* (The Hague: Nijhoff, 1962), pp. 260–86, esp. pp. 277 ff.

the focusing of so many pathologists on isolated "symptoms," to the exclusion of other features of the total phenomenon. The real task of the biologist was "to record in an open-minded fashion *all* phenomena." This first postulate implied the rejection of the familiar principle of economy, also labeled "Ockham's razor," and the premature strait-jacketing of the phenomena by preconceived theories. The second postulate stressed the correct description of these phenomena in themselves rather than in terms of their effects, on the basis of a thorough analysis. Finally, according to the third postulate, each phenomenon was to be seen in relation to the organism and the situation in which it appeared. While this method was clearly formulated with an eye to the study of the organism, it also had bearing on general methodology, in which it was rooted. Goldstein's conception of the phenomenon and its proper analysis became particularly clear when he referred to it in his critique of Freud's theory of the unconscious (p. 205; Eng. trans., p. 310). Here, in contrast to Freud's negative concept, Goldstein characterized his own goal as "to describe in positive statements those phenomena which have induced scientists to assume such a structure as it is conceived by psychoanalysis."

However, it would not be safe to identify Goldstein's concept of the phenomenon with that of the merely phenomenal. That his view was broader can be seen from his friendly dispute with the gestaltists, whose conception he considered as too exclusively based on the phenomenal as the merely given. Goldstein thought that he could determine more about the *Gestalt* phenomenon than its mere givenness—namely, its root in the organism. A fortiori, Goldstein's phenomenon differs of course from Husserl's conception of phenomenon. In this sense and to this extent Goldstein transcended the phenomenal interpretation of the phenomena from the outset in the direction of Goethe's concept of the *Phänomen*. In other words, Goldstein's concept of the phenomenon is ontological in the widest sense.

But in this connection a conception in Goldstein's later thought must not be overlooked: his emphasis on "the sphere of immediacy." [13] Previously, Goldstein had distinguished clearly between two fundamental attitudes in the human organism, the concrete and the abstract attitude, one directed to specific situations, the other to general types of such situations. Here Goldstein had in mind a sphere of immediate contact between human

13. *The Organism*, 1964 paperback edition, pp. xiv ff.

beings, expressed particularly in the smile of the human baby. This sphere of immediacy was primarily a social phenomenon. But it also implied a new type of access to the phenomena, more direct and less articulate than the usual objectifying scientific approach. It widened the dimension of intuitive givenness in the context of or approach to the world. The very fact that Goldstein related this phenomenon to his interest in Buytendijk's concept of the "encounter" shows how much he was aware of its phenomenological significance.

B. *Goldstein's Conception of Essence* (Wesen)

For anyone approaching Goldstein from the direction of phenomenology as a study of essences, one of the more suggestive features of his theory of organism is its pervading interest in the discovery of the essence (*Wesen* or *Wesenheit*). The fact that Goldstein very often surrounds this term (both in German and in English) with quotation marks makes this feature even more intriguing. Was he aware of its proximity to phenomenology? All I can say is that my attempt in 1964 to elicit a comment about this point from the octogenarian did not yield either a confirmation or a denial.

Only once in *Der Aufbau des Organismus* did Goldstein raise the question of the meaning of the word "essence" and our ways of knowing about "essence" (p. 80; Eng. trans., p. 120). The immediate context suggests that Goldstein understood by it simply the "whole," which in his opinion could not be obtained by adding up our knowledge of the parts in accordance with the procedure of natural science.[14] In the English version, Goldstein usually used the term "essence" interchangeably with nature. But he still left those puzzling double quotation marks around the synonymous term "essence." Later in the text Goldstein did return to this general question, but from then on he concentrated completely on the question of the nature of the organism and our ways of knowing about it. Any attempt to answer explicitly the question of the meaning of "essence" and our ways of knowing it requires a study of the role of this term in context. I shall discuss some of the major usages.

14. There is an interesting and perhaps significant difference beween the German (p. 81) and the English versions (p. 120). The German speaks of the acquisition of an idea *vom Ganzen, vom "Wesen,"* the English of a "concept of the whole of the essence." Does this suggest that in 1938 Goldstein no longer wanted to identify essence and whole?

1. "Essence" makes its first appearance in the organism book in the first chapter, which starts with observations on brain-injured human beings. It is introduced when the hierarchy in the disintegration (*Abbau*) of the functions of the brain is described. Here Goldstein distinguishes between higher and lower functions on the basis of what is more or less important for the "essence" of the organism. As a criterion for the higher rank, he uses what he calls *Wesenswertigkeit*, which is rendered in English as "functional significance or value," as opposed to *Lebenswichtigkeit*, or "survival importance." The normal organism preserves not only its life but its *Wesenheit* (intrinsic nature), while the pathologically changed organism can preserve its life but loses its *Wesenheit*. What is here understood by "essence" seems to be the most characteristic feature of a thing, whose loss affects its identity though not its mere being. It comes close to, even if it does not coincide with, the Aristotelian conception of the substantial form. There are also similar conceptions of essence in phenomenology (e.g., in Jean Hering).

2. The "essence" is discussed further when in his holistic theory of the organism (Chapter 6; Eng. trans., Chapter 7) Goldstein tries to determine what the "constants" are within an "essence." Goldstein defines these constants by the organism's "preferred" or "ordered" behavior and distinguishes between two kinds of constants, those "characteristic of the essential nature of the species," perhaps better called the "generic" ones, and the individual's normal constants, which are characteristic of the nature of the individual (*individuelle Wesenheit*). There is no mention of variables as distinguished from these constants. Whether or not they are also part of the essence is not easy, but neither is it probably very important, to ascertain. The concept of constants must not be understood in the sense of something static. Especially in the case of an organism, they consist of preferred types of behavior. They can even be lost. But in that case the organism also loses its identity, acquiring a new and possibly a stunted essence. This may not be quite in accord with some of the earlier conceptions of the essence as conceived by Husserl. But it is certainly compatible with the one which can be found in Pfänder's view of the essence of a living being.

3. Even more significant is Goldstein's view that the essence is something which has to be actualized or realized, as the organism comes to terms with its world (*Umwelt*) (p. 197; Eng. trans., p. 305). This implies that the essence is at first some-

thing merely potential, in this sense unreal or ideal, hence in need of realization. This adds of course a Platonic ingredient to Goldstein's conception. As far as phenomenology is concerned, similar conceptions occur primarily in Pfänder (*Die Seele des Menschen*).

4. A good deal of Goldstein's inspiration seems to come from Goethe, whose ideas he invokes for confirmation repeatedly. In particular it is the idea of *Urbild* or prototype for life-forms which Goldstein often identifies with his own "essence." Goethe's theory is in fact a form of phenomenology in a wider sense, insofar as Goethe the "scientist" is an important ally of the phenomenological tradition, not only through his theory of colors but also through his philosophy of biology.

5. In this connection Goldstein's theory of biological knowledge or, more specifically, of its "essence," is important and revealing. Here in raising the question of how biological knowledge can decide what is essential to an organism, Goldstein rejected both induction and deduction as inadequate methods. Instead he advocated a "creative activity," also called "ideation" (*Schau*), in which, on the basis of empirical facts, we can reach an "experience" of the idea of the organism. Goldstein denied that there is anything mystical about it and saw in it a process of gradual approximation to the essence, comparable to what happens as we learn a skill such as bicycle riding. In this connection Goldstein also spoke of a dialectically progressing experience (pp. 241, 261; Eng. trans., p. 421). He was fully aware of the fact that such a procedure cannot and must not claim any exactness in the sense of mathematical science, which is inappropriate in biology. While biological science is symbolic too, in the sense of Cassirer, Goldstein stressed that its symbols or prototypes, being images (*Bilder*), can and must come closer to the concrete facts of phenomena than those of the mathematical sciences.

This "ideation" or *Schau* in Goldstein's sense sounds of course very much like Husserl's *Wesensschau* or *Ideation* (*idealisierende Abstraktion*). But this does not mean that their meanings coincide or, much less, that Goldstein borrowed the idea from Husserl. After all Husserl's ideation had a much wider scope than Goldstein's in its concern with the turn from the particular to the universal essence. On the other hand, there are striking similarities between the two approaches to essences, since both are neither inductive nor deductive. They suggest that there must be more than a parallel between these two conceptions; there may well have been a kind of intellectual osmosis.

C. *Goldstein's Conception of Anxiety*

The place where Goldstein seems to come closest not only to phenomenology but to existentialism is in his studies of the phenomenon of anxiety. Goldstein showed his awareness of Kierkegaard's and Heidegger's discussions of anxiety to the extent of referring to them in passing (p. 189; Eng. trans., p. 294). But he mentioned them only after he had discussed Freud, William Stern, and others, and he remained non-committal about Kierkegaard's and Heidegger's attempts to link up anxiety with the phenomenon of "nothingness." In fact, in private conversation Goldstein told me that his own interest in the subject of anxiety had preceded his acquaintance with the existentialists. Perhaps even more important is the fact that, presumably both in Frankfurt and later in America, he had been in close touch and communication with Paul Tillich, who confirmed to me that they had exchanged thoughts on the subject of anxiety. This interchange seems particularly plausible, though it is not expressed in the text, by the fact that Goldstein, like Tillich, saw anxiety as the counterpart of courage (the final answer in coping with anxiety) and as the affirmative answer to the shocks of existence, much in the spirit of Tillich's "courage to be." And yet Goldstein's interest in anxiety is not a case of a mere loan from the philosophers or theologians of anxiety. It has to be understood as stemming from independent firsthand observation of brain-injured patients as they confronted situations which they could no longer master.

Goldstein's own stake in the phenomenon of anxiety was related to his primary interest in the attempt of the organism in its environment to maintain its constancy, or rather to actualize its essence "adequately." This organism has to face the challenges of an unpredictable universe. Nothing can guarantee that it will always be a match for them. In fact, it is undeniable that eventually it no longer will be, and that death, the supreme biological catastrophe, is the end. In the meantime, the organism is vulnerable to all kinds of shocks, which it either can or cannot meet. When it can, the challenge leads to growth; when it cannot, a catastrophe results, either a temporary or a permanent one. Chances are that even after such a catastrophe the organism will find a new balance, although on a reduced scale.

In the catastrophic reaction, the central control breaks down and behavior becomes disorganized. The conscious expression of this disorganization is the state of anxiety. In contrast to fear, which is always fear of something, anxiety is "essentially" without object and attacks us from the rear, as it were. Fear is a defensive condition, expressible in bodily action. In anxiety we find "meaningless frenzy, with rigid or distorted expression, accompanied by withdrawal from the world, a shut-off affectivity in the light of which the world appears irrelevant, and any reference to the world, any useful perception and action is suspended" (p. 189; Eng. trans., p. 293).

Such a description is considerably more concrete than those of the existentialists, mostly by its addition of the organismic dimension. Yet it fails to utilize the phenomenon as a springboard for "ontological interpretations." Eventually, however, in the context of Goldstein's philosophy of organism, anxiety is one of the most important clues for understanding the organism's relation to its world in which it occupies a precarious, though not hopeless, position.

D. *Goldstein's Conception of "Existence" as Self-Actualization*

The account of Goldstein's conception of anxiety obviously has existential aspects. In fact, Goldstein himself frequently referred to anxiety as the expression of a threat to human existence. All the more important is it to realize that, as Goldstein himself insists, his concept of existence does not simply coincide with the existence of the existentialists in its many interpretations. Goldstein's concept is probably closer to the traditional uses of the word, but it also differs from it to the extent that he often surrounds it with quotation marks.

"Existence" in quotation marks can be found in Goldstein as early as 1934, when he introduced it in *Der Aufbau des Organismus* in connection with the interpretation of disease as a shaking (*Erschütterung*) and threatening of existence (pp. 268 ff.; Eng. trans., p. 432), adding that such threats are not restricted to biological existence. Since then Goldstein has defined this concept of existence more explicitly as "the condition in which an individual is able to actualize his essential capacities or what he considers to be such." [15] Such existence "does not

15. "The Idea of Disease and Therapy," *Review of Religion,* XIII (1949), 230.

mean survival. Survival, as important as it is, is not really a value in itself. . . . Existence means the realization of the individual, of the individual's intrinsic nature, the fulfillment of all his capacities in harmony with each other." [16] Thus, "existence" means an ideal state rather than a fact, such as the utterly contingent fact of the being of the single individual thrown into the world of the existentialists. It also coincides with health in a new normative sense that is for Goldstein primarily a value concept. This confronts Goldstein with certain "epistemological problems," which I shall consider briefly in their significance for Goldstein's relation to phenomenology.

E. *Biological Knowledge and Phenomenology*

In his study of the structure of the organism, Goldstein already had come to the conclusion that biological knowledge, based on the holistic approach, was essentially different from that of the non-biological sciences, which was based on analytic or isolating methods. In fact, in his autobiography he went so far as to say that such knowledge cannot be derived from the results of a natural-science methodology in which "natural science" is clearly used in the restrictive sense of the physicochemical sciences.[17]

This realization led Goldstein to a growing interest in "epistemology," [18] which became even more urgent as he developed his new ideas of health and "existence" and tried to justify them epistemologically. The first result of these efforts was an attempt to interpret biological knowledge as knowledge of the whole by a "creative act" through which the idea of the organism becomes a lived experience (*Erlebnis*), a kind of intuition (*Schau*), in Goethe's sense, that is always based, however, on "very empirical facts." [19] Goldstein tried to clarify this conception by invoking such philosophers as Ernst Cassirer with his ideas of symbolic knowledge. But he did not make it clear how far such holistic knowledge consists in the construction of a mere ideal model (*Bild*) or in the intuitive grasp of a whole underlying the partial phenomena. However, the very

16. "Health as Value," in *New Knowledge in Human Values,* ed. A. H. Maslow (New York: Harper & Row, 1959), pp. 178 ff.

17. *History of Psychology in Autobiography,* p. 153.

18. "Notes on the Development of My Concepts," pp. 10 ff.

19. *Der Aufbau des Organismus,* p. 242; Eng. trans., p. 402.

appeal to intuition of the essence already expresses a certain affinity with the essential insight (*Wesensschau*) claimed by Husserlian phenomenology. The fact that at times Goldstein even speaks of "ideation," a term introduced by Husserl, again suggests the possibility of some kind of osmosis.

But this is not the only rapprochement that occurs in the later Goldstein. In trying to account for his concept of "existence" as self-actualization, Goldstein realized that the "methods of natural science" are incapable of supporting value concepts.[20] Here too he appeals to a "special mental procedure which I have characterized as a creative activity based on empirical data, by which the 'nature' [*Wesen*] comes, as a Gestalt, increasingly within the reach of our experience." Goldstein himself admitted that this procedure will at first seem strange, and tried to make it more palatable by reminding us of the way in which we achieve "adequacy" in learning a skill.

In the light of this difficulty, it is revealing that toward the end of his "Notes," Goldstein, in rejecting the existentialists' concept of existence, called his own "an epistemological concept based on phenomenological observations, which enables us to describe normal and pathological behavior and to give a definite orientation to therapy" (p. 13). What exactly this "phenomenological observation" implies and how it is related to the biological knowledge of essences and to that of the values of existence cannot be clearly determined from such an isolated phrase. But it seems significant that at this point in his epistemological efforts Goldstein no longer hesitated to use the term "phenomenological" as the most appropriate characterization for the observations at the base of his holistic approach.

F. *Goldstein's Relation to Other Phenomenological Psychologists*

In addition to primary interactions between Goldstein's organismic biology and phenomenology, there are also some secondary ones. I am thinking here of relations between his theory and those of the schools of psychology mentioned in the previous sections, in which we have found definite traces of influence issuing from Husserl's inspiration.

Let us first consider the Göttingen group. Of particular im-

20. "Notes on the Development of My Concepts," p. 11.

portance here is the case of Edgar Rubin. In characterizing the holistic structure of the organism, Goldstein believed that the relation among different processes in the organism could be said to be a relation between foreground and background. It was in this context that he referred to Rubin's observation of figure and ground, and their reversibility, as particularly illuminating. However, it must be realized that the reference to Rubin's distinction served chiefly as an analogy and a means for demonstrating the role of various parts of the organism in their alternation. What Goldstein added about the possibility that an active approach could stop the ambivalence of the figures exceeded Rubin's merely psychological or "phenomenological" description.

Of even greater significance was the affinity between Goldstein and the gestaltists, whose relations with phenomenological philosophy were originally much looser than those of the Göttingen group. Special opportunity for contact and discussion between the two groups was provided by the close academic contact between Gelb and Goldstein on the one hand and Wertheimer, Koffka, and Köhler on the other at the University of Frankfurt. The high degree of congeniality between them can also be illustrated by the frequent contributions of Gelb and Goldstein to *Psychologische Forschung*, the main organ of the gestaltist group.

Nevertheless, there were differences in method and emphasis, and one of them may well have been the difference in attitude toward the phenomenological approach. Goldstein himself devoted an entire chapter of his organism book to a discussion of the relationship. The central issue here was the difference between the concepts of the whole and of *Gestalt*. Köhler in particular had always avoided the term "wholeness" (*Ganzheit*), perhaps in order to set himself apart from the Leipzig *Ganzheitspsychologie* of Felix Krüger and Fritz Sander. In Goldstein's chapter, and even more pronouncedly in its original German version, Goldstein, without making direct priority claims, pointed out the independent origins of his holistic conception.

[5] How Phenomenological Was Goldstein?

Toward the end of his autobiography, which he had almost completed shortly before his death at 87, Goldstein stated, "My main interest now is directed toward the problem of the relation between biology and philosophy." He referred to a passage in the Final Remarks of his organism book (repeated almost literally in the Preface to his second large work, *Language and Language Disturbances*), in which he stated that the demarcations usually couched in the contradistinctive terms "empirical research" and "philosophic reasoning" are irrelevant: "When we approach the material with as unbiased an attitude as possible and allow ourselves to be guided by the material itself and employ that method which the factual material dictates, the necessity of considerations customarily called philosophic may become apparent" (p. xii).

In other words: "going to the things" and letting the things speak for themselves is bound to lead us to philosophy, or more specifically to phenomenology—the kind of philosophy that was based on that very motto. For Goldstein, the path from empirical findings obtained by an analytic approach led first to holism, then to reflections on biological knowledge in general, and finally to the kind of intuition which, while primarily invoking Goethe, Kant, and Cassirer, comes very close to Husserl's ideation. Ultimately, the need for understanding existence made Goldstein appeal to phenomenology by name.

Would it be appropriate, then, to characterize the relationship between Goldstein and phenomenology as resonance? "Resonance" is a term with several meanings. In its strongest sense it signifies the reinforcement and prolongation of a sound by reflection or by vibration of other bodies. In this sense it is certainly not justified to claim an interaction between Goldstein's position and that of the phenomenologists. There was no cumulative chain reaction. But resonance may also stand for the echoing response of mutual sympathetic recognition of one another's parallel efforts and results.

As far as the phenomenologists were concerned, some of them not only recognized the importance of Goldstein's findings but received valuable impulses from them; this would be particularly true in the case of Merleau-Ponty. But here the "resonance" came to an end.

As far as Goldstein himself was concerned, his realization of parallelism apparently only came late and as a result of information he received from such philosophical friends as Aron Gurwitsch. But there were at least signs of a more active involvement in Goldstein's utilization of "phenomenological analysis" and in his final claim that phenomenological observations were the basis of biological knowledge. It would be unwise to overestimate these interactions. Yet there is reason to rejoice in the convergence of two philosophies: one based on empirical research and directed by the "nature of the material toward philosophy" and another increasingly responsive to the findings of a trail-blazing scientist like Goldstein.

13 / Paul Schilder (1886–1941): Between Psychoanalysis and Phenomenology

[1] General Orientation

"The only man in whose works real insights in the Freudian direction of a grand theory of drives are integrated in a rare though colorful unity with a universally critical (though not always equally thorough) knowledge of experimental psychology, pathopsychology and psychopathology and the pertinent parts of physiology and morphology plus the evolutionary history of the nervous system, finally of the phenomenology of the drives and affects, based on considerable clinical experience in the living person, which is often brilliantly screened and analyzed and on often considerable philosophical background, this man is, as far as I can see, Paul Schilder. To me his *Medical Psychology* seems to contain by far the best we possess in the German language concerning the question here raised." [1]

This glowing, if somewhat cumbersome, commendation for Schilder in one of Scheler's last works may seem a bit extravagant more than forty years later. Today, especially in America, Schilder is known at best as a psychiatrist of Austrian descent who was in the main line of psychoanalytic succession.[2] While his book on the body image has achieved a certain independent fame, his stake in phenomenology, secondary even in Scheler's eulogy, is practically unknown.

1. Max Scheler, *Die Wissensformen und die Gesellschaft* (1925), in *Gesammelte Werke* (Bern: Francke, 1960), VIII, 332 ff.; for other references, see *The Nature of Sympathy,* trans. Peter Heath (New Haven, Conn.: Yale University Press, 1954), pp. 20 ff.

2. Isadore Ziferstein, "Paul Schilder," in *Psychoanalytic Pioneers,* ed. Franz Alexander, Samuel Eisenstein, and Martin Grotjahn (New York: Basic Books, 1966), 457–68.

Where, then, did Schilder himself pitch his tent? He was not an easy joiner. But there is evidence that during his life in Vienna, where there was no active phenomenological group, he identified principally with the psychoanalytic movement. Certainly, his autobiography of 1940 shows much greater interest in psychoanalysis than in phenomenology. Yet it is important not to overlook the outspoken interest in, and explicit use of, phenomenology that are shown in Schilder's earlier writings, including *Medical Psychology* (1924). Obviously, Schilder believed that these two interests were compatible. Thus it will be all the more meaningful to study this case of "divided loyalty" in greater detail and to determine just how far Schilder went in subscribing to each of these disciplines. Only then can we determine the extent to which Schilder either remained an eclectic or achieved a real synthesis.

[2] Schilder's Attitude toward Phenomenology

In his autobiography, Schilder made it fairly clear that his acquaintance with phenomenology preceded his contacts with psychoanalysis, a significant contrast to the pattern of Binswanger's development. Since Schilder related this interest to his studies of psychopathology, one may suspect that it had been fed by his exposure to Jaspers' early phenomenological writings. Actually his first book, on self-consciousness and consciousness of personality,[3] starts out immediately from phenomenology and contains no references to psychoanalysis. Only after the First World War, in his survey of the new trend in psychopathology, did he mention psychoanalysis as a possible supplement to phenomenology.[4]

But it was in his book on psyche and life (1923) that Schilder first discussed phenomenology and psychoanalysis as the two basic approaches (*Anschauungsweisen*) to psychology. Even here he began with phenomenology. Brentano is mentioned as the originator of a "subtle" analysis of psychic experience, Husserl as the one who deepened it and strove for the essential. Scheler is given credit for his "really marvellous" (*geradezu wunderbare*) descriptions. This does not mean that Schilder was

3. *Selbstbewusstsein und Persönlichkeitsbewusstsein* (Berlin: Springer, 1914).

4. "Die neue Richtung in der Psychopathologie," *Monatschrift für Psychiatrie und Neurologie,* L (1921) 127–34.

uncritical of phenomenology, though some of his criticisms are, in fact, based on misunderstandings. For one thing, he thought that phenomenology was unsuited for investigating dynamic, and especially causal, relationships. It was at this juncture that psychoanalysis was to step in. Thus, at the very end of this discussion, Schilder suggested that Freud's psychoanalysis had opened up causal connections to our phenomenological viewing. However, this did not mean that the whole psychological field was to be covered by phenomenological and psychoanalytic approaches. Increasingly, Schilder stressed the importance of additional methods. Already, in *Medical Psychology*, he had mentioned four of them. Eventually he concluded that phenomenology and psychoanalysis could explore only limited aspects of psychic reality and had to take their places in the framework of a comprehensive "organismic" approach.

There is probably little chance, and less need, for reconstructing the story of how Schilder, the Vienna student of medicine and psychiatry, became acquainted with and won over by Husserl's phenomenology. Even after Brentano's resignation, remnants of his descriptive psychology had survived in Vienna, and it is possible, too, that at the time when Schilder studied psychiatry in Halle, traces of Stumpf's and Husserl's teaching in the nineties were still around. Anyway, the plain fact was that for Schilder phenomenology meant primarily Husserl, although he does not seem to distinguish him clearly from Brentano. Nor did he see much of a difference between Husserl and Scheler, whom he mentioned repeatedly along with Pfänder and Geiger. It may also be significant that Schilder chose phenomenology as his original method in connection with his initial and pervading interest in the experience of the ego and of depersonalization.[5]

In his most comprehensive work, *Medical Psychology*, he stated that his basic goal was "to unify in one framework phenomenology, psychoanalysis, experimental psychology, and brain pathology," and admitted that this implied a certain type of eclecticism justified by its yield of factual knowledge.[6] But among these approaches phenomenology came first; it was also the one about which he tried to give a detailed account in the Introduction. This emphasis makes it important to take notice of

5. *Selbstbewusstsein*, p. 2.

6. *Medizinische Psychologie* (Berlin: Springer, 1924). English translation by David Rapaport, *Medical Psychology* (New York: International Universities Press, 1953), p. 19. Subsequent page references are to the English edition.

Schilder's conception of phenomenology without paying too much attention to his later departures from it.

To Schilder phenomenology was primarily a study of conscious acts which intend objects. To this extent intentionality was central to his understanding. Schilder also stressed the identifying function of consciousness in relating several acts synthetically to identical objects, very much in the way Husserl himself had done. He assigned the root of these acts to the ego. He even used such Husserlian terms as "noesis" for act and "noema" for object. He saw that for Husserl phenomenology was primarily concerned with essences without regard for actual facts, and he acknowledged this as his basis for distinguishing it from empirical psychology. However, at this point Schilder, very much like August Messer, stopped following Husserl. To him, phenomenology simply meant descriptive psychology (p. 38). It should also be realized that Schilder, though clearly familiar with Husserl's *Ideen,* never mentioned phenomenological reduction or constitution, which from then on had become basic constituents of Husserl's own conception. Another limitation of Schilder's conception of phenomenology, suggesting the influence of Jaspers, was that to him it dealt only with the description of static phenomena and did not handle genetic and dynamic connections. This limitation allowed him, without fear of a clash, to add psychoanalysis to phenomenology as the supplementary study of the temporal dynamics of the psyche.

But Schilder had other reservations about accepting phenomenology wholesale. Thus, from the very start he expressed criticism of Husserl's trust in self-evidence as the guarantee of phenomenological insights, since in his view this criterion was incurably "subjective." [7] In fact, I sense an increasingly skeptical trend in Schilder's statements about the epistemological values of phenomenological insight. Thus, in 1934 Schilder expressed a rather doubtful view of phenomenology and especially of Husserl's claims to "essential insight":

> Husserl believed that the data obtained [by intuitive insight] constituted a fundamental science, phenomenology, which, he thought, went far beyond mere careful psychological description. This claim has not been substantiated. Husserl's phenomenology is just psychology, and as such an empirical science.[8]

7. *Selbstbewusstsein,* pp. 12 ff.

8. P. Schilder and D. Wechsler, "Children's Attitudes toward Death," *Journal of Genetic Psychology,* XVL (1934), 406–7.

Next Schilder refers to the use of the phenomenological method by Heidegger, who "stated that death and absolute nothingness are constantly before the inner eye of man. . . . He was even of the opinion that the fact of death enables us to perceive time." [9] This misinterpretation of Heidegger's views, puzzling as they must have been to Schilder, makes it understandable that Heidegger never figures in his conception of phenomenology.

However, Schilder's later statements on phenomenology, especially during his American period, must not be interpreted as a complete abandonment of its basic goals. Even his final posthumous work on *Goals and Desires of Man* acknowledges that "against the intention of their creators" phenomenology qua psychology "has offered new vistas, especially in the hands of Husserl and Scheler. To the latter we owe deep insights into emotional problems." [10]

[3] Schilder's Attitude toward Psychoanalysis

In order to understand and appraise Schilder's relation to phenomenology, one must also consider his more direct and more conspicuous ties with Freud and the Vienna psychoanalysts. In his autobiography Schilder mentioned the fact that he had not only attended Freud's lectures (remaining "refractory to his ideas"), before turning to phenomenology, but that later he had had personal contacts with Freud, though they were "never particularly close." [11] Freud himself mentioned Schilder as the first psychoanalyst to hold a chair in psychiatry at the University of Vienna. But in a letter to Karl Abraham of March 22, 1918, he also commented on Schilder's neglect of the Oedipus complex in his *Wahn und Erkenntnis*. Schilder's autobiography further mentions "closer association with the Vienna psychoanalytic society." But later, in America where he was invited to Johns Hopkins University by Adolf Meyer, Schilder abandoned organized psychoanalysis, ostensibly because of "changed interests and minor conflicts." Being un-analyzed, "he considered himself always on

9. *Ibid.*, pp. 406–51; see also Schilder, *Contributions to Developmental Neuropsychiatry* (New York: International Universities Press, 1964), pp. 132–33.

10. *Goals and Desires of Man* (New York: Columbia University Press, 1942), p. 241.

11. *Journal of Criminal Psychopathology*, II (1940), 221–25.

the periphery of the movement" with all its subdivisions. However, as he himself put it in his third-person autobiography:

> Schilder considers himself a psychoanalyst in the true sense of the word, feeling that he has kept the heritage of Freud better than many of those who were closer to him personally and who followed, at least for a while, his words more or less mechanically (p. 224).

There would be no point in trying to plot here all the agreements and disagreements between Freud's and Schilder's shifting positions. The only relevant question is how far phenomenology in Schilder's sense had any bearing on their differences. Schilder himself did not state this explicitly, but there are indications that some of his departures from Freud were at least related to his phenomenological orientation.

Apparently, it was not until 1921, in his report on the new trend in psychopathology, that Schilder mentioned psychoanalysis as a possible supplement to a phenomenology which dealt only with the description of static phenomena. But he did not yet enter into the subject. In 1922 a long article on the unconscious rejected Freud's conception of it but expressed high admiration for his psychodynamics. In his *Medical Psychology* Schilder did not deny the unconscious but interpreted it differently, as we shall see below. Several other works of Schilder's showed that his general adherence to psychoanalysis was much more explicit than his allegiance to phenomenology.[12] But in addition to his variant interpretation of the unconscious, Schilder departed from other basic views of Freud's as well.

As his fundamental point of dissent from Freudian analysis, Schilder himself singles out its "regressive character," i.e., the allegation that life has a tendency to return to prior stages of satisfaction and to rest, as expressed in Freud's death instinct, the later counterpart of his original libido. This theory simply did not agree with Schilder's general holistic philosophy of life, oriented as it was primarily toward the future and to the "constructive psychology" which he tried to build upon it. In fact, Schilder believed that in spite of Freud's disclaimers psychoanalysis implied a philosophy, and that this philosophy was irreconcilable with Freud's occasional materialistic and mechanistic pronouncements. Specifically, Schilder felt that Freud's

12. See, e.g., *Introduction to a Psychoanalytic Psychiatry* (New York: International Universities Press, 1928); *Psychoanalysis, Man, and Society*, ed. Lauretta Bender (New York: Norton, 1951).

seeming allegiance to associationism concealed his fundamental teleological orientation, according to which psychic life even in its unconscious regions is determined by meanings.[13]

But apart from these general and philosophical reservations, one can sense Schilder's desire to put psychoanalysis on a more phenomenological basis than can be traced in Freud. Thus in Schilder's *Introduction to Psychoanalytic Psychiatry* (1928), which approaches psychoanalysis by way of a study of the ego, the entire fourth section consists of a phenomenology of the ego experience, implying the need for an additional phenomenological exploration of what Freud had introduced as a mere hypothesis in *Das Ich und das Es* (1923). In *Medical Psychology* a six-page section on the phenomenology of the ego-experience puts special emphasis on the fact that the ego is directly experienced. Moreover, in a paper of 1933, included in *Psychoanalysis, Man and Society,* Schilder criticizes the psychoanalytic theory of instincts as not being sufficiently phenomenological. Phenomenology, Schilder felt, refutes Freud's theory of the regressive character of instincts (p. 13): "When we speak from a phenomenological viewpoint . . . there are not only two instincts, but innumerable instincts which drive to different goals. Every attempt to classify the instincts transgresses phenomenology and deviates from the immediate experience" (p. 11).

[4] Phenomenological Themes in Schilder's Work

Phenomenology was more than a label for Schilder. He tried to put it to work in connection with some of his special concerns. While there are no areas in psychology and psychopathology which he did not enter at times, there are some fields in which he applied phenomenology with particularly telling results. As examples I shall single out his phenomenologies of the ego, the body image, and the unconscious.

A. *The Ego*

This topic was clearly of basic importance for Schilder. His very first book on *Selbstbewusstsein und Persönlichkeitsbewusstsein* begins with a discussion of the ego and introduces phenomenology as the most adequate approach to it. The ego is

13. "Psychoanalysis and Philosophy," *Psychoanalytic Review,* XXII (1935), 274–85.

especially relevant to the discussion of the main psychopathological problem in phenomenology, that of depersonalization. Here Schilder claimed that depersonalization and the so-called multiple egos do not affect the identity of the ego. While there can be far-reaching transformations in cases of depersonalization, which affect even the "personality," the identity of the ego is never destroyed. For Schilder, it is another question whether careful investigation can also take care of cases of "possession," which need not affect, however, the essential identity of the ego itself.

What in many ways is Schilder's most interesting contribution to the phenomenology of the ego is the only publication which in its subtitle he designated as "a phenomenological study": the one on the "ego-sphere" (*Ichkreis*) of 1924.[14] Without offering a structural model of the ego, Schilder pointed out that as a phenomenon the ego is a circular or spherical entity with a center (*Ichmittelpunkt*) and a periphery. The experiences of the ego are distinguished by their degree of closeness to or distance from the center and by transitions from one position to the other. However, it is not the content of an experience that determines its distance from the center; thus bodily sensations may be at different distances from the ego center and may form a "jagged line." Schilder also makes interesting phenomenological observations about the closeness of parts of the body to the ego, especially in the case of sickness. The distinction is then applied to different parts of Freud's ideal ego (superego), which may be more or less close to the ego. Further differentiations lead to a dimension of ego-depth in which past items are anchored after they are no longer close (p. 651); hence the ego not only has dimensions of closeness and distance but is four-dimensional, as it were.

In the section of *Medical Psychology* on phenomenology of experience of the ego, Schilder begins by insisting that the ego is "directly experienced and is a priori inherent to every experience: it is not a postulated reference point of thought, but an undeniable experience" (p. 298). In fact the knowledge of the ego is even a matter of an "essential insight." It is experienced as the source of acts from which the "intendings" emanate. Schilder also mentions the ambiguous relations of the ego to the body, pointing out that the experienced body always appears in the context of a surrounding world.

14. *Zeitschrift für die gesamte Neurologie und Psychiatrie,* XCII (1924), 644–54.

B. *The "Body Image"*

Schilder was not the first to pay attention to the phenomenon of the body as given to our consciousness, and distinguished from its biological reality. He himself referred to Sir Henry Head as his main predecessor in pointing out the importance of the "postural model" of the body or of "organized models of ourselves, which may be termed 'schemata.'" From Schilder's quotations, it could appear that Head's schemata are something like maps of the body with a certain normative significance, i.e., yardsticks against which all postural changes are measured. This is hardly Schilder's own conception. In any case, he goes far beyond Head's articles by exploring the body image, ideal and real, in its entirety.

In what sense and to what extent can Schilder's book on *The Image and Appearance of the Human Body* (1935) be considered phenomenology? The term "phenomenology" itself hardly ever occurs in it. It figures in the Preface, when Schilder quotes his own earlier German book of 1923 on *Das Körperschema* and points out that phenomenology, psychoanalysis, and brain pathology are not enough, and that what is needed is a comprehensive psychological doctrine of life and personality as a whole. Otherwise, it is mentioned only in a discussion of Köhler's Gestalt theory.

Perhaps the main basis for interpreting the book as a piece of phenomenology comes from the title itself. Actually this title is never fully explained, and the distinction between image and "appearance" can only be guessed at from the context. At least the "image" of the body is clearly defined as "the picture of our own body which we form in our own mind, that is to say the way in which the body appears to ourselves." [15] But if this were all there were to it, the addition of the word "appearance" to "image" in the title would be strange, since the two would almost coincide. By observing the further uses of the term "appearance," and even more of "disappearance," I have just about come to the conclusion that what Schilder had in mind was the dynamic process by which the body image develops and changes all through our life.

Even the organization of the book does not show any preference for phenomenology. The titles of its three parts indicate

15. *The Image and Appearance of the Human Body* (New York: International Universities Press, 1935), p. 11.

Schilder's concern with the physiological basis of the image, its libidinous structure, and its sociology. But despite this emphasis on the somatic, the psychoanalytic, and the sociological angles, and the seeming disclaimer of the phenomenological approach, closer inspection reveals not only that all these sections are permeated with phenomenological observations, but that the near-absence of the label might be explained by a narrow interpretation of phenomenology which made Schilder avoid the term at the time. Thus the "physiological part," especially in its later sections (after section 17) dealing with the importance of the vestibular apparatus, contains some striking reports on how the body is given in experience, beginning with the way in which one's own face is presented and how the surface of the body, its openings, and its mass are experienced. In the part on the "libidinous structure of the body," Schilder shows how the image of the body is shaped by the dynamics of libidinal forces centering around the erogenous zones, a field which Schilder thought had been neglected thus far by the psychoanalysts (p. 201). In the sociological part we learn that the body image, which expands beyond the physical body, is essentially related to the body images of others and even allows for such functions as identification with the body of others.

In this connection it is important to pay attention to the subtitle of the book: "Studies on the Constructive Energies of the Psyche." For one must remember that Schilder, in contrast to Freud, wanted psychoanalysis to stress the constructive rather than the regressive features of the psyche. The experience of the body is a case in point. The construction of the body image is actually one of our constant and never completed tasks. For Schilder insisted that the common view according to which the body is the most familiar and best known part of our world—an error which he attributed to "most philosophical speculations" (p. 297)—is actually a very uncertain possession.

Thus the body image as a phenomenon, to be distinguished from the body itself, and its "appearance" are largely the result of the constructive energies of the psyche. Actually, this conception fits surprisingly well into the kind of constitutive phenomenology which Husserl developed in his later years. This is perhaps the main reason why Schilder's late strictures against the phenomenological approach to the problem of the body image need not be taken too seriously. When, in the Conclusion of the book, on the last page, Schilder contrasts the phenomenological method with the empirical and realistic point of view that he wants to contribute, he actually overlooks how much the phenomenological method has widened since he restricted it to the description of static phenomena. "Going back to the life situations, the libidinous and emotional striving" is by no means beyond the range of a constitutive phenomenology. It fully concurs with the view that "even our own body is beyond our immediate reach." Sentences such as "a discussion of the body-image as an isolated entity is necessarily incomplete. A body is always the expression of an ego and of a personality and is in a world" (p. 304) fit straight into Husserl's phenomenology of the life-world and perhaps even more into the phenomenology of Merleau-Ponty, who was familiar with and fond of Schilder's shorter German work on *Das Körperschema.*

Schilder's study of the body image transcends phenomenology, especially in the many physiological and causal explanations which it includes, in much the same way as does James's *Principles.* But as far as its descriptive parts are concerned, it is phenomenological in a much more advanced sense than Schilder himself realized.

C. *The Unconscious*

Psychoanalytically, Schilder's most original and heterodox enterprise was probably his handling of that pivotal conception of Freud's system, the unconscious. In view of Schilder's understanding of phenomenology, which seems never to have gone beyond the stage of Husserl's *Ideen,* his work on the unconscious becomes especially illuminating.

At first sight, Schilder's essay of 1922 would understandably have shocked orthodox psychoanalysts and would have disqualified him from their ranks. For, after a careful examination of the possible meanings and uses of the term "unconscious," Schilder admitted that he had looked in vain for the psychically unconscious. "I therefore advocate the arrogant conviction, untenable according to Freud, that everything psychic is conscious." [16]

But this did not mean that Schilder denied the phenomena of the unconscious, but only that he felt it could no longer claim to be "psychic." Instead it would have to be "somatic." In particular, the drives, unconscious according to Freud, are to Schilder cases of directedness in Husserl's sense and as such can be

16. *Zeitschrift für die gesamte Neurologie und Psychiatrie,* LXXX (1922), p. 114.

experienced (*erlebt*), though not primarily given as objects, and can only later be converted into objects of consciousness. They are part of the stream of consciousness which to Schilder has not only breadth but depth and different speeds. Even in hypnosis, to Freud the first manifestation of the psychic unconscious, Schilder sees merely repressed conscious experiences which are still there in a corner of consciousness, repression being not necessarily repression into the unconscious.

Here Schilder developed a conception which was to a large extent to take over the functions of the psychically unconscious, that of the "sphere" (*die Sphäre*). It included everything which resembled an object of consciousness. Schilder credited Karl Bühler and the Külpe school with the conception of this "sphere" (*Sphärenbewusstsein*) that accompanied each consciousness. It formed the background of what was given as foreground, as it were, and was related to James's conception of "fringes." Schilder transferred Freud's concrete accounts of the dynamics of the unconscious, which he accepted completely, to this "sphere."

How is one to interpret Schilder's seemingly ambiguous position in accepting Freud's dynamic system of the unconscious and yet denying its psychic character? To some extent this is an expression of his organismic position, which allows him to place part of the unconscious on the somatic side. But it also expresses his prior phenomenological commitment. What he objected to was an unconscious which cannot be verified by direct experience but must be merely inferred as an unconfirmable hypothesis. That is his reason for confining the unconscious to the background of the "sphere" of what is given—into which the conscious can be repressed—but never beyond it. In this sense and to this extent, Schilder's theory of the unconscious can be considered a first attempt at a phenomenological assimilation of the unconscious. Obviously, such an assimilation can only go as far as the preconscious. Freud's absolutely unconscious remains beyond the pale of such a phenomenological "reclamation."

[5] Schilder's Synthesis

The evidence here presented may suggest the conclusion that Schilder was the first psychiatrist to combine phenomenology and psychoanalysis into a harmonious system. But such a claim needs modification. Insofar as it is true, it must be understood that his conception of phenomenology was selective, restricting itself to the early Husserl and to Max Scheler, and that he was certainly not an orthodox Freudian, much as he stressed the role of psychoanalysis, especially during his American period, as can be seen from the very titles of his late books. Schilder was simply an independent thinker, concerned chiefly about the practical task of the psychiatrist in our time, who felt compelled to utilize all the methods and insights that he found helpful, omitting what seemed to him unessential and fruitless. He was not a system builder. This also means that he never attempted to fuse phenomenology and psychoanalysis. Phenomenology was simply to supply the basic method, while psychoanalysis was to provide some central insights which would add to his "holistic constructive interpretation of the psychic phenomena." In this sense and to this extent it may indeed be said that Schilder was the pioneer in later attempts toward a synthesis of phenomenology and psychoanalysis.

Schilder's attempt to synthesize phenomenology and psychoanalysis suggests a comparison with Binswanger's later and much more sustained enterprise. Almost surprisingly, both men refer to each other merely in passing, mostly for bibliographical references and seemingly unaware of their common concern.

But despite this striking parallel, important differences can be pointed out, which go beyond the simple fact that Binswanger's exposure to phenomenological philosophy was much more extensive than was Schilder's. Binswanger's phenomenological anthropology or *Daseinsanalyse* was a throughgoing attempt to interpret man and his world in the light of the major phenomenological insights. Schilder was interested merely in the descriptive approach of phenomenology, its direct enrichment of the phenomenal base for the psychiatric and psychoanalytic construction, and its role in dovetailing the two. In this sense and to this extent Schilder's use of phenomenology compares with that of Jaspers, who however had rejected psychoanalysis almost completely. Both Binswanger and Schilder show that there can and must be fruitful exchanges between the two approaches. While Schilder's contribution to such an enterprise was the more modest one, it may also be more accessible and a good point of departure for more ambitious projects such as Binswanger's.

14 / Medard Boss (b. 1903): Phenomenological *Daseinsanalytik**

[1] Boss's Place in Phenomenological Psychiatry

THE MAIN REASON for including Boss, who occupies a major chair in psychotherapy at the University of Zurich and is also a frequent visitor on the American scene, in the framework of the present study is the fact that his work has the active and apparently unqualified support of Martin Heidegger—although I am not aware that Heidegger has thus far acknowledged this in print. Boss himself told us in 1969 that "for more than ten years" the septuagenarian Heidegger had taken part in their joint "Zolliker Seminare" for "dozens of Swiss doctors and foreign participants" and had come to Zurich from Germany between one and three times each semester.[1] Arranged by Boss, the seminar had attracted former foreign participants as well as Swiss psychiatrists. Rarely if ever has a philosopher literally gone to such lengths in order to aid and abet the enterprise of a non-philosopher and specifically a practicing psychiatrist. In

* The term *Daseinsanalytik,* in contrast to *Daseinsanalyse* (*Daseinsanalysis*), as used in the English version of Boss's basic work of 1957, which is discussed below on p. 334, n. 2), indicates some of the difficulties in interpreting this new type of existential analysis. The word *Analytik* forms part of the German title, where it makes clear the difference between Boss's complete allegiance to Heidegger's existential analytics in *Being and Time* and Binswanger's *Daseinsanalyse,* which is based on a much freer understanding of the early Heidegger, if not a misunderstanding, however productive, of his intentions. The exclusive use of *Daseinsanalysis* for both is apt to conceal the difference between the two phenomenologies of *Dasein.* The price of leaving the title even more Germanic than in Boss's book title seems to me worth paying here.

1. "Ein Freundesbrief," *Neue Zürcher Zeitung,* 10 May 1969, p. 50.

addition to this aid, Boss acknowledges Heidegger's "untiring personal help in compiling the summary of the preceding chapter," i.e., Chapter 2, an "Outline of Analysis of *Dasein*," in his major English book.[2] To what extent does this imply that Boss, in contrast to Binswanger, is not only Heidegger's authorized spokesman in psychiatry but also is considered by Heidegger to be an outstanding representative of phenomenological psychiatry? The answer will depend largely on the appraisal of Heidegger's final commitment to phenomenology. But it will, of course, also depend on the intrinsic merits of Boss's own work. It may well be added that, despite Boss's academic position and following in Zurich and his international reputation and role, he is by no means universally regarded as a phenomenologist by other psychiatrists, those in Switzerland or Germany, for example, or by the phenomenological anthropologists in the wake of Binswanger. In order to fully evaluate his role, at least something of the relationship, still largely unknown publicly, between Boss and Binswanger, would have to be explored.

[2] Boss's Way to Heidegger via Freud, Jung, and Binswanger

Like Binswanger, Boss started his search for psychiatric understanding with a study of Freud. But his was of course a later search than Binswanger's, and he never seems to have been in personal touch with Freud. Even Boss's alienation from Freud was never total. Inasmuch as Freudian psychoanalysis is primarily a psychotherapeutic technique and only secondarily a theory of human nature, Boss is a supporter of the former aspect, but developed into an opponent of the latter. He found in the "immediate reality of Freud's psychoanalytic practice an attitude which helps the patient to open himself to his own being and listen to it." He became more and more suspicious, however, of the naturalistic theory which Freud had erected above this therapeutic foundation and which in fact even interfered with its application. Thus, to explain feelings of guilt by the Oedipus complex and the consequent fears of castration simply did not help the type of patient Boss described. But Boss's major opposi-

2. *Psychoanalyse and Daseinsanalytik* (Bern: Huber, 1957). English translation by Ludwig B. Lefebvre. *Psychoanalysis and Daseinsanalysis* (New York: Basic Books, 1963).

tion concerned the type of theorizing which led Freud to the hypothesis of the unconscious and its mechanisms and specifically to his symbolic theory of dreams. Freud's preference for constructive theory over direct understanding of the phenomena which we perceive signified for Boss an exclusively "natural-scientific" approach. It also meant that Freud had failed to attend to the phenomena and their message.

Boss's interest in and eventual disillusionment with Carl Gustav Jung are of a considerably different nature. In fact, there had been personal contacts between the two. Boss belonged to Jung's Zurich circle, and for a considerable time he practiced Jungian analysis. What attracted him about it was its early opposition to Freud's abstractions and constructions. Jung, as Boss saw him, wanted to stick to the phenomena and even proclaimed his strict adherence to the phenomenological principle.[3] However, Jung's actual analysis had taken him far beyond the description of the phenomena of direct experience into the kind of theorizing about archetypes and similar constructs which in Boss's view could not be supported phenomenologically; for the archetype is not a "true phenomenon" (p. 39). A Jungian analysis is superior to Freud's inasmuch as here the analyst confronts his patient in a face-to-face relationship and pays more attention to the dignity of the individual than did Freud. But, according to Boss, it diverts him from his concrete troubles instead of helping him to come to grips with them. In Boss's eyes the analytic interpretation of symbols proves to be an ultimately ineffective construction. In Jung, as in Freud, philosophical presuppositions which have been taken over uncritically and not recognized as such have crushed the true phenomenology (p. 44). What is needed instead is the direct interpretation of the phenomena themselves, not of their symbols. This does not mean mere description. For purposes of therapy, these phenomena must be made to speak in the way they do to Heidegger.

For a Swiss psychiatrist, the most obvious way to such a hermeneutic phenomenology clearly led to and via Binswanger, with whom Boss also shared the common background of training and association at the Burghölzli clinic in Zurich with its early psychoanalytic sympathies. While Boss never stayed at Kreuzlingen, Binswanger's sanatorium, for more than occasional visits, it was indeed Binswanger, who, according to what Boss told me, first drew his attention to Heidegger. However, Boss ap-

3. *Psychoanalyse und Daseinsanalytik* (German version), p. 36.

parently never was quite satisfied with the uses to which Binswanger had put Heidegger's analytics of *Dasein*. So, after considerable solitary struggles with Heidegger's *Being and Time* during the War, Boss decided to seek direct contact with its author, who at that time was being widely shunned and ostracized because of his role in the early phases of the Nazi regime. But this was no longer the Heidegger of *Being and Time*, who had inspired Binswanger, but the "thinker of Being" who had given up the completion of his magnum opus. As a result, Boss not only achieved a much more intimate relationship with Heidegger than with Binswanger but also was able to draw on Heidegger's final philosophy. From this position, Boss could still acknowledge Binswanger's pioneer discovery of the psychopathological possibilities in Heidegger's philosophy, especially the conception of being-in-the-world as a condition of a subject. For Boss, Heidegger has settled once and for all that the Cartesian conception of the subject as taken up by Husserl and also by Binswanger is the basic fault of modern philosophy. It has therefore no place in *Daseinsanalytik*, which considers *Dasein* only as man in his total relationship to Being itself. What Binswanger, according to Boss, chiefly overlooked was the characteristic of *Dasein* as a clearing (*Lichtung*) within Being, toward which *Dasein* is opened in such a way that it has an original understanding of Being (p. 61).

As to Heidegger's thought as a whole, Boss expresses no reservations whatsoever. He even presents it very much in Heidegger's terminology, in a way which does not diminish the notorious difficulties for the reader and compounds them for the translator.

What is puzzling about this *Daseinsanalytik*, as used here by Boss, is that it is not exactly identical with its meaning in *Being and Time*, where it coincides with the "fundamental ontology" that is to focus on the peculiar type of Being of *Dasein*, rather than on *Dasein* in its full concreteness as an entity (*Seiendes*). For Heidegger the theme of his analytics is only the categories of existence, the "existentialia," not the properties of the existing human being. Apparently this difference does not matter to Boss and—in view of the master's supervision—one might almost think it no longer does to Heidegger himself. In any case, Boss's *Daseinsanalytik* is a study of *Dasein* for its own sake in all of its characteristics. However, it is its relation to Being itself which turns out to be basic, not its being-in-the-world, as it was for Binswanger.

[3] Boss's Conception of Phenomenology

I HAVE FOUND no specific statement of Boss's about his conception of phenomenology and its functions. But it is obvious that he simply takes over Heidegger's interpretation of it, especially in his German version. The only surprising thing is that he speaks so often about phenomenology, while Heidegger has dropped the term almost completely. Husserl and Scheler are practically ignored. In his *Einführung in die psychosomatische Medizin*, Boss merely discusses French "existential phenomenology" as background for the Heideggerian conception of man and his living body—and finds it wanting. However, more recently, in his Harvard Lecture of 1963, Boss has described the phenomenological approach as the rival of the "natural-science approach to [the] behavioral sciences," understanding by it a "science which simply wants to stay with the phenomena themselves . . ." and "lets the objects themselves tell us about their immediately given, inherent meaning-content." But Boss protests sharply against all identification of this phenomenology with the existentialism based on Sartre's distortions of Heidegger. Instead, Boss wants us to return to the phenomenology of Goethe, to Husserl's motto "to the things" (as interpreted by Heidegger), and to "the greatest phenomenological thinker of modern times, Martin Heidegger," who alone succeeded in implementing Husserl's program.[4] The goal of such a phenomenology differs fundamentally from that of science, which can only supply an x-ray diagram, as it were, of the phenomena, useful for certain practical purposes but obviously not a total picture of the human world. Phenomenology, then, as Boss interprets it, consists in receiving the message of Being as it speaks to us. Man as the "clearing" in Being is the receiver of it in the attitude of reverence for Being. Specifically, phenomenology is to refrain from the kind of theoretical interpretations in which Freudian or Jungian psychoanalysis indulge. But, while Heidegger's "hermeneutics" is not mentioned explicitly, such a phenomenology clearly allows for the hermeneutics of the immediate meanings of the phenomena as they appear, e.g., in our dreams. In this sense even Boss does not simply remain inactive in the face of the self-revealing phenomena. How far he is to go in interpreting,

4. "What Makes Us Behave At All Socially?" *Review of Existential Psychology and Psychiatry*, IV (1964), 62.

for example, the silver bowl of his model dream as the gift of love from mother to son, would call for further exploration. In the meantime, one might acknowledge that Boss's "phenomenological interpretation" tries to avoid the artificiality of a special dream language and to make dreams speak as much as possible for themselves before any explanatory hypothesis is imposed upon them.

Boss's attempt to develop Heidegger's thought of Being into a full-fledged conception of *Dasein* is certainly a feat, and the fact that Boss has done so with Heidegger's apparent approval (although none of his works has an explicit preface by Heidegger), would seem to imply that Heidegger does not object. But I cannot suppress the suspicion that this utilization of Heidegger's ontology is at last an expansion of Heidegger's "openness to Being" into "openness to the world," i.e., to beings, which seems to ignore the rigor of Heidegger's original division of being and Being (the so-called "ontological difference"). To a Heideggerian, insisting on the purity of ontology, this must sound like a relapse into metaphysics. But apparently this need not worry the psychiatrist and the therapist. However, it should be of concern to the philosopher who sees in metaphysics the original sin of philosophy. This is not merely *existential* analytics of the mode of Being of *Dasein* but *existentiell* analysis of *Dasein,* i.e., of the total being called man.

[4] Applications

Boss HAS PUT this conception of *Daseinsanalytik* to use in a considerable variety of contexts, the most significant of which are the fields of sexual perversions, dreams, and psychosomatic illnesses. What is remarkable about these studies is that Boss undertakes to show that, contrary to frequent charges that Heidegger ignored such phenomena as love and the body, raised particularly by the French existential phenomenologists, his thought contains at least implicitly the makings of a full Daseins-analytic philosophy of these phenomena with their normal and abnormal modifications.

A. *Sexual Perversions*

In this area Boss offers first a critical examination of the main rival conceptions, beginning with the psychoanalytic ones, concentrating on the inadequacies of "phenomenological anthropology," in this case particularly von Gebsattel's studies, with their emphasis on the destructive or nihilistic factors in sexual perversions and addictions. Perhaps the most noteworthy thing about Boss's new use of Heidegger's analytics is the way in which he derives a conception of the essence and meaning of love out of Heidegger's fundamental ontology. Existence, to be interpreted as ek-sistence, i.e., as being outside oneself, involves being with things and one's fellow-beings and has a special tuning (*Stimmung*). Apparently, this tuning necessarily includes the tuning of love.[5] In the light of this interpretation of *Dasein,* the various perversions can be seen as based on interferences with the possibilities of love through constrictions and anxiety. In his special case studies Boss tries to show concretely how various perversions, such as fetishism, can be understood as ways in which the tuned ek-sistence of love gets "out of tune."

B. *Dreams*

The emphasis on the dream in psychoanalysis and psychotherapy might make one expect that the phenomenology of the dream had been equally developed. But Freud's classic on the interpretation of dreams simply presupposed an adequate understanding of their structure as phenomena—as did most post-Freudian studies, for example, those of C. G. Jung and his school. Binswanger had made the dream the subject of a series of lectures, which appeared later as a book, in which he chiefly traced the historical conceptions and interpretations of the dream,[6] before using it for a first demonstration of his new anthropological approach to the modes of being-in-the-world (*"Dream and Existence"*). But Binswanger's work, too, was at best a sample of an applied phenomenology of the dream.

Philosophers also would seem to have a special stake in the strange phenomenon of the dream, particularly after Descartes's famous challenge to our capacity for distinguishing dream and reality. But here too no complete phenomenological answer has been forthcoming. A beginning has been made by Alfred Schutz.[7]

5. *Sinn und Gehalt der Sexuellen Perversionen* (Bern: Huber, 1947), p. 32. The English translation of this passage by L. L. Abell, *Meaning and Context of Sexual Perversions* (New York: Grune & Stratton, 1949), p. 30, diverges considerably from the original in content and form.

6. *Wandlungen in der Auffassung und Deutung des Traumes von den Griechen bis zur Gegenwart* (Berlin: Springer, 1928).

7. "On Multiple Realities," *Collected Papers,* Vol. I, *The Problem of Social Reality,* ed. Maurice Natanson (The Hague: Nijhoff, 1962), pp. 240 ff.

For a full-scale if not exhaustive ontological and phenomenological investigation I refer to the book on dreams by Detlev von Uslar.[8]

Psychoanalyse und Daseinsanalytik, which was stimulated by Binswanger's preceding work but opposes it, is meant as a completely phenomenological study in the sense of Heidegger's later perspective. Early in the book Boss tries to dispose of all preceding theories. On the negative side the most significant aspect of his approach to the dream is his rejection of Freud's and Jung's theories that the dream is a symbol for unconscious and normally repressed wishes and fears. Not only does Boss challenge the assumptions and the hypotheses underlying such an interpretation, but he also claims to have concrete and even experimental evidence to prove that in normal cases there is no dream censor who interferes with the fulfillment of repressed desires. On the positive side Boss describes the dream as primarily a way of *Dasein*, with the same right and significance as awakeness. Its phenomena require as much and as little interpretation as those of wakeful life. Both must speak for themselves. On this basis Boss explores the various dimensions of dreaming existence, based on a vast number of observations from his therapeutic practice. Thus he distinguishes dreams that repeat a wakeful experience (traumatic shock dreams), dreams in which active decisions are made, dreams in which we reflect on our freedom of the will, dreams with the possibility of imagining something in the realm of rational investigation (e.g., Kekulé's dream of the benzol ring), dreams of mistakes (*Fehlhandlungen*), dreams of moral appraisal and control, dreams of genuine religious experiences. He also considers the possibility of dreaming of dreaming, of analyzing one's dream while dreaming, of dreams being converted into things (e.g., soil) or animals.

This does not mean that dream existence has the same structure as wakeful existence. Dreams are discontinuous; they do not link up with one another; they do not allow for one continuous life history. In fact, according to Boss, all dream interpretation depends essentially on being awake. But this does not preclude the fact that phenomenologically the dream world has its rights as a part of the existence to which we must open ourselves.

8. *Der Traum als Welt: Zur Ontologie und Phänomenologie des Traums* (Pfullendorf: Neske, 1964).

C. *Psychosomatic Phenomena*

As in the case of love, Boss tries to show that the charge of the French existential phenomenologists that Heidegger has neglected the human body is unjustified, inasmuch as his analytics includes the possibility of a medically adequate understanding of psychosomatic phenomena. In fact, Boss maintains that Sartre, Merleau-Ponty, de Waelhens, and Ricoeur fail to account for the phenomena that can be understood by seeing the body in the context of Heidegger's conception of *Dasein.*

For Boss, *Dasein* as primarily being-in-the-world is not a mere subject set apart from other objects. It transcends itself toward the world, including the body. It includes this body as medium in its relation to the world beyond the body in a way which involves its animal, vegetative, and hormonal processes. By contrast Sartre had not freed himself from Cartesian dualism. In fact, for all of the French phenomenologists of the body, *Dasein* remains a subject, however incarnated.

On this foundation Boss presents several case studies showing how specific psychosomatic disturbances can be understood as based on special projects of *Dasein* and on successful or unsuccessful ways of relating to the world through the body as a part of *Dasein* itself. Boss finds this conception confirmed by the major types of psychosomatic ailments and eventually tries to show how such interpretations can be put to use in therapy.

[5] Implications for Psychotherapy

Boss makes no claims that his approach offers new methods of therapy. In his own belief he is still adhering to fundamental Freudian principles, even including at times such techniques as the use of the couch "for long phases of the analytic treatment."[9] The main difference is the removal of the Freudian theoretical framework and in its replacement by the Heideggerian non-naturalistic conception of man as an opening for Being. The chief function of therapy is therefore the complete release or "liberation" of the patient's phenomenal experience, which the therapist has to accept for whatever it presents itself to be, beginning with his dreams, and without imposing upon it any symbolic interpretations.

9. *Psychoanalysis and Daseinsanalysis,* p. 63.

This reverence for the phenomena [10] not only permits the patient to accept himself and the world but makes it possible for "Being to speak to him in a way which allows him to respond to it in harmonizing fashion," even when it speaks in the language of old or new religion or "even of demons." Clearly, this is a therapy of adjustment, but of adjustment on a cosmic, ontological scale. As such it involves a metaphysical optimism, where all is well when man "lets being be" (*Gelassenheit*), as the later Heidegger puts it. In this sense, it becomes understandable why Boss, like Carl Rogers, is shocked by Binswanger's fatalistic capitulation at Ellen West's suicide.

[6] Toward an Appraisal

This is not the place for an appraisal of Boss's work in its entirety, or especially, an evaluation of its psychopathological and psychiatric adequacy. Compared with the complexity of Binswanger's conception and the scope and detail of his analyses, what Boss offers appears stunningly simple, even though the Heideggerian formulations in the background may seem mystifying enough to the uninitiated.

What matters here is merely Boss's new use of phenomenology. In Boss's hands phenomenology has become the means to overcome the symbolism and constructivism of classic psychoanalysis and to replace it by the simple profundity of Heidegger's vision. It is another question, not to be pursued here, whether this simplicity and profundity also guaranty clarity and truth in a sense accessible to non-believers.

10. "Ehrfurcht vor dem vollen und eigenen, unmittelbar zugänglichen Wesensgehalt aller wahrgenommenon Erscheinungen, die uns die Daseinsanalytik zurückgibt," *Psychoanalyse und Daseinsanalytik*, p. 152.

15 / Viktor Frankl (b. 1905): Phenomenology in Logotherapy and *Existenzanalyse*

[1] General Orientation

The case for including Frankl's work in the present series of studies is by no means clear. Much as his vigorous and enthusiastic personality in its unique mixture of militancy and conciliatoriness, humility and self-assurance calls for admiration, the role of phenomenology as a part of and foundation for his therapy needs cautious consideration. Here the initial interest that attaches to the work of this prophetic psychogogue is the fact that he repeatedly has given phenomenology generous, and perhaps over-generous, credit for his own new approach.

Frankl did not label his own contribution to the First Lexington Conference of 1961 on "Phenomenology Pure and Applied" as phenomenological, but called it "The Philosophical Foundations of Logotherapy." Here he stated his underlying philosophy of life in the form of three assumptions: (1) freedom of will, (2) will to meaning, and (3) meaning of life, for which he claimed phenomenological support based on the immediate data of life experience.[1]

However, the major names for his own enterprise are *Existenzanalyse* and *Logotherapie*. It is not always clear whether the two are not simply synonymous. But it seems safe to say that

1. *Psychotherapy and Existentialism* (New York: Clarion Books, 1968), see esp. pp. 2, 11, 14.

the first term puts more emphasis on the patient to be treated ("explication of ontic existence"), the second on the cure to be applied.[2]

As far as *Existenzanalyse* is concerned, Frankl makes it clear that his "analysis" has little if anything to do with such enterprises as Binswanger's *Daseinsanalyse* or Boss's *Daseinsanalytik* (p. 21). His is not primarily an attempt to understand man anthropologically or ontologically, but to influence him therapeutically. In this respect, Frankl's main ambition is to find an alternative to Freud's and Alfred Adler's techniques by a new way of practical analyzing. The "Third Vienna School of Psychoanalysis," as it has been called, concentrates on helping people who suffer from a kind of neurosis neglected by the two earlier schools—a spiritual or "noogenic" neurosis, which Frankl called the "existential vacuum" or "frustration" expressed in the sense of meaninglessness.

"Logotherapy" is the term which focuses on the means of this approach. In this new invention the Greek term "Logos," as Frankl interprets it, does not signify reason or logic but "meaning." Logotherapy tries to cure meaninglessness by helping the victims of existential frustration to find new meanings for their existence.

Thus, in its concern with an area of suffering not touched by either, Frankl's enterprise transcends psychopathology and psychiatry in the traditional sense. It deals, by means of a new type of counseling, with the failure of man's practical philosophy of life. It might be considered primarily as a contribution to an applied philosophy of life for otherwise normal patients, especially at times of major stress. As a psychiatrist who has put this philosophy to the "crucial" test (in more than one sense) of surviving several years in Nazi concentration camps, where he lost his entire family, Frankl has given logotherapy a verification which few other contemporary philosophies of life can claim—and without making any explicit theological assumptions. In this sense, Frankl's little book, *Man's Quest for Meaning: A Psychiatrist Experiences the Concentration Camp,* may well be considered one of the great human documents of our time. The title of three untranslated lectures, "*Nevertheless say*

2. See especially *Theorie und Therapie der Neurosen* (Vienna: Urban & Schwarzenberg, 1957), B, "Logotherapie und Existenzenanalyse," p. 118.

'yes' to life"; expresses this heroic "courage-to-be" most challengingly.[3]

But while Frankl's enterprise is thus mostly reformatory in the sense of offering first and lasting aid for the sick in spirit (rather than in psyche), like all such enterprises, it has its roots in a theoretical framework, an understanding of man, his needs, and his destination. At this point it involves not only a theory of man and his existence but also a theory of ends and values. It is for these theoretical foundations that Frankl sought and found reinforcements, if not new foundations, in phenomenology.

Two of Frankl's collaborators, Matthias E. Korger and Paul Pollak, have gone so far as to claim that *Existenzanalyse* not only represents a phenomenological way of procedure (*Verfahrensweise*),[4] but has grown out of the soil of the phenomenological perspective and considers itself to be a phenomenological method. Moreover, "it presents itself as a further development and continuation of phenomenology; especially in regard to the theory of being and concept of being it goes considerably beyond the doctrines of classical phenomenology" (p. 652). No explicit documentation is added to these claims. How far Frankl himself would back them I have not been able to determine. But the fact that Frankl, who was both a collaborator and coeditor of the *Handbuch*, let these claims pass without comment is probably significant. In the light of the texts and other information available about Frankl's development and contacts with phenomenology, these claims deserve closer examination.

[2] Frankl's Relations to Phenomenology

Judging from the number of explicit references in Frankl's prolific publications, phenomenology in the technical sense plays only a minor part in his work. It contains only a few references to Husserl, giving him credit for having initiated a new kind of empirical approach to the immediate data of experi-

3. ". . . *trotzdem Ja zum leben Sagen*"; *Ein Psycholog erlebt das Konzentrationslager* (Vienna: Jugend und Volk, 1946). English translation, revised and enlarged, by Ilse Lasch, *Man's Search for Meaning: From Death-Camp to Existentialism* (Boston: Beacon Press, 1963).

4. *Handbuch der Neurosenlehre* (Munich: Urban & Schwarzenberg, 1959), III, 639.

ence but characterizing his essential insights as inferior to existential knowledge.[5] Yet no explicit acknowledgment is needed to realize that Frankl's battle against psychologism owes a special debt to Husserl's pioneer work.

Frankl's major guide to phenomenology was clearly Max Scheler, although he never met him in person. In fact, at one time Scheler's central work on ethics (*Der Formalismus*) became something like a philosophical Bible to Frankl.[6] His name appears most frequently among all the references to phenomenologists in Frankl's writings—and almost uniformly with high praise. Scheler is for him not only the major ally in fighting "biologism," "psychologism," and "sociologism," but his main support for a new theory of values and meanings.

There are also a few references to Heidegger, but rarely specific ones. In fact in the fifties there was at least one personal contact with Heidegger, according to Frankl at Heidegger's initiative, during which he left an entry in Frankl's guestbook expressing his sympathy with Frankl's position on his "optimistic views on the past."[7] But these contacts do not seem to have made much of a difference to Frankl's approach to phenomenology as such.

However, Frankl rejects completely the existentialism of Sartre, in which he sees nothing but a new kind of nihilism. Apparently, he did not become aware of Sartre until his own *Existenzanalyse* was already well under way. There have been more friendly overtures in the direction of Gabriel Marcel, himself only a temporary acceptor of the label "Christian existentialism."

As to other phenomenological psychiatrists, Frankl maintained at least a sympathetic relation with Jaspers, understandable in view of the congenial stress on existential appeal in Jaspers' elucidation of existence. Frankl's relation to Binswanger is ambiguous. While he sees in Binswanger's *Daseinsanalyse* an aid to understanding others, he suspects it of therapeutic pessimism. Apparently there has been no personal relationship. However, such contacts do exist to a considerable degree between Frankl and von Gebsattel, with whom he joined forces in editing the monumental *Handbuch der Neurosenlehre und Psychotherapie*, and there is also evidence that von Gebsattel influenced

5. See, e.g., *Der unbedingte Mensch* (Vienna: Deuticke, 1949), pp. 22 ff., 30; *Psychotherapy and Existentialism*, p. 2.

6. Personal letter to the author, May 26, 1962.

7. "Existential Dynamics and Neurotic Escapism," in *Psychotherapy and Existentialism*, pp. 31 ff.

him in other ways as well. Frankl also turns repeatedly to Erwin Straus for support, although personal contacts between them do not seem to have taken place until after World War II.

[3] The Role of Phenomenology in the Development of Logotherapy

Frankl, as a medical student in Vienna with a pronounced interest in psychiatry, found himself exposed at once to the rivalry of the "two only great systems in the psychotherapeutic field," those of Sigmund Freud and Alfred Adler. He credited Freud with a "huge achievement" as far as his uncovering of the repressed facts of human sexuality was concerned but, like the later Binswanger, he saw Freud's main limitation in his naturalism, i.e., in his one-sided conception of man.

So Frankl first joined the Adlerian group, which attracted him particularly because of its appeal to the sense of individual responsibility. In fact, he wrote his first piece, "Psychotherapy and *Weltanschauung,*" for one of its journals.[8] Here Frankl focused immediately on the neurotic who bases his attitude toward life on a certain philosophy. In accordance with the Adlerian position, Frankl still assumed that it was essential to undermine the superstructure of such a *Weltanschauung* by breaking down its psychological substructure. But Frankl also believed that before this was possible, it would be necessary to meet this *Weltanschauung* with counterarguments on its own grounds. This could be done only by criticizing the neurotic's value system itself—especially if he was an intellectual. To be sure, as Frankl saw it at the time, "values cannot be proved a priori. In fact, there are no absolute values independent of a valuing will." All we can do is to point out that we have to accept *some* values in any case, and that we have to affirm community as the task of life. Eventually, the biological unity of happiness and virtue (*Tüchtigkeit*), in the sense of Spinoza, is held up to the neurotic, but it is again interpreted in the sense of the life value of the community.

Frankl soon came to reject Adler's exclusive emphasis on biological and social values and particularly on the will to power (*Geltungsstreben*). Other targets of Frankl's criticisms of Adler included his interpretation of all our concrete enterprises in life as "maneuvers" (*Arrangements*) and his suspicion of the seri-

8. *Internationale Zeitschrift für Individualpsychologie*, III (1925), 250–52.

ousness, genuineness, and immediate character of the patients' expressions. In fact, Frankl eventually charged this "restriction of phenomenal reality" against both psychoanalysis and individual psychology. Apparently, from what Frankl has told me, he was so outspoken in his criticism that Adler insisted in 1927 on his "excommunication." It was at this stage that Frankl, through Rudolf Allers, "my teacher" at the University of Vienna, became acquainted with Max Scheler's writings.

Rudolf Allers (1883–1963) was an Austrian psychiatrist, who later (especially during his American phase, which began in 1938) turned scholastic philosopher.[9] During medical studies in Munich, and as a *Privatdozent* there until 1913, he was in touch with the Munich phenomenologists and particularly with Scheler. After World War I, when he returned to Vienna, he joined the Adler group as a "Catholic Adlerian." During this period he contributed an article on the concept of community to Adler's journal, in which he referred specifically to Scheler's phenomenology of values.[10] According to Frankl, Allers left Adler around 1927.[11]

Frankl not only shared with Allers his interest in Adler but also absorbed from him Scheler's phenomenology, though not his later Thomist philosophy. He leaves no doubt about the fact that this indirect encounter with Scheler was decisive for his emancipation from the first and second Viennese analytic schools, although Scheler's writings did not deal with Adler explicitly, as they did with Freud. As to the positive effects of Frankl's Scheler studies, later statements make it clear that he was impressed particularly by Scheler's phenomenology of values, his anti-relativism and anti-subjectivism, as well as by his views about the "intentional" character of value feeling as a source of value knowledge—all of which helped him overcome his early value subjectivism and develop the philosophical foundations of his logotherapy.

There is a conspicuous gap in Frankl's list of publications between 1924 and 1938, the year when the important article on the spiritual problems of psychotherapy appeared.[12] Presumably,

9. See James Collins, "Rudolf Allers," *The New Scholasticism*, XXXVIII (1964), 281–307.

10. "Die Gemeinschaft als Idee und Erlebnis," *Internationale Zeitschrift für Individualpsychologie*, II (1924), 7–10.

11. "Rudolf Allers als Philosoph und Psychiater," *Gedenkrede*, 24 March, 1964.

12. "Zur geistigen Problematik der Psychotherapie," *Zentralblatt für Psychotherapie*, X (1937), 33–45.

this was a period of incubation and gestation, aggravated by Frankl's considerable professional struggles to establish himself in relation to his colleagues. It also must have been the period in which he absorbed a good deal of philosophical and phenomenological literature. The article of 1937 criticized both psychoanalysis and individual psychology not only as one-sided but also as guilty of restricting the phenomenally-given psychic reality. Both require mutual supplementation as well as the addition of what Frankl now calls *Existenzanalyse,* encompassing human existence in its entirety with its "heights" as well as with its "depths" (p. 36), the heights in this case standing for the meaning of life to be fulfilled by the realization of the highest possible objective values, in the sense of Scheler. There are reflections on "the deepest content of human *Dasein,*" on "the phenomenal original data [*phänomenaler Urtatbestand*]" which are to supply the concept of the responsibility of the human person, the anthropological center and the basis of a psychotherapeutic theory of values. In accordance with these insights, Frankl develops here for the first time the program of logotherapy as the parallel of what he calls *Logizismus*, the answer to psychologism in philosophy, a therapy which includes the discussion of *Weltanschauung* in the therapeutic process. The same ideas are developed more concisely in an article on "Philosophy and Psychotherapy," published in 1939 in Switzerland with the subtitle "Concerning the Foundations [*Grundlegung*] of an *Existenzanalyse,*[13] but now emphasizing also the relations of the new therapy to philosophy as such. In particular, it pleads for the inclusion of ethical considerations in psychotherapy, since human existence embraces the trinity of eros, logos, and ethos. But Frankl opposes any imposition of values on the patient, except for the formal one of responsibility as essential to human existence.

It was clearly this conception which Frankl was developing in a manuscript which represented a first version of his first book on *Ärztliche Seelsorge* (Medical Ministry) which he had taken along to Nazi concentration camps. Its loss there was one of the many tests to which Frankl and his logotherapy were put and which both passed in a way which has added personal credibility and weight to his offering. After his return, Frankl not only became the director of the Neurological Department

13. "Philosophie und Psychotherapie: Zur Grundlegung einer Existenzanalyse," *Schweizer Medizinische Wochenschrift,* LXIX (1939), 707–9.

of the Vienna Polyklinic Hospital, but began to publish the stream of books and articles which have now made him and his work known all over the world, beginning with *Ärztliche Seelsorge,* dedicated to the memory of his murdered wife, now rewritten and revised in English translation (*The Doctor and the Soul*). Starting with the more extended discussion of the need for logotherapy to fill the vacuum in therapy between psychoanalysis and individual psychology, it discusses in the central part on "General Existential Analysis" the meaning of life, including that of death, suffering, work, and love, and offers in a shorter special part an analysis of various kinds of neuroses (anxiety and obsession), and even of melancholia and schizophrenia, in the light of the new approach. For the first time phenomenology is mentioned as having shown that its "intentionality" refers essentially to a transcendent real object (Sartre might agree, but not Husserl), and particularly that intentional feelings point to transcendent values. Besides, it attests that man is not a prey of his drives, and that the pleasure principle is in conflict with the phenomenological facts (*phänomenologischer Tatbestand*) —one of Frankl's favorite claims based on phenomenology.

Frankl's subsequent books and essays would defy any attempt at a developmental analysis. Many have grown out of his lectures and articles. On the whole, they merely interpret and clarify his position with regard to various situations and other viewpoints in philosophy and psychiatry. Some try to formulate a more theoretical framework. Usually, phenomenology is invoked only in passing, in close connection with existential analysis, and particularly in connection with assertions about values (see, e.g., *Homo Patiens* [14]) But no basic modifications seem to have occurred.

[4] Frankl's Phenomenology in Action: Logotherapy and Its Values

Frankl is no methodologist. It is therefore not surprising that he does not take any interest in the theory of phenomenology. Only once does he give an explicit characterization, namely, in the form of a footnote to his Lexington lecture of 1963 on "The Philosophical Foundations of Logotherapy" [15] which reads:

14. (Vienna: Deuticke, 1950).
15. *Psychotherapy and Existentialism,* p. 2.

> Phenomenology, as I understand it, speaks the language of man's pre-reflective self-understanding rather than interpreting a given phenomenon after preconceived patterns.

This formulation was clearly conceived in response to the special occasion of the Conference on "Phenomenology: Pure and Applied." It hardly indicates any special interest in phenomenological language in contrast to other languages, but rather shows Frankl's determination to stay close to the "immediate data" of "pre-reflective experience." It does imply disinterest in the more technical aspects of phenomenology beyond mere attention to the given.

However, this does not mean that in practicing this approach Frankl did not utilize and develop some of the results of previous phenomenologists, especially those of Max Scheler. The clearest case is the pattern of values that Frankl used as the foundation for his logotherapeutic meanings of life—and that show him as both dependent on and independent of Scheler.[16] Frankl distinguishes three types of such values:

(1) *creative values*, i.e., values that can be realized by creative activity;

(2) *values of experience*, i.e., values that are realized by receptive surrender (*Hingabe*), as in aesthetic enjoyment of nature and art;

(3) *values of attitude* (*Einstellung*), or better, response, expressed by the way in which we respond to the inevitable suffering that limits our access to creative and experiential values. In fact, Frankl considers these not only equal but superior to the two other groups.

Now these values, which allow any conscious being to find some meaning for his life under any conceivable circumstances, are according to Frankl not only objective, but in a sense absolute. They even belong to a special realm. This does not mean that the values essential for the existential meaning are eternal in the sense that they are valid at all times and for everybody. They are, rather, "situational values," i.e., values geared to particular situations to which they apply uniquely and specifically. But, even so, there is no "subjectivity" about them.

Frankl credits Scheler especially with this last conception and with general support for his theory of values. However, Frankl's trinity of values is no mere loan from Scheler. Scheler's

16. See especially *The Doctor and the Soul*, 2d ed., trans. Richard and Clara Winston (New York: Knopf, 1965), pp. 43 ff.

phenomenological ethics, to which Frankl refers so fondly as his main philosophical support, indeed contains a rich and almost bewildering collection of values.[17] But neither the terms "creative values," "experiential values," "attitudinal values," or their equivalents occur in Scheler's German text, though some equivalents to Scheler's terms can be found in Frankl's own rather summary collection. These may very well have inspired Frankl. But the actual development of his particular triad is clearly his own. In this sense and to this extent, Frankl's triad is more than a streamlining of Scheler's more comprehensive survey. It is geared to "existential" needs, based on the varying accessibility in man's concrete situations, not on any structural difference in the values thus attained or attainable, which may be aesthetic, ethical, or religious in themselves. One may question the bases for Frankl's claiming the highest place for the attitudinal values; a ranking which may arouse the suspicion that such a preference is based on *ressentiment* ("sour grapes"). But Frankl's three values are clearly suited for those in search and need of meanings, especially *in extremis*.

How far can Frankl's theory of values and existential meaning claim to be phenomenological? As we have seen, Frankl is never explicitly concerned about matters of method. While it is true that he appeals to phenomenology as the basis for his philosophical assumptions, he makes no explicit attempt to support these assertions by any specific descriptions or discussion of alternative answers. Clearly, Frankl is not interested in phenomenology for its own sake. He merely wants to apply it. In his writings he implies only that he has consulted it in reaching his conclusions. He leaves it to others like Scheler to buttress his doctrine of values systematically.

It should be realized that, while Frankl's view of values is objectivistic, it is not absolutistic in the sense of independence of time and place. In fact all the values which are relevant to the meaning of life in logotherapy are situational values, applicable only to specific situations, in that sense temporal but still objective, fitting each particular situation uniquely.

It should also be noted that even in his phenomenological phase Frankl is anxious never to impose any values upon his patients. The reasons for this restraint may be merely pedagogical and therapeutic: imposed values simply are unlikely to help.

17. See *Der Formalismus in der Ethik und die materiale Wertethik* (Halle: Niemeyer, 1913–16); in *Gesammelte Werke* (Bern: Francke, 1954), II, 120–25.

Nevertheless, what Frankl has to offer does not depend on the acceptance of an objectivistic position in axiology.

The example of Frankl's triad of values does not mean that other parts of his logotherapy cannot be interpreted as ultimately based on phenomenological description. Some of his original therapeutic innovations such as "paradoxical intention," i.e., the technique of curing the patient of a particular symptom by asking him to produce it deliberately, may have some phenomenological foundation in experience, although Frankl does not show it. In other cases, such as Frankl's discussion of the "will to meaning" as a basic fact of human existence, one receives the impression that at least Frankl's invocation of the "will" is less phenomenological than an attempt to match, ingeniously at that, the slogans of the "will to life" or the "will to power" as the primary drives and needs of man. As such this topic constitutes more of a challenge to phenomenology than an actual achievement.

[5] The Role of Phenomenology in Frankl's Work

The preceding study should make it clear that phenomenology cannot claim Frankl as one of its major practitioners; nor can Frankl (nor does he) make phenomenology a major part of his message, which is not only "trans-clinical," but missionary. At best phenomenology plays for him the role of a minor auxiliary. As such it has obviously helped him in his emancipation from the two earlier forms of Viennese analysis, Freudian psychoanalysis and Adlerian individual psychology, by allowing him to return to a less sophisticated description of immediate experience within a framework of a simplified value theory inspired by, but not simply taken over from, Scheler.

Frankl's use of phenomenology in developing and expounding his logotherapy does not characterize his work as particularly phenomenological. His way of presenting his insights is certainly less that of description than of proclamation, without any attempts to produce detailed analyses. His main evidences are case histories, surely relevant, but not always subjected to the test of critical interpretation.

Frankl's tribute to phenomenology is certainly gratifying. This does not mean that phenomenology deserves it. Nor does it necessarily mean that Frankl has done more than pioneer in an area where phenomenology could and should give more support to the therapist than it has done thus far.

16 / Concluding Reflections

IT IS TIME to conclude this story. Inconclusive and incomplete though it is, it needs an ending. Thus I shall offer some retrospective and prospective reflections that may aid the reader in drawing his own conclusions. These offerings will consist of summary reminders, tentative appraisals, and a guarded look ahead.

[1] LOOKING BACK

NOT ONLY the patient reader of this book but also its judicious sampler should be warned that what he will find here is not a concentrate of the material in the preceding chapters. There are always limits to a meaningful condensation of evidence, and a mere summary of the highlights makes less sense than ever in an account that aims at developing understanding rather than mere factual information.

Instead, I intend to offer a retrospective analysis of some of the major findings about the historical significance of phenomenological philosophy for psychology and psychiatry. In so doing I want to sum up the main evidence for the impact of phenomenology on two major human sciences. As a guideline for this analysis, I will not repeat the names of the protagonists in this story—looking up the conclusions of the chapters, the table of contents, and the indexes should serve this purpose for the reader—but I will refer to the patterns of influence that were discussed in the introduction.

I have distinguished between "non-personal" and "interpersonal," direct and indirect, influences and have divided their "degrees" into total and partial influences.

Here I will concern myself chiefly with the last distinction, though I will begin by reflecting briefly on the two earlier divisions:

1. On the whole, the influences that I have traced have been on the "non-personal" side. Few, if any, of the major philosophical phenomenologists have been interested in, or have had the chance to, teach psychologists and psychiatrists in person, as did their forerunners, Brentano and Stumpf. The psychologists and psychiatrists mentioned in this book who did visit Husserl's, Scheler's, or Pfänder's classes or seminars apparently carried away no specific inspirations for their own research. There were some more personal contacts later on, but few of them had lasting results. The relationships between Scheler and Buytendijk or Heidegger and Boss may serve as examples. Most of the non-personal influences emanated from the writings of the philosophers, Husserl's *Logische Untersuchungen* and Heidegger's *Sein und Zeit* being the major sources. But philosophical ideas can also travel by word of mouth; this was especially true in the case of the earlier Heidegger. Nor should one overlook the role of personal exchanges among students and young researchers in circles that often formed independently of the central figures. The Göttingen psychologists and the gestaltists are perhaps the most conspicuous examples of such personal interaction in groups based on the ideas supplied by the "masters."

2. The picture is much the same as far as the distinction between direct and indirect influences is concerned. The direct influence of the philosophers and even of their books upon the psychologists and psychiatrists was relatively minor. None of the philosophers instructed the psychologists to carry out specific research or suggested fruitful areas for study. But some of their ideas did have a direct influence, especially when the philosophical terminology was taken over, as in the case of "intentionality" or "being-in-the-world." Binswanger is probably the clearest illustration of this, in spite of the fact that his personal contacts with the phenomenological philosophers were brief and intermittent.

However, there is clearly no limit to the indirect influences that are actually the major basis for any movement, once it has spread beyond a closed circle of disciples and "cliques." It would be hopeless and of little meaning to trace these influences from their center to the perimeter. It is more important to pay attention to the transformations, distortions, and dilutions which occurred in the spreading itself. Heidegger's ontology and Sartre's existentialism, especially in their popularized forms, provide the best examples of such wide but scattered and distorted influences. As a consolation one might remember Etienne Gilson's dictum that the history of philosophy is mostly the result of productive misunderstandings.

3. But in this context my major concern is with the degree and quality of such influences.

A. Again, "total influence," meaning the influence that amounts to exclusive responsibility for effecting the influenced medium, is not likely to occur in the field of ideas. There are of course wholesale transfers of ideas by way of loans. And in some cases psychologists and psychiatrists have taken over parts of phenomenological philosophy wholesale and built upon them as unquestioned foundations for their other work. The clearest case is that of Medard Boss in his relation to Heidegger. As for Binswanger, one should realize that neither Husserl nor Heidegger, nor both together, were the only influences he experienced. And even more important, Binswanger's creative use of these ingredients on his own makes it impossible to explain his work merely as a result of influences, total or partial.

B. The really important questions concern the partial influences: To what extent and in what way have psychology and psychiatry been influenced in this manner by philosophical phenomenology?

(1) I shall first discuss influence by *stimulation*. A complete listing of all the stimuli that phenomenological philosophy has provided for psychologists and psychiatrists would almost amount to a repetition of the preceding chapters. Some reminders must suffice. Perhaps the major stimulus that has issued from Brentano's and Stumpf's work is the device of describing prior to explaining. In Husserl's case the appeal to go "to the things," especially in the form in which it was understood in the early days of phenomenology, is reflected in the perceptiveness for new phenomena that characterizes the work of the "second generation" of Göttingen psychologists and the gestaltists. Sartre's excitement upon hearing that phenomenology allowed him to phenomenologize about everything including his glass of absinthe on the table was another instance. But there are of course more specific motifs for stimulation in the philosophical arsenals of Husserl and others. Perhaps the greatest stimulation that has come from Husserl is that of his posthumous and little developed

conception of the "life-world"; it is reflected especially in the work of the psychiatrists. But even earlier, Heidegger's conception of being-in-the-world had been a major stimulus for the further differentiations made by Binswanger in his own work. Scheler was probably the most effective stimulator, as evidenced in the work of Kurt Schneider, Eugène Minkowski, and Viktor Frankl. Sartre's poignant observations on the human gaze have inspired Jürg Zutt and C. Kulenkampff.

In all such cases phenomenology has had at least a triggering effect. But this stimulation has certainly not determined the further fates of the stimulating ideas in psychology and psychiatry and therefore need not be credited to or blamed on the initiating philosophical stimulators.

In speaking of stimulation, one must not overlook the case of negative or "dialectical" stimulation. Husserl's "egology" led in Gurwitsch and Sartre to the attempt to get rid of the transcendental ego through a non-egological interpretation of consciousness. Heidegger's emphasis on care (*Sorge*), however misunderstood, led Binswanger, by way of protest, to the development of his phenomenology of love. Sartre's social phenomenology of conflict, as the basic form of coexistence, induced the more balanced phenomenologies of dialogue and encounter.

(2) Philosophical influences can also be *reinforcing*. In this role Husserl's ideas have been an aid to the Würzburg school, whose imageless thought found backing through Husserl's "*kategoriale Anschauung*" (non-sensuous intuiting) in the *Logische Untersuchungen*. On more general grounds the gestaltists too have become increasingly interested in phenomenology. Jaspers, at least at the time of his *Allgemeine Psychopathologie*, found important support in Husserl's early work. This also seems to have been true of Erwin Straus and of such French psychiatrists as Henri Ey (through Husserl) and Hesnard (through Merleau-Ponty). Cases of mutual reinforcement usually presuppose some active cooperation on a project. In the case of phenomenology there seems to have been regrettably little of that. Gurwitsch's cooperation with the gestaltists, which resulted in his amendments to Husserl's constitutional analyses, may come closest.

(3) *Corroboration* as distinguished from reinforcement means subsequent confirmation and strengthening of one's independent findings. Donald Snygg's phenomenology seems to have been such a case, as contrasted with the work of Carl Rogers, who received some reinforcement from phenomenology as he developed his theory of personality. Perhaps the most interesting

results of a corroboration based on belated discovery and pleased recognition occurred in the work of Kurt Goldstein. Corroboration of the work of Piaget cannot yet be claimed, although there are indications that it might develop. Thus far, one can find only parallels in his work and that of the phenomenologists.

Philosophical purists have denied at times that there is any such thing as a phenomenological psychology and psychiatry with legitimate philosophical credentials. It is certainly true that phenomenology and existentialism have had a fatal appeal for a good many band-wagon climbers and freeloaders on the fringes of scientific psychology and psychiatry who try to profit from the prestige of the new movement by name-dropping or even without it. But this is no good reason for rejecting the legitimate claims of those who have taken serious account of the philosophical foundations of their enterprises. The preceding retrospect at least should have reassured skeptics that there are demonstrable connections between phenomenological philosophy and such sciences as psychology and psychiatry. Moreover, it should have demonstrated that phenomenology is more than a mere philosophical theory and that it can have far-reaching consequences for the human sciences.

[2] Assessing

Having established that phenomenology qua philosophy has had an impact on some of the non-philosophical sciences, I now would like to face the much graver question of whether this influence has been a "good" thing or a "bad" thing for them. My criterion for answering this point-blank question will be whether phenomenology has added to or detracted from their growth.

I would like to examine first the case against phenomenology. And to counterbalance my bias, I shall call on one of the leading psychologists of our days as the chief witness for the prosecution.

In a recent book [1] Jean Piaget sounds the alarm against "philosophical psychology," whose chief contemporary representative is to him phenomenology, and particularly the French phenomenology of Sartre and Merleau-Ponty (his academic

1. *Sagesse et illusions de la philosophie* (Paris: PUF, 1965). English translation by Wolfe Mays, *Insights and Illusions of Philosophy* (New York: World, 1971).

predecessor at the Sorbonne). Its major danger as he sees it is that it claims to supply genuine knowledge independent of and superior to that of "scientific," i.e., empirical, psychology—in fact that it is fundamentally anti-scientific. Actually, as far as Husserl is concerned, Piaget, who read him only after 1939 (p. 35), expresses considerable sympathy with his ultimate objectives. He even subscribes to the idea of a convergence of his own genetic epistemology with Husserl's conception of constitutive intentionality, and with its stress on the role of the subject, as suggested by Aron Gurwitsch (pp. 150, 178)—a sentiment which Piaget had already expressed in his *Introduction à l'épistémologie génétique* [2] with regard to the *Logische Untersuchungen.* But what alarms him is the supposed claim of Husserl's "eidetic psychology" to supersede scientific psychology in its investigation of the facts by objective empirical methods.

Now apart from a number of misunderstandings about Husserl's attitude toward psychology, which certainly was ambivalent and was based on insufficient information about more recent developments in the field, there is unfortunately a good deal of reason for sharing Piaget's concern about a tendency among some phenomenologists to ignore or minimize the work of empirical psychologists. But fortunately there is no good reason for suspecting phenomenology as such of an anti-psychologism which would reject "scientific," and particularly experimental, psychology on principle. Even for Sartre there is the area of the "probable" which only empirical research can explore. But it may well be the case, and Piaget gives disturbing instances for this possibility, that the interest in phenomenological psychology has undermined the respect for those contingent facts which phenomenological a priori methods, actually for essential reasons, can never reach and determine.

Specifically, and going beyond Piaget, I would like to point out that too many phenomenologists, in asserting their essential insights, have failed to realize the need for making sure of the initial phenomena to which they apply. They also have overlooked the fact that it is very often the scientific approach that can enrich such pre-scientific experience. The everyday life-world is not the only world to be experienced. Phenomenologists also have often been guilty of summary contempt of experimental research (which Husserl was not). They might as well remember that claims to essential insights have to be verified

2. *Introduction à l'épistémologie génétique* (Paris: PUF, 1950), I, 29 ff.

by the kind of experiment in thought which Husserl retained in the form of free variation in the imagination. On the whole they should not have forgotten that the empirical research of Stumpf, Michotte, Goldstein, and the gestaltists has not only yielded new phenomena but has confirmed some of the essential insights of phenomenological philosophy. To miss out on such confirmations is poor strategy at the very least.

Apart from such dangers, which for the most part can be and have been avoided, if the evidence here presented is correct, there is of course the question of an essential danger inherent in the nature of the phenomenological approach. Piaget suspects that this is the case because of phenomenology's essential commitment to the introspective approach. But while it is true that phenomenology starts from the subjective phenomena as an essential, and in fact the initial, part of the total evidence, the charge that phenomenology is committed to merely personal subjectivity is certainly ill-founded. It is precisely one of the functions of the eidetic approach to widen the merely personal perspective by systematic variation, to one of intersubjective essential insight.

Once the objectives of a phenomenological psychology are clearly understood, there should be no question about the fact that it has essential limitations and that it cannot and must not be considered as a serious rival of "scientific" research. Its main *raison d'être* is to serve as an ally to the scientific enterprise. This makes it all the more urgent to define their mutual relationship. But as far as the essential danger of phenomenological psychology is concerned, it should be removable once it is realized that phenomenology too has its criteria of "rigorous science," and that phenomenological claims require and receive verification as do any other claims to knowledge. Only the means of verification may differ.

But, then, what is the "good thing" about phenomenology in its relation to psychology and psychiatry? Again, the record here presented should provide the basis for any systematic reflection. I submit that at least some of the influences I have been able to trace have been for the good.

But if so, one may still wonder whether these results could not have been achieved without the aid of philosophical phenomenology. This is what Jaspers, for instance, claimed in retrospect. Ultimately, of course, such a question cannot be answered as long as we cannot run historical control experiments. But there is at least the indisputable fact that some of the main agents of this drama have testified to the importance of the phenomenological inspirations, confirmations, and corroborations in their research. And even if these should not have been indispensable, chances are that they have accelerated progress in the respective fields.

It may be argued further that the philosophical infiltration cannot have been accidental. Enough has been said in the Introduction about the fact that there can never be influence without a receptive soil. There is ample evidence to show that the scientific soil in the early twentieth century was ready for new fertilization; phenomenology provided the seeds. Chances are that it accelerated, rather than retarded, new growth. But only concrete case studies can show how and why the needs of science were met by the phenomenological influx.

However, more detail is required in order to demonstrate the specific good that phenomenology has achieved thus far for psychology and psychiatry. I submit that phenomenology has made a major contribution on several levels: by enriching the field through drawing attention to new and neglected phenomena, by providing new patterns for understanding these phenomena and hypothesizing beyond them, and by showing new ways for verifying such hypotheses. I shall attempt to substantiate these claims by more specific references.

1. By stressing the need for description of the phenomena and by urging the direct approach to these phenomena prior to description, phenomenology has discouraged the trend in science, based on the misinterpretation of Ockham's razor, to reduce the phenomena to the indispensable minimum, instead of merely not multiplying them beyond necessity. Phenomenology is not afraid of variety. As such it has not only encouraged and supported the exploration of neglected and overlooked phenomena but has actively participated in spotting them.

2. By aiming at insights into essential structures and relationships, phenomenology has supplied new patterns of understanding for relating phenomena, which are otherwise merely juxtaposed in time and space except for the functional relations of "explanatory" covering laws. By putting the phenomena into the context of lived experience in a "life-world," by exploring the meaningful connections experienced in motivation, by using methods of interpretation sometimes called "hermeneutic," phenomenology has added new dimensions to empirical exploration.

3. By providing patterns for going beyond experience, phenomenology has helped in the development of meaningful hy-

potheses. It is a well-known quandary in the methodology of science that there is no department store for scientific hypotheses, that science itself has to appeal to the "scientific" imagination, and that there are no patent prescriptions for its use. It has even been suggested that this is the function for "intuition," in the Bergsonian sense. At least in the area of psychology and psychiatry, phenomenology can suggest interpretative patterns to the imagination. Here I have in mind such patterns as intentionality, constitutive processes, and fundamental choices. These may again sound like speculative constructions. The difference is that such phenomenological patterns of interpretation are based on experience, though it is a widened and deepened experience. Phenomenology appeals to imaginative variation of this experience, but it does not replace rigor by fancy. Henri Ey's and Binswanger's studies illustrate this expansion of the phenomenological enterprise.

4. By widening the possibilities of verification, phenomenology makes it possible to test such hypotheses in new and enriching ways. Often phenomenology is suspected, not without some reason, of ignoring the problems of verification and of having no criteria for testing its sometimes sweeping claims. But it must not be forgotten that Husserl was deeply concerned about the problem of ultimate justification and that for him all meanings had to be supported by intuitive fulfillment. This fulfillment did not necessarily come through factual, and especially sense experience. Different kinds of intuitive evidence were appropriate in mathematics and in the normative sciences. While the theory of phenomenological verification is still very much in need of clarification and development, it may at least be suggested that the phenomenological liberalization of epistemology opens up new opportunities for scientific verification.

This, then, is the "good" of the philosophical contributions of phenomenology to scientific psychology and psychiatry as I see it: Not to rival science or to replace it, but to aid it by enriching and strengthening it in its foundations as well as in its powers of understanding and guiding. In striving to be itself a "rigorous science," phenomenology also wants to buttress other sciences, particularly those which are not yet firmly established. Its basic function is that of an eye-opener and eye-widener. As such it aims to help psychology and psychiatry not only in breaking fresh ground but also in cultivating the newly won territory. It also wants to keep them close to the earth of direct intuitive evidence. Thus, in its relations to science, phenomenology can assume the complementary roles of scout and pioneer, as well as of designer and supervisor.[3]

[3] Looking Ahead

WHAT ABOUT the future? In the case of an ongoing development, even the historian may be expected to put on the phophets' mantle. But I confess that I feel little desire to do so. Predictions can never be better than the factual evidence on which they are based, and here the evidence is certainly inconclusive. Anyway, one of the ironies of science is its own unpredictability. One merely has to recall the prediction made at the end of the nineteenth century that all that physics would add in the twentieth would be one more decimal to the accuracy of its measurements. Moreover, where the future depends in part on our own doing, valid predictions are perhaps impossible in principle. They may also be self-fulfilling or, worse, self-defeating.

Nevertheless, at least a sober assessment of the present basis for all such predictions is in order. For one must be under no illusions: The present role of phenomenology in the total picture of psychology and psychiatry, particularly in the Anglo-American world, is a minor one and has not shown significant growth in recent years except at the "fringes." Even a look at such ecumenically-minded reviewing organs as *Contemporary Psychology*, the publishers' catalogues, or the programs of the professional meetings, makes it clear that phenomenology is the concern of only a small and unrepresentative minority. Its academic influence in the major universities and departments is likewise unimpressive.

There is certainly good reason for sobriety. The kind of window-dressing publicity which phenomenology has enjoyed in recent decades has been anything but a blessing. What has gone on behind the display window, if anything at all, often has been more than questionable. But yet there is no sign of a deliberate turning away from or a turning against phenomenology. There is still enough ongoing activity, even among the younger

3. In this connection I would like to mention the related controversy between behaviorism and phenomenology started by Nathan Browdy and Paul Oppenheim under the title "Tensions in Psychology between the Methods of Behaviorism and Phenomenology," in *Psychological Review*, LXXIII (1966), 295–305; with important replies by Richard M. Zaner, *ibid.*, LXXIV (1967), 318–24, and Mary Henle and Gertrude Baltimore, *ibid.*, pp. 325–29; rebuttal, *ibid.*, pp. 330–34.

scholars, to preclude pessimism, although certainly one's optimism should be guarded and conditional. What we must look for are new concrete and limited projects in depth, instead of the sweeping promises of the more existentialist-minded phenomenologists. Even more important, however, is the need for the development and application of more critical standards. Thus all I am ready to predict is that there is still a future for phenomenology in psychology, and perhaps even more of one in psychiatry. But the shape and size of this future is something on which I am not prepared to commit myself—it depends, and not a little, on us. Specifically, it depends on the training of qualified workers. We do not seem to have adequate training facilities, and there is hardly any thought about how to develop them.

But there is another way of looking ahead, by way not of prophecy but of program. Far be it from me to end up with a blueprint for the future of phenomenology in psychology and psychiatry, particularly since I do not intend to do much about following it myself. All I can offer are some reflections about the kinds of programs which would seem to me to make special sense at this juncture.

When on August 15, 1923, Husserl paid a visit to Binswanger at his sanatorium in Kreuzlingen, he left the following entry in the guestbook:

> We shall not enter the kingdom of a true psychology unless we become like children. We must look for the A B C of consciousness and thus become really A B C beginners [*ABC Schützen*]. The way to the ABC and from there upwards to elementary grammar and step by step to the universal a priori of concrete organizations [*Gestaltungen*] is the way which makes true science possible and the universe intelligible (my translation).[4]

This ambitious program, about which Binswanger was so enthusiastic, need not be interpreted literally. While its beginning seems to suggest a return to the naïveté of the pre-scientific life-world, it soon proceeds to the more rigid methods of the Pestalozzi approach to teaching the elements. And while there is no explicit mention of "reductions" and "transcendental constitution," this is clearly what Husserl was aiming at.

The question is whether this kind of program holds any

4. "Dank an Husserl," in *Edmund Husserl, 1859–1959*, ed. H. L. Van Breda (The Hague: Nijhoff, 1959), p. 65. The same language of the ABC occurs in a letter to Ernst Cassirer of April 3, 1925 (see also Iso Kern, *Husserl und Kant* [The Hague: Nijhoff, 1964], pp. 301 ff.).

promise today for a phenomenological psychology and psychiatry. To some extent Binswanger seems first to have striven only for the naïveté of true children by studying the worlds of his patients prior to all theory. But in his last period he turned to an attempt to understand the genesis of the illusions of his patients by means of Husserl's constitutional phenomenology.

Both programs continue to make sense. There is need for more descriptive work on the "life-worlds." [5] But there is also need for studying the way in which they typically establish themselves in consciousness (constitution). This does not mean an orthodox return to Husserl. On the contrary, the more this approach can be freed from the technicalities of Husserl's language and from his assumptions, the better. But against the background of such philosophical patterns even empirical work can be enriched and deepened.

Such a program might be interpreted as a plea for a return of philosophy to empirical science, from which it has been (supposedly) expelled with so much difficulty and so much benefit. But certainly this is not my point if philosophy is understood as a speculative philosophy in the grand manner, which imposes its unexamined concepts and axioms upon empirical research. I am not even thinking of a philosophy of science, whose auxiliary services have proved to be indispensable to any self-critical science. The real question is whether and in what sense phenomenology, as it now proves relevant, if not essential, to psychology and psychiatry, can and must be considered as philosophy.

It can be argued that it is not philosophy but the kind of pre-science and pre-philosophy that gives access to the basic phenomena prior to all factual research and meta-scientific reflection. Descriptive phenomenology in this sense of going to the pristine phenomena is not yet philosophy in any technical sense. Hence the plea for such a phenomenology is definitely not to be identified with that of a return to "metaphysics."

On the other hand, phenomenology is philosophically not as innocent as such a plea for "presuppositionless" description might make it out to be. For phenomenology also wants first to be philosophy, a philosophy that re-examines all presuppositions of human knowledge and practice. Phenomenology certainly

5. See my article, "The Relevance of Phenomenological Philosophy for Psychology," in *Phenomenology and Existentialism*, ed. E. N. Lee and M. Mandelbaum (Baltimore, Md.: Johns Hopkins University Press, 1967), pp. 219–41.

does fulfill some, if not all, of the requirements of such an enterprise. But under whatever name, programs like the ones here suggested might make phenomenology more meaningful as an aid to specific psychological and psychiatric research.

I would certainly not want to restrict the program for phenomenology in psychology and psychiatry to as narrow and dated a range as seems to be suggested by Husserl's Kreuzlingen entry. My plea is for a study of the specific needs of psychology and psychiatry in order to see where phenomenological clarifications and explorations may be welcome. At the moment such needs may be found especially in the areas of ego-psychology, motivation, and social psychology. Whatever the topic, the most important requirements seem to me concreteness, limited scope for the sake of greater penetration, and relevance. Once phenomenology has proved itself in specific areas of research by the fruitfulness of its concrete descriptive analyses, the time may have arrived for more ambitious undertakings. Given a chance, phenomenology also should be eager and willing to enter teamwork with open-minded specialists in the field. Only by a pooling of subjectivities is there a real chance to achieve intersubjectivity and to lay the specter of introspective subjectivism.

This final suggestion is meant merely as an example. I have no intention of legislating for the future of phenomenology. I merely want to suggest that this future offers an open chance. How this opening will be filled must not be dictated a priori; it must be governed by the phenomena themselves. Their autonomy and their primacy is the first and ultimate message of phenomenology.

Selected Bibliography

THE PURPOSE of this limited bibliography is to give readers wanting to go beyond the text of this book aids for further orientation and study. In using the bibliography, readers should also consult the footnotes to the relevant discussion in the text; specific references can be found by consulting the Index of Names or the Table of Contents. In a few cases this bibliography includes authors not mentioned in the main text.

It should be noted that under "Primary Sources" only such texts are listed as are relevant to phenomenology in psychology and psychiatry; texts of importance also to general philosophy and its branches, as listed in the bibliographies of my book *The Phenomenological Movement* (The Hague: Nijhoff, 1965), have been omitted. "Secondary Sources" also are restricted to books and articles which are helpful to an understanding of phenomenology in psychology and psychiatry. The bibliographies I have listed are the most comprehensive and up-to-date ones known to me.

As to the psychologists discussed in Chapter 2 on "Phenomenological Philosophy in Some Major Schools of Psychology," there seemed to be no point in repeating information that can be found in such standard works as E. G. Boring's *History of Experimental Psychology*, 2d ed. (New York: Appleton-Century-Crofts, 1950). References up to 1932 are listed also in the *Psychological Register*, Vol. III, ed. Carl Murchison (Worcester, Mass.: Clark University Press, 1932). For living authors, such sources as *American Men of Science: The Social and Behavioral Sciences* (New York: Bowker), *Kürschners Deutscher Gelehrtenkalender* (Berlin: de Gruyter), and various national *Who's Whos* provide helpful guides for research. As to the psychoanalysts mentioned in Chapter 4, "Phenomenology in Psychoanalysis," all that seems possible and sensible is to direct the reader to general reference works, especially the *Index of Psychoanalytic Writings*, ed. Alexander Grinstein, 10 vols. (New York: International Universities Press, 1956–66). The Subject Index in these volumes includes "Phenomenology" and gives a number of scattered titles, among which the following entries, not listed above in the main text, seem noteworthy:

15110 Van der Hoop, J. H. "Phénoménologie en Psychoanalyse," *Psychiatry en Neurology*, IV–V (1932), 473–82.

61689 Vergote, A. "Psychanalyse et Phénoménologie," in *Problèmes de Psychanalyse* (Paris: Fayot, 1927), pp. 125–44.

Narziss Ach (1871–1946)

I. *Bibliography*

Psychological Register, p. 772.

Ludwig Binswanger (1881–1966)

I. *Primary Sources*

A. Books

Einführung in die Probleme der allgemeinen Psychologie. Berlin: Springer, 1922.

Über Ideenflucht. Zurich: Orell Fuessli, 1933.

Grundformen und Erkenntnis menschichen Daseins. Zurich: Niehans, 1942; 3d ed., 1962; 4th ed., Munich: Reinhardt, 1964.

Ausgewählte Vorträge und Aufsätze. 2 vols. Bern: Francke, 1942–55.

Drei Formen missglückten Daseins. Tübingen: Niemeyer, 1956.

Schizophrenie. Pfullingen: Neske, 1957.

Melancholie und Manie. Pfullingen: Neske, 1960.

Wahn. Pfullingen: Neske, 1965.

B. Articles in Translation *

"Dream and Existence" (1930). In *Being-in-the-World*, edited by Jacob Needleman, pp. 222–48. New York: Basic Books, 1963.

* The dates of the original publication in German are given in parentheses.

"Freud's Conception of Man in the Light of Anthropology" (1936). In *Being-in-the-World,* pp. 149–81.
"Freud and the Magna Charta of Clinical Psychiatry" (1936). In *Being-in-the-World,* pp. 182–205.
"On the Manic Mode of Being-in-the-World" (1944). In *Phenomenology: Pure and Applied,* edited by E. Straus, pp. 127–41. Pittsburgh, Pa.: Duquesne University Press, 1964.
"The Case of Ellen West" (1944–45). In *Existence,* edited by Rollo May, Ernest Angel, Henri F. Ellenberger, pp. 237–364. New York: Basic Books, 1958.
"Insanity as Life-Historical Phenomenon and as Mental Disease: The Case of Ilse" (1945). In *Existence,* pp. 214–36.
"The Existential Analysis School of Thought" (1945). In *Existence,* pp. 191–213.
"The Case of Lola Voss" (1949). In *Being-in-the-World,* pp. 266–301.
"Heidegger's Analytic of Existence and Its Meaning in Psychiatry" (1949). In *Being-in-the-World,* pp. 206–21.
"Extravagance [*Verstiegenheit*]" (1949). In *Being-in-the-World,* pp. 343–50.
"Existential Analysis and Psychotherapy" (1954). *Psychoanalytic Review,* XLV (1958–59), 79–83.
Sigmund Freud: Reminiscences of a Friendship (1956). New York: Grune & Stratton, 1957.
"Introduction to *Schizophrenie*" (1957). In *Being-in-the-World,* pp. 249–65.

II. *Secondary Sources*

Cargnello, Danilo. "Dal Naturalismo Psichoanalitico alla Fenomenologia antropologica della Daseinsanalyse. (Da Freud a Binswanger)." *Archivio di Filosofia* (1961), pp. 127–91.
Edelheit, Henry. "Binswanger and Freud." *Psychoanalytic Quarterly,* XXXVI (1967), 85–90.
Ellenberger, Henri. "Binswanger's Existential Analysis." In *Existence,* pp. 120–24. A highly condensed first orientation, stressing Buber's role in the development of Binswanger's thought.
Kuhn, Roland. "Daseinsanalyse und Psychiatrie." In *Psychiatrie der Gegenwart,* edited by H. W. Gruhle et al., I / II, 853–902. Berlin: Springer, 1963. Kuhn, who worked particularly closely with Binswanger, is also his best qualified interpreter.
———. Obituary of Binswanger in *Schweizer Archiv für Neurologie und Psychiatrie,* XCIX (1966), 113–17.

Needleman, Jacob. Translation of and critical introduction to Binswanger's *Being-in-the-World.* New York: Basic Books, 1963. This book is actually a composite of Needleman's introduction to Binswanger's work and his translation of seven independent texts of Binswanger's. The introduction, a Yale dissertation, is admittedly merely an attempt to comprehend Binswanger in the light of Kant and Heidegger and makes no attempt to show his development—especially in terms of the role of Husserl in his thinking. The attempt to relate Binswanger to Sartre is certainly not in line with Binswanger's own rejection of Sartre. The selections from Binswanger belong to the period between 1930 and 1957; the dates of individual articles are not identified, and the arrangement is not chronological. The first and last periods of Binswanger's production, in which the influence of Husserl was prevalent, are not represented. The major emphasis is on Binswanger's relation to Freud and Heidegger. The translation is usually adequate.

III. *Bibliographies*

Cargnello, Danilo. In "Filosopfia della Alienazione e Analisi Existentiale," *Archivio di Filosofia* (1961), pp. 193–98. Contains a chronological arrangement of 84 items up to 1968, repeating book publications at the end.

Larese, Dino. *Ludwig Binswanger: Versuch einer kleinen Lebensskizze.* Amriswiler Bücherei, 1965. Pp. 17–30. Apparently the most complete bibliography available.

Sneessens, Germaine. In *Revue philosophique de Louvain,* LXIV (1966), 594–602. Almost as complete as Larese's bibliography, but differently grouped. It includes publications until Binswanger's death, arranged in groups, beginning with books and collections and followed by articles and brochures, and finally by titles of unpublished lectures. Translations into other languages are listed separately.

Medard Boss (b. 1903)

I. *Primary Sources*

Sinn und Gehalt der sexuellen Perversionen. Bern: Huber, 1947; 2d ed., 1952. English translation by Liese Luise Abell.

Meaning and Context of Sexual Perversions: A Daseinsanalytic Approach to the Psychopathology of the Phenomenon of Love. New York: Grune & Stratton, 1949.

Der Traum und seine Auslegung. Bern: Huber, 1953. English translation by Arnold J. Pomerans. *The Analysis of Dreams.* New York: Philosophical Library, 1958.

Einführung in die psychosomatische Medizin. Bern: Huber, 1954.

Psychoanalyse und Daseinsanalytik. Bern: Huber, 1957. English translation by Ludwig B. Lefebvre. *Psychoanalysis and Daseinsanalysis.* New York: Basic Books, 1963. The English translation is really a new version, three times as long as the German original, but omitting some important parts of it to which my account in the main text also referred.

Grundriss der Medizin: Ansätze zu einer phänomenologischen Physiologie, Psychologie, Therapie und zu einer daseinsgemässen Präventiv-Medizin in der modernen Industriegesellschaft (Bern: Huber, 1971).

Franz Brentano (1838–1917)

I. *Major Primary Sources*

Psychologie vom empirischen Standpunkt. Vol. I. Leipzig; Dunkker & Humblot, 1874; 2d ed., 1911 (includes chaps. V–IX and supplements). These texts and others not previously published were included in the posthumous edition in 3 vols. by Oskar Kraus. Leipzig: Meiner, 1924–28. English translation of Book I, chap. I, and Book II, chap. VII by B. D. Terrell in *Realism and the Background of Phenomenology,* edited by R. M. Chisholm, pp. 39–70. Glencoe, Ill.; Free Press, 1960.

Vom Ursprung sittlicher Erkenntnis. Leipzig; Duncker & Humblot, 1889. English translation by R. M. Chisholm and E. H. Schneewind. New York: Humanities Press, 1969.

II. *Secondary Sources*

Chisholm, R. M. "Brentano's Descriptive Psychology." In *Akten des XIV-Internationalen Kongresses für Philosophe,* II, 164–74. Vienna: Herder, 1968. A discussion of Brentano's still unpublished Vienna lectures on "Psychognosie" (EL 74).

Gilson, Lucie. *La Psychologie descriptive selon F. Brentano.*

Paris: Vrin, 1955. Deals mostly with principles, less with content, and is based only on texts published thus far. Contains a bibliography, pp. 11–17.

Rancurello, Antos C. *A Study of Franz Brentano: His Psychological Standpoint and His Significance in the History of Psychology.* New York: Academic Press, 1968.

III. *Most Comprehensive Bibliography*

Rancurello, *Study of Franz Brentano.* Pp. 134–69 (annotated).

Karl Bühler (1879–1963)

I. *Major Primary Sources*

Wahrnehmungstheorie. Jena: Fischer, 1922.
Die Krise der Psychologie. Jena: Fischer, 1927.
Sprachtheorie. Jena: Fischer, 1934; 2d ed., 1965.

II. *Secondary Sources*

"Symposium on Karl Bühler's Contributions to Psychology." *Journal of General Psychology,* LXXV (1966), 181–219.

III. *Bibliography*

Psychological Register, pp. 587–88.

F. J. J. Buytendijk (b. 1887)

I. *Primary Sources*

A. Books

Über das Verstehen der Lebenserscheinungen. Habelschwerdt: Francke, 1925.
Psychologie des animaux. Paris: Payot, 1928.
Wesen und Sinn des Spiels. Berlin: Wolf, 1933.
The Mind of the Dog. London: Allen & Unwin, 1935.
Wege zum Verständnis der Tiere. Zurich: Niehans, 1938.

Pain. Translated by Eda O'Shiel. Chicago: University of Chicago Press, 1962. Dutch original, Utrecht: Spectrum, 1943.

Phénoménologie de la rencontre. Paris: Desclée de Brouwer, 1952. German original in *Eranos Jahrbuch,* XIX (1951), 431–86.

Allgemeine Theorie der menschlichen Haltung und Bewegung. Heidelberg: Springer, 1956. Dutch original, *Allgemeine theorie van de menselijke honding und beweging.* Utrecht: Spectrum, 1948. French version, *Attitudes et mouvements.* Paris: Desclée de Brouwer, 1957.

Das Menschliche. Stuttgart: Koehler, 1958.

De vrouw. Utrecht: Spectrum, 1958. English translation by Dennis J. Barret. *Woman.* Glen Rock, N. J.: Newman Press, 1968.

Prolegomena van een anthropologische fysiologie. Utrecht: Spectrum, 1965.

B. Articles in Translation

"The Phenomenological Approach to the Problems of Feeling and Emotions." In the Second Moosehart Symposium on *Emotions and Feeling* (1948), 127–41. Also in *Psychoanalysis and Existential Philosophy,* edited by H. Ruytenbeck, pp. 155–72. New York: Dutton, 1962.

"Experienced Freedom and Moral Freedom in the Child's Consciousness." *Educational Theory,* III (1953), 1–13.

"Femininity and Existential Psychology." In *Perspectives in Personality Theory,* edited by H. P. David and H. von Bracken, pp. 197–211. New York: Basic Books, 1957.

"The Body in Existential Philosophy." *Review of Existential Psychology and Psychiatry,* II (1961), 149–72.

II. *Secondary Source*

Grene, Marjorie. *Approaches to a Philosophical Biology.* New York: Basic Books, 1968.

III. *Bibliography*

Rencontre/Encounter/Begegnung: Contributions toward a Human Psychology. Utrecht: Spectrum, 1957. Pp. 508–20. Complete bibliography up to 1957.

KARL DUNCKER (1903–1940)

I. *Primary Sources*

"Über induzierte Bewegung." *Psychologische Forschung,* XX (1929), 180–259. Translated in part by Willis D. Ellis. In *A Source Book of Gestalt Psychology,* pp. 164–72. New York: Humanities Press, 1966.

Zur Psychologie des produktiven Denkens. Berlin: Springer, 1935. English translation by Lynne J. Lees. "On Problem Solving." In *Psychological Monographs,* LVIII (1956), 1–113.

"Ethical Relativity? An Inquiry into the Psychology of Ethics." *Mind,* XLVIII (1939), 39–57.

"On Pleasure, Emotion, and Striving." *Philosophy and Phenomenological Research,* I (1941), 392–430.

"Phenomenology and Epistemology of Consciousness of Objects." *Philosophy and Phenomenological Research,* I (1941), 505–42.

HENRI EY

I. *Major Primary Sources*

Etudes psychiatriques. Vol. I: *Historique, Méthodologie, Psychopathologie generale.* Paris: Desclée de Brouwer, 1948; 2d ed., 1952. Vol. II: *Aspects séméiologiques.* Paris: Desclée de Brouwer, 1950; 2d ed., 1957. Vol. III: *Structure des psychoses aigües et déstructuration de la conscience.* Paris: Desclée de Brouwer, 1954; 2d ed., 1960.

La Conscience. Paris: PUF, 1963; 2d ed. (enlarged), 1968.

"Esquisse d'une conception organo-dynamique de la structure, de la nosographie et de l'étiopathogenie des maladies mentales." In *Psychiatrie der Gegenwart.* Berlin: Springer, 1963. English translation by S. L. Kennedy. In *Psychiatry and Philosophy* edited by E. Straus. New York: Springer, 1969.

VIKTOR FRANKL (B. 1905)

I. *Primary Sources*

Ärztliche Seelsorge. Vienna: Deuticke, 1948. English translation by Richard and Clara Winston. *The Doctor and the Soul.* 2d ed. New York: Knopf, 1965. This translation in the revised edition contains an added chapter.

Ein Psycholog erlebt das Konzentrationslager. Vienna: Jugend und Volk, 1946. English translation by Ilse Lasch. *Man's Search for Meaning: From Death-Camp to Existentialism*. Boston: Beacon Press, 1963. A newly revised and enlarged edition.

Der unbedingte Mensch: Metaklinische Vorlesungen. Vienna: Deuticke, 1949.

Homo patiens: Versuch einer Pathodizee. Vienna: Deuticke, 1950.

Theorie und Therapie der Neurosen: Einführung in die Logotherapie und Existenzanalyse. Vienna: Urban & Schwarzenberg, 1957.

Psychotherapy and Existentialism: Selected Papers on Logotherapy. New York: Clarion Books, 1968.

II. *Secondary Sources*

Tweedie, Donald F. *Logotherapy and the Christian Faith: An Evaluation of Frankl's Existential Approach to Psychotherapy*. Grand Rapids, Mich.: Buker Book House, 1961.

Ungersma, Aaron. *The Search for Meaning: A New Approach to Psychotherapy*. Philadelphia, Pa.: Westminster Press, 1968.

III. *Bibliographies*

Tweedie, Donald F. *Logotherapy and the Christian Faith*, pp. 181–83.

Frankl, Viktor. *Theorie und Therapie der Neurosen*. Pp. 201–4.

———. *Psychotherapy and Existentialism: Selected Papers on Logotherapy*. New York: Clarion Books, 1968. Pp. 223–29. These bibliographies are most detailed, but apparently not complete.

Viktor von Gebsattel (b. 1883)

I. *Primary Sources*

A. Books

Prolegomena zu einer medizinischen Anthropologie. Berlin: Springer, 1954.

Imago Hominis. Schweinfurt: Neues Forum, 1964.

B. Articles in Translation

"The World of the Compulsive." Translated by Sylvia Koppel and Ernest Angel. In *Existence,* ed. Rollo May, Ernest Angel, Henri F. Ellenberger, pp. 170–90. New York: Basic Books, 1958. An abridgement of a text that originally appeared in *Prolegomena zu einer medizinischen Anthropologie,* pp. 74–127. Berlin: Springer, 1954.

II. *Bibliographies*

Prolegomena zu einer medizinischen Anthropologie. Pp. 413–14.

Werden und Handeln. Stuttgart: Hippokrates, 1963–66. A continuation of the bibliography in *Prolegomena;* it also contains a biographical introduction by Eckart Wiesenhütter, pp. 9–16.

Moritz Geiger (1880–1937)

I. *Major Primary Sources*

"Beiträge zur Phänomenologie des ästhetischen Genusses." *Jahrbuch für Philosophie und phänomenologische Forschung,* I (1913).

"Das Unbewuste und die psychische Realität." *Jahrbuch für Philosophie und phänomenologische Forschung,* IV (1921).

Zugänge zur Ästhetik. Leipzig: Der neue Geist, 1928.

II. *Secondary Source*

Zeltner, Hermann. "Moritz Geiger zum Gedächtnis." *Zeitschrift für Philosophische Forschung,* XII (1960), 452–66.

III. *Bibliography*

Psychological Register, pp. 707–8.

Kurt Goldstein (1878–1965)

I. *Primary Sources*

Psychologische Analysen hirnpathologischer Fälle (with A. Gelb). Leipzig: Barth, 1920.

Der Aufbau des Organismus: Einführung in die Biologie unter besonderer Berücksichtigung der Erfahrungen am kranken Menschen. The Hague: Nijhoff, 1934. English translation, *The Organism: A Holistic Approach to Biology Derived from Pathological Data in Man.* New York: American Book, 1939. With a foreword by K. S. Lashley. The text of this translation contains "some changes in the arrangement of the material as well as a number of additions and omissions" (Preface to the English edition). This is true particularly of the sequence of the chapters after VI. New paperback edition. Boston: Beacon Press, 1964.

Human Nature in the Light of Psychopathology. William James Lectures. Cambridge, Mass.: Harvard University Press, 1940; 2d ed., New York: Schocken, 1963.

Language and Language Disturbances: Aphasic Symptoms and Their Significance for Medicine and Theory of Language. New York: Grune & Stratton, 1948.

II. *Secondary Sources*

Grene, Marjorie, *Approaches to a Philosophical Biology.* New York: Basic Books, 1968. Chapter 5, especially pp. 257 ff., discusses some of the phenomenological aspects of Goldstein's work.

Simmel, Marianne L., ed. *The Reach of Mind: Essays in Memory of Kurt Goldstein.* New York: Springer, 1968.

III. *Bibliography*

Meyer, Joseph. In *The Reach of Mind,* pp. 271–83. A comprehensive bibliography of 328 items.

Hans Gruhle (1880–1958)

I. *Bibliography*

Psychological Register, pp. 804–5.

Aron Gurwitsch (b. 1901)

I. *Major Primary Sources*

The Field of Consciousness. Pittsburgh, Pa.: Duquesne University Press, 1964.

Studies in Phenomenology and Psychology. Evanston, Ill.: Northwestern University Press, 1966.

II. *Bibliography*

Life-World and Consciousness: Essays for Aron Gurwitsch. Edited by Lester E. Embree. Evanston, Ill.: Northwestern University Press, 1972. Pp. 391–400.

Nicolai Hartmann (1882–1950)

I. *Major Primary Source*

Das Problem des geistigen Seins. Berlin: de Gruyter, 1933.

II. *Most Comprehensive Bibliography*

Ballauf, Theodor. In *Nicolai Hartmann: Der Denker und sein Werk*, edited by Heinz Heimsoeth and Robert Heiss, pp. 286–308. Göttingen: Vanderhoeck, 1952.

Martin Heidegger (b. 1889)

I. *Major Primary Sources*

Sein und Zeit. Halle: Niemeyer, 1927. English translation by J. Macquarrie and E. Robinson. *Being and Time*. London: SCM Press, 1962.

Was ist Metaphysik. Bonn: Cohen, 1929. English translation by E. C. Hull and A. Crick in *Existence and Being*. Chicago: Regnery, 1949.

II. *Secondary Sources*

Binswanger, Ludwig. "Die Bedeutung der Daseinsanalytik Martin Heideggers für das Selbstverständnis der Psychiatrie." In *Martin Heideggers Einfluss auf die Wissenschaften*, pp. 58–72. Bern: Francke, 1949.

Boss, Medard. "Martin Heidegger und die Ärzte." In *Martin Heidegger zum siebzigsten Geburtstag*, pp. 276–90. Pfullingen: Neske, 1959.

Heiss, Robert. "Psychologismus, Psychologie und Hermeneutic." In *Martin Heideggers Einfluss auf die Wissenschaften*, pp. 9–21.

Kunz, Hans. "Die Bedeutung der Daseinsanalytik Martin Heideggers für die Psychologie und die philosophische Anthropologie." In *Martin Heideggers Einfluss auf die Wissenschaften*, pp. 22–57.

III. *Most Comprehensive Bibliography*

Sass, Hans Martin. *Heidegger Bibliographie*. Meisenheim: Hain, 1968.

Fritz Heider (b. 1896)

I. *Major Primary Source*

The Psychology of Interpersonal Relations. New York: Wiley, 1958.

II. *Bibliography*

Psychological Register, p. 607.

A. L. Hesnard (1886–1969)

I. *Major Primary Sources*

La Psychanalyse des névroses et des psychoses. Paris: Alcan, 1914.

L'Univers morbide de la faute. Paris: PUF, 1949.

Morale sans péché. Paris: PUF, 1954.

Psychanalyse du lien interhumain. Paris: PUF, 1957.

L'Oeuvre de Freud et son importance pour le monde moderne. Paris: Payot, 1960.

II. *Bibliography*

Hesnard, A. L. *De Freud à Lacan*. Paris: Les Editions ESF, 1970. **P. iv.**

Edmund Husserl (1859–1938)

I. *Major Primary Sources*

Über den Begriff der Zahl: Psychologische Analysen. Halle: Heynemann, 1887. Reprinted in *Husserliana* XII, 289–339.

Philosophie der Arithmetik. Vol. I. *Logische und psychologische Studien.* Halle: Pfeffer, 1894. Reprinted in *Husserliana* XII, 1–288.

Logische Untersuchungen. 2 vols. Halle: Niemeyer, 1900–1901. Especially Vol. 1, chaps. 3–8, and Vol. 2, Investigations I, V, and VI. English translation by J. N. Findlay. *Logical Investigations.* New York: Humanities Press, 1970. With minor exceptions, reliable and as readable as faithfulness to the original permits.

"Philosophie als strenge Wissenschaft." *Logos* I (1911), 289–341. English translation by A. Lauer. In *Phenomenology and the Crisis of European Philosophy.* Chicago: Quadrangle Press, 1965. Not free from errors.

Ideen I. Halle: Niemeyer, 1913. Especially Section III. English translation by W. R. Boyce Gibson. *Ideas: General Introduction to Pure Phenomenology.* New York: Collier, 1962. Conscientious, but not always reliable.

Phänomenologische Psychologie (1925, 1928). Reprinted in *Husserliana* IX, 1–236.

"Phenomenology." 14th edition (1929) of the *Encyclopaedia Britannica.* The German original of this misleading paraphrase, published in *Husserliana* VIII, 278–301, is now available in an unabridged translation by Richard E. Palmer in *Journal of the British Society for Phenomenology,* II (1971), 77–90.

Cartesianische Meditationen (1929), especially IV and V. First published in French. Paris: Colin, 1931. Reprinted in *Husserliana* I. English translation by Dorion Cairns. *Cartesian Meditations.* The Hague: Nijhoff, 1960.

Die Krisis der europäischen Wissenschaften und die tranzendentale Phänomenologie (1935–37), especially Section III B (incomplete). Reprinted in *Husserliana* VI. English translation by David Carr. *The Crisis of the European Sciences and Transcendental Phenomenology.* Evanston, Ill.: Northwestern University Press, 1970.

Erfahrung und Urteil. Developed and edited by L. Landgrebe. Prague: Academia, 1939.

II. *Secondary Sources*

A. Books

Drüe, Hermann. *Husserls System der phänomenologischen Psychologie*. Berlin: de Gruyter & Co., 1963. A very helpful attempt to organize systematically Husserl's ideas on psychological topics—but not a "system." The "Phenomenologische Psychologie," published in 1962, is not considered.

Kockelmans, Joseph J., *Edmund Husserl's Phenomenological Psychology: A Historico-Critical Study*. Pittsburgh, Pa.: Duquesne University Press, 1967. This revised translation by the author of an earlier Dutch book is the most complete study of the development of Husserl's phenomenological psychology thus far. Its final critical rejection is based on existentialist premises.

B. Articles

Buytendijk, F. J. J. "Die Bedeutung der Phänomenologie Husserls für die Psychologie der Gegenwart." *Phaenomenologica* II (1959), 78–114. Emphasizes Husserl's general inspiration for psychology.

Fluckiger, Fritz A., and Sullivan, John J. "Husserl's Conception of a Pure Psychology." *Journal of the History of the Behavioral Studies*, I (1965), 262–77. Based merely on Husserl's *Crisis of the European Sciences*.

Gurwitsch, A. "Husserl's Conception of Phenomenological Psychology." *Review of Metaphysics*, XIX (1965), 689–727. An expository essay with critical questions at the end.

Spiegelberg, H. "The Relevance of Phenomenological Philosophy for Psychology." In *Phenomenology and Existentialism*, edited by E. N. Lee and M. Mandelbaum, pp. 219–41. Baltimore, Md.: Johns Hopkins Press, 1967. See especially pp. 223–32.

III. *Most Comprehensive Bibliographies*

A. Of Primary Sources up to 1959

Van Breda, H. L. In *Edmund Husserl 1859–1959, Phaenomenologica* IV, pp. 288–306. The Hague: Nijhoff, 1959; continued by Gerhard Maschke and Iso Kern in *Revue internationale de philosophie*, XIX (1965), 156–60.

B. Of Secondary Sources

Patočka, Jan. "Husserl-Bibliographie." *Revue internationale de philosophie,* I (1939), 374–97.
Raes, Jean. "Supplément à la Bibliographie de Husserl." *Revue internationale de philosophie,* IV (1950), 469–75.
Eley, Lothar. "*Husserl-Bibliographie,* 1945–1959." *Zeitschrift für philosophische Forschung,* XIII (1959), 357–67.
Maschke, G., and Kern, I. "Ouvrages et articles sur Husserl de 1951 à 1964." Revue *internationale de philosophie,* XIX (1965), 160–202.

C. In Preparation

A new comprehensive bibliography under the auspices of the Husserl Archives in Louvain.

Erich Jaensch (1883–1940)

I. *Bibliography*

Psychological Register, pp. 817–19.

Karl Jaspers (1883–1969)

I. *Primary Sources*

Allgemeine Psychopathologie. Berlin: Springer, 1913; 4th ed., 1946; 7th ed., 1959 (with new preface). English translation by J. Hoening and Marion W. Hamilton. *General Psychopathology.* Chicago: University of Chicago Press, 1963. While this translation claims that in all major matters the intention of this great work has been served by the English rendering, it is far from literal, particularly in the phenomenological and philosophical sections; it is not always reliable as far as technical points are concerned.
Gesammelte Schriften zur Psychopathologie. Berlin: Springer, 1963. This collection contains eight psychopathological papers that precede Jaspers' larger books, e.g., his paper on "Die phänomenologische Forschungsrichtung in der Psychopathologie."

II. *Secondary Sources in English*

Curran, J. N. "Karl Jaspers (1883–1969)." *Journal of the British Society for Phenomenology,* I (1970), 81–83.

Havens, Lester L. "Karl Jaspers and American Psychiatry." *American Journal of Psychiatry,* CXXIV (1967), 66–70.

Kolle, Kurt. "Jaspers as Psychopathologist." In *The Philosophy of Karl Jaspers,* ed. Paul Schilpp, pp. 437–66. La Salle, Ill.: Open Court, 1957. German edition, Stuttgart: Kohlhammer, 1957.

Lefebvre, Ludwig B. "The Psychology of Karl Jaspers." In *The Philosophy of Karl Jaspers,* pp. 467–97.

Schrag, Oswald O. *Existence, Existenz and Transcendence: An Introduction to the Philosophy of Karl Jaspers.* Pittsburgh, Pa.: Duquesne University Press, 1971. Mostly an expository conspectus focusing on Jaspers' three-volume *Philosophie* of 1931.

Wallraff, Charles F. *Karl Jaspers: An Introduction to His Philosophy.* Princeton, N J.: Princeton University Press, 1970. Presenting the major topics of Jaspers' philosophy without stress on his relation to phenomenology or his psychopathology.

III. *Bibliographies*

Rossman, Kurt. Bibliography of the Writings of Karl Jaspers to 1957. In *The Philosophy of Karl Jaspers,* pp. 871–86.

Saner, Hans. "Bibliographie der Werke und Schriften." In *Karl Jaspers, Werk und Wirkung.* Munich: Piper, 1963. Pp. 169–216 (to 1962).

David Katz (1889–1953)

I. *Major Primary Sources (see also footnotes, pp. 42–52)*

"Die Erscheinungsweisen der Farben und ihre Beeinflussung durch die individuelle Erfahrung." *Zeitschrift für Psychologie* (1911), Erganzungsband 7. 2d ed., *Der Aufbau der Farbwelt,* 1930. English translation by Robert B. MacLeod and G. W. Fox. *The World of Colour.* London: Kegan Paul, Trench, Trubner, 1935. Professor MacLeod has told me that the cuts in this translation had been indicated by Katz himself, under pressure from the publisher, and that Katz was unhappy about them. Unfortunately, the cuts are not indicated in the translation;

the whole organization of the book consequently no longer agrees with that of the German original.

II. *Secondary Sources*

Arnheim, Rudolph. "David Katz: 1889–1953." *American Journal of Psychology,* LXVI (1953), 638–44.
MacLeod, Robert B. "David Katz." *Psychological Review,* LXI (1954), 1–4.

III. *Bibliography*

Psychological Register, pp. 821–22.

KURT KOFFKA (1885–1941)

I. *Major Primary Sources*

"Psychologie." In *Die Philosophie in ihre Einzelgebieten,* edited by Max Dessoir, pp. 497–608. Berlin: Ullstein, 1924.
The Growth of the Mind. New York: Harcourt, 1925.
Principles of Gestalt Psychology. New York: Harcourt, 1935.

II. *Secondary Source*

Heider, Grace. "Kurt Koffka." In *International Encyclopedia of the Social Sciences,* 2d ed., VIII, 435–38.

III. *Bibliographies*

Harrower, Molly. "A Note on the Koffka Papers." *Journal of the History of the Behavioral Sciences,* VII (1971), 141–53.
Psychological Register, pp. 285–87.

WOLFGANG KÖHLER (1887–1967)

I. *Major Primary Sources*

Die physischen Gestalten in Ruhe und in stationärem Zustand. Erlangen: Philosophische Akademie, 1924.
Gestalt Psychology. London: Bell, 1929.

The Place of Value in a World of Facts. Philadelphia: Liveright, 1938.
Selected Papers. Edited by Mary Henle. Philadelphia: Liveright, 1970.

II. *Secondary Source*

Zuckermann, Carl Z., and Wallach, Hans. "Wolfgang Köhler." In *International Encyclopedia of the Social Sciences,* 2d ed., VIII, pp. 438–45.

III. *Bibliography*

Newman, E. B. In *Selected Papers,* pp. 437–49.

Arthur Kronfeld (b. 1882)

I. *Bibliography*

Psychological Register, pp. 829–31.

R. D. Laing (b. 1927)

I. *Major Primary Sources*

The Divided Self: A Study of Sanity and Madness. Chicago: Quadrangle Books, 1960.
Interpersonal Perception: A Theory and a Method of Research (with H. Phillipson and A. R. Lee). New York: Springer, 1960.
The Self and Others: Further Studies in Sanity and Madness. Chicago: Quadrangle Books, 1962.
Sanity, Madness, and the Family. Vol. I: *Families of Schizophrenics* (with A. Esterson). New York: Basic Books, 1964.
The Politics of Experience. New York: Pantheon, 1967.

Kurt Lewin (1890–1947)

I. *Main Primary Sources*

A Dynamic Theory of Personality. New York: McGraw-Hill, 1935.

Principles of Topological Psychology. New York: McGraw-Hill, 1936.

Field Theory in Social Science. New York: Harper, 1951.

II. *Secondary Sources*

Heider, Fritz. "On Lewin's Methods and Theory." In *On Perception, Event Structure, and Psychological Environment*, pp. 108–20. New York: International Universities Press, 1959.

Marrow, Alfred J. *The Practical Theorist: The Life and Work of Kurt Lewin*. New York: Basic Books, 1969.

Spiegelberg, H. "The Relevance of Phenomenological Philosophy for Psychology." In *Phenomenology and Existentialism*, edited by E. N. Lee and M. Mandelbaum, pp. 219–41. Baltimore, Md.: Johns Hopkins Press, 1967.

III. *Bibliography*

Marrow, Alfred J. *The Practical Theorist*. Pp. 238–43.

Robert B. MacLeod (b. 1907)

I. *Primary Sources*

"The Phenomenological Approach to Social Psychology." *Psychological Review*, LIV (1947), 193–210.

"The Place of Phenomenological Analysis in Social Psychological Theory." In *Social Psychology at the Crossroads*, edited by J. B. Rohrer and M. Sherif, pp. 215–41. New York: Harper, 1951.

Gabriel Marcel (b. 1889)

I. *Major Primary Sources*

Journal métaphysique. Paris: Gallimard, 1927. English translation by B. Wall. London: Rockliff, 1952.

Etre et avoir. Paris: Aubier, 1935. English translation by K. Farrer. *Being and Having*. London: Collins, 1965.

Homo viator. Paris: Aubier, 1945. English translation by E. Crawford. Chicago: University of Chicago Press, 1951.

L'Homme problématique. Paris: Aubier, 1955. English translation by B. Thompson. New York: Herder, 1967.

II. *Secondary Source*

Mushuoto, M. A. "Existential Encounter in Gabriel Marcel: Its Value in Psychotherapy." *Review of Existential Psychology and Psychiatry*, I (1961), 53–62.

III. *Most Complete Bibliographies*

A. Of Marcel's Own Writings

Troisfontaines R. *De l'existence à l'être*. Louvain: Nauwelaerts. 1952. II, 381–425.

B. Of Writings about Marcel

Wenning, Gerald G. "Works by and about Gabriel Marcel." *Southern Journal of Philosophy*, IV (1966), 82–96.

Willy Mayer-Gross (1889–1961)

I. *Secondary Source*

Jung, R. "Willy Mayer-Gross." *Zeitschrift für Psychiatrie*, CCIII (1962), 123–36, with bibliography ("Die wichtigsten Arbeiten"), pp. 134–36.

II. *Bibliography*

Psychological Register, p. 880.

Maurice Merleau-Ponty (1908–1961)

I. *Major Primary Sources*

La Structure du comportement. Paris: PUF, 1942. English translation by Alden L. Fisher. *The Structure of Behavior*. Boston: Beacon Press, 1963.
Phénoménologie de la perception. Paris: Gallimard, 1945. Eng-

lish translation by Colin Smith. New York: Humanities Press, 1962. Not free from mistakes.

II. *Secondary Sources*

A. Books

Bannan, John F. *The Philosophy of Merleau-Ponty.* New York: Harcourt, Brace, 1967.

Geraets, Theodore F. *Vers une nouvelle philosophie transcendentale: La Genèse de la philosophie de Merleau-Ponty jusqu'à la Phénoménologie de la Perception.* The Hague: Nijhoff, 1971.

Rabil, Albert. *Merleau-Ponty: Existentialist of the Social World.* New York: Columbia University Press, 1967.

B. Articles

Kockelmans, Joseph A. "Merleau-Ponty's View on Space-Perception and Space." *Review of Existential Psychology and Psychiatry,* IV (1964), 69–105.

______. "Merleau-Ponty on Sexuality." *Journal of Existentialism,* VI (1965), 9–30.

III. *Bibliographies*

A. Of Primary Sources

Geraets, Theodore F. *Vers une nouvelle philosophie transcendentale,* pp. 200–9.

B. Of Secondary Sources

Lapointe, François H. "Bibliography of Works on Merleau-Ponty." *Journal of the British Society for Phenomenology,* II, no. 3 (1971), 99–112.

August Messer (1867–1937)

I. *Bibliography*

Schmidt, R., ed. *Die Philosophie der Gegenwart in Selbstdarstellungen.* Leipzig: Meiner, 1922. III, 175–76.

Albert Michotte (1881–1965)

I. *Bibliography*

Miscellanea psychologica. Louvain: Institut supérieur de philosophie, 1948. Pp. xxxiii–xxxv.

Eugène Minkowski (b. 1885)

I. *Primary Sources*

A. Books

La Schizophrénie: Psychopathologie des schizoïdes et des schizophrènes. Paris: Payot, 1927; 2d ed., Paris: Desclée de Brouwer, 1953.

Le Temps vécu: Etudes phénoménologiques et psychopathologiques. Paris: D'Artrey, 1933; 2d printing, Neuchâtel: Delachaux & Niestlé, 1968. English translation by Nancy Metzel. *Lived Time.* Evanston, Ill.: Northwestern University Press, 1970.

Vers une cosmologie: Fragments philosophiques. Paris: Aubier, 1936.

Traité de psychopathologie. Paris: PUF, 1968.

B. Articles in Translation

"Findings in a Case of Schizophrenic Depression." In *Existence,* ed. Rollo May, Ernest Angel, Henri F. Ellenberger, pp. 127–38. New York: Basic Books, 1958.

"Phenomenological Approaches to Existence." *Existential Psychiatry,* I (1966), 292–315.

II. *Secondary Source*

Laing, R. D. "Minkowski and Schizophrenia." *Review of Existential Psychology and Psychiatry,* VI (1966), 292–315.

III. *Bibliography*

Cahiers du Groupe Françoise Minkowska, No. 15 (December, 1965). This bibliography appears at the end of a selective

"Receuil d'articles 1923–1965" (including five at the end under "Phénoménologie"), pp. 169–75. It does not claim to be quite complete and does not include translations.

Maurice Natanson (b. 1924)

I. *Major Primary Source*

"Philosophy and Psychiatry." In *Psychiatry and Philosophy,* edited by M. Natanson, pp. 85–110. New York: Springer, 1969.

Alexander Pfänder (1870–1941)

I. *Major Primary Sources*

Phänomenologie des Wollens. Leipzig: Barth, 1900; 2d ed., 1930, including the essay "Motive and Motivation" (1911). English translation by Herbert Spiegelberg. *Phenomenology of Willing and Motivation.* Evanston, Ill.: Northwestern University Press, 1967.

Einführung in die Psychologie. Leipzig: Barth, 1904; 2d ed. 1920.

"Zur Psychologie des Gesinnungen." In *Jahrbuch für Philosophie und phänomenologische Forschung,* I (1913), and III (1916).

"Grundprobleme der Charakterologie." In *Jahrbuch der Charakterologie,* I (1924), 289–335.

Die Seele des Menschen: Versuch einer verstehenden Psychologie. Halle: Niemeyer, 1933.

II. *Secondary Sources*

Büttner, Hans. "Die phänomenologische Psychologie Alexander Pfänders." *Archiv für die gesamte Psychologie,* XCIV (1935), 317–46.

Spiegelberg, Herbert. *Alexander Pfänders Phänomenologie.* The Hague: Nijhoff, 1963. With bibliography, pp. 69–71.

In preparation

Schuhmann, Karl. *Husserl über Pfänder.* The Hague: Nijhoff. Will contain the most comprehensive bibliography.

Hans Reiner (b. 1897)

I. *Primary Sources*

Freiheit, Wollen und Aktivitat: Phänomenologische Untersuchungen in Richtung auf das Problem der Willensfreiheit. Halle: Niemeyer, 1927.

Das Phänomen des Glaubens. Halle: Niemeyer, 1934.

II. *Secondary Source*

Spiegelberg, H. *The Phenomenological Movement,* pp. 602, 757.

Géza Révész (1878–1955)

I. *Bibliography*

Psychological Register, pp. 992–94.

Paul Ricoeur (b. 1913)

I. *Major Primary Sources*

Philosophie de la volonté. I. *Le Volontaire et l'involontaire.* Paris: Aubier, 1950. English translation by E. Kohák. *Freedom and Nature.* Evanston, Ill.: Northwestern University Press, 1966.

Philosophie de la volonté. II: *L'Homme fallible.* Paris: Aubier, 1960.

De l'interprétation: Essai sur Freud. Paris: Seuil, 1965. English translation by Denis Savage. *Freud and Philosophy: On Interpretation.* New Haven, Conn.: Yale University Press, 1970.

II. *Secondary Source*

Ihde, Don. With a foreword by Paul Ricoeur. *Hermeneutic Phenomenology: The Philosophy of Paul Ricoeur.* Evanston, Ill.: Northwestern University Press, 1971. An attempt to show Ricoeur's development from "structural phenomenology" to hermeneutic phenomenology. Includes the best English survey of English translations and secondary sources up to 1971.

III. *Most Comprehensive Bibliography*

Vansina, Dirk R. In *Revue philosophique de Louvain,* LX (1962), 395–413; LXVI (1968), 85–101.

CARL ROGERS (B. 1902)

I. *Bibliography*

On Becoming a Person. Boston: Houghton Mifflin, 1961. Pp. 403–11.

EDGAR RUBIN (1886–1951)

I. *Bibliography*

Psychological Register, pp. 669–70.

H. C. RÜMKE (B. 1893)

I. *Bibliography*

Eine blühende Psychiatrie in Gefahr. Berlin: Springer, 1967. Pp. vii–viii.

JEAN-PAUL SARTRE (B. 1905)

I. *Major Primary Sources*

L'Imagination. Paris: Alcan, 1936. English translation by F. Williams. Ann Arbor: University of Michigan Press, 1962.

Esquisse d'une théorie des émotions. Paris: Herrman, 1939. English translation by B. Frechtman. *The Emotions: Outline of Theory.* New York: Philosophical Library, 1948.

L'Imaginaire. Paris, Gallimard, 1940. English translation, *Psychology of Imagination.* New York: Philosophical Library, 1948.

L'Etre et le néant. Paris: Gallimard, 1943. English translation by

H. Barnes. *Being and Nothingness*. New York: Philosophical Library, 1956. Not free from mistakes.

Saint Genet: Comédien et martyre. Paris: Gallimard, 1952. English translation by B. Frechtman. New York: Braziller, 1969.

Critique de la raison dialectique. Vol. I. Paris: Gallimard, 1960.

L'Idiot de la famille: Gustave Flaubert de 1821 à 1857. 2 vols. Paris: Gallimard, 1971.

II. *Secondary Sources*

A. Books

Dempsey, J. R. Peter. *The Psychology of Sartre*. Westminister, Md.: Newman Press, 1950.

Fell, Joseph P. *Emotion in the Thought of Sartre*. New York: Columbia University Press, 1965. A developmental, comparative, and critical study, perceptive and judicious.

B. Articles

Bannon, John F. "The Psychiatry, Psychology and Phenomenology of Sartre." *Journal of Existentialism*, II (1960), 176–86.

Elkin, Harry. "Comment on Sartre from the Standpoint of Existential Psychotherapy." *Review of Existential Psychology and Psychiatry*, II (1961), 189–94.

Olson, Robert G. "The Three Theories of Motivation in the Philosophy of J. P. Sartre." *Ethics*, LXVI (1956), 176–87.

Stern, Günther Anders. "Emotion and Reality." *Philosophy and Phenomenological Research*, X (1951), 553–62.

III. *Most Comprehensive Bibliography*

Contat, Michel, and Rybalka, Michel. *Les Ecrits de Sartre*. Chronologie, bibliographie annotée. Paris: Gallimard, 1970.

MARTIN SCHEERER (1900–1961)

I. *Major Primary Sources*

Die Lehre von der Gestalt: Ihre Methode und ihr psychologischer Gegenstand. Berlin: de Gruyter, 1931.

Cognition: Theory, Research, Promise. Papers edited by Constance Scheerer. New York: Harper, 1964.

Max Scheler (1874–1928)

I. *Major Primary Sources*

Zur Phänomenologie und Theorie der Sympathiegefühle und von Liebe und Hass. Halle: Niemeyer, 1913; 2d ed., *Wesen und Formen der Sympathie.* Bonn: Cohen, 1923. English translation by Peter Heath. *The Nature of Sympathy.* New Haven, Conn.: Yale University Press, 1954. At times very free, but generally reliable.

Der Formalismus in der Ethik und die materiale Wertethik. Halle: Niemeyer, 1913–16; 3d ed., 1926. *Gesammelte Werke,* Vol. II.

Abhandlungen und Aufsätze. Leipzig: Der neue Geist, 1915. Reprinted in *Vom Umsturz der Werte.* Bern: Francke, 1954. *Gesammelte Werke,* Vol. III. Includes an essay on "Das Ressentiment im Aufbau der Moralen" (1912). Translated as a separate book, by W. H. Holdheim. *Ressentiment.* New York: Free Press, 1971.

Vom Ewigen im Menschen. Leipzig: Der neue Geist, 1921. *Gesammelte Werke,* Vol. V. English translation by B. Noble. *On the Eternal in Man.* London: SCM Press, 1960.

Die Stellung des Menschen im Kosmos. Darmstadt: Leuchter, 1928. English translation by Hans Mayerhoff. *Man's Place in Nature.* Boston: Beacon, 1961.

II. *Secondary Sources*

Frings, Manfred. *Max Scheler: A Concise Introduction into the World of a Great Thinker.* Pittsburgh, Pa.: Duquesne University Press, 1965.

Lorscheid, Bernhard. *Max Scheler's Phänomenologie des Psychischen.* Bonn: Bouvier, 1957. Deals chiefly with the ontology and epistemology of the psychic in general, but not with Scheler's concrete contributions.

Ranly, Ernest W. *Scheler's Phenomenology of Community.* The Hague: Nijhoff, 1966.

Rüttishauser, Bruno. *Max Schelers Phänomenologie des Fühlens.* Bern: Francke, 1969.

III. *Most Comprehensive Bibliography*

Hartmann, Wilfried. *Scheler Bibliographie.* Stuttgart: Fromman, 1963.

Paul Schilder (1886–1941)

I. *Primary Sources*

Selbstbewusstsein und Persönlichkeitsbewusstsein. Berlin: Springer, 1914.

Wahn und Erkenntnis. Berlin: Springer, 1918.

Das Körperschema. Berlin: Springer, 1923.

Seele und Leben. Berlin: Springer, 1923.

Medizinische Psychologie. Berlin: Springer, 1924. English translation by David Rapaport. *Medical Psychology.* New York: International Universities Press, 1953.

Introduction to a Psychoanalytic Psychiatry. New York: International Universities Press, 1928.

The Image and Appearance of the Human Body. New York: International Universities Press, 1935.

Psychotherapy. New York: Norton, 1938; rev. ed., 1951.

Goals and Desires of Man. New York: Columbia University Press, 1942.

Mind: Perception and Thought in Their Constructive Parts. New York: Columbia University Press, 1951.

Psychoanalysis, Man, and Society. Edited by Lauretta Bender. New York: Norton, 1951.

Contributions to Developmental Neuropsychiatry. New York: International Universities Press, 1964.

II. *Secondary Source*

Ziferstein, Isidore. "Paul Schilder." In *Psychoanalytic Pioneers,* edited by Franz Alexander, Samuel Eisenstein, and Martin Grotjahn, pp. 457–68. New York: Basic Books, 1966.

III. *Bibliography*

Journal of Criminal Psychopathology, II (1940), 226–34. Complete up to 1940. For later major works (posthumous), see *Psychoanalytic Pioneers.*

Kurt Schneider (1887–1963)

I. *Bibliography*

Psychological Register, p. 869.

Otto Selz (1881–1944)

I. *Bibliography*

Psychological Register, p. 873.

Wilhelm Specht (b. 1874)

I. *Bibliography*

Psychological Register, pp. 874–75.

Kurt Stavenhagen (1885–1951)

I. *Primary Source*

Absolute Stellungnahmen. Erlangen: Weltkreis, 1925.

II. *Secondary Source*

Spiegelberg, H. *The Phenomenological Movement,* pp. 220–21.

Edith Stein (1891–1942)

I. *Primary Sources*

Zum Problem der Einfühlung. Halle: Waisenhaus, 1917. English translation by Waltrant Stein. *On the Problem of Empathy.* The Hague: Nijhoff, 1964.

"Beiträge zur philosophischen Begründung der Psychologie und der Geisteswissenschaften." *Jahrbuch für Philosophie und phänomenologische Forschung,* V (1922), 1–264.

Erwin Straus (b. 1891)

I. *Primary Sources*

Geschehnis und Erlebnis. Berlin: Springer, 1924.

Vom Sinn der Sinne. Berlin: Springer, 1935; 2d ed., 1956. English translation by Jacob Needleman. *The Primary World of Senses: A Vindication.* Glencoe, Ill.: Free Press, 1963.

On Obsession: A Clinical and Methodological Study. New York: Nervous and Mental Disease Monographs #373, 1948.

Psychologie der menschlichen Welt: Gesammelte Schriften. Berlin: Springer, 1960.

Psychiatrie und Philosophie. In *Psychiatrie der Gegenwart* I/II. Berlin: Springer, 1963. English edition by Erwin Straus, M. Natanson, and H. Ey. *Psychiatry and Philosophy.* New York: Springer, 1969.

Phenomenological Psychology: Selected Papers. Translated by Erling Eng. New York: Basic Books, 1966.

II. *Secondary Source*

Grene, Marjorie. *Approaches to a Philosophical Biology.* New York: Basic Books, 1968. Pp. 183–218.

III. *Bibliography*

Von Bayer, W., and Griffiths, R., eds. *Conditio Humana: Erwin Straus on His 75th Birthday.* Berlin & New York: Springer, 1966. Pp. 334–37. The bibliography is complete up to 1966.

Carl Stumpf (1848–1936)

I. *Primary Sources*

Tonpsychologie. 2 vols. Leipzig: Hirzel, 1883–90.

"Erscheinungen und psychische Funktionen." *Abhandlungen der Berliner Akademie* (1907).

"Zur Einteilung der Wissenschaften." *Abhandlungen der Berliner Akademie* (1907).

"Selbstdarstellung." In *Philosophie der Gegenwart in Selbstdar-*

stellungen, edited by R. Schmidt. Leipzig: Meiner, 1924. V, 205–65, with bibliography, pp. 262–65. English translation in *History of Psychology in Autobiography,* edited by Carl Murchison. Worcester, Mass.: Clark University Press, 1930. Pp. 389–441.

Viktor von Weizsäcker (1886–1957)

I. *Secondary Source*

Vogel, P. *Viktor von Weizsäcker.* Berlin: Springer, 1956. Bibliography, pp. 318–26.

Max Wertheimer (1880–1943)

I. *Major Primary Sources*

Über Gestalttheorie. Erlangen: Weltkreis, 1925. English translation in *A Source Book of Gestalt Psychology,* edited by Willis D. Ellis, pp. 1–11. London: Kegan Paul, 1938.

Drei Abhandlungen zur Gestalttheorie. Erlangen: Weltkreis, 1925.

Productive Thinking. New York: Harper, 1959.

II. *Secondary Source*

Luchins, Abraham S. "Max Wertheimer." In *International Encyclopedia of the Social Sciences,* 2d ed., XVI, 622–27.

Index of Names

THE FOLLOWING INDEX is meant to include all references to persons, other than editors and translators, mentioned in the text of the book. The one exception is Edmund Husserl; for his name appears on almost every page, and the reader will be served best by being given only those page numbers that refer to sustained discussions. Page numbers in italics refer to material that is especially significant.

Index of Subjects

THE ITEMS SELECTED for this index are only those likely to be consulted for information about the phenomenological position on topics of major interest to psychologists and psychiatrists. Some important technical terms such as "Intentionality" are also included, but no definitions are added; for these I would like to refer the reader to the Glossary in my book on *The Phenomenological Movement* (The Hague: Nijhoff, 1965), pp. 709–28.